The Public Value of the Humanities

The WISH List
(Warwick Interdisciplinary Studies in the Humanities)

**Series editors: Jonathan Bate, Stella Bruzzi, Thomas Docherty
and Margot Finn**

In the twenty-first century, the traditional disciplinary boundaries of
higher education are dissolving at remarkable speed. The last decade
has seen the flourishing of scores of new interdisciplinary research
centres at universities around the world and there has also been a
move towards more interdisciplinary teaching.

The WISH List is a collaboration between Bloomsbury Academic and
the University of Warwick, a university that has been, from its foundation,
at the forefront of interdisciplinary innovation in academia. The series
aims to establish a framework for innovative forms of interdisciplinary
publishing within the humanities, between the humanities and social
sciences and even between the humanities and the hard sciences.

Also in *The WISH List*:

Reading and Rhetoric in Montaigne and Shakespeare
Peter Mack
ISBN 978-1-84966-061-7 (Hardback); ISBN 978-1-84966-060-0 (Ebook)

*Raising Milton's Ghost: John Milton and the Sublime of Terror in the
Early Romantic Period*
Joseph Crawford
ISBN 978-1-84966-332-8 (Hardback); ISBN 978-1-84966-419-6 (Ebook)

Open-space Learning: A Study in Trans-disciplinary Pedagogy
Nicholas Monk, Carol Chillington-Rutter, Jonothan Neelands,
Jonathan Heron
ISBN 978-1-84966-054-9 (Hardback); ISBN 978-1-84966-055-6 (Ebook)

The Public Value of the Humanities

Edited by
JONATHAN BATE

BLOOMSBURY ACADEMIC

First published in 2011 by:

Bloomsbury Academic

An imprint of Bloomsbury Publishing Plc
36 Soho Square, London W1D 3QY, UK
and
175 Fifth Avenue, New York, NY 10010, USA

CIP records for this book are available from the British Library and the Library of Congress

ISBN (paperback) 978-1-8496-6062-4
ISBN (hardback) 978-1-8496-6471-4
ISBN (ebook) 978-1-8496-6063-1

This book is produced using paper that is made from wood grown in managed, sustainable forests.
It is natural, renewable and recyclable. The logging and manufacturing processes conform to the
environmental regulations of the country of origin.

Printed and bound in Great Britain by the MPG Books Group, Bodmin, Cornwall.

www.bloomsburyacademic.com

Foreword

Onora O'Neill

As the economic downturn that began in 2008 deepened, a partly phony war about the value of research and reasons for taxpayers to fund it grew. Some held that in straitened times all public funding should go to research that can lead to innovation and economic growth, and thought that public support should go only to research in science, technology, engineering and medicine. They were content (perhaps even eager) for research in the humanities and social sciences to receive little funding, in the (arithmetically rather implausible) hope that this would protect scientific research with its greater 'impact' from funding cuts.

That is the context of which this book has been written. In a world in which public expenditure must be cut, it is tempting to think that research funding should serve economic recovery in very direct ways. But research is not like that: in the nature of the case, results are not known before research is undertaken, and the 'impact' of results is uncertain. Even when results are known and published, the road to innovation – let alone marketable products, economic growth and new jobs – is long, bumpy and often peters out. We can seldom be sure in advance which research will contribute most to, or indeed be essential for, securing which economic or other benefits. We know that research often leads to unexpected results, and that many innovations draw on research in many different fields. None of the early twentieth century philosophers and mathematicians whose work in logic lies behind the development of information technology foresaw that their arcane work would transform our world. That is why research funders distribute money across many projects and proposals, in the full knowledge that not all will bear fruit, and the pleasant anticipation that some will have fruits not imagined when the work was undertaken.

Why Humanities?
This collection of essays on the value of research in the humanities was initiated by the Arts and Humanities Research Council. Each paints a vivid and variegated picture of changes and activities to which research in the humanities can lead, and collectively they show that there is and can be no single or simple metric for the value of this – or perhaps of other – research. Work in the humanities is fruitful. It has many valuable effects, but there is no bureaucratically convenient way of measuring or aggregating them.

Some effects are indeed straightforwardly economic: many of the UK's very successful 'cultural industries', from publishing and higher education to theatre and broadcasting, depend on humanities research to shape and refresh their 'products'. Other effects are evidently valuable, but their value may not be reducible to economic value. Research that establishes historical evidence or understanding of other cultures may be indispensable for foreign and domestic policies; work that establishes more reliable texts or superior interpretations may be necessary to raise and maintain the standard of legal and cultural work.

The value of humanities research is neither negligible nor ineffable. Research of all sorts can change individuals and societies. It changes what we believe and what we do, the technologies we rely on, and the things we value. The changes to which it leads may follow in short order or lag for many years, and can surprise even those who do the research. And once changes that depend on research have taken place, it is often hard to remember how things used to be. We cannot now recapture an understanding of the natural world untouched by scientific work done across many generations. Equally we cannot now imagine an understanding of the human world that is not deeply shaped by the accumulated work in the humanities across many generations. Our understanding of places and pasts, and of our own place and past, indeed our own present, is steeped in past work on the languages and texts, representations and artefacts that shape our memories and perception, our understanding and feeling, and our very sense of the human world we inhabit.

Why Humanities Research?

It might be said that nobody doubts that there are excellent reasons to support the objects and activities investigated by research in the humanities, but that this does not show that there is a case for public funding of research in the humanities. Even those who are wholly convinced of the importance of supporting literature and art, music and theatre may hold that supporting research into art and literature, music and theatre, history and philosophy, is another matter. They may insist that our lives are shaped not by the findings of research in the humanities, but rather by the objects of that research – by music and buildings, by languages and literatures, by cultures and religions. They doubt whether the research is needed.

However, cultural objects are not self-interpreting. Just as we draw on accumulated scientific research to understand and to engage with the natural world, so we draw on accumulated research in the humanities to understand and engage with the human world of cultural objects. Inquiry in the humanities begins with attempts to *interpret representations*, whether words, texts, symbols, images, musical scores or performances, and *artefacts*, whether pictures, manuscripts, tools, furniture or buildings. It also seeks to interpret uses of representations and artefacts as found in action and practices, beliefs and attitudes, mentalités and performances, discourse and communication, as well as constellations of these that constitute more abstract cultural objects such as languages, genres, traditions, and what are now called identities – or indeed cultures.

Interpretation is not, however the only task of research in the humanities. As in the natural sciences, a lot of research in the humanities aims at establishing what is or has been the case. Empirical enquiry in the humanities, as elsewhere, aims at truth; it seeks to follow where evidence leads, and to point out where evidence is absent or unclear. It is as open to refutation as other empirical claims: just as a beautiful scientific theory may have to give way to an unaccommodating fact or experiment, so a beautiful historical account may be undermined by an inconvenient document. In the absence of historical research a society will have to fall back on received opinions or ideologies; self-flattering and inaccurate accounts of past glories and grievances may cast dark shadows on present policy making and self-perception.

Nobody does research except in the hope that their work will at some point make some difference, although they are not likely to think of that difference simply as a matter of economic benefit or gain. Those who do research variously hope to establish new truths, more penetrating interpretations, or better arguments, or to call in question unconvincing beliefs or assumptions or to provide more accurate or perspicuous ways of measuring, classifying and connecting. The fruits of research are marvellously and gloriously diverse, and wonderfully illustrated by the essays collected here.

Of course not all research succeeds: some proves useless, or pointless, and some is rapidly superseded by better and more convincing work. Some experiments fail; some interpretations are refuted or discarded for good reasons; some conjectures turn out to be false. Research findings are necessarily fallible: research would be beside the point – either in the natural sciences or in the humanities – if its results were known or its success could be guaranteed in advance. Despite the fallibility of research findings, some prove lasting and can alter what people believe what they can do, what they value, and how they change the world we inhabit. That is why research in the humanities as in the natural sciences matters, and why funding of that research should not be a matter of indifference, even in hard times.

Onora O'Neill writes on ethics and political philosophy, including the philosophy of Immanuel Kant, questions of international justice, issues of trust and accountability, as well as medical and research ethics. She was Principal of Newnham College, Cambridge from 1992–2006, is professor emeritus in the Faculty of Philosophy in Cambridge, and was President of the British Academy from 2005–9. She is a crossbench member of the House of Lords (Baroness O'Neill of Bengarve).

Acknowledgements

The writing of these essays was made possible by the Arts & Humanities Research Council, to whom the publisher, the editor and the contributors are most grateful. Special thanks to Philip Esler for initiating the process.

Jonathan Bate would also like to thank Adam Putz for editorial assistance and our swift and eagle-eyed copy editor at Bloomsbury Academic, Howard Watson.

 Arts & Humanities
Research Council

Contents

Part Three: Informing Policy

Part Four: Using Words, Thinking Hard

Contributors

Jonathan Bate is Professor of Shakespeare and Renaissance Literature at the University of Warwick; his many books include *John Clare: A Biography* (2003), *Soul of the Age: The Life, Mind and World of William Shakespeare* (2008) and *English Literature: A Very Short Introduction* (2010).

Mary Beard is Professor of Classics at the University of Cambridge and a Fellow of Newnham College; her many books include *The Invention of Jane Harrison* (2000), *The Roman Triumph* (2007) and *Pompeii: The Life of a Roman Town* (2008).

Iain Borden is Professor of Architecture and Urban Culture at University College London; his books include *Skateboarding, Space and City* (2001) and *Manual: The Architecture and Office of AHMM* (2003).

Christopher Breward is Head of Research at the Victoria and Albert Museum, London; he is the author of *The Culture of Fashion* (1995), *The Hidden Consumer: Masculinities, Fashion and City Life 1860–1914* (1999), and *Fashioning London: Clothing and the Modern Metropolis* (2004).

Ben Cowell is Assistant Director, External Affairs, at the National Trust, and author of *The Heritage Obsession* (2008).

Stephen Daniels is Professor of Cultural Geography at the University of Nottingham and Director of the AHRC Landscape and Environment programme. His publications include *Humphry Repton: Landscape Gardening and the Geography of Georgian England* (1999) and *Paul Sandby: Picturing Britain* (2009).

Nicholas Davey is Professor of Philosophy at the University of Dundee and author of *Unquiet Understanding: Gadamer's Philosophical Hermeneutics* (2006).

Chris Gosden is Professor of European Archaeology at University of Oxford; his books include *Knowing Things: Exploring the Collections of the Pitt Rivers Museum 1884–1945* (with Frances Larson) (2007) and *The Oxford Handbook of Archaeology* (with B. Cunliffe and R. Joyce) (2009).

Robert Hampson is Professor of Modern Literature at Royal Holloway, University of London; his books include *Joseph Conrad: Betrayal and*

Identity (1992), *Cross-Cultural Encounters in Joseph Conrad's Malay Fiction* (2000) and various editions of Conrad, Kipling and Rider Haggard.

Deborah Howard is Professor of Architectural History at the University of Cambridge and Fellow of St John's College, Cambridge; her books include *Venice and the East* (2000) and *The Architectural History of Venice* (revised edn, 2002).

Richard Howells is Reader in Cultural and Creative Industries at King's College, London; his books include *Visual Culture* (2003) and *The Myth of the Titanic* (1999).

Matthew H. Johnson is Professor of Archaeology at the University of Southampton: His books include *Archaeological Theory: An Introduction* (1999), *Ideas of Landscape* (2006) and *English Houses 1300–1800* (2010).

Michael Kelly is Professor of French at the University of Southampton and Director of the UK Subject Centre for Languages, Linguistics and Area Studies; his books include *The Cultural and Intellectual Rebuilding of France after the Second World War* (2004) and *The European Language Teacher* (2003).

Catherine Leyshon is Associate Professor of Historical and Cultural Geography at the University of Exeter. She has recently published an edited collection entitled *Process: Landscape and Text* (2010). Many of her publications are as Catherine Brace.

Rónán McDonald holds the Chair in Modern Irish Studies at the University of New South Wales; his publications include *Tragedy and Irish Literature* (2002) and *The Death of the Critic* (2008).

April McMahon is Forbes Professor of English Language and Vice Principal for Planning, Resources and Research Policy at the University of Edinburgh; her books include *Lexical Phonology and the History of English* (2000) and *Language Classification by Numbers* (2005). **Will Barras, Lynn Clark, Remco Knooihuizen, Amanda Patten** and **Jennifer Sullivan** are her graduate students at Edinburgh.

Francis O'Gorman is Professor of Victorian Literature at the University of Leeds; his publications include *Victorian Literature and Finance* (2007) and *The Cambridge Companion to Victorian Culture* (2010).

Katie Overy is Director of the MSc in Music in the Community and Co-Director of the Institute for Music in Human and Social Development

(IMHSD) at the University of Edinburgh; her publications include *Dyslexia and Music: From Timing Deficits to Musical Intervention* (2003) and *Being Together in Time: Musical Experience and the Mirror Neuron System* (2009).

Mike Parker Pearson is Professor of Archaeology at the University of Sheffield; he has directed excavations at Stonehenge, in the Outer Hebrides and Madagascar, and his many books include *Bronze Age Britain* (1993) and *The Archaeology of Death and Burial* (1999).

Mike Press is Professor of Design Policy at Duncan of Jordanstone College of Art and Design, University of Dundee; his books include *The Design Agenda* (1995) and *The Design Experience* (2003).

Simon Szreter is Professor of History and Public Policy at the University of Cambridge and Fellow of St John's College; he is co-founder and editor of www.historyandpolicy.org and has most recently published *Health and Wealth: Studies in History and Policy* (2005) and (with Kate Fisher) *Sex Before the Sexual Revolution. Intimate Life in England 1918–1963* (2010).

Vanessa Toulmin is Chair in Early Film and Popular Entertainment at the University of Sheffield and Director of the National Fairground Archive; her publications include *Electric Edwardians: The Story of the Mitchell & Kenyon Collection* (2006) and *Blackpool's Winter Gardens: The Most Magnificent Palace of Amusement in the World* (2009).

Gary Watt is Professor of Law at the University of Warwick; he is the author of *Equity Stirring: The Story of Justice Beyond Law* (2009) and founding co-editor of the journal *Law and Humanities*.

John Wolffe is Professor of Religious History at The Open University; his publications include *God and Greater Britain* (1994), *Great Deaths* (2000) and *The Expansion of Evangelicalism* (2006).

Jürgen Zimmerer is Professor of African History at the University of Hamburg and Reader in International History at the University of Sheffield, where he founded the Centre for the Study of Genocide and Mass Violence. He is currently president of the International Network of Genocide Scholars (INoGS) and Senior Editor of the Journal of Genocide Research.

Introduction

Jonathan Bate (University of Warwick)

Seven lean cows

In chapter 41 of the Book of Genesis, Pharaoh has two troubling dreams. In the first, seven lean cows rise out of the river and devour seven fat cows. And in the second, seven withered ears of grain swallow up seven healthy ears. Pharaoh sends for experts and wise men, but they are unable to interpret these dreams. Then, however, his chief cupbearer tells him of a young captive Jew named Joseph who has proved himself adept in the art of interpretation. Joseph is called for. He suggests that the dreams are predicting that seven years of abundance will be followed by seven years of famine. Pharaoh should accordingly store up surplus food supplies during the good years. He must find a wise and discerning man to take charge of the process. Pharaoh responds by giving the job to Joseph, who builds massive grain stores in the good years, with the result that Egypt thrives during the years of famine – not least by exporting grain to other countries that have not shown such foresight.

In public life in the twenty-first century, the experts who are usually asked to predict the future are scientists (for example, climatologists) and social scientists (for example, economists). The scientists offer warnings that anthropogenic global warming will lead to famine and flood, causing mass migration and widespread disruption to settled ways of life. The economists advise on the setting of bank interest rates as a predictive mechanism for the control of inflation. But scientists cannot yet predict when earthquakes and volcanic eruptions will take place. And economists signally failed to predict the banking crisis of 2008.

Joseph, who did such a good job of predicting the future, was neither a scientist nor an economist. He was an interpreter of narrative, for which another name would be a literary critic. At another level, of course, Joseph is not a real expert but a character within a narrative: the Book of Genesis is not a factual document but a story about the origins and values and cultural identity of the Jewish people. Stories – myths, plays, pictures, novels, histories – are among humankind's chief instruments for understanding ourselves and our world.

The Book of Genesis is one of the foundational texts of the Western and Middle-Eastern worlds. The three great religions that have shaped the history of those worlds – Judaism, Christianity, Islam – all have their origins in the Abrahamic stories that are recorded there. In order to understand the meaning of what we read in Genesis and its sequels we need the expertise of language scholars (to translate from Hebrew and Greek), of palaeographers and bibliographers (to decipher the manuscript and print traditions that have transmitted the Bible to us), of historians and archaeologists (to locate the Abrahamic narrative in time and place), and of anthropologists and theologians (to explain what the stories tell us about humankind and our need for divinity). There is a collective name for all these experts: a faculty of humanities. In the light of the recent historical developments for which '9/11' serves as shorthand, it was perhaps unfortunate that the swingeing funding cuts to higher education in the early 1980s fell with particular severity on supposedly marginal areas of the humanities such as Islamic Studies.

At one level, Joseph succeeds in predicting the future when all the acknowledged experts have failed because he sticks to common sense. It is not rocket science to see that both the weather and the economy move in cycles and that it is accordingly a good idea to 'put something away for a rainy day' or to build up your financial reserves during the boom years so that you will be better prepared for the recession that will inevitably follow. At another level, the story is much more complicated, tapping into deep archetypal structures of narrative that occur in many different cultures and eras: reversal and recognition, the wisdom of the fool, the exile and the prisoner who rises to power and eminence. The person who appears to be useless turns out to be very valuable indeed.

Joseph's predictive skill is a little allegory of what faculties of humanities can do for society. Humanists look long and hard at the past, and at stories and ideas. They can impart some common sense to our public debates by way of the lessons of the past and the understanding of human nature. But they can also impart some healthy scepticism regarding easy solutions by way of their demonstration that, when humankind is involved, things are usually more complicated than they first seem.

On 'value'

In 2010, a number of governments committed themselves to a new age of austerity. A time of restraint upon public spending is a good moment for asking fundamental questions about value. What are the things that *must* be financed from the public purse? A health service, counter-terrorism, public transport, basic literacy and numeracy, housing for the poor and advanced research into non-carbon energy sources? What possible case could be made for, let us say, the budget of the Arts & Humanities Research Council when measured against these more urgent demands? Should governments that have overspent in the years of plenty continue to spend 'taxpayers' money' funding research into ancient Greek tragedy, philosophical conundrums, the history of landscape, literary value and the aesthetics of design? Is it possible to demonstrate that such research delivers 'value for money' and 'public benefit'? And what exactly *is* research in the humanities? People readily grasp the idea of scientific research (discovering a new star, a new cell, a new source of fuel, a cure for cancer), but humanities scholars are often met with puzzlement when telling taxi drivers that they conduct 'research'.

There is, however, a simple answer to the question 'what is the value of research in the humanities?' It is that research in the humanities is the only activity that can establish the meaning of such a question.

What do we mean by 'value', by 'research' and by 'the humanities'? These are questions that can only be answered by means of the tools of the disciplines of the humanities. They are questions of semantics and interpretation. And they require philosophical and historical understanding. Language, history, philosophy: the humanities.

By the same account, a further value of research in the humanities is that it is the only activity that can answer the question 'what is the value of research in the sciences?' It is generally assumed that the value of research in the sciences is to advance knowledge so as to improve the quality of human life. The value of medical research is to cure disease, relieve suffering and lengthen life. Among the potential values of research in climatology, biochemistry, physical engineering and several other scientific disciplines might be the discovery of various means to fix an array of environmental problems. But questions such as why we should value long life and what ethical obligations we might have to future generations, to other species, or indeed to the planet itself, are 'humanities' questions, only answerable from within the framework of disciplines that are attentive to language, history and philosophy.

In Act 2, Scene II of Shakespeare's rigorously intellectual (and wildly bawdy) tragedy *Troilus and Cressida*, the Trojan lords debate whether it is worth fighting a war for the sake of the beautiful Helen. Hector proposes that 'she is not worth what she doth cost / The keeping.' 'What's aught but as' 'tis valued?' asks Troilus in reply. 'Value' here is initially conceived in economic terms. According to the *Oxford English Dictionary* – an essential product of humanities research – the primary meaning of the word value is 'That amount of some commodity, medium of exchange, etc., which is considered to be an equivalent for something else; a fair or adequate equivalent or return. [As in the] phr[ase] value for money (freq[uently] attrib[uted, used metaphorically]).' Value, then, is a term referring to a commodity, a medium of exchange, something quantifiable. It is interpreted in terms of the market, of 'economic impact'. According to this argument, there will always come a point where the price is simply not worth paying.

Hector, though, comes back with a counter-argument that shifts the meaning of the term:

> But value dwells not in particular will:
> It holds his estimate and dignity
> As well wherein 'tis precious of itself
> As in the prizer. 'Tis mad idolatry

To make the service greater than the god. (Shakespeare, Act 2, Scene 2, lines 58–62)

The word 'value' must now be understood in the light of another of its definitions in the *Oxford English Dictionary*:

The relative status of a thing, or the estimate in which it is held, according to its real or supposed worth, usefulness, or importance. In Philos[ophy] and Social Sciences, regarded esp[ecially] in relation to an individual or group; gen[erally] in pl[ural], the principles or standards of a person or society, the personal or societal judgement of what is valuable and important in life.

The relativism of Troilus (things only have value in so far as they are valued by particular people who prize them and who can accordingly put a price on them) is replaced by the proposition that there can be essential values, that a thing might be intrinsically valuable ('precious of itself'). As the dictionary definition reminds us, this essentialism may eventually have to be dissolved into another relativism: 'society' will make judgements as to 'what is valuable and important in life'. We need historians, anthropologists and researchers in comparative literature to show us how different societies have different values. Shakespeare, following Montaigne, was very interested in the idea that what one society regards as the product of 'nature', another society will regard as mere 'custom'. In a world of globalized communication, international exchange and migratory labour, this knowledge of difference is especially important.

But every society has gods of one kind and another. In response to the commodified understanding of value with which he and Troilus began, Hector reminds us that it is mad idolatry to make the service greater than the god. This is as if to say: a merely economic understanding of value makes the service – the instrumentality – greater than the thing served, the real value. The value of humanities research is to identify the nature of the god.

In the arena of higher education in the early twenty-first century, the relationship between the service and the god appears to be changing. Universities had their origins in the service of first the church (the centrality of theology in the medieval curriculum) and then the state (the idea extending from Tudor reforms to the last days of the British Empire that one of the primary functions of universities was to form the minds of civil administrators). But for Cardinal Newman at the high water mark of the Victorian era, the *idea* of the university was premised upon a god: the university was 'a place of teaching universal knowledge' (Newman 1852: v). Historically, the idea of 'education', deriving from '*educere*', the Latin for 'to lead out', is intimately bound to the notion of character formation. The model for the university tutorial is the classical sage – Plato in his academy or Epicurus in his garden – in dialogue with his pupils, imparting wisdom by example and through training in the art of argument. The platonic university is a place where young people learn to think. Their starting-point must be the art of thinking disinterestedly, not instrumentally.

The Victorians were the first generation in this country to believe that the state should be the principal agency to take responsibility for education. They created a government department to oversee the process. Whilst the main educational business of nineteenth-century politicians and civil servants was the provision of universal school education, they also initiated processes that led to the reform of Oxford and Cambridge, and the growth of civic universities elsewhere, especially in the north. Interestingly, the running in this latter regard was made within local, not national, government – a model worth pondering in the context of the various other kinds of devolution that are reshaping our society today.

Victorian educational ideals in general and Cardinal Newman's idea of the university in particular are a far cry from the rhetoric of the servants of the early twenty-first century British government who are responsible for the funding of higher education. If a Tardis were to transport Newman to the year 2010, so that he could attend his own beatification by the Pope in the Archdiocese of Birmingham, he would be surprised to discover that universities come within the remit not of the Department of Education but of the Department of Business, Innovation and Skills (BIS). The function of the modern university is now officially linked not to 'teaching universal knowledge' but to 'the innovation and skills agenda'. Crudely put, academic research must pay its way by generating real returns in the wider economy.

One of the big new ideas is 'knowledge transfer'. This is defined on the website of Research Councils UK (RCUK), the quango charged by BIS with the delivery of research funding, as 'improving exploitation of the research base to meet national economic and public service objectives', to be achieved by means of 'people and knowledge flow', together with 'commercialisation, including Intellectual Property exploitation and entrepreneurial activities'. These ambitions do sound very much like the service becoming greater than the god: the predominant language ('exploitation', 'economic', 'commercialisation', 'entrepreneurial') is that of the commodity and the marketplace.

However, even in the hard sciences, the relationship between original research and commercial exploitation is usually indirect and long-term. More than half a century passed between Arthur C. Clarke's visionary conception of the communication potential of orbital satellites and the massive economic impact of the manufacture and sale of GPS devices to individual motorists. Medical research, too, has a long history of vast sums of money being spent on journeys up blind alleys, with new breakthroughs often coming by chance in quite unexpected places. Ciclosporin (formerly Cyclosporin), the immunosuppressive agent that revolutionized organ transplantation, was discovered as part of a general screening programme, not through a funded research project specifically addressing the problem of graft rejection. Medical history is full of stories of this kind.

Government and its officers have a prime duty to account for the expenditure of taxpayers' money, but in measuring the value of research a much subtler style of accountancy is required. There is something especially inappropriate about the attempt to *quantify* the 'value' and 'impact' of work in the humanities in economic terms, since the very nature of the humanities is to address the messy, debatable and unquantifiable but essentially human dimensions of life, such as history, beauty, imagination, faith, truth, goodness, justice and freedom. The only test of a philosophical argument, an historical hypothesis or an aesthetic judgement is time – a long period of time, not the duration of a government spending review.

One phrase in the RCUK definition of 'knowledge transfer' stands out: 'exploitation of the research base to meet national economic and public service objectives'. Public service, a concept most often used in relation to the charter of the BBC ('public service broadcasting'), comes from a different lexicon to that of economic objectives and commercial exploitation. It actually takes us back to some of the historical functions of the university. Like the BBC, the universities are in the business of *educere* as a public service. In this regard, their most significant form of 'knowledge transfer' goes under another name: teaching.

One of the most important answers to the question of what kind of public service is provided by humanities research is that it feeds into teaching: in good universities, research questions emerge through teaching and new hypotheses are tested out on students. An artificial barrier between research and teaching in the provision of government funding for universities – exacerbated by the impact of the 'Research Assessment Exercise' that has determined funding for the past two decades – has obscured this obvious answer. The division is sometimes justified on the grounds that the university teacher needs only 'scholarship', not new 'research', but such a distinction between scholarship and research simply does not hold water in any humanities discipline. To take an example from one of the most widely studied humanities disciplines, English literature: to teach a literary work well at university level, one requires a good text of that work; the establishment and creation of such texts through the discipline of textual bibliography is a highly advanced, technical and time-consuming form of research (my new recension of the text of Shakespeare's complete works required more than fifteen person years' research time); the resulting product cannot be described as 'merely a textbook' in the way that synthesis of existing scientific or medical knowledge into a textbook for students could be described as 'scholarship' rather than 'research'.

The primary impact of humanities research will always be within the educational system – which now means the global educational market. The universities that promote the best research and scholarship in the humanities will attract graduate students from around the world, thus greatly stimulating the economy and increasing our international competitiveness. The universities that build research into the undergraduate 'learning experience' will produce the most able students, who will bring their 'innovation' and 'skills' to every sector of the economy. A variety of metrics have provided empirical demonstration that UK humanities researchers lead the world in their disciplines, and that the quality of research and graduate education in British universities attracts overseas graduate students who bring a benefit of at least £2 billion a year to the UK economy (Arts & Humanities Research Council 2009: 11–13).

The relationship between academic research and teaching is paramount, but other answers are also needed to the question of the value of humanities research of the kind that is funded by Research Councils UK. I polled a random sample of colleagues, within my own university and beyond, with a hypothetical question (developing the art of posing hypothetical questions is, of course, another of the values of the humanities):

> Imagine a civil servant responsible for the distribution of the research budget. Imagine them saying 'I don't lose any sleep at night over the spending of taxpayers' money on medical research, but I do lose sleep over the spending of it on humanities research; I like riding my horse, but I don't expect the taxpayer to pay for me to do so.' Imagine, then, that you have the ear of that civil servant, or for that matter the minister to whom they report, for a few sentences. What will you say to help them to rest more easily at night on this matter of the taxpayer and humanities research?

Here are the – representative – replies of ten colleagues:

1. Britain is a major world centre of publishing and intellectual life. Research in humanities makes possible the intellectual property and the cultural institutions that sustain this position. Without British humanities academics there would be no *Oxford English Dictionary*, no *Macmillan Dictionary of Art*, no *Grove Dictionary of Music*, no *Routledge Encyclopedia of Philosophy*, no Oxford Classical Texts, all of which are sold on to the world and whose publication in turn guarantees Britain's place as a world intellectual centre. Furthermore, humanities research provides an infrastructure that maintains Britain's place as an intellectual and cultural centre, a place of publishing and reviewing, which enriches the work of our composers, artists, playwrights and novelists, whilst attracting creators from other countries and cultures to live here. We abandon this at our peril.

2. Humanities research engenders and fosters *critical thinking*, which is indispensable to innovative work in any field whatsoever.

3. One of the research councils' strategic priorities is 'global security'. If George W. Bush's and Tony Blair's security and strategic advisors had

been educated in the historical research of Erez Manela, the world would be a less dangerous place (see Mishra 2008).

4. To a person dying from cancer, the 'cure for cancer' is abstract and meaningless. It will only come after they are dead. What is needed by a dying person, beside the palliative medical care that is now available, are resources for working through their grief and anger and fear. Recent research in 'bibliotherapy' suggests that reading – reading in groups in particular – provides an extremely effective (and cost-effective) resource for this purpose. That is hardly surprising. The links between poetry and mental health have long been established. After all, William Wordsworth was the effective inventor of cognitive behavioural therapy – an initiative that has proved to be highly economic and effective. It is not entirely frivolous to suggest that literature offers public benefit in the arena of healthcare.

5. If the civil servant's horse-riding were of a standard to make her a potential Olympic competitor, wouldn't the taxpayer be content to fund her? National prestige need not be confined to sport: What is the objection to funding the research that allows our best historians, literary scholars, classicists and philosophers to be the Olympians of their disciplines?

6. A great deal of humanities research has to do with the question of how we have come to be who we are and what we might come to be as a community in the future – locally, nationally and globally. Government nowadays frequently asks questions about 'Britishness' and cultural identity: these are questions that can only be answered with any rigour through the historical and analytic perspectives offered by research in the humanities.

7. Anyone who thinks the arts and humanities are equivalent to leisure activities should probably stop using the word 'education' and just say 'training' instead. University teaching and research in the arts and humanities are essential to the maintenance of cultural heritage and cultural value. Only university teaching that is directly informed by high-quality research can sustain standards of international excellence. The fact that medical research requires money is no argument for reducing the money for other kinds of research to zero. What can the beneficiaries of advances in medical science do with the health they retain or recover? Read books, debate ideas, go to plays and movies, develop their capacity for thinking, speaking and writing – at work no less than at play. These are activities to which teaching in the arts and humanities – and the research that underpins and extends it – makes an essential contribution.

8. For every pound that the UK government spends on supporting academic work in the arts and humanities, it spends twenty-five on research into destroying human beings (the Arts & Humanities

Research Council budget is around £100 million, the Ministry of Defence Research Budget is £2.5 billion, almost exactly equal to that of the seven RCUK research councils put together). Work in the humanities includes what Matthew Arnold called 'disinterested endeavour to learn and propagate the best that has been known and thought in the world'. Are we to deprive future generations of that learning and propagation? But the humanities do not end there. They include understanding ourselves and other peoples through the language, literature, art, music, history, religion, philosophy, sense of identity, politics, desires, fears and ambitions, all of which animate ourselves and others, whether these are the best or not. We are asked whether this understanding is a public good, deserving public support, or merely a private hobby. The answer is that if you believe knowledge is too expensive, try ignorance. The human world is one in which we move and act, just as much as the natural world, which is the object of science. Misunderstanding either is the road to catastrophe; understanding each of them is our only salvation.

9. Your analogy with horse riding is fallacious since it implies that humanities research is purely recreational and confers no public good. However, the slightest acquaintance with the history of ideas supplies numerous examples of curiosity driven enquiry in the humanities having great social consequences. For example, Bertrand Russell's philosophical investigations into logic and language paved the way for the artificial languages essential to computer science; historical and cultural research fills bookshelves and museums that would otherwise be empty; and, in general, the knowledge and learning of the universities inspires cultural production and artistic endeavour. Exposure to the intellectual culture of academic research enriches the lives of countless students whose education would be greatly impoverished were they not taught by active scholars. Finally, a great proportion of academic books, journals and presses originate in the UK, and many students and foreign academics visit our shores only because of the academics that study in our public universities. Many jobs are created to service their needs while they are here and then there are the fees and taxes they pay. The total budget of the Arts & Humanities Research Council for a year is less than the cost of the average completely failed and written off National Health Service IT initiative.

10. A personal anecdote: something that pleased me more than anything for a long time was an email out of the blue from a Syrian asking permission to translate my little book *Think* (Blackburn 1999) into Arabic; he pleaded that there was no royalty he could pay, but he thought the Islamic world desperately needed an introduction to secular philosophy. Given the billions that the military option wastes, I think I can claim at least a small probability of being economically more efficient!

The purpose of the chapters in this book – a deliberately eclectic mix of case studies and reflective essays – is to offer a wide range of examples of humanities research in action, so demonstrating the strength of the many and varied claims made by my respondents.

Bentham v Coleridge

Several of the respondents make a comparison or contrast between military spending and spending on humanities research. These would appear to be two very different spheres of public life, but the juxtaposition is worth pursuing.

One of the values of humanities research is that it teaches us that all controversies have historical precedents – the lessons of which we are very good at ignoring. The debate between those who look for the 'economic impact' of academic research and those who appeal to the pursuit of knowledge as a civilizing virtue replicates a dichotomy identified by John Stuart Mill in the early Victorian era, in his pair of essays on Jeremy Bentham (written in 1838) and Samuel Taylor Coleridge (1840).

Mill contends that Bentham and Coleridge are the two 'great seminal minds' of the age. Britain, he proposes, is indebted to them 'not only for the greater part of the important ideas which have been thrown into circulation among its thinking men in their time, but for a revolution in its general modes of thought and investigation'. Bentham and Coleridge, he argues:

> were destined to renew a lesson given to mankind by every age, and always disregarded – to show that speculative philosophy, which to the superficial appears a thing so remote from the business of life and the outward interests of men, is in reality the thing on earth which most influences them, and in the long run overbears every other influence save those which it must itself obey. The writers of whom we speak have never been read by the multitude; except for the more slight of their works, their readers have been few: but they have been the teachers of the teachers; there is hardly to be found in England an individual of any importance in the world of mind, who (whatever opinions he may have afterwards adopted) did not first learn to think from one of these two. (Leavis 1959: 39)

To effect a revolution in 'general modes of thought'; to inhabit a realm ('speculative philosophy') that seems utterly remote from 'the business of life' and yet to influence society more than anyone else; to be 'the teachers of the teachers'; to be the figures from whom all serious minds 'learn to think' – even if these claims were to be greatly diluted, the implication would still be that the intellectual work of Bentham and Coleridge was of extraordinary value to society, although its *direct* impact (in terms of the number of people who read their major books) was minimal. Their importance is in itself is a salutary warning against the danger of taking the short view of the question of public value.

What, then, were their great innovations? Bentham, says Mill, was 'the great *critical* thinker of his age and country', 'the great questioner of things established'. He was the iconoclast who was no respecter of institutions and traditions. A latter-day Benthamite might well say: Why should we fund research in the humanities just because we have funded it in the past? Bentham, continues Mill, 'introduced into morals and politics those habits of thought and modes of investigation, which are essential to the idea of science'. A latter-day Benthamite might very well say: Prove the value of what you do by *quantifying* it. Be precise, be empirical, do not rely on windy rhetoric. Give me a *metric*. Famously, Bentham's utilitarian principle was 'the greatest happiness of the greatest number'. If push-pin (a children's game) gives happiness to more people than poetry, then push-pin is more valuable than poetry. 'Quantity of pleasure being equal, push-pin is as good as poetry.' In this view, quantity – or, as we would now say, 'access' or 'inclusion' – trumps intellectual athleticism and aesthetic value. By this logic, government might well find itself subsidizing access to push-pin's modern equivalents – computer games – and leaving poetry to the mercy of the market.

Mill admires the modernity and the democracy of Bentham's utilitarian position, but deplores its lack of imagination: 'He committed the mistake of supposing that the business part of human affairs was the whole of them.' Bentham failed to take into account other aspects under which human activities should be judged – the moral, the aesthetic and the sympathetic (a modern term for the latter might be 'the socially cohesive'). Bentham must therefore be balanced against Coleridge.

Whereas Bentham began by asking of every received opinion 'Is it true?', Coleridge began by asking 'What is the meaning of it?' How can society foster those dimensions of human life that Benthamite utilitarianism cannot account for – the ethical, the beautiful, the cohesive force? Through the creation, Coleridge suggests, 'of an endowed class, for the cultivation of learning, and for diffusing its results among the community'. Mill describes how, in his treatise *On the Constitution of the Church and State*, Coleridge (who was actually developing an idea first put forward in Germany by Friedrich Schiller) proposed that there should be what he termed a 'nationalty' or 'national property' in the form of a fund – derived from taxation – dedicated to 'the advancement of knowledge, and the civilization of the community'. This national fund should support and maintain what he called a 'clerisy', a kind of secular clergy, with the following duties:

A certain smaller number were to remain at the fountain-heads of the humanities, in cultivating and enlarging the knowledge already possessed, and in watching over the interests of physical and moral science; being likewise the instructors of such as constituted, or were to constitute, the remaining more numerous classes of the order.

The members of this latter and far more numerous body were to be distributed throughout the country, so as not to leave even the smallest integral part or division without a resident guide, guardian, and instructor; the objects and final intention of the whole order being these – to preserve the stores and to guard the treasures of past civilization, and thus to bind the present with the past; to perfect and add to the same, and thus to connect the present with the future; but especially to diffuse through the whole community, and to every native entitled to its laws and rights, that quantity and quality of knowledge which was indispensable both for the understanding of those rights, and for the performance of the duties correspondent; finally, to secure for the nation, if not a superiority over the neighbouring states, yet an equality at least, in that character of general civilization, which equally with, or rather more than, fleets, armies, and revenue, forms the ground of its defensive and offensive power. (Coleridge 1972: 34)

Researchers and teachers in the humanities are of value to the state if and when they fulfil the function of the Coleridgean clerisy. They must remember, though, that they are a form of 'national property': their work must be for the benefit not of themselves but of the entire nation. Reading Coleridge's definition of the clerisy in the light of twenty-first century debates about research funding, what is most striking is the huge emphasis that he places on what is now called 'dissemination'. The results of our research must be 'distributed throughout the country, so as not to leave even the smallest integral part or division without a resident guide, guardian, and instructor'.

The investment must be large, the responsibility – the public duty – placed upon the latter-day clerisy is heavy, but in the 'knowledge economy' and faced with the global insecurity of the twenty-first century, the return on the investment is potentially vast. Even more than in Coleridge's day, the work of the clerisy in binding past, present and future, in yoking inheritance to aspiration and tradition to innovation, and in maintaining the understanding of 'those rights' and 'correspondent duties' that are at the core of national identity, can play a major role in 'securing for the nation' that 'character of general civilization, which equally with, or rather more than, fleets, armies, and revenue, forms the ground of its defensive and offensive power'.

Research in the humanities is often regarded as a superficial ornament of society. Those who undertake it are sometimes accused of obscurantism, of being all too eager to show off the amazing technicolor dreamcoat of their academic jargon at the expense of communicating clearly with a wide public. But if Coleridge is to be believed, it might just be that among the faculties of humanities we will find the Josephs who will guide us through the seven lean years.

Bibliography

Arts & Humanities Research Council (2009), *Leading the World: The Economic Impact of UK Arts and Humanities Research*, http://www.ahrc.ac.uk/About/Policy/Documents/leadingtheworld.pdf [accessed 10 July 2010].

Blackburn, S. (1999), *Think: A Compelling Introduction to Philosophy*, Oxford: Oxford University Press.

Coleridge, S.T. (1972), *On the Constitution of the Church and State*, edited by J. Barrell, London: Dent.

Leavis, F.R. (ed.) (1959), *Mill on Bentham and Coleridge*, London: Chatto & Windus.

Mishra, P. (2008), 'Ordained as a nation', review of E. Manela's *The Wilsonian Moment*, *London Review of Books*, 30: 4: 3–8, http://www.lrb.co.uk/v30/n04/misho1_.html.

Newman, J.H. (1852), *Discourses on the Scope and Nature of a University Education*, Dublin: James Duffy.

RCUK, http://www.rcuk.ac.uk/aboutrcs/activities/default.htm [accessed 10 July 2010].

Shakespeare, W. (2007), *The RSC Shakespeare: The Complete Works*, edited by J. Bate and E. Rasmussen, New York and Basingstoke: Macmillan.

PART ONE

Learning from the Past

1. Live Classics: Or 'What's the use of Aeschylus in Darfur?'

Mary Beard (University of Cambridge)[1]

Fram, *Trackers* and classics

Tony Harrison's play, *Fram*, brought the Arctic icecap to the British stage in 2008. It traces the career of Fridtjof Nansen from polar explorer ('*Fram*' was the name of his ship) to philanthropist, campaigner and Nobel Laureate for his efforts in relieving the Russian famine of 1922. Quirky as well as brilliant, written in rhyming couplets, the play is partly the resurrection of a forgotten hero: for Nansen's polar exploits were soon surpassed by Roald Amundsen's, and his beloved League of Nations was quickly sidelined by the events of the 1930s. It is also a play of big questions and ideas: on the nature of heroism, the fragility of human survival and the power of language to change the world. In one memorable scene, a group of well-meaning but ineffectual do-gooders, who are debating the relative merits of colour and black-and-white photography to open the eyes of the world to the suffering of Russia, are upstaged, literally, by the character of Sybil Thorndike, who in a mesmerizing speech demonstrates the power of words alone to evoke the horrors of starvation (Nemser 2008: 149–56).

Yet there is another set of questions to which Harrison repeatedly returns in *Fram*. In what ways does the classical world still make a difference our own? What is the point of Greek tragedy now? How can its study be justified? Or, as one of the play's first reviewers put it, 'What's the use of Aeschylus in Darfur?' (Nightingale 2008) At first sight these questions make an incongruous pairing with the story of polar exploration and interwar famine relief. But the play has a second hero, in the character of Gilbert Murray, Professor of Greek at the University of Oxford between 1908 and 1936. Like Nansen, Murray had several strings to his bow. He was a prolific and immensely successful translator of Greek tragedy, and almost single-handedly responsible for bringing ancient drama to a wide popular audience in Britain. His research was instrumental in changing forever our assumptions about ancient Greek culture and religion: Murray and his friends showed that underneath its calm, intellectual, apparently rational exterior, Greek culture retained a primitive, bloody and irrational side. He was also, like Nansen, a driving force behind the League of Nations and other liberal causes. His translation of Euripides' *Medea* was performed at women's suffrage meetings, as the tale of a woman provoked to the most terrible acts of infanticide by her powerlessness in a man's world; and his translation of *Trojan Women*, a tragedy about the terrible consequences that war wreaks on non-combatants, was famously staged in thirty-one locations through the American Mid-West in 1915 as part of the Women's Peace Movement. In *Fram*, Tony Harrison gives Murray an unlikely new role: emerging from his tomb in Westminster Abbey, on the fiftieth anniversary of his death and with Dame Sybil in tow, he is to write a play – a play within a play – on the life of Fridtjof Nansen.

Murray's part in *Fram* prompts all kinds of questions about the value of research in classics; and about what counts as worthwhile discovery and exploration, from the polar wastelands to the world of the ancient Greeks. 'Tragedy was my *Fram*', as Murray remarks at one point (Harrison 2008: 78). In characteristic fashion, Tony Harrison's answers are simultaneously trenchant, visionary and ambivalent. For although Murray in the end smashes to the floor the Greek tragic mask that has been his classical symbol and totem throughout the play, there are many occasions earlier where his engagement with the ancient world has proved not only eye-opening, but central to the political and humanitarian goals the drama espouses. In fact, Sybil Thorndike's brilliantly persuasive soliloquy on the horrors of famine derives directly from the conventions of Greek tragedy, which always chose words over images when it came to conveying agony, violence and brutality. Murray is our guide in trying to understand quite how, and why, those words could be so powerful – and why they cannot be written off, to quote one of the boorish bit-part players, who has no truck with culture of any sort, as 'ancient tragic shit' (Harrison 2008: 41).

Harrison had explored some of these themes before. His 1988 *The Trackers of Oxyrhynchus* brought to life a play by the Athenian tragedian Sophocles, which had been rediscovered in 1907 by a couple of British classicists digging in the buried piles of wastepaper in a small town of Roman Egypt. *Trackers* is not itself a tragedy, but a burlesque in which the god Apollo, with the help of some grossly phallic 'satyrs', tries to track down his herd of cows, stolen by a prankster junior deity, the baby Hermes. It is a rare survival of the bawdy, subversive comedies conventionally performed for light relief, after the original fifth-century audience had sat through several hours of wrenching tragic drama. For Harrison, *Trackers* was an opportunity to explore this lusty populist side of classical culture. His production, first at Delphi and then at London's National Theatre, was almost the first time the play had been performed in over 2,000 years.[2]

The 'Trackers' of the title has two senses, for Harrison frames the performance of the ancient comedy with the story of its two young discoverers, Bernard Grenfell and Arthur Hunt, who are also in the business of 'tracking': not stolen cattle, but the material from the classical world that we have lost. They are searching in the rubbish dumps of Roman Egypt for the precious fragments of Greek and Roman writing. Here too, in the different priorities of Grenfell and Hunt, Harrison focuses on the question of why we want to study the classical world. What are we doing it *for*? Both men are keen to recover the rich scraps from the Roman wastepaper baskets, but they are after scraps of a different sort: the down-to-earth Hunt is entranced by the documents of real life in the ancient world (the desperate petitions of the Roman homeless, for example); the donnish and slightly dotty Grenfell has eyes only for the remains of ancient poetry. What, Harrison is asking, is the study of the ancient world all about? Is it a history of politics, power, deprivation, slavery and misogyny? Or of creative literature that can still engage and inspire? (Parsons 2007)

Greek drama now

Harrison himself has done much to prove the extraordinary power that Greek drama can still have over a modern audience – from his prize-winning translation of Aeschylus' *Oresteia*, directed by Peter Hall in 1981, to his version of Euripides' *Hecuba* for the Royal Shakespeare Company almost three decades later, which played in London, the USA and Greece, with Vanessa Redgrave in the title role. But Harrison is only one voice – uniquely privileged though he is, as both dramatist and classicist by training – in an extraordinary flowering of ancient drama on the contemporary British stage. Greek plays are now performed more often than they have been at any time since the second century AD. In Britain, more than anywhere else, a series of notable productions over the last thirty years has had enormous cultural and political impact, as well as critical and commercial success. They have played both in London and the regions (*Trackers* itself moved to Saltaire in Yorkshire after the National), both in mainstream and experimental theatre. For example, Punchdrunk, a radical theatre company singled out by one Labour minister of culture for its commitment to 'access' combined with 'excellence', reconfigured *The House of Oedipus* as a live action installation within a vast garden at Poltimore House in Devon in 2000.[3] Several of these productions have turned into distinguished British cultural exports, from Bombay (Liz Lochhead's *Medea*) to Broadway (both Jonathan Kent's and Deborah Warner's *Medea*, as well as Harrison's *Hecuba*).

The best of them have prompted admiration, reflection and debate, going beyond the array of prizes that they have won. True, Diana Rigg's role as Medea (in Kent's production) brought her a Tony Award in New York; Fiona Shaw and Deborah Warner both won Evening Standard Awards in 2001 as actor and director, for their *Medea*; and an Olivier Award went to Clare Higgins for her part in Jonathan Kent's *Hecuba* in 2004 (one of three *Hecubas* playing on the London stage in the space of a year). But even more impressive has been the powerful cultural resonance of these performances. In addition to the trio of *Hecubas*, with their stark focus on the human cost of war, director Katie Mitchell's productions for the National Theatre and the Royal Shakespeare Company have memorably linked Euripides' war tragedies (*The Phoenician Women, Iphigenia at Aulis* and *Women of Troy*) to new areas and methods of military conflict, from the Balkans to Iraq. Even closer to home, in the spring of 1992 the

Royal Shakespeare Company's *Electra* was performed to nightly standing ovations in a sports stadium in Londonderry. A terrifying analysis of revenge, passed down from generation to generation, corrupting human feelings, values and aspirations, the play coincided with one of the bloodiest weeks of sectarian violence in the province. The audience got the point.

As Harrison suggests in *Fram* and *Trackers*, the success of ancient drama on the modern stage depends on a dynamic collaboration between the theatre and the academy, a symbiosis of stage professionals and academic research. Brilliant as the ancient plays are, they are not transparent timeless creations, waiting to be rediscovered by an enterprising director and a talented company of actors. They are difficult texts. In many cases the Greek is very difficult to understand, and the underlying sense of the words is often elusive. It takes years of learning to begin to make sense of Aeschylus' *Oresteia* in Greek. The texts are also culturally very dense. For, although tackling issues that are as close to universal as we could imagine (passion, incest, jealousy, betrayal, cruelty...), these plays are also deeply embedded in the society, politics, myth and religion of the ancient Greeks. They are simultaneously familiar to us and very foreign indeed. It requires knowledge, expertise and hard work to see how their significance can best be represented for a wide modern audience. Greek drama does not simply speak for itself.

One aspect of that symbiosis is the practical collaboration between theatre professionals and academic researchers. Oliver Taplin (University of Oxford), for example, has worked side by side with Harrison and Mitchell; Edith Hall (Royal Holloway, University of London) has collaborated with Colin Teevan, who translated Euripides' *Bacchae* for the National Theatre, and with Peter Hall (no relation); Ian Ruffell (University of Glasgow) worked with John Tiffany and David Greig on a National Theatre of Scotland production of the *Bacchae*; Vanessa Redgrave read and talked to Simon Goldhill (University of Cambridge) in preparing the part of Hecuba. This is not merely to cast the academic in the role of pronunciation adviser and fact-checker, though I am sure they sometimes do both. Nor is it simply a question of commissioning a likely 'expert' to write the programme notes, though such experts have been responsible for excellent, accessible essays to accompany many a production. In the most fruitful of these collaborations, it is the interaction and dialogue between the scholar and the director, translator or actor that lies at the very heart of the production and its interpretation of the dramatic text.

However, at a deeper level than that, the freshness and innovation of these productions depends on their engagement with up-to-date British research in ancient Greek literature more generally. One of the clearest examples of this lies in the whole area of theatrical technique and staging. How Greek tragedies were performed in antiquity itself, and in what kind of space, has exercised classical research for generations. In fact, it was precisely this issue that first stimulated the revival of wider interest in stage performances of Greek drama at the end of the nineteenth century. The most influential productions of that period were devised not by dramatists, but by archaeologists attempting to solve what they called the 'Greek theatre question': namely, did Greek actors originally perform on a raised platform? The answer proved to be a definite 'no', and that once bitterly fought controversy has long been forgotten. But these practical archaeological simulations of the Greek theatre turned out to be successful in theatrical terms and kick-started the modern tradition of Greek drama in performance. It is a nice example of the serendipity and unpredictable consequences of so much research. A narrowly archaeological puzzle opened the way for more than a century of creative theatrical productions.

More recently academic concerns have focused on the problems of *masking* in Greek drama: not whether the actors were originally masked (they were), but rather what difference the masks must have made to the articulation and scripting of the play, to the characterization of the actors and to the effect of the performance on the audience. This strand of research was developed by Peter Hall, both in his production of Harrison's *Oresteia* and in his later *Oedipus Plays* at the National Theatre, where the actors were all masked. This was not merely an experiment in archaeological authenticity. Hall has come to see masks as essential to the performance of Greek tragic drama and, in particular, to the effective recreation of a Greek chorus. 'I think the plays were telling us to go back to masks,' Hall has said (Hall 1996). Not all would agree, but this stress on masking has been taken up, very differently, by Punchdrunk. Their radical redefinition of the theatre as an all-encompassing artform (which at the same time liberates the audience from the prison of their seats) owes much to questions about theatrical space raised in academic work on ancient drama. Although its repertoire extends a long way beyond the classical, the company's slogan is a quotation from Sophocles' *Oedipus at Colonus* ('These things are mysteries not to be explained. But you will understand when you get there alone') and one of its devices is to put masks not the actors, but on the audience. There is a direct, if nicely subversive, link here between the development of artistic form and research in the ancient world (Smith 2009: 166–8).

It is, however, in changing interpretations of the ancient texts that research in classics has had most to contribute to Greek drama on stage, and to its power to affect and attract modern and diverse audiences. Research in the classical world is neither a narrowly antiquarian pursuit, nor is it a desperate search for cheap contemporary relevance. At its best, it sets up a dialogue between our own concerns and those of the ancients, prompting new understandings of the ancient world as our concerns change – and vice versa. In these terms, research into any aspect of the classical world can never be finished. Each generation finds something new, and often mind-changing, in material that has for the most part (notwithstanding notable discoveries among the wastepaper of ancient Egypt) been known and studied for centuries.

Translation is a good case in point. Why bother with further expensive work on Greek texts when we have sometime hundreds of translations of the major plays? Harrison answers this question in *Fram*. Returning to London after fifty years in the grave, Murray is aware that his translations would now sound ridiculous. 'All translations date', he says, defensively, 'I don't for a minute imagine that I dare aspire / to a National Theatre revival of my *Oresteia*' (Harrison 2008: 80) – Harrison's rhyming couplets here echoing some of the worse of Murray's verse.[4] It would take no more than a minute's glance at Murray's translations to see that, hugely successful though they once were, they would never attract an audience now, still less earn a transfer to Broadway. So why do they not work for us? T.S. Eliot's view was entirely aesthetic: they were in his view bad poetry (Eliot 1920).[5] But that hardly explains their influence and wide popularity. The answer must be that, in the continuing dialogue with the past, Murray's concerns and Murray's Greek tragedy are not ours. For all our admiration for Murray, our Greek drama is not the same as his.

We can see that difference, and the effect of new research, in some of the most successful productions of the last thirty years. Hall's production of Harrison's *Oresteia* did not merely exploit recent work on masks, it reflected other lines of research on Aeschylus' trilogy. One case in point was the highly ritualized style of the performance, which would have been impossible without a renewed scholarly interest in the ritual element of tragedy. (For all Murray's concern with religion and the irrational, his theatrical versions were frankly rather polite and stately.) Several critics saw that the National Theatre production had turned the tragedy back into a ritual event, in which the audience was encourage to share – and almost believe in (Wiles 2000). Another important aspect was language and, in particular, the sonorous emphasis on the gender markers of the original Greek: 'he-god', 'she-god', 'man-child'. Disliked by some reviewers, this feature reflected much new research on these plays, which sees highly gendered language underlining the trilogy's role as a charter myth for the subordination of women.[6] The National Theatre of Scotland's *Bacchae* similarly exploited new academic approaches to the play: Ian Ruffell writes of exploring with the director and translator 'many of the key themes in recent research into Greek tragedy ... questions of identity (particularly gender identity), of the self-reflexivity, playfulness and humour of (in particular) Euripidean tragedy'. The result challenged the old familiar play about madness and possession, to suggest a story of the collapse of identities, especially sexual ones – in an extraordinarily powerful, disconcertingly modern, as well as authentically ancient, production.

The message is very clear: that this internationally acclaimed tradition of British theatre is unthinkable without a thriving tradition of classical research. It is through the contemporary re-readings of these plays within the academy – time-consuming, intensive scholarly work – that they retain a capacity to speak to audiences today. Or, as Alan Davey, the Head of the Arts Council, puts it: 'a dynamic research base into classical culture is important for the effective presentation and understanding of classical drama on the stage and elsewhere, and is essential for the development of theatrical form'.[7]

Classical research: discovery, rediscovery and distinction

Classical research, of course, extends far beyond Greek drama to all aspects of Greek and Roman culture, from the unsavoury remains of Pompeian latrines to the origin of law in early Greece, from the relationship between Greco-Roman and Chinese science to the religious conflicts of the Roman Empire. Nonetheless, research in drama and its successful public dissemination offers a useful paradigm for work in the subject more broadly.

As already mentioned, *The Trackers of Oxyrhynchus* was set in an Egyptian rubbish dump, with an odd pair of Oxford classicists on the hunt for lost evidence of the ancient world: poetry, drama, petitions, laundry-lists and tax receipts. Classics remain a discipline of discovery. The scraps of paper which Grenfell and Hunt unearthed early last century are still, even now, being deciphered – a highly skilled task – in Oxford. There are, in fact, 50,000 pieces that remain not yet fully studied; these will take 40 more volumes over 40 years to put into the public domain (Parsons 2007: 25–30). Grenfell and Hunt differed, as we saw, on exactly what it was they hoped to track down. Grenfell's passion for the lost poetry of antiquity would not have been wholly disappointed. Some 95 per cent of Greek literature did not make it through the Middle Ages. Most of it did not appeal to the tastes of the medieval monks on whose choices in preservation our own libraries now largely depend. The sands of Egypt, and the wastepaper stuffing used in mummies, have produced several 'new' works of literature. These include substantial parts of the Athenian comic dramatist Menander, and of the poetry of Sappho, the most famous female writer of the classical world and not a favourite in the monasteries.[8] Recently, in Grenfell and Hunt's scraps, more than twenty lines of a new poem by the sixth-century BC poet Archilochus has been deciphered (Gonis *et al.* 2005). But it is the more sober Hunt who would probably have been most pleased with the results of their wastepaper finds. Thanks to the everyday, throw-away documents that have now been decoded – contracts, letters, tax-demands and so on – a vivid picture of life in an Egyptian town from the ancient world to the early Middle Ages can be reconstructed. Here we find inflation and famine, the grassroots effects of Roman imperialism, the rough-edges of multiculturalism, the beginnings of Christianity and, towards the end, the growth of Islam. A hundred years of hard research has opened an entirely new window on to the day-to-day life of an ancient town. And it is brilliantly captured for a non-specialist, as well as a specialist, audience in Peter Parsons' best-seller: *City of the Sharp Nosed Fish* (which is what the word 'Oxyrhynchus' actually means).

There are discoveries of this kind on our own doorstep, too. On a BBC television programme broadcast to a huge audience on New Year's Day 2003, a 'panel of experts' judged the Roman writing tablets found at the Roman fort of Vindolanda near Hadrian's Wall to be Number One of the British Museum's 'Top Ten Treasures'. More than 400 of these tablets have been excavated at Vindolanda since the early 1970s, and – in addition to all kinds of new evidence about the Roman army – they include such evocative vignettes of ancient life as a birthday party invitation from one Roman soldier's wife to another and a note enclosed with a gift of socks and pants to a soldier. It is these, along with hundreds of so-called 'curse tablets' ('May whoever it was who stole my cloak suffer agonies', etc.) found in and near Bath, that have given Britain a surprising claim to fame (Tomlin 1988; Woodward and Leach 1993). Over the last twenty years or so, more 'new' Latin has been unearthed here (as distinct from the Greek texts from Egypt) than anywhere else in the world.

The discovery of the Vindolanda tablets had a powerful effect on the popular imagination, as the BBC accolade suggests. On Hadrian's Wall itself, it launched a series of wide-ranging heritage and cultural events, notably from 2001 to 2006 an Arts UK creative writing project called 'Writing on the Wall'. This not only showcased the tablets and the archaeology of the surrounding area; it involved the local community, museums and schools in workshops and events which explored the multicultural character of the Roman Empire (and modern Britain) by bringing to the region writers from all the countries that had garrisoned the Wall in the Roman Empire, from Iraq to Morocco, Bulgaria to Wales. Hugely successful, it was a direct consequence of the charismatic discovery – and would have been impossible to imagine if the tablets had remained illegible (Chettle 2006).

The reading of these documents is, in fact, even more difficult than that of the Oxyrhynchus papyri. They were originally written on wax smeared over a wooden board. The wax has long since disappeared, and the writing survives only as the stylus' scratches on the wood beneath. Two things were needed to make any sense of these. The first was the most advanced technology of 'imaging', simply to reveal what was there, though invisible to the naked eye. This was achieved in Oxford by collaboration with those in the forefront of medical imaging. And, in fact, in one of those unexpected research spin-offs (such as those prompted by the 'Greek Theatre Question'), some of the techniques developed for the tablets turned out to have applications in clinical medicine. But, even then, the words would have remained undecipherable without the highest level of skill in Latin, historical linguistics and palaeography (that is, the reading of the handwritten language), nurtured and honed in British research centres for centuries. This kind of expertise cannot simply be re-learnt when you just happen to decide you need it again. The ability to exploit key discoveries depends on continuity and long-term investment in these highly technical research skills.

The success of Greek drama in the contemporary theatre is not, however, based on new finds. *Trackers* aside, we are watching plays that have been part of Western culture for millennia. What is new is what we make of them, and the changing interpretations and associations that allow them to speak afresh to us. Likewise classical research more generally is revolutionary in its capacity to reinterpret, and to see new things and new areas of study in what we thought we understood. Every area of the subject can produce notable examples of this. Ancient historians are now looking much more directly at the cultural and religious identities that marked the diverse communities of the Roman Empire. In what sense, for example, was the Roman world racist? And, if not, why not? They are using new demographic techniques to examine the movements of populations in antiquity, and thinking again about the patterns of migration and asylum. Ancient philosophers have started to reassess the many works of philosophy that followed the period of Plato (still probably the most read and best-selling philosopher in the world) and Aristotle. Partly stimulated by the recent decipherment of the philosophical papyri discovered at Herculaneum (on the Bay of Naples) in the eighteenth century, this new work has focused particularly on the school of Epicurus. This was not the hedonism that the term 'Epicurean' was often taken to mean, but a rigorous school of thought, hugely influential on Jeremy Bentham, British Utilitarianism and, ironically, the cost-benefit philosophy that now underlies much public policymaking.

But perhaps the most striking rediscovery of the last twenty years has been the literature and culture of Greece under the Roman Empire, in the first and second centuries AD. This was once written off as decidedly second rate compared with that of the fifth and fourth century BC (the great tragedians, Herodotus and Thucydides, Plato and Aristotle) – the work of fawning provincials under an oppressive empire, rather than free citizens of a democracy. Re-read in a 'post-colonial' world, this imperial literature can now be seen as a clever, careful and sometimes very witty response to a new world order and imperial domination. It has prompted some of the most innovative literary and cultural studies of ancient texts, some of which have not seriously been thought about for centuries – Lucian, Plutarch's *Essays*, Dio Chrysostom. At the same time it has turned attention to the Roman emperors of the second century AD, in particular Hadrian, whose sponsorship of Greek architecture, whose self-presentation as a Greek philosopher and whose attachment to a young Greek boy, Antinous, are all part of the same cultural phenomenon – albeit from the Roman side.

The influence of this work in the public sphere has been particularly impressive. An exhibition on *Antinous: the face of the Antique* was staged at the Henry Moore Institute in Leeds in 2006. Co-curated by a young Cambridge classicist, it featured some of the exquisite statues that the grieving Hadrian erected to the boy after his tragic and mysterious death in the Nile. The catalogue accompanying this show won the inaugural Art Book

Award, and was particularly praised for making 'the art of antiquity relevant to twenty-first-century viewers' (Vout *et al.* 2006). In 2008 a major exhibition on Hadrian himself opened in the British Museum, taking the place recently vacated by the terracotta warriors. The museum's summer blockbuster, devised in collaboration with university academics, it made accessible to hundreds of thousands of visitors some of the fruits of this important new strand of research (Opper 2008).

In the end, there is the issue of distinction. One major reason for the international renown of British 'classical' theatre is simply quality. These productions are innovative, challenging, accessible – world leading. The same is true of classical research overall. Classics is an international community, a subject shared through old and new Europe, as well as the USA, Australia and further afield (the subject flourishes in Japan, China, Brazil, Mexico, South Africa – even Zimbabwe and Congo). In this context, British classical research is world-leading, punching well above its weight. British books of classical scholarship (as well as newer electronic forms of dissemination) are sold and translated throughout the world. British classical scholars continue to win far more than their fair share of the international marks of esteem. Of the last twenty-five annual Sather Professors at Berkeley (invited to deliver what are generally acknowledged to be the most prestigious lectures in the field) ten either teach or were educated in Britain. Of the four 'ancient' prize-winners of the International Balzan Prize, since its foundation in 1961, two have been based in the United Kingdom.

The truth is that classics is a subject at which the British do very well indeed. Classical researchers here are working on a subject that is radical and innovatory, at the same time as it is a traditional and indispensable part of Western culture. Within and beyond the universities, it has an enduring value and significance.

You could want no better proof of that – to take one final example from Europe – than the events of summer 2008 in the town of Braunschweig in Saxony, Germany. In the Second World War Braunschweig was the major base to the SS and the home garrison of many of the German soldiers who died at Stalingrad. With Claudia Bosse as director and Edith Hall (of Royal Holloway) as advisor, the town recently hosted a performance of Aeschylus' *Persians*, the earliest Greek tragedy to survive, telling the story of the defeat of the Persians by the Greeks in the early fifth century BC – from the Persian point of view. Following a similar experiment by Bosse, on a slightly smaller scale, in Geneva the year before, 500 of the 'ordinary' citizens of Braunschweig played the part of the chorus (of defeated Persians). This was not only an attempt – in the style of Punchdrunk's audience masking – to subvert the hierarchy of actor and audience; there was a more directly political point, too. For Bosse (as for Harrison), Greek tragedy forces the modern world to confront its demons (Müller-Schöll 2004: 51–3).

Notes

1   I owe thanks for helpful conversations and correspondence on 'Live Classics' to many, especially Alan Bowman, Alan Davey, Simon Goldhill, Edith Hall, Charlotte Higgins, Ian Ruffell, Peter Stothard, Oliver Taplin and Peter Parsons.

2   There is a complex textual history to this play, and significantly different versions. Tony Harrison, *The Trackers of Oxyrhynchus* (Harrison, 1990) publishes the version of the play first played at Delphi in 1988; the second published edition, in 1991, includes both the version played at Delphi and at the National Theatre 'revival' in 1990. The play is acutely discussed by Oliver Taplin (Taplin 1991). The Oxford Archive of Performances of Greek and Roman Drama (www.apgrd.ox.ac.uk) references five earlier performances of Sophocles' satyr play since its rediscovery – in Germany (1913), Czechoslovakia (1921), Italy (1927), UK (1959), USA (1988).

3   The praise was from James Purnell in a speech at the National Portrait Gallery, London, on 6 July 2007 (www.culture.gov.uk/reference_library/minister_speeches/2058.aspx/, accessed 10 July 2010).

4   Some of the more hostile critics of *Fram* and its rhymes failed to see that Murray's own verse (or, rather, how it now sounds to us) was being parodied. See, for example, Michael Coveney (Coveney 2008): 'the tone hovers between trite pantomime couplet and a joltingly overcrowded metrical system'.

5   Harrison's Murray on several occasions fights back, attacking 'rhymeless poetry like you-know-who's' (Harrison 2008: 14).

6   Benedict Nightingale (Nightingale 1981) was not the only critic to find this turning of language irritating: 'sounding like a collaboration between the author of "Beowulf" and some street-café poetaster in jeans [it] gives unnatural and sometimes specious to the trilogy's concerns with matters sexual and cosmosexual'. Yet important classical work on the conflicts of gender within the trilogy, such as that by Froma Zeitlin (Zeitlin 1978), was surely influential on Harrison. As Ruth Padel later observed (Padel 1996: 216): 'New interpretative work by classicists does eventually filter through to the outside world. You could hear Froma Zeitlin in Tony Harrison's *Oresteia*, Richard Seaford [University of Exeter] in *Trackers*'.

7   Ian Ruffell and Alan Davey: personal communications.

8   Almost all that survives from Menander's plays is owed to papyrus discoveries of the last 100 years or so – the most substantial being the more or less complete *Dyskolos* (or 'Bad-tempered Man'), edited by E.W. Handley (Handley 1965). A 'new' poem of Sappho was reconstructed as recently as 2004, by combining part of a poem found at Oxyrhynchus with another part on a papyrus now in Cologne (Gronewald and Daniel 2004).

Bibliography

Astley, N. (ed.) (1991), *Tony Harrison*, Newcastle-upon-Tyne: Bloodaxe.

Beard, M. (2002), *The Invention of Jane Harrison*, Cambridge, MA: Harvard University Press.

Bowman, A.K. (1998), *Life and Letters on the Roman Frontier: Vindolanda and its People*, London: British Museum Press.

Chettle, S. (ed.) (2006), *Writing on the Wall*, Newcastle-upon-Tyne: Arts UK.

Coveney, M. (2008), 'Fram', 18 April, http://www.whatsonstage.com/reviews/theatre/london/E8821208509195/Fram.html [accessed 18 July 2010].

Easterling, P. (1999), 'The Early Years of the Cambridge Greek Play: 1882–1912', in Christopher Stray (ed.), *Classics in 19th and 20th Century Cambridge: Curriculum, Culture and Community*, Supplement 29, Cambridge: Cambridge Philological Society.

Eliot, T.S. (1920), 'Euripides and Professor Murray', in *The Sacred Wood: Essays in Poetry and Criticism*, London: Methuen, 71–7.

Goldhill, S. (ed.) (2001), *Being Greek under Rome: Cultural Identity, the Second Sophistic and the Development of Empire*, Cambridge: Cambridge University Press.

Goldhill, S. (2007), *How to Stage Greek Tragedy Today*, Chicago and London: Chicago University Press.

Gonis, N., Obbink, D. *et al.* (eds and trans) (2005), *Oxyrhynchus Papyri*, vol. LXIX, London: Egypt Exploration Society.

Gronewald, M. and Daniel, R.W. (2004), 'Ein neuer Sappho-Papyrus', *Zeitschrift für Papyrologie und Epigraphik* (International Journal for Papyrology and Ancient Epigraphics), 47: 1–8.

Hall, E., Macintosh, F. and Wrigley, A. (eds) (2004), *Dionysus since 69: Greek Tragedy at the Dawn of the Third Millennium*, Oxford: Oxford University Press.

Hall, E. (2010), *Greek Tragedy: Suffering under the Sun*, Oxford: Oxford University Press.

Hall, E. (1999), 'Sophocles' *Electra* in Britain', in J. Griffin (ed.), *Sophocles Revisited: essays presented to Sir Hugh Lloyd-Jones*, Oxford: Oxford University Press, 261–306.

Hall, P. (1996), *Exposed by the Mask: Form and Language in Drama*, quoted in 'Platform Papers' (2000), London: National Theatre, 21 September, http://www.nationaltheatre.org.uk/2626/platform-papers/peter-hall.html [accessed 10 July 2010].

Handley, E.W. (ed.) (1965), *Dyskolos*, London: Methuen.

Harrison, T. (2008), *Fram*, London: Faber and Faber.

Harrison, T. (1990; 2nd edn 1991), *The Trackers of Oxyrhynchus*, London: Faber and Faber.

Horden, P. and Purcell, N. (2000), *The Corrupting Sea: A Study of Mediterranean History*, Oxford and Malden, MA: Oxford University Press.

Isaac, B. (1994), *The Invention of Racism in Classical Antiquity*, Princeton, NJ: Princeton University Press.

Müller-Schöll, N. (2004), 'Theatre of Potentiality. Communicability and the Political in Contemporary Performance Practice', *Theatre Research International*, 29: 42–56.

Nemser, R. (2008), 'The Scream', *Arion*, 16: 149–56.

Nightingale, B. (1981), *New York Times*, 20 December.

Nightingale, B. (2008), *The Times*, 1 April.

Opper, T. (2008), *Hadrian: Empire and Conflict*, Exhibition Catalogue, London: British Museum Press.

Padel, R. (1996), '*Ion*: Lost and Found', *Arion*, 4: 216–24.

Parsons, P. (2007), *City of the Sharp-Nosed Fish: Greek lives in Roman Egypt*, London: Weidenfeld & Nicolson.

Scheidel, W. (2004), 'Human Mobility in Roman Italy, I: The Free Population', *Journal of Roman Studies*, 94: 1–26.

Scheidel, W. (2005), 'Human Mobility in Roman Italy, II: The Slave Population', *Journal of Roman Studies*, 95: 64–79.

Sedley, D. (1998), *Lucretius and the Transformation of Greek Wisdom*, Cambridge: Cambridge University Press.

Smith, P. (2009), 'Actors as Signposts: A Model for Site-Based and Ambulatory Performances', *New Theatre Quarterly*, 25: 159–71.

Stray, C. (ed.) (2007), *Gilbert Murray Re-assessed: Hellenism, Theatre and International Politics*, Oxford: Oxford University Press.

Taplin, O. (1991), 'Satyrs on the Borderline: *Trackers* in the Development of Tony Harrison's Theatre Work', in N. Astley (ed.), *Tony Harrison*, Newcastle-upon-Tyne: Bloodaxe, 458–64.

Taplin, O. (2001), 'Masks in Greek Tragedy and in Tantalus', *Didaskalia*, 5, http://.didaskalia.net/issues/vol5no2/taplin.html [accessed 10 July 2010].

Terras, M. (2006), *Image to Interpretation: An Intelligent System to Aid Historians in Reading the Vindolanda Texts*, Oxford: Oxford University Press.

Tomlin, R.S.O. (1998), 'The Curse Tablets', in B.W. Cunliffe, *The Temple of Sulis Minerva at Bath Vol. 2. The Finds from the Sacred Spring*, Oxford: Oxford University Press, 59–280.

Vout, C. *et al.* (2006), *Antinous: The Face of the Antique*, Exhibition Catalogue, Leeds: Henry Moore Institute.

Wahl, C. (2008), 'Mehr Demokratie klagen', *Der Tagesspiegel* (Daily Mirror), 9 June.

Whitmarsh, T. (2001), *Greek Literature and the Roman Empire: The Politics of Imitation*, Oxford: Oxford University Press.

Wiles, D. (2000), *Greek Theatre in Performance: An Introduction*, Cambridge: Cambridge University Press, 26–47.

Woodward, A. and Leach, P. (1993), 'The Inscribed Lead Tablets', in *The Uley Shrines. Excavation of a Ritual Complex on West Hill, Uley, Gloucestershire, 1977–79*, English Heritage Archaeological Reports 17, London: English Heritage, 113–26.

Woolf, G. (1998), *Becoming Roman: The Origins of Provincial Civilization in Gaul*, Cambridge: Cambridge University Press.

Zeitlin, F. (1978), 'The Dynamics of Misogyny: Myth and Mythmaking in the *Oresteia* of Aeschylus', *Arethusa*, 11: 149–84.

2. The Value of Archaeological Research

Mike Parker Pearson (Sheffield University)

Archaeology is one of the most popular intellectual pursuits for people in Britain and around the world. It sells newspapers, television programmes, websites, magazines and books, and supports the tourist industries of many nations. Millions of people benefit from and enjoy archaeological research, either by following it in the media or by taking part as volunteers and amateurs alongside the professionals. In Britain each week, viewers are usually offered at least one terrestrial television programme featuring archaeological research, and it is daily fare for some of the cable channels. Many television archaeologists are household names and formerly arcane archaeological techniques such as geophysical surveying ('geofizz') are understood by millions.

Yet only two to three decades ago archaeologists were worrying about how they could communicate the results of archaeological research to the public. How could such a minority interest be successfully taken up by the wider population? Could its elitist image be shaken off in favour of a more accessible approach to finding out about the past? As the editor of the popular magazine *British Archaeology* commented last year, 'our heritage has never been more popular and archaeology never stronger' (Pitts 2007). Yet archaeology is rarely taught in schools, other than covering, say, the ancient Egyptians (among seven options within a world history study) at Key Stage 2 (for children aged 7–11). Archaeology A-level is a minority subject and the annual intake of archaeology students into British universities is under 1,500 undergraduates, a drop in the ocean in comparison with school subjects such as history and geography. Perhaps it is the very fact that archaeology is not forced on to schoolchildren, but has to be sought out, that helps to preserve its mystique and to generate the passion and commitment which it engenders among people of all ages and walks of life.

We should always be careful of what we wish for, in case we get it, and that moment has already come in archaeology. As in other fields, the media's need to entertain has overtaken its responsibility to educate. The expectations of television producers and other media professionals have been fuelled by make-believe Hollywood characters such as Indiana Jones and Lara Croft: makers of factual television want pyramids, mummies, hidden treasure and high adventure. The value of archaeological research, it cannot be denied, lies partly in entertainment (or 'edutainment', as it has been dubbed) but there are many other aspects of human life to which it contributes.

What is archaeology?

Archaeology is a relatively young discipline within the humanities, created out of antiquarian and social evolutionary studies in the late nineteenth century, through the work of pioneers such as John Lubbock and Augustus Pitt Rivers. In many ways it is the child of both Charles Darwin and Karl Marx, whose influences have shaped its development to the present day. By the middle of the twentieth century, its methodological and theoretical basis was developed in particular by Gordon Childe (McNairn 1990). As in other social sciences, archaeological theory has gone through a series of transformations since the 1960s, from 'culture history' (the study of cultural change through diffusion and migration) to the New Archaeology (study of processes of change or 'processual archaeology') and post-processual archaeology (a variety of postmodernist and post-structuralist perspectives). If archaeology lost its innocence in 1973 (Clarke 1973), it developed its social conscience in the 1980s and 1990s.

Archaeology's scope is truly breathtaking: the last four million years of human behaviour across the entire planet. From the earliest hominins (human ape-like ancestors) to practices of waste disposal in the present, archaeologists study all aspects of material culture and the material conditions of human life. Formerly dubbed the 'handmaid of history', archaeology addresses the entire span of human history, 99.9 per cent of which has no written documentation. It also sheds light on the lives of the millions within the historical era who otherwise have no documents to record their existence – the common people, the poor and the enslaved (Orser 2007).

To study people long dead who have left few or no written records of their lives is no easy task. Mute stones and artefacts present tremendous challenges to the researcher, requiring the mobilization of a rich variety of source materials and methods. It is the greatest detective story on earth, uncovering the remains of events, people and processes that form the path that has led from our earliest beginnings to the present world. The past is one of the great frontiers of knowledge, where exploration and discovery can still thrill and astound us in the search for the origins and development of our humanity from mobile, small-scale hunter-gatherers to the global urbanized nation states of today. It is a means of finding out just who we are by way of where we have come from.

Archaeology never sits easily within the straitjacket-like categorizations of arts and sciences, and it bridges that outmoded and relict distinction in a way that few other academic disciplines can echo. In contrast to geography – split into physical and human – archaeology has this synthesis of arts and science at its core. Researchers apply an ever-widening range of sophisticated scientific techniques – radiocarbon-dating, chemical analysis, geophysical analysis, isotopic measurement, ancient and modern DNA analysis, palynology, faunal analysis, human osteology, computer simulation, multivariate statistics, metallurgical analysis, etc. – directed at answering questions about humanity. This ability to fully develop the scientific study of human history has been with us for only half a century and part of archaeology's excitement is the fast rate at which new scientific advances can be harnessed to answer questions about the human past. Aspects of human life that once seemed unreachable – plotting human migrations from isotopes, reconstructing diet from proteins and lipids preserved within pots, and recovering DNA from Neanderthals – are now firmly on the research agenda.

Archaeological research increasingly needs its archaeological scientists to be archaeologists trained in the natural sciences rather than scientists trained in archaeology. The questions that are asked are fundamentally about human beings and human history. Our interest in the chemical composition of lipid residues, for example, is only a means to an end, aimed at answering questions about people and their daily lives – what foods were prepared, how, when and why?

As archaeology has become more scientific in its techniques and methods, it has also forged new links to the arts. Indeed, today's research often goes hand in hand with artistic presentations, in which archaeologists develop new ways of telling through experimental writing and imagery, or by working with artists who use excavations as contexts for art installations of many kinds. Recent examples have been the use of artists in residence at Gardom's Edge (Derbyshire) to display landscape art, the integration of artists within the Stonehenge Riverside Project in 2007 and 2008, and Colin Renfrew's long-running collaboration with landscape artists such as Richard Long.

Archaeology draws upon all academic disciplines in some form or another. This extraordinary eclecticism is a measure of archaeology's breadth and one of the reasons why so many professionals in other disciplines are drawn to it as a fascinating hobby and pastime. Philosophy, engineering, medicine, anthropology, languages, biomolecular science, geology, palaeontology, climatology, botany, zoology, physics, mathematics, law, economics and politics are some of the more obvious disciplines which contribute to archaeology. In many ways, archaeology is the precocious child of their union.

Who values archaeological research?

For most of the twentieth century, archaeology was practised by upper-class academics who provided high culture for a cultured minority. As one retired archaeologist recalls from his boyhood in the 1950s, he was advised by Kathleen Kenyon, one of the *grandes dames* of archaeology, that he should acquire a private income if he wanted to become an archaeologist – scant comfort for this son of a Welsh miner (Wainwright 2000). Yet the early television shows such as 'Animal, Vegetable, Mineral?' (1952–9) and 'Buried Treasure' (1955–9), presented by archaeologists Mortimer Wheeler and Glyn Daniel, reached Britain's entire television-owning public. Despite its high-brow content and bow-tie dress requirement, it kindled a level of public interest touched previously only by Howard Carter in the Valley of the Kings and C. Leonard Woolley at Ur, and created two of Britain's first television celebrities.

During the 1960s and 1970s grassroots organizations such as 'Rescue' galvanized a new generation of volunteers and enthusiasts into salvaging Britain's buried heritage as historic city centres were bulldozed and motorways were built across swathes of countryside. In 1984 the first heritage centre opened on the site of a Viking dig: crowds queued around the block to visit the Jorvik Viking Centre in York, to experience the sights, sounds and smells of life on the streets a thousand years ago. In the same year, English Heritage was formed as a government quango with a brief to conserve and promote the archaeological remains and historic environment of England. Its remit was defined by the 1983 National Heritage Act which is unique in UK legislation: it is the only Act of Parliament to enshrine in law a primary duty to promote public enjoyment and advance public knowledge, in this case of ancient monuments and historic buildings (Breeze 2006).

In 1992 'Time Team' was first aired on terrestrial television, the start of a seventeen-year long career, still continuing, that has changed the culture. As one of the first examples of 'reality TV', it depicted real archaeologists carrying out real excavations. Both loved and hated, its substantial viewing figures marked archaeology's full emergence from minority enthusiasm to national obsession. Many imitations followed over the next decade as television producers vied with each other to commission documentaries on the latest archaeological research. Newspapers began to report archaeological research in greater depth (Ascherson 2004). Many of their stories were of astonishing discoveries – Britain's first prehistoric mummies, an Alpine migrant buried near Stonehenge, and Britain's first Palaeolithic cave art, to name a few.

Yet the success of 'Time Team' lay in the discovery of the mundane and the ordinary. As Peter Fowler has remarked, 'Time Team' has never excavated anything significant enough to find its way into the textbooks. The value of their findings lies in people's fascination with local places and local pasts. Attempts to film 'Time Team' in exotic holiday destinations such as Majorca and the Caribbean met with disappointing viewing numbers. What it demonstrates is the general public's fascination with places that are meaningful because they are where we all live. According to the programme's creator Mick Aston, Britain's ethnic minorities, resident for only a generation or two in the UK, are well represented among the viewers of programmes researching the localities in which they live.

Archaeological research has much to contribute to understanding and living with Britain's multicultural present and future. We are a nation of mongrels, as the late social anthropologist Sir Edmund Leach proclaimed many years ago, referring to Britain's historically documented immigrations over the last two millennia. New developments in sequencing ancient as well as modern DNA, together with strontium and oxygen isotopic studies, are enabling archaeologists to track prehistoric migrations into Britain, to evaluate the long-term impacts of incomers upon culture change. The Beaker People Project, funded by the Arts & Humanities Research Council (AHRC), is one such example, investigating processes of immigration to Britain 4,000 years ago by groups from continental Europe, among whom were migrants who grew up in the foothills of the Alps and in Brittany. Coming to an island which had been culturally as well as physically isolated from the Continent for the previous thousand years, these Beaker people of the Bronze Age brought with them practices such as gold-working and horse-riding, cultural imports that had a profound impact on prehistoric Britain's social and economic future.

The sea-change in televised research, brought about by programmes such as 'Time Team', coincides with a growing interest in archaeology by non-professional researchers. After years of angry confrontation, archaeologists have finally developed a *modus vivendi* with metal detectorists, with most of these treasure-seekers working within the law and contributing their results to the Department for Culture, Media and Sport-funded Portable Antiquities Scheme (Bland 2004). Whilst they and landowners can still maximize the economic value of coins, brooches and other finds, the research value of these discoveries is no longer being lost. Finding a brooch or a coin in a muddy field provides a tangible connection to the ancient past, even when that item is to be sold for personal gain or kept in a private collection. The Portable Antiquities Scheme ensures that these finds are logged and recorded, regardless of their ownership, so that the precious information about their context can be studied by specialists and the wider public alike. Such discoveries by amateur enthusiasts are often the first step to reading about ancient civilizations and even developing specialist knowledge to rival that of professional archaeologists.

Since the 1980s, community archaeology has been a major element in research projects both in Britain and abroad. This is one of several ways in which archaeologists engage with the problems facing the modern world, in this case through the fostering of community identities by working *for* those communities. Within Britain this has worked in both town and country, with exemplary projects run by the Museum of London for the people of Shoreditch and by Leicestershire Museums – where the concept was first developed – for rural groups in that county. The remains of the past can act as powerful symbols that build and strengthen community and local identities, especially in times of rapid change. On the island of South Uist in the Outer Hebrides, a twenty-year project by Sheffield University and other academic institutions has seen the construction of a new museum, the presentation of archaeological sites to the public, and the provision of guide books, signposts and information boards to enhance the tourist experience and also to provide Hebrideans with a fuller understanding of their prehistoric past. Together with the revival in Gaelic language and culture, this new-found awareness of archaeology provides a valued material dimension which has been hitherto neglected.

The concept of community archaeology has had a global impact (Merriman 2004). Principles of good practice for archaeologists working throughout the world include the need to engage local and/or indigenous people in the planning and execution of archaeological projects (Broadbent 2004). The 'Time Team' series of Big Digs, begun in 2003, has brought this sense of archaeology of the people to the British viewing public, filming many hundreds of households in each event excavating their gardens and recording their finds. Archaeologists carrying out research excavations today count visitor access and information as one of the major factors to be included in project planning.

The professionalization of archaeology in the 1980s in Britain created a split between professionals and amateurs which, for a time, threatened to return the subject to its former exclusivity. In the space of just twenty years, archaeologists have fought back to regain the deep link between the practice of archaeology and its ownership by the public. New posts of heritage interpreters and education officers, together with a new level of public awareness amongst archaeologists more generally, have helped to create a sense of archaeology's prime mission to serve its public. Commercial archaeology has spread around the world, as developers are required by UNESCO guidelines and national legislation and codes of practice to provide for investigations prior to development. In England alone, developers pay over £50 million a year for archaeological research – far greater than any research council or government funding – in mitigation of damage to the archaeological heritage. Efforts are often made to publicize this research but legal issues generally prevent members of the public from actively participating in these commercial-sector projects. Consequently, it is important that research projects outside the commercial sector integrate with local communities, providing facilities for interested amateurs to work alongside university-trained professionals and students.

Of all the historical professions, archaeology is fortunate to have so many aspects with wide appeal: its emphasis on teamwork, its mix of practical and academic study, and its direct accessibility to the past through tangible, material remains make it very attractive in this modern-day office-bound existence. Not only can amateurs attend evening classes and part-time courses, but volunteers can find themselves shovelling alongside university professors on summer excavation projects.

The economic value of archaeology

Archaeology is ostensibly about the past but it can have considerable impact on the present and future. Some archaeological projects have a direct economic value in rebuilding ancient facilities to be used for future economic benefit. One of the earliest of these, the UNESCO-sponsored Libyan Valleys project, set out to not only map and understand the Roman cultivation and irrigation systems within the Sahara but also repair them, so that Libyan farmers might be able to cultivate in areas that had become too arid for crops to grow (Barker and Jones 1982). Similarly, the British-led Cusichaca Trust project in the Central Andes has applied archaeology to revive Peruvian agriculture by repairing and reopening abandoned irrigation canals that Inca farmers once used to irrigate their crops (Kendall 1984).

In the last thirty years, similar projects have been initiated in various parts of the world, such as the Raised Field Agricultural Project around Lake Titicaca (Erickson 2002; Sabloff 2008: 20–7). One of the most recent of these is the ARCHAEOMEDES project investigating land-use and degradation in the western Mediterranean (van der Leeuw *et al.* 2004). Among its findings is the observation that landscape processes operate over centuries rather than decades and may not be identified by short-term studies. This archaeological research reveals that agricultural expansion to natural limits in the good years was followed by land crises and abandonments when the region was hit by a succession of poorer years. Conditions leading to environmental crisis may not be apparent for many decades beforehand. Societies also become increasingly vulnerable to environmental crisis as they become less adaptable to environmental change. Only archaeology can reveal these build-ups to moments of crisis over previous millennia.

In North America, important knowledge about the Western world's mounting rubbish problem comes from the Tucson Garbage Project. This started out in 1973 as a scheme to help students learn from contemporary waste disposal about consumption and identity. The project uncovered startling differences between what people claim they do and what they actually do. It has evolved into a series of multi-themed investigations into problems of landfill, degradability of materials, contamination and pollution, and disposal practices (Rathje and Murphy 1991). All of these research directions have public policy implications which have been taken up by local authorities in planning for a less polluted world with improved arrangements for recycling and sustainability.

The innovations of the ancient world generate considerable interest among the public who find 'what the Romans did for us' and 'what the Ancient Britons did for us' to be very entertaining. Rarely, though, do such inventions have a practical and economic application in this 'high-tech' modern world. There are exceptions, however, such as the rediscovery of how to make a particular pigment known as Maya Blue from indigo and palygorskite, as used by the people of Mesoamerica in the first millennium AD (Arnold *et al.* 2008). Today this sky-blue colour is produced industrially from a cobalt-based pigment whose heavy-metal content is harmful to our environment. The recipe for Maya Blue now offers the opportunity to produce an acceptable non-polluting substitute.

Discoveries from human osteoarchaeology and palaeopathology provide significant medical information on the history of specific diseases and pathologies. From a long-term perspective, archaeologists can demonstrate that health in the Americas was in decline well before Columbus and worsened with the rise of agriculture, government and urbanization (Steckel and Rose 2002). Even in Britain, where people are generally much better off in terms of health than their prehistoric ancestors, we are less well off in terms of respiratory diseases, poor diet, lack of exercise, allergies, drug abuse, exposure to tropical diseases, infections due to antibiotic resistance, and growing rates of tuberculosis and HIV (Roberts and Cox 2003: 397).

A recent spin-off from osteoarchaeology has been the development of forensic archaeology (Hunter *et al.* 1996). Britain's police forces now routinely incorporate archaeological researchers, experts in excavation and identification of human remains, in their search teams when looking for the buried remains of murder victims. Forensic archaeologists also excavate buried remains of the victims of genocide in Rwanda, Congo, Argentina, Chile, Bosnia and Afghanistan. Where archaeologists once dug to uncover the glories of ancient Mesopotamia, they currently excavate to reveal the atrocities of modern Iraq.

Archaeological research mostly provides economic value indirectly, supporting tourist industries, media communications, and museums and heritage centres. People pay to visit heritage centres, touring exhibitions, re-enactment displays and archaeological sites. Despite critics' predictions in the 1980s of doom and gloom for the heritage industry and the British economy (Hewison 1987; Wright 1985), the marketing of Britain's past has gone from strength to strength. Today's research is tomorrow's museum exhibition. Cresswell Crags, the gorge where Britain's first known Palaeolithic cave art was discovered in 2003, is now a thriving heritage centre whose development has helped economic and cultural regeneration of a coalfield community blighted by recession and the closure of mines.

The discoveries made on the AHRC-funded Stonehenge Riverside Project have revolutionized our understanding of how the builders of Stonehenge lived by uncovering the remains of their houses and everyday items, providing new insights into prehistoric daily life. Plans to open a new visitor centre for Stonehenge by 2012 have been put on hold because of government cutbacks but, at the time of writing, English Heritage are still hoping to raise enough funding to build a new centre to display these findings to around 0.8 million people a year from around the world.

The Stonehenge Riverside Project also helps to sell newspapers, magazines and television programmes. A press release of our discoveries in January 2007 led to worldwide interest, much of it on the front pages of the world's leading newspapers. Stonehenge research sells books, magazine articles and an entire catalogue of Stonehenge memorabilia. People are drawn to find out about the mysterious past and Stonehenge is iconic as a representation of ancient mystery and lost civilization. The present time is particularly important for research into Stonehenge, with colleagues in a complementary project excavating at the monument in the full glare of publicity and our own field season promising to further rewrite much of what we thought we knew about this enigmatic landscape.

The economic value of archaeology to national economies is perhaps best appreciated when the tourist industry is threatened. Egypt's economy is estimated to have lost $700 million as a result of foreign tourists being massacred at Luxor in 1997, having already lost an estimated $2 billion from previous terrorist outrages up to 1995 (Renfrew and Bahn 2004: 557). The 2006 London bombings similarly put off many tourists to Britain whose itineraries would have included archaeological sites such as Stonehenge and Roman Bath.

Archaeological research, like other forms of historical inquiry, often gains new insights from study of its archives as well as from changed perspectives on the past, but it has a fundamental advantage over other forms of history. Most of our information about the past still remains buried and unknown to us. A new find of a single hominin fossil, like the 2004 discovery of the Flores 'hobbit', can rewrite what we know about human evolution. A frozen mummy or a deep-sea shipwreck can provide intimate, hitherto undreamt of details of ancient life. For archaeologists, most of our past lies in the future, awaiting discovery. Not a year goes by without an extraordinary find to whet the appetite of millions of people.

Are there lessons from the past?

'My name is OZYMANDIAS, king of kings:
Look on my works, ye Mighty, and despair!'
Nothing beside remains. Round the decay
Of that colossal wreck, boundless and bare
The lone and level sands stretch far away
(From 'Ozymandias' by Percy Bysshe Shelley, 1817)

The future of humanity is a topic of increasing concern to governments and governed around the world. Archaeologists study humanity's long-term successes and failures, and contribute to an information bank from which we draw to envision our possible, sustainable futures. In his study of how societies collapse or succeed, the geographer and biologist Jared Diamond concludes that there is hope for the future through the application of knowledge gained from the archaeological past: 'Past societies lacked archaeologists and television ... Thus, we have the opportunity to learn from the mistakes of distant peoples and past peoples. That's an opportunity that no past society enjoyed to such a degree. My hope in writing this book has been that enough people will choose to profit from that opportunity to make a difference' (Diamond 2005: 525).

In a similar vein, Jonathan Friedman and Christopher Chase-Dunn point to the past as a means of preparing for the future:

> The possible futures of the global system are illuminated by careful study of its past and comparisons with power processes in previous eras ... in which there are similarities as well as differences with the past. If the similarities are taken seriously, then we must be driven to reconsider many of our assumptions about the state of the world today and the direction it is taking. If history is replete with replays of notably similar scenarios, then we must ask what we have learned as a species and whether we can avoid such 'repetition compulsion' in the future. (Friedman and Chase-Dunn 2005: 2)

Archaeologists have a unique insight into the long-term trajectory of human societies, capable of assessing the sustainability of different subsistence practices in a variety of environments from tropical rainforests to temperate regions. We unravel the processes that lead to soil erosion, loss of freshwater supplies, soil salinization and depletion of marine and terrestrial resources. We study the long-term outcomes of the astonishing range of social systems devised by past peoples around the world, from empires to utopian communities.

This long-term perspective is of course useful for viewing today's climate change and global warming. Humans have adapted successfully to successive Ice Ages and we have shown ourselves to be one of the most versatile species on the planet, capable of inhabiting the most hostile of environments with relatively low levels of technology. The present interglacial, whose end is thought by many to be already overdue, has been a period in which our species has changed its social and economic nature entirely, evolving from small-scale, mobile hunter-gatherers to global urbanism in which more than half of the world's exponentially growing population now live in towns and cities. This transformation has taken place in the last 12,000 years, in less than 500 generations, beginning during a period of rapid climate change known as the Younger Dryas when temperature changes were even more rapid than today, initially falling 6° C in a decade and then rising 4° C, just 600 years later. Changes in human behaviour within the Younger Dryas included our first steps towards agriculture in the Middle East as well as the abandonment of cave-dwelling in northern Europe.

It may well be that the causes of global warming lie not simply in the last two centuries of the industrial age but in changes that humans have wrought over the last 8,000 years. The climatologist William Ruddiman has linked the long-term rise in carbon dioxide with increases in forest clearance over the last 6,000 years, and the rise in methane with the development of rice farming and irrigation about 3,000 years ago (Ruddiman 2005). Archaeological research is able to test and fine-tune this hypothesis by documenting the precise dating and extent of these transformations within regional and global perspectives.

Large, complex civilizations, which developed from the fourth millennium BC, have proved to be vulnerable to climatic variations in tandem with a wide variety of processes such as agricultural degradation, warfare, population pressure, technological stagnation and economic depression. Growth cycles, together with rates of change in artefact styles, have also accelerated, leading to a shortening of the lifespans of states and empires from millennia to a few centuries.

This may not be our final century (*contra* Rees 2003) and, over the millennia to come, humans will probably adapt in some form or other to whatever car-crash of a world we create for the future, but the present course of civilization and the current world order have not much longer to run on an archaeological timescale. As the sixth 'extinction-level event' unfolds on our little planet, we are seeing the failure of conservation efforts to support the survival in the wild of, for example, the big cats and great apes beyond the next few decades, whilst the prospect of large-scale starvation lurks outside the developed world whose consumption footprint is pressing heavily on natural resources.

Attempts to address global sustainability by examining it within the long term have already affected archaeological research. In the USA, archaeologists are increasingly researching issues of how to improve agricultural yields, limit soil erosion and plan for long-term water use (van der Leeuw and Redman 2002). For example, Arizona State University has established a School of Sustainability, led by an archaeologist, in which archaeology is part of a collaborative venture to tackle the environmental, economic and social challenges of the twenty-first century.

Conclusion

Archaeology is one of the youngest of the human sciences, appearing on the scene at the eleventh hour as humanity faces a great crisis, to provide a much-needed long-term perspective on the current world's problems. Its task, to recover the memory of humankind by documenting our largely unwritten past, leads us to glimpse new and unfamiliar worlds, and to recover and learn new stories about human history. Our research and exploration on the frontier of our past feeds a modern world hungry for mysteries and adventure. Within just three decades, archaeology's public has grown from a motley band of cranks and enthusiasts to a global audience of many millions who follow research on cultural icons such as Stonehenge, the terracotta army from Xi'an and ancient Egyptian pyramids, as well as the local findings of a myriad of research projects throughout the world.

British archaeologists are among the very best in the world, leading their counterparts in advances in theory and method, writing major syntheses, and passing to the next generation the highest skills in excavation and fieldwork.

Through joint research projects, conferences and cultural links to China, Japan, India and many other nations, British archaeologists are sharing their skills and expertise with researchers in other countries. For example, at 2008's Society of American Archaeology conference in Vancouver, the AHRC-funded Stonehenge Riverside Project's session attracted the largest audience of the conference, closely followed by British archaeologist Ian Hodder's Çatalhöyük project. British archaeological research, whether carried out by amateurs or professionals, at home or abroad, is the envy of colleagues the world over; it is a strength we must continue to build upon.

Archaeological research underpins and contributes to entire industries of heritage promotion, media and publishing, merchandising of reworked ancient spirituality, and science-fantasy projections of imagined futures that draw heavily on researched pasts. By providing new and varied perspectives on the past, we also demonstrate how the future might be different rather than merely a continuation of the present.

Archaeological research is one of the ways in which Jared Diamond's world-saving combination of 'televisions and archaeologists' is contributing to educating and informing the wider global public of just how tight a corner we are in and what steps need to be taken to provide for a sustainable future. Yet its value runs much deeper than economic payoff and apocalyptic messenger. We must also remember that value is integral to the very enterprise of doing research into the human past: 'Historians are also urged to make history "relevant" … Like philistines, the politically correct scorn "academic" interests as spineless, selfish and effete. Ashamed to confess that they enjoy the past for its own sake, not for its immediate relevance, historians [and archaeologists] cloak high-minded scholarship behind some fabricated "useful" motive' (Lowenthal 1998: 119).

Most archaeologists would agree to some extent with Lowenthal: alongside the 'relevance' of archaeology, we never forget the sheer wonder of discovery and the satisfaction of telling new stories to the world. Fortunately the value of archaeological research in many aspects of life can be demonstrated without much difficulty, but let us not forget that this young hybrid discipline is one of humanity's most revelatory projects, to find out who we are by way of where we have come, and to question and advise where we may go.[1]

Note

1   I thank Graeme Barker for providing the opportunity to write this essay for the Arts and Humanities Research Council. Many colleagues have participated in discussions about the value of archaeological research over the years but I particularly thank Robin Dennell for lengthy discussion on this topic. My participation in the National Geographic Society's Explorers Symposium in Washington DC in April 2007 provided the opportunity to discuss these matters with Roland Fletcher, Jared Diamond and many wildlife conservationists and social analysts, and to appreciate how much closer to global catastrophe we may be than many realize.

Bibliography

Arnold, D.E., Branden, J.R., Ryan Williams, P., Feinman, G.M. and Brown, J.P. (2008), 'The first direct evidence for the production of Maya Blue: rediscovery of a technology', *Antiquity*, 82: 151–64.

Ascherson, N. (2004), 'Archaeology and the British media', in N. Merriman (ed.), *Public Archaeology*, London: Routledge, 145–58.

Barker, G. and Jones, G.D.B. (1982), *The UNESCO Libyan Valleys Survey 1979–1981: Palaeoeconomy and Environmental Archaeology in the Pre-desert*, London: Society for Libyan Studies.

Bland, R. (2004), 'The Treasure Act and the Portable Antiquities Scheme: a case study in developing public archaeology', in N. Merriman (ed.), *Public Archaeology*, London: Routledge, 272–91.

Breeze, D.J. (2006), 'Ancient monuments legislation', in J. Hunter and I. Ralston (ed.), *Archaeological Resource Management in the UK: An Introduction*, 2nd edn, Stroud: Sutton, 57–68.

Broadbent, N. (2004), 'The ethics of collaborative research in Sweden. Finding common ground with local and indigenous people', in H. Karlsson (ed.), *Swedish Archaeologists on Ethics*, Göteborg: Bricoleur, 87–98.

Clarke, D.V. (1973), 'Archaeology: the loss of innocence', *Antiquity*, 47: 6–18.

Diamond, J. (2005), *Collapse: How Societies Choose to Fail or Succeed*, New York: Viking Penguin.

Erickson, C.L. (2002), 'Agricultural landscapes as world heritage: raised field agriculture in Bolivia and Peru', in J.-M. Teutonico and F. Matero (eds), *Managing Change: sustainable approaches to the conservation of the built environment*, Los Angeles, CA: Getty Conservation Institute, 181–204.

Friedman, J. and Chase-Dunn, C. (eds) (2005), *Hegemonic Declines: Past and Present*, Boulder, CA: Paradigm.

Hewison, R. (1987), *The Heritage Industry: Britain in a Climate of Decline*, London: Methuen.

Hunter, J., Roberts, C. and Martin, A. (1996), *Studies in Crime: An Introduction to Forensic Archaeology*, London: Batsford.

Kendall, A. (1984), *Current Archaeological Projects in the Central Andes*, International Series 210, Oxford: BAR.

Lowenthal, D. (1998), *The Heritage Crusade and the Spoils of History*, Cambridge: Cambridge University Press.

McNairn, B. (1980), *The Method and Theory of V. Gordon Childe*, Edinburgh: Edinburgh University Press.

Merriman, N. (ed.) (2004), *Public Archaeology*, London: Routledge.

Orser, C.E. (2007), *The Archaeology of Race and Racialization in Historic America*, Gainesville, FL: University Press of Florida.

Pitts, M. (2007), 'Editorial', *British Archaeology*, 95: 5

Rathje, W.L. and Murphy, C. (1991), *Rubbish! The Archaeology of Garbage*, New York: Harper Collins.

Rees, M. (2003), *Our Final Century: Will the Human Race survive the Twenty-first Century?*, London: Heinemann.

Renfrew, C. and Bahn, P. (2004), *Archaeology: Theories, Methods and Practice*, 4th edn, London: Thames and Hudson.

Roberts, C. and Cox, M. (2003), *Health and Disease in Britain: From Prehistory to the Present Day*, Stroud: Sutton.

Ruddiman, W.F. (2005), *Plows, Plagues, and Petroleum: How Humans took Control of Climate*, Princeton, NJ: Princeton University Press.

Sabloff, J. (2008), *Archaeology Matters: Action Archaeology in the Modern World*, Walnut Creek, CA: Left Coast Press.

Steckel, R.H. and Rose, J.C. (eds) (2002), *The Backbone of History: Health and Nutrition in the Western Hemisphere*, Cambridge: Cambridge University Press.

van der Leeuw, S.E. and Redman, C.L. (2002), 'Placing archaeology at the center of socio-natural studies', *American Antiquity*, 67: 597–606.

van der Leeuw, S.E., Favory, F. and Girardot, J.-J. (2004), 'The archaeological study of environmental degradation: an example from southeastern France', in C.L. Redman, S.R. James, P.R. Fish and J.D. Rodgers (eds), *The Archaeology of Global Change: The Impact of Humans on Their Environment*, Washington DC: Smithsonian Books, 112–29.

Wainwright, G.J. (2000), 'Time please!', *Antiquity*, 74: 909–43.

Wright, P. (1985), *On Living in an Old Country: The National Past in Contemporary Britain*, London: Verso.

3. Why Religious History Matters: Perspectives from 1851

John Wolffe (The Open University)

'The Sea of Faith'

In the early 1980s it seemed easy for both academics and the media to characterize religion as a steadily receding and increasingly marginal force in human affairs. A quarter of a century later, despite the specific reality of continuing decline in British church attendances, overall perceptions have changed very substantially. Although committed adherents of the churches are dwindling in numbers, the pronouncements of their leaders on political and moral issues, whether the Iraq war or bioethics, have gained a high public profile. In 1989 Muslims reacted with great hostility to Salman Rushdie's recently published and allegedly blasphemous novel *The Satanic Verses*, thus giving decisive notice to secular liberals that religion was pivotal to the culture of ethnic minorities in Britain. In 1997, the response to Princess Diana's death indicated that, despite popular British ambivalence towards traditional Christianity, alternative spiritualities were widespread.

Above all, although the situation in Britain remained variegated, in the 1990s religious issues moved increasingly to the centre of the world stage. The explosion of the 'Rushdie affair' in the same year, 1989, as the fall of the Berlin Wall was symbolic of a trend that had begun with the Iranian revolution of 1978. Before the turn of the millennium, not only the resurgence of political Islam, but also the influence of the 'new Christian right' in the United States, the growth of Hindutva nationalism in India, and the increasing social importance of Pentecostalism in Africa, Asia and Latin America all belied previous assumptions that religion would retreat to marginality in a modernized and secularized world. Then, as the new century dawned, terrorists claiming Islamic inspiration stunned the world with their suicide attacks on the World Trade Center and the Pentagon on 11 September 2001 and on the London Underground on 7 July 2005.

There is currently considerable confusion and doublethink regarding the trajectory of religion in the contemporary world. It is possible to argue, depending on one's geographical and confessional frame of reference, that religion is either resurgent or declining, and that religion itself is either a major world problem or a panacea for other difficulties. The effect of 9/11 and 7/7 has been to change the debate from one primarily of academic and insider interest, to one that is perceived to be a matter of major public concern, and moreover one that opens up highly disturbing possibilities. In that respect it has significant parallels with the recent foregrounding of public concern over climate change. Indeed anxieties over religious change and over climate change may well show common patterns of thought and collective insecurity, grounded in underlying anxiety about the stability and long-term viability of the current social order. It will be argued in this essay that an informed historical perspective has much to contribute to reasoned engagement with such concerns.

In 'Dover Beach', first published in 1867 but probably written in June 1851,[1] Matthew Arnold evoked a world in which the tide of faith was already retreating:

> The Sea of Faith
> Was once, too, at the full, and round earth's shore
> Lay like the folds of a bright garment furl'd.
> But now I only hear
> Its melancholy, long, withdrawing roar ... (Ricks 1999: 453)

Today there is no consensus as to whether the tide is going in, or out, or on the turn; but there is a consciousness that there are some vicious eddies and rip currents around. At the end of the poem Arnold changed his metaphor with a chilling allusion to the ancient battle between the Athenians and the Syracusans at Epipolae in Sicily described in Thucydides' history of the Peloponnesian War (Thucydides 1973: 358–60). This fight took place at night, with the soldiers unable to see what was going on. In the consequent chaos and confusion, there were unnecessary Athenian casualties, a classical parallel for what would nowadays be called a 'friendly fire' incident.

> And we are here as on a darkling plain
> Swept with confused alarms of struggle and flight
> Where ignorant armies clash by night. (Ricks 1999)

The lapse of time between composition and publication altered perceptions of these lines. By 1867, in the wake of the publication of Charles Darwin's *On the Origin of Species* and of controversy over liberal theology in the Church of England, they appeared to be a comment on the existential chaos arising from the decline of traditional religion. In 1851, however, when Christianity still seemed very much in the ascendant but was bitterly divided, they were more likely to have been intended as an observation on the perplexing internecine struggles of contemporary believers. Arnold's evocation of 'ignorant armies' clashing by night may therefore aptly be applied to characterize attitudes to religion in the early twenty-first-century world. There is a collective confusion and fearfulness about religious commitments and influences that are not adequately understood. Actions intended to calm or neutralize religious difficulties have a disconcerting tendency to inflame them further.

Past and present: parallels and differences

Let us look more closely at Britain in the early 1850s as a vantage point from which to view the early 2000s. Three features of these years are worthy of particular attention: the 1851 Religious Census offers a comparator for present-day religious practice; strong anti-Catholicism bears a striking resemblance to contemporary Islamophobia; and exploration of the interface between religion and national consciousness stimulates an enhanced understanding of current debates over citizenship, the nature of the United Kingdom and its role in the wider world.

First, the 1851 Religious Census was a survey, unique until very recent times, of every identified place of worship in Britain and of attendances on 30 March 1851. The surviving documentation consists of printed parliamentary reports containing copious statistical tables covering the whole of Great Britain, and most of the original manuscript returns for England and Wales (those for Scotland have disappeared) which still survive in the National Archives. There are numerous limitations in the data, and problems with interpretation, but it is still an invaluable document.

The Religious Census indicates that overall between a third and a half of the British population attended Christian worship on the Census Sunday, with a few thousand Jews present on the preceding Sabbath. Participation was thus very substantially higher than present-day rates (6.3 per cent in 2005),[2] but it also fell a long way short of universal. Indeed when the results were published three years later contemporaries were alarmed at the extent of non-attendance, especially in working-class districts. Horace Mann, the official responsible for compiling the report, coined the memorable phrase 'unconscious Secularists' (*Census of Great Britain 1851* 1853: clviii) to characterize the attitudes of the absentees. He argued that their non-participation did not generally arise from conscious opposition to Christianity, but rather from the distractions and preoccupations of the 'passing hour', which meant that organized religious activity was not a priority for them. He might well have been describing still widespread attitudes in contemporary Britain, where opinion poll evidence indicates that the level of professed Christian or at least supernatural belief greatly exceeds actual church attendances. Awareness that such a state of mind has a long history is important in qualifying the facile but influential assumption that it is a distinctive feature of a 'postmodern' and 'post-Christian' culture.

Research on the 1851 Religious Census is also important in revealing the highly diverse particularities of regional and local religious practice (Wolffe 2005).[3] One standard statistic derived from the Census, the Index of Attendance, shows total attendances as a proportion of population. Double-counting of people who went to church more than once meant that this figure could exceed 100 per cent. To some extent the census data confirms conventional assumptions about the negative effect of industrialization and urbanization on religious observance. For example, some predominantly agricultural counties such as Bedfordshire, with an Index of Attendance (IA) of 104.6, and Buckinghamshire, with an IA of 87.3, were highly observant. Forty miles to the south, in already highly urbanized Middlesex (IA 37.2), there was much lower church attendance. However, the figures for Herefordshire (49.0) and the West Riding of Yorkshire (52.9) should immediately serve to check simplistic generalization. Crude urban/rural, industrial/agricultural, 'modern'/'premodern' dichotomies give us little help in explaining why attendance was dramatically lower in Herefordshire than in Bedfordshire, and even somewhat lower than in industrial Yorkshire.

The closer one looks at the Census the more complex and variegated the picture appears. Mappings of patterns of attendance and their denominational distribution at registration district or parish level tend to look like patchwork quilts with no straightforward socio-economic explanations for the significant differences between nearby localities. Why for example, in North Yorkshire, was attendance in the Bedale registration district (IA 79.1) more than 20 per cent higher than in the seemingly very similar Northallerton district (IA 57.0) immediately to the east? Why were there significant variations in attendance between different parts of the densely populated West Riding textile conurbation? For example, inner Leeds had an IA of 50.9, but the suburbs only 45.0, whereas the nearby town of Dewsbury was much higher at 62.9. The answers to such questions require study of the detailed contingencies of previous local history and events, geographies and personalities. When we bring other documentary evidence into the picture, it becomes apparent that not only did the snapshot of this particular Sunday reveal very different pictures in particular localities, but that medium-term trajectories were often also different. Congregations were growing in one village while they were stagnant or declining in another nearby similar settlement.

The importance of studying organized religion in its local context may seem obvious once the point is made, but it is too often forgotten in more general assessments. Historical legacies can be very longstanding, for example in the physical siting and layout of places of worship. They continue to exercise a significant influence on present-day religious behaviour. Moreover, in view of the frequently formative role of churches and chapels in the development of village and urban settlements, such awareness also informs appreciation of the local heritage and its role in contemporary community life. When read carefully alongside other evidence, the Census can yield valuable clues to other aspects of religious practice – for example the frequency with which individuals attended Sunday worship – that enable better understanding of the role of churches and of Christian belief in people's lives. Awareness of complex local variation in the past alerts the observer to look out for it in the present, where indeed motives for active practice of religion continue to be diverse and where numerous instances of successful growing churches can be obscured by overall statistics of Christian decline. Are such varying local experiences specific to their context, or do they suggest alternative wider potentialities for a future in which organized Christianity recovers some lost ground? The incidence of Islam and of other faiths is also, like that of Roman Catholicism in the nineteenth century, highly geographically specific, and needs to be carefully mapped if its impact and significance are to be properly understood.

A second feature of the early 1850s is highlighted by the fact that at the very time that the Religious Census was being conducted, many days of parliamentary time were being devoted to debate on the Ecclesiastical Titles Act, the sole purpose of which was to make the titles of Roman Catholic bishops illegal.[4] This somewhat surreal climax of Victorian anti-Catholicism had been provoked by the Pope's creation (or, from a Catholic point of view, restoration) of a hierarchy of bishops with territorial titles. Hostile Protestants viewed this action as a carving up of English territory by a foreign power. The analogies with present-day suspicions of Muslims are striking. Exploration of this historical perspective, as well as analysis of the long-term pattern of interactions between Christianity and Islam, hence offers a valuable enhancement to the growing social scientific literature on Islamophobia.

Roman Catholics were a small and semi-invisible minority in early nineteenth-century Britain. Then in 1829 Catholic Emancipation gave them something close to civil equality. Migration from Ireland gathered momentum in the following two decades and they became a much more numerous and conspicuous presence. Similarly, there was a small Muslim community in Britain from at least the late nineteenth onwards, but only in the 1970s and 1980s did Muslims, now much more numerous, develop a visible public profile.

A small minority of nineteenth-century Catholics, like a small minority of early twenty-first-century Muslims, were indeed dangerously alienated from the British state because of its longstanding repression of the political aspirations of their co-religionists in Ireland. And Catholics like Muslims appeared to have divided loyalties because of their recognition of an extra-territorial spiritual tie to the papacy. They also represented a genuine spiritual challenge: nineteenth-century Catholic leaders dreamed of the reconversion of England; contemporary Muslims also seek conversions from the majority community and aspire to develop an Islamic vision of society. In both cases, however, the extent of popular antagonism became grossly disproportionate to the objective threat. Victorian Protestants were apt to see a Jesuit conspirator in every inoffensive professing Catholic; just as some are likely to perceive every contemporary Muslim as at least a potential terrorist. Sexual undercurrents also run deep. Both groups were associated with practices seen as fundamentally unnatural by Western cultural Protestants: celibacy in the case of Catholics, and arranged marriage and the supposed repression of women among Muslims. In both cases, too, anxieties have a significant apocalyptic dimension: the nineteenth-century expansion of Catholicism was often interpreted as a manifestation of evil powers foretold in the biblical Book of Revelation; contemporary Islamophobics perceive Muslim growth as presaging the collapse of existing Western society.

In a pamphlet published in 1852, John MacGregor, secretary of the Protestant Alliance, envisaged a future in 1900 in which Britain would be controlled by over a thousand district courts of Inquisition, English replaced by Anglo-Latin and the satirical magazine *Punch* suppressed (MacGregor 1852). In 1865 James Wylie articulated the views of many when he wrote that 'the civil liberty of the country is at this hour in very great peril' from the perceived aggression of the papacy (Wylie 1865: iv). A century-and-a-half later, it is true that Catholicism is still perceived as somewhat distinctive and the papacy's authoritarian and conservative tendencies are regarded with concern in some quarters. Nevertheless, even the most forceful critics of recent popes would take a much milder view of their potential influence. Contemporary recognition of the exaggerated and irrational nature of much Victorian antagonism to Catholicism should thus stimulate a caution towards similarly alarmist views of the future impact of Islam. It is especially important to place such concerns in due proportion because they are given credibility by influential academic commentators, notably Samuel Huntington, with his scenario of a 'clash of civilizations' (Huntington 1996), and Niall Ferguson, with his endorsement of the view that growing Muslim influence could see Europe transformed into 'Eurabia' during the course of this century (Ferguson 2004).

There is, though, one very significant contrast. Nineteenth-century anti-Catholicism was a multifaceted phenomenon, but its central driving force was Protestant belief. Conviction derived originally from the sixteenth-century Reformation view that Rome's doctrinal teachings and religious practices were fundamentally erroneous and spiritually corrupting. By contrast contemporary Islamophobia, and indeed residual anti-Catholicism, evident for example in the parliamentary controversy in 2008 over the Human Fertilization and Embryology Bill, is much more secular in its ethos. Huntington, Ferguson and others perceive a clash between Islam and Christianity, but they do so from a perspective of attachment to what Sir Winston Churchill in 1940 called 'Christian civilization' (Robbins 1985: 279) rather than from the personal theological and faith commitments that inspired nineteenth-century anti-Catholics. Moreover, the ideological Protestantism that characterized mid-nineteenth-century anti-Catholicism was bound up with positive assertion of a 'Britishness' that had been a central strand in the forging together of the nation in the eighteenth century. On the other hand, present-day Islamophobia lacks such strong links to a focused religio-nationalist ideology: while the rhetoric of groups such as the British National Party and the English Defence League includes appeals to residual Christian identity, their underlying ethos is a secular one.[5]

Contemporary official Christian leaders, for their part, have generally appeared to be seeking rapprochement rather than confrontation with Islam.

In 1991 George Carey explicitly addressed other faiths in his enthronement sermon as Archbishop of Canterbury, saying 'I trust I can listen to your story and respect your integrity, even though having listened I may still want to present to you, as to all, the claims of my Lord' (British Council of Churches 1991: 17). More recently, in February 2008, his successor Rowan Williams spoke positively of the possibility of allowing some kind of limited space for *shar'ia* law in relation to Muslim communities in Britain, framing his argument by reference to the established accommodations already existing for other religious communities, for example, in allowing Christian medical professionals conscientiously to refuse to be involved with performing abortions (Williams 2008). The widespread hostile reaction that greeted a scholarly and nuanced lecture, in which the Archbishop had already anticipated and addressed most of the potential objections, was very revealing of the force of contemporary secular prejudice against Islam.

A third prominent feature of Britain in the early 1850s was strong links between Christianity and national consciousness. Following the assertion of Protestantism in the Ecclesiastical Titles Act of 1851, the Duke of Wellington's funeral in 1852 was a spectacular pageant bringing together the religious and military resonances in mournful celebration of the final passing of the era of the Napoleonic Wars. Then in 1854, the Crimean War broke out, with the subsequent course of the conflict marked by national days of prayer and a seemingly perverse sense that national mission was being advanced amidst the messy military realities.

During the later nineteenth and early twentieth centuries British national consciousness, and indeed more strident forms of imperialist and nationalist self-assertion, continued in general to grow out of Christianity rather than to be in conflict with it. The monarchy gave particular focus to that linkage of the secular and sacred. The Duke of Clarence, Queen Victoria's grandson who died in 1892 at the age of twenty-eight, was cast as an unlikely St George in the stained glass window of Sand Hutton village church in the Vale of York (Wolffe 2000: plate 9). The connections of religion, monarchy and nation were particularly apparent at events such as the Diamond Jubilee and death of Queen Victoria, and the interment of the Unknown Warrior in Westminster Abbey in 1920, at which George V was chief mourner (Wolffe 2000: 222–42, 261–4). It still appeared plausible at the time of the coronation of 1953 to describe it, in a serious academic journal, as 'a great act of national communion' (Shils and Young 1953).

Since the 1960s, however, declining conventional Christian observance has been paralleled by a decline in popular enthusiasm for the monarchy. These processes had a common root in a weakening sense of collective overall British identity. Indian independence in 1947 and the dismantling of most of the remainder of Britain's overseas empire in the 1960s left a more introverted and insecure nation at home. From the 1960s onwards nationalist movements in Scotland and Wales gathered momentum. They manifested a substantially more secular ethos than their nineteenth- and early twentieth-century antecedents which were primarily rooted in the distinctive religious cultures of the two nations. In Ireland, north and south, church attendances remained much higher and the sectarian roots of the Troubles in Northern Ireland gave religion a consistently high political profile. Even there, however, religious influences appear to have receded somewhat in recent years, despite the Christian symbolism of the Good Friday Agreement of 1998.

This historical perspective is very relevant to contemporary debates over citizenship and 'Britishness'. The endeavour to reinvent 'Britain' is shown to be a challenging undertaking in a society where religious commitments are pluralist rather than exclusively Christian, and where secular forces are increasingly strong. There are two discernible approaches to this challenge. First, there is inclusive religion, as symbolized for example by the prominent seating of representatives of non-Christian faiths under the dome of St Paul's at the Golden Jubilee service in 2002. Second, there is an essentially secular strategy that consigns religious faith and activity to the private sphere and seeks public consensus in non-religious language and ritual. It is apparent that the Queen, and in a different way the Prince of Wales, would prefer the former, while many elected politicians would support the latter, which might perhaps have negative implications for the monarchy. Organized religion is itself divided depending on whether more sectarian or more universalistic impulses predominate. Future debate on such issues needs to be rooted in an informed sense of history, not in a misplaced endeavour to resurrect an anachronistic, narrowly Christian construction of British identity, but in order to ensure that any new model can both have the credibility that comes from awareness of past tradition and be responsive to the realities of the twenty-first century (Wolffe 1993; Wolffe 2010a).

Britain in the past lacked the sharp distinctions between the religious and the secular that have been present in French public life since the revolution of 1789, but recent trends indicate a sense of heightened tension, and sometimes confrontation between the religious and the secular. The traditional middle ground of nominal Anglicanism and cultural Nonconformity has been steadily eroded. It leaves on the one hand a highly diverse minority of committed believers and, on the other, a probably somewhat larger minority with firmly secular outlooks. The middle ground remains, but it looks more contested and variegated than it was, with Arnold's night battlefield analogy appearing to be an apt one. For example, church schools, having until the early twentieth century been a bone of contention between Anglicans and Nonconformists, subsequently became an effective channel for the diffusion of nominal Christianity. Nowadays, however, faith schools again increasingly look like becoming a battleground between a variety of committed religious groups and a secular constituency that perceives them as a divisive anomaly in contemporary Britain.

The conclusion that the current historical trend is to the clearer polarization of the religious and the secular helps to make sense of the rather contradictory impressions with which this essay opened. Organized religion, or at least organized Christianity, may still be in statistical decline, but the context has stimulated a greater assertiveness by both religious and secular camps which paradoxically makes religion more visible.[6] It is very conceivable such attention will stimulate a degree of religious revival. Minority groups are prompted to perceive their religion as a key marker of identity and culture, while a sense of mild persecution may well prove more galvanizing for the Christian churches than the consciousness of complacent but limited acceptance that characterized their situation in Britain for much of the twentieth century. Comparative history indeed suggests alternative possibilities: although in France organized Christianity has declined even more precipitately than in Britain, in the United States, which also has a constitutional separation of church and state, church attendances have continued at a much higher level.

Partnership

There are therefore extensive contemporary applications for the work of historians of religion. Indeed, if the field of vision is widened beyond the primarily British perspective explored here, to consider the role of religion on the world stage, the importance and urgency of objective historical research and analysis is magnified further. Historians have, however, hitherto been somewhat coy about acknowledging a contemporary application for their work: one leading practitioner of religious history has pithily remarked that they 'had better be content to decline the role of saviours of the nation' (Bossy 1975: 1). Inflated claims for any single academic discipline are inadvisable, but there is a converse danger of false modesty and academic isolationism. In reality the insights arising from religious history have much to contribute to an interdisciplinary process of knowledge exchange to inform understanding of present-day issues.

These opportunities have been facilitated by the development of the subject area itself since the 1960s. An earlier generation of church historians primarily concerned with the institutional and theological development of Christian religious organizations has given way to religious historians who have moved the field outwards to engage in much wider ranging assessment of religious influences in society, culture and politics. The pioneers in this respect have tended to be medievalists and early modernists, for whom the historical centrality of religion is hard to question. However, leading researchers such as Hugh McLeod, David Hempton and Callum Brown have pursued similar approaches in relation to the nineteenth and twentieth centuries. The parallel development of religious studies as a discipline distinct from theology has also served to facilitate this process by stimulating scholars to analyse forms of religion other than the narrowly institutional, and encouraging an historical engagement with major religious traditions other than Christianity. The field has also developed a methodological maturity that facilitates objective inquiry and debate. Researchers inevitably have personal commitments, both religious and non-religious, which may legitimately shape their agendas and the manner in which they weigh the evidence, but there is a consensus that academic religious history should not on the one hand be subordinated to Christian theology nor on the other be utilized to support a secular or atheist polemic (Wolffe 2010b).

Three avenues for knowledge exchange call for exploration. First, there is significant potential for work with religious organizations themselves. These face two converse dangers in their approach to their own history. On the one hand there is the risk of an uncritical traditionalism that risks condemning them to marginality and irrelevance in a fast-changing world. On the other hand there are the perils that come from wholesale rejection of the past in the endeavour to be as contemporary as possible, leading to a sense of rootlessness and a tendency unwittingly to repeat previous mistakes. A constructive middle course implies a readiness to engage critically and reflectively with the past, not in order to replicate it, but as a route to better understanding of their present-day situation, and a resource both of ideas for the future and of cautionary tales.[7]

Second, there is value in working with the media to advance public understanding of a longer term view of topical contemporary issues, as in the BBC-Open University series, *A History of Christianity*, presented by Diarmaid MacCulloch and screened in 2009 and 2010. Awareness of the complexity of the religious past is a valuable corrective to simplistic and short-term interpretations of present-day religious problems. An enhanced knowledge of the situation of religious minorities in earlier periods, and of attitudes towards them, would help to advance better community and inter-faith relations in the twenty-first century.

Third, there is considerable unrealized potential for partnership both with religious organizations and with the heritage industry to advance informed understanding of the past. Religious buildings, notably cathedrals, may be popular tourist sites, but visitors need to be helped to understand them in their evolving historical context. Museums remain liable to ignore or to marginalize religion. There may well be a perceived difficulty in a multicultural society in drawing too much attention to a national religious past that in institutional terms was primarily Christian, but carefully considered modes of interpretation should facilitate constructive engagement with that legacy rather than its simplistic glorification or its implicit rejection.

If such partnerships can be developed, religious history offers valuable potential to assist in bridging divides between different communities as well as between the religious and the secular. Scholars also need to give priority to historical engagement with non-Christian religions and with non-European

Christianity. Such a process should immediately stimulate awareness not only that the paradigm of religious decline in the twentieth century is a distinctively European one rather than a global one, but also that the very polarity of the secular and religious either operates in different ways, or does not really exist at all. The very numerical strength of organized Christianity in the United States or in sub-Saharan Africa implies a different kind of relationship to the surrounding 'secular' culture and society from that operating in Western Europe with its much smaller active Christian minorities. And when one turns to look at majority Muslim, Buddhist or Hindu societies, underlying religious and cultural values imply the integration of the secular and the sacred much more than their separation.

An historical perspective suggests that the best way of understanding the situation of religion in our day may well be to think not so much of the decline of religion, but of a sharpened polarization on the ground between the religious and the secular. That polarization brings with it numerous possibilities, some of them alarming, others much more constructive. At the same time, the development of religious history offers a growing opportunity for a positive dialogue between religious and secular perspectives, and for facilitating a realistic response to contemporary religious challenges.

Notes

1   For a summary of literature on the dating of 'Dover Beach' see Weinstock (Weinstock 1981: 73, footnote 1).

2   Christian Research Press Release, 18 September 2006.

3   The figures stated below are calculated from the tables in the census report.

4   For the specific context of mid-nineteenth-century anti-Catholic agitation see Wolffe (1991), and for discussion of longer-term trends see Wolffe (2004), especially chapters 4 and 10.

5   http://www.bnp.org.uk; http://www.englishdefenceleague.org [accessed 11 July 2010].

6   For a specific example see the Bishop of Durham's critique of legislation inspired by the 'militantly atheist and secularist lobby' in his Easter Day sermon in 2008 (Wright 2008) and the response from the 'Godfree' columnist David Aaronovitch (Aaronovitch 2008).

7   I am pleased to acknowledge ongoing support from the Arts & Heritage Research Council and the Economic and Social Research Council for three current projects of my own, designed to advance this agenda in relation to changing approaches to the Christian formation of youth; the role of the Church of England in London; and Protestant-Catholic conflict.

Bibliography

Aaronovitch, D. (2008), *The Times*, 25 March.

Bossy, J. (1975), *The English Catholic Community 1570–1850*, London: Darton, Longman and Todd.

British Council of Churches, Committee for Relations with People of Other Faiths (1991), *In Good Faith: The Four Principles of Inter-faith Dialogue*, London: Council of Churches for Britain and Ireland.

Census of Great Britain 1851: Religious Worship, England and Wales – Report and Tables (1853), House of Commons Sessional Papers, 1852–3, vol. 89, London: House of Commons.

Ferguson, N. (2004), 'Decline and Fall of the Christian Empire', *Sunday Times*, 11 April.

Huntington, S.P. (1996), *The Clash of Civilizations and the Remaking of World Order*, New York: Simon & Schuster.

MacGregor, J. (1852), *Popery in 1900*, London: Seeleys.

Ricks, C. (ed.) (1999), *The Oxford Book of English Verse*, Oxford: Oxford University Press.

Robbins, K. (1985), 'Britain, 1940 and "Christian civilization"', in D. Beales and G. Best (eds), *History, Society and the Churches*, Cambridge: Cambridge University Press.

Shils, E. and Young, M. (1953), 'The meaning of the Coronation', *Sociological Review*, 1: 63–82.

Thucydides (1973), *The History of the Peloponnesian War*, edited by R. Livingstone, Oxford: Oxford University Press.

Weinstock, D.J. (1981), '"Say not we are on a darkling plain": Clough's response to "Dover Beach"', *Victorian Poetry*, 19.

Williams, R. (2008), 'Civil and Religious Law in England: A Religious Perspective', speech, 7 February, http://www.archbishopofcanterbury.org [accessed 10 July 2010].

Wolffe, J. (1991), *The Protestant Crusade in Great Britain 1829–1860*, Oxford: Oxford University Press.

Wolffe, J. (1993), '"And there's another country...": Religion, the State and British Identities', in G. Parsons (ed.), *The Growth of Religious Diversity: Britain from 1945, Vol. II, Traditions*, London: Routledge, 85–121.

Wolffe, J. (2000), *Great Deaths: Grieving, Religion and Nationhood in Victorian and Edwardian Britain*, Oxford: Oxford University Press.

Wolffe, J. (ed.) (2004), *Religion in History: Conflict, Conversion and Coexistence*, Manchester: Manchester University Press.

Wolffe, J. (2005), *The Religious Census of 1851 in Yorkshire*, Borthwick Paper 108, York: Borthwick Institute.

Wolffe, J. (2010a), 'Protestantism, Monarchy and the Defence of Christian Britain 1837–2005', in C. Brown and M. Snape (eds), *Secularization in the Christian World*, Aldershot: Ashgate.

Wolffe, J. (2010b), 'Religious History', in J.R. Hinnells (ed.), *The Routledge Companion to the Study of Religion*, 2nd edn, London: Routledge, 56–72.

Wylie, J.A. (1865), *Rome and Civil Liberty*, London: Hamilton, Adams.

Wright, N.T. (2008), 'The uncomfortable truth about Easter', http://www.ntwrightpage.com/sermons/EasterDay08.htm [accessed 11 July 2010].

4. The Use and Abuse of National History and the National Poet

Jonathan Bate (University of Warwick)

To be sure, we need history. But we need it in a manner different from the way in which the spoilt idler in the garden of knowledge uses it, no matter how elegantly he may look down on our coarse and graceless needs and distresses. That is, we need it for life and for action, not for a comfortable turning away from life and from action or for merely glossing over the egotistical life and the cowardly bad act. We wish to serve history only insofar as it serves living. (Nietzsche 2010)

Essentially British?

On 20 February 2008, Prime Minister Gordon Brown said in a speech on 'Managed Migration and Earned Citizenship' that:

> Citizenship is not an abstract concept, or just access to a passport. I believe it is – and must be seen as – founded on shared values that define the character of our country. Indeed, building our secure and prosperous future as a nation will benefit from not just common values we share but a strong sense of national purpose. And for that to happen we need to be forthright – and yes confident – about what brings us together not only as inhabitants of these islands but as citizens of this society. Indeed there is a real danger that while other countries gain from having a clear definition of their destiny in a fast changing global economy, we may lose out if we prove slow to express and live up to the British values that can move us to act together. So the surest foundation upon which we can advance socially, culturally and economically in this century is to be far more explicit about the ties – indeed the shared values – that make us more than a collection of people but a country. This is not jingoism, but practical, rational and purposeful – and therefore, I would argue, an essentially British form of patriotism.[1]

Brown's rhetoric was symptomatic of a series of anxieties about cultural identity, immigration, and notions of belonging in a multicultural and globalized society that were highly characteristic of Britain in the early twenty-first century. This essay will suggest that humanities research alone has the capacity to test the meaning and validity of claims about what is or is not 'essentially British'.

Without knowledge of history, the phrase 'essentially British' is essentially meaningless. Is there, has there even been, could there be an essentially British form of patriotism? Both 'Britain' and 'patriotism' are ideas with complicated histories. Recent research in the humanities has done much to untangle those histories and to reveal the complicated intertwining of the terms. A kneejerk patriot wrapped in the Union Jack might be surprised to learn that when the word 'patriot' entered the English language during the reign of Queen Elizabeth I, the nation of Great Britain – let alone the United Kingdom – did not exist. By the time the conceptual term 'patriotism' emerged in the eighteenth century, 'Britain' had come into being. But for much of that century, 'patriot' was a term associated with oppositional politics, not support for the government. And at the end of the eighteenth century, to be a 'patriot' sometimes meant to be a supporter of the French Revolution, which was little short of treasonable.

Before we talk about certain values being 'essentially British', we need to remember that these islands are not essentially British. We might begin with the national poet. William Shakespeare is a regular fixture in lists of national icons, Great Britons and the like. But was he an English dramatist or a British one? The answer to this question is surprisingly simple but all too often neglected. It is that during the reign of Queen Elizabeth I Shakespeare considered himself English, and indeed devoted a large portion of his writing time to plays that dramatized the history of England, but in the early years of the reign of James VI of Scotland as James I of England he began writing about 'British' matter (notably in *King Lear* and *Cymbeline*) because James had hopes of creating a British state. Those hopes were dashed by the parliaments in both London and Edinburgh. The British state did not come into being until 1707 (except, briefly and somewhat theoretically, in republican form between 1654 and 1660).

Storytelling has always played an important part in the shaping of national identity. The Victorians believed in a seamless bond between 'our English Literature' – that great body of national self-expression with Shakespeare and John Milton at the centre – and 'our island story' (Brooke 1877: 1). But, as modern historians have frequently emphasized, the forms of nationhood within these islands have been highly varied. Every different 'state' formation has had its own narratives of identity and belonging (see Davies 1999).

There were High Kings in Ireland until the year 1169. Before the Romans came, the larger of the two big islands was divided among many different tribal principalities. The name 'Britannia' was imposed by the Roman invaders, who never colonized 'Hibernia', which we call Ireland, and who built a wall to protect themselves from the Picts, whom we call Scots, in the north. After the Roman retreat in the fifth century, the country was again divided, this time among Anglo-Saxon principalities and independent Celtic domains such as Cornwall and Cumbria.

There was an independent kingdom of the Scots from the ninth century to 1651, and again from 1660 to 1707. Between the tenth century and 1536, the kingdom of England, together with its dependencies including the Channel Islands, the Isle of Man, the Welsh March, and English-occupied Wales and Ireland, went through several changes of dynasty – Norman, Angevin, Lancastrian, Yorkist and Tudor. There were times when politically England was in effect part of what we now call France and others when much of what we now call France was in effect part of England.

From 1536 to 1649 and again from 1660 to 1707, England and Wales formed a single kingdom, with a change of dynasty bringing a new king and queen from the Netherlands, and a shift in the balance of power between monarchy and Parliament, at the 'Glorious Revolution' of 1688. The Kingdom of Ireland was ruled by England from 1541 to 1649 and again from 1660 to 1800. In 1649 Parliament declared and enacted:

> That the People of England and of all the Dominions and Territories thereunto belonging [including Wales and Ireland] are, and shall be, and are hereby Constituted, Made, Established, and Confirmed to be a Commonwealth and Free State; and shall henceforward be Governed as a Commonwealth and Free State by the Supreme Authority of this Nation, the Representatives of the People in Parliament, and by such as they shall appoint and constitute as Officers and Ministers for the good of the People, and that without any King or House of Lords. (Adams and Stephens 1930)

In 1654 the name was changed from the Commonwealth and Free State of England to the Commonwealth of Great Britain and, though the state continued to be a republic by virtue of the absence of a monarch, the Lord Protector Oliver Cromwell governed very much in the style of a king. At the end of the decade, the Commonwealth was briefly re-established before the Restoration of the monarchy.

The United Kingdom of Great Britain came into being in 1707, following the Act of Union with Scotland, and with a new succession of kings from Hanover taking the throne with effect from 1714. The United Kingdom of Great Britain and Ireland came into being on 1 January 1801, following the previous year's Acts of Union with Ireland. It endured until 1922, when the Irish Free State (later Éire, then the Republic of Ireland) was born. The United Kingdom of Great Britain and Northern Ireland came into being in 1922. It endures at the time of writing, though since 1998 with varying degrees of devolved powers for Scotland, Wales and Northern Ireland.

For several centuries, the English/British were part of a theological entity called 'Christendom', which was often assumed (incorrectly) to overlap with a geographical entity called 'Europe'. English members of the original diasporic nation, the Jews, have long been considered 'outsiders' because they do not belong to 'Christendom': this is a key point in several major nineteenth-century novels, most notably *Daniel Deronda* (1876) by George Eliot and *The Wondrous Tale of Alroy* (1833), *Coningsby* (1844) and *Tancred* (1847) by Benjamin Disraeli, himself a Jew by birth (though baptized a Christian in his teens).

Following UK entry into the 'European Economic Community' or 'Common Market' in 1973 and the transformation of that alliance of preferentially trading states into a more legally homogenized 'European Union' at Maastricht in 1993, the British are part of Europe once more. There is, however, markedly less enthusiasm for this secular union than there was for the old spiritual idea of Christendom, and no major work of English-language literature or drama has yet been written from the distinctive standpoint of the European Union.

The earning of citizenship and the right to pronounce about national identity really should be dependent, at the very least, on an outline knowledge of this extraordinarily complicated story, which can only be unpacked and interpreted by means of the research of our historians.

The invention of Britannia

The Reformation in religion, and more particularly Henry VIII's break from Rome, was decisive in shaping the modern English, and then British, state and, at the same time, the idea of love of one's country ('patriotism'). The culture of England was until the early sixteenth century always implicitly part of something larger: the culture of Catholic Europe. After 1536–39, when Henry VIII dissolved the monasteries and proclaimed the supremacy of the English crown and the independence of the English church, it became necessary to forge a new kind of national culture.

A key work in this project was a huge book called *Britannia*, by William Camden, antiquarian and second master at Westminster School. Published in Latin in 1586, it went through six editions by 1607, and was translated into English by Philemon Holland in 1610.

Dedicated to William Cecil, Baron Burghley, Lord Treasurer and chief minister to Queen Elizabeth, Camden's weighty book began with a history of early Britain, then proceeded to a county-by-county guide to the topography, history and antiquities of the nation. *Britannia* was an attempt to write the nation into being. Britain is proclaimed as a chosen land, symbolically set apart from the European mainland.

The opening of Camden's text implies that Britain is one nation, if with several names, played off against 'the continent of Europe'. But his title page presents a more complicated picture. Holland translated it as follows: *Britain, or a Chorographicall Description of the most flourishing Kingdomes, England, Scotland, and Ireland, and the ilands adjoyning, out of the depth of Antiquitie* ('chorographical' means 'the writing of regions', as opposed to 'geography', the writing of the whole earth). The county-by-county survey begins with Cornwall in the extreme south-west, goes across to Kent in the extreme south-east, then criss-crosses northward until it reaches Cheshire, at which point Camden writes, 'I Thinke it now my best way, before I treat of the other parts of England, to digresse a while and turne a little aside toward Wales, called in Latin *Cambria*, or *Wallia*, where the ancient Britans have yet their seat and abode' (Camden 1637: 615). Wales is thus subsumed into England, though with the recognition on the one hand that it is marginal – you must turn a little aside to acknowledge it – and on the other hand that it is special, since the Celtic or ancient British heritage remains unusually alive there. The latter acknowledgment might look to a Welshman like condescension masked as flattery.

From Wales, Camden proceeds through the northernmost counties of England and into Scotland, which he says that he will willingly enter into, 'but withall lightly passe over', since he does not know its customs well and will not presume to trespass upon them. His text passes it over in a score of leaves, whereas it has dwelt in England for hundreds of pages. Camden quotes an apt Greek proverb, 'Art thou a stranger? Be no Medler'. One senses that Camden is a little uneasy about subsuming the Scots into his treatment of England-as-implicitly-Britain, as he had subsumed the Welsh. His task became much easier after King James united the thrones of Scotland and England in 1603. Holland's 1610 translation proceeds with a passage that Camden added to his 1607 edition:

> Certes, I assure my selfe that I shall bee easily pardoned in this point, the people them selves are so courtuous and well meaning, and the happinesse of these daies so rare and admirable, since that by a divine and heavenly opportunity is now fallen into our laps, which wee hardly ever hoped, and our Ancestours so often and so earnestly wished: Namely, that Britaine so many ages disjoigned in it selfe and unsociable, should all throughout like one uniforme City, under one most sacred and happie Monarch, the founder of perpetuall peace, by a blessed Union bee conjoyned in one entire bodie. (Camden 1637: 3 in separately paginated section on Scotland)

Because Scotland has a court, unlike Wales, it is thought of as a place of courtesy. The joining of the two courts is conceived as a knitting together of the body politic. King James is then praised for bringing a long history of 'dismale DISCORD', which has set the two 'otherwise invincible' nations at long debate, to 'sweet CONCORD', so that '*Wee all one nation are this day*'.

The lifetime of Queen Elizabeth was a unique period for England, lying between the schism from Rome and the union with Scotland. The special conditions of the period 1533–1603 gave birth to a recognizably modern sense of the nation. It is no coincidence that in the late sixteenth century the term 'the nation' took on the meaning of 'the collectivity of the people' and the word 'national' enters the language, as did the grammatically absolute usage of 'country' as a personification of the native land – as in Shakespeare's 'Forgive me, country, and sweet countrymen' in *Henry VI Part One*. In 1615, Camden dedicated his *Annals* of Queen Elizabeth's reign to 'God, my country, and posterity' ('DEO, PATRIAE, ET POSTERIS'). Such a trinity would have been inconceivable a century earlier.

Nor is it coincidental that in the 1560s Laurence Nowell applied to William Cecil for aid in mapping the entire realm, county-by-county; in the next decade Christopher Saxton completed the first comprehensive *Atlas* of England and Wales. The Elizabethans did not only 'discover' new worlds across the ocean: they also discovered England. And, despite – or because of – a succession of rebellions and the constant persecution of Roman Catholic recusants, they unified England. By the end of the sixteenth century, the government's administrative machinery had put in place a nationwide network of civic and legal officers ultimately answerable to the crown, while the ecclesiastical settlement had established the supremacy of Anglicanism. Most importantly for our purposes, a national culture had come to full flower, thanks in large measure to the educational advances effected by the grammar schools, the translation into English of the foundation texts of Western culture (the Bible, Homer and the major authors of classical Rome), the writing of national history, the increased availability of books of all kinds and, for Londoners at least, the completely new cultural arena of the public playhouse. Anticipations of some of these individual factors may be found in earlier periods, but it is their concatenation in the aftermath of the break from Rome that marks the distinctively Elizabethan image of the nation.

Wales was absent from Camden's title page because it was regarded as part of England; in 1536 Henry VIII had given royal assent to a bill formally uniting the two countries. Scotland, as we have seen, was deferred to as a separate nation. Ireland represented more of a problem. It had its distinctive topography and its independent history, which Camden duly and indeed respectfully recorded, but since Henry II's conquest in 1172 it had been under the rule and power of England. Camden, with his immense reverence for Christian learning, was fascinated by the figure of St Patrick and the Irish monastic tradition that extended back to the fifth century. He even suggested that the English Saxons learned literacy from the Irish. This led him, in a fascinating sentence added to *Britannia*'s sixth edition, to formulate and resolve a paradox:

And no cause have we to mervaile, that Ireland which now for the most part is rude, half-barbarous, and altogether voide of any polite and exquisite literature, was full of so devout, godly and good wits in that age, wherin good letters throughout all Christiendome lay neglected and half buried; seeing, that the Divine providence of that most gratious and almighty ruler of the world, soweth the seeds and bringeth forth the plantes of

Sanctity and good arts, one whiles in one nation and other whiles in another, as it were in garden beds and borders, and that in sundry ages: which being removed and translated hither and thither, may by a new grouth come up one under another, prosper, and be preserved to his owne glory, and the good of mankind. (Camden 1637: 68 in separately paginated section on Ireland)

Camden's expectation was clearly that a reader might well marvel at the transformation of Ireland from centre of erudition and holiness to cultural and moral desert. His explanation for the change relied on a providential and cyclical view of history, in thorough accordance with the Elizabethan theory of the translation of empire and learning (*translatio imperii et studii*) in which England was regarded as the nation chosen by God to succeed Greece and Rome as the pre-eminent home of world power and high culture – and indeed to exceed the ancients, since imperial glory and 'good arts' were combined with Christian 'Sanctity'. The providential explanation diverts the reader from another possibility: namely that all traces of high culture have been extinguished from Ireland because it has been so long subjugated to England, that it is the English who have made the Irish 'rude' and 'half-barbarous'. Between 1586, when *Britannia* was first published, and 1607, when this passage was added, Tyrone's rebellions had been suppressed and the English crown's stranglehold on Ireland tightened. Though strangers in Ireland, the English did not hesitate to meddle. You can only invent a nation by positing its other, by creating an outside, by denominating and demonizing aliens. Ireland, Catholic Spain, the Ottoman Empire, Italy – paradoxically regarded as the source of both artistic sophistication and Machiavellian decadence – and the New World served the Elizabethans well in this respect.

At first sight, the above piece of research may appear antiquarian, parochial, even pedantic. An examination of the textual changes between the Elizabethan and Jacobean versions of Camden's *Britannia* does not sound like the kind of thing that has 'relevance' to the early twenty-first-century debate about 'earned citizenship' and 'national identity'. But it is precisely in Camden's negotiations of the relationship between 'England' and 'Britain', between service to God and love of 'patria', that modern notions of citizenship, patriotism and national identity begin to emerge.

The 'British question', as historians call it, has been the focus of much of the most innovative and provocative historical and literary-historical research in the last twenty years – the line of distinguished work extends from Hugh Kearney's *The British Isles: A History of Four Nations* (1989) to John Kerrigan's *Archipelagic English* (2008). The fostering and dissemination of that research, through teaching, through books aimed at a wide intelligent readership, through broadcasting and – why not? – even through seminars for the education of politicians and civil servants can play a major role in raising the level of debate about nation and devolution, arrival and belonging.

Shakespeare raises an army

Samuel Taylor Coleridge once remarked that the English get their history from Shakespeare, just as they get their theology from Milton. Research in recent decades has indeed done much to show how the creation of national identity is as much a cultural – a literary and theatrical – phenomenon as an historical and political one. It was in the eighteenth century, following the 1707 Acts of Union between England and Scotland, that politicians, polemicists and writers forged a sense of 'Britishness' (see Colley 1992; Weinbrot 1993). It was also in the eighteenth century, and by a parallel process, that Shakespeare was elevated to the role of national poet (see Bate 1989; Dobson 1992). His history plays are central to English conceptions of their past. Whether it is the left-wing theatre director Michael Bogdanov bringing on to the stage of his English Shakespeare Company in the 1980s a group of squaddies carrying a banner proclaiming 'F--- the Argies' or the BBC broadcasting a Royal Shakespeare Company actor reciting 'God for Harry, England, and St George' in the build-up to a World Cup rugby match, the reanimation of Shakespeare's history plays offers a prime example of what Friedrich Nietzsche in his essay 'The Use and Abuse of History for Life' calls 'history for life and for action' (Nietzsche 2010).

Shakespeare excelled in every available genre of Elizabethan drama, but in the two parts of his *King Henry IV* he achieved his generic full house, hitting the jackpot identified by Polonius in *Hamlet*: 'tragical-comical-historical-pastoral' are rolled into one. As history, the plays paint a panorama of England, embracing a wider social range than any previous historical drama, as the action moves from court to tavern, council-chamber to battlefield, city to country, Archbishop and Lord Chief Justice to whore and thief. As comedy, they tell the story of a prodigal son's journey from youth to maturity and an old rogue's art of surviving by means of jokes, tall tales and the art of being not only witty in himself but the cause that wit is in other men. As tragedy, they reveal the slow decline of a king who cannot escape his past, along with the precipitate demise of an impetuous young warrior (the hotly named Hotspur) who embodies both the glory and the futility of military heroism, and finally the heart-stopping dismissal of a substitute father.

The action of *The First Part of Henry the Fourth* (as *Part One* was known) begins some time after the events that ended Shakespeare's earlier play, *The Tragedy of Richard the Second*. Henry Bullingbrook has usurped the throne of King Richard, but now the rebels who helped him to the throne have turned against him. Whereas *Richard the Second* conformed to the traditional structure of tragedy – the story of the fall of a powerful man – the *Henry the Fourth* plays adopt a wider perspective. *Richard the Second* had been written entirely in measured iambic verse, the medium of royal and aristocratic characters, whereas long stretches of the *Henry the Fourth* plays are in supple and inventive prose, the medium of the common people.

The scenes in *The Second Part* with Justice Shallow in his Gloucestershire orchard are the closest that Shakespeare ever came to a stage representation of the rural England of his own early life in Stratford-upon-Avon.

Part One has a good claim to be regarded as Shakespeare's most popular play in his own time. In the absence of box office numbers, such a claim has to be measured by a variety of inferential indicators. It wins on all of them: number of times the published script was reprinted before the works were collected in the First Folio (six, more than any other Shakespeare play); frequency of quotations, allusions and imitations in works by others (on this count, Falstaff is up there with Hamlet); demand for sequels (*Part Two* and then *The Merry Wives of Windsor* to give audiences another dose of Falstaff, and *Henry V* to follow through the story of Prince Hal).

It sustained its position in the ratings long after Shakespeare's death. Most of his plays had to be heavily rewritten in order to keep their place in the repertoire after the reopening of the theatres with the Restoration of the monarchy in 1660, and through the eighteenth century: so as to conform to the theatrical taste of the age, *King Lear* was decked out with a happy ending and *Macbeth* with all-singing, all-dancing witches. But *Henry IV Part One* held the stage, and was revived almost as frequently as *Hamlet* and *Romeo and Juliet*, with only the most minor alterations.

In the twentieth century, Orson Welles stitched the two parts together, threw in a chunk of *Henry V* for good measure, and created *Chimes at Midnight*, one of the all-time great Shakespeare movies. In his *Henry V* film Kenneth Branagh used flashbacks to key moments in each part, illuminating King Harry's back story. And in *My Own Private Idaho* (1991) Gus Van Sant quirkily but brilliantly updated the script into a world of gay street hustlers and rich boys on the run from their origins. Through such adaptations, Shakespeare has offered living history for four centuries.

The sheer richness and variety of the *Henry IV* plays is such that they continue to offer historical lessons in an extraordinary variety of ways. So it is that one finds the character of Sir John Falstaff evoked in the most unlikely places: for instance, an article on the history of military contracting in the *Journal of International Peace Operations*. This is not, as the title might suggest, the august organ of a think-tank for NGOs in the aid trade, but rather the house magazine of the International Peace Operations Association, the trade organization of the burgeoning private military industry. Its operatives do not, of course, call themselves 'private armies', but rather 'the Stability Operations Industry'.

The article in question is entitled 'Shakespeare on Military Contracting: Lessons from History about Private Contracting'. Its author is Gary Sturgess, formerly head of the New South Wales Cabinet Office, 'during which time,' Wikipedia tells us, 'he introduced a number of major policy initiatives including the Independent Commission Against Corruption'. Sturgess is now executive director of the Serco Institute, 'a research facility studying competition and contracting in public services'. A 2006 article in the *Sydney Morning Herald* credited him as a key figure in the move towards the contracting out of state functions in Australia. The Serco Group now runs everything from prisons to railways in over thirty countries, combining, in the words of its website, 'a deep public service ethos with the commercial know-how that gives us the ability to deliver'.

Sturgess turns out to be extremely well informed about the tricky issue of the resemblances and differences between the character of Sir John Falstaff in *Henry IV* and Sir John Fastolf in *Henry VI*. He is also aware of the complicated history whereby Falstaff's original name was Sir John Oldcastle, but this had to be changed because his drunkenness, sloth, gluttony and cowardice traduced the historical figure of that name, who was a revered Lollard (proto-Protestant) martyr. It was unfortunate for Shakespeare and his acting company that the office of Lord Chamberlain, the man in charge of censoring plays, passed to a descendant of Oldcastle just as *Henry IV* was entering the repertoire.

But where Sturgess has really done his homework is with regard to the finances of raising an army in the early modern period, when there was no state standing army. He offers a crisp introduction to the intriguing subject of Falstaff's role as a military entrepreneur:

> Under the proprietary system that prevailed in England and the rest of Europe until the 18th century, regiments were owned by the colonels and the captains who recruited them. Their proprietors usually supplied arms, food and clothing, and their bright livery was a means of distinguishing them from other corps.
>
> Until the middle of the 19th century, the British military also relied on 'touts' or 'crimps,' men who recruited soldiers for a commission. Without close regulation, such a system was open to abuse. Both crimps and recruiting sergeants were widely accused of signing men up under the influence of liquor and holding them against their will.
>
> At the very least, Falstaff is a crimp who fills up his muster book with 'shadows' – men recruited, but never actually supplied – and allows draftees to purchase their release. Until the late 18th century, his admissions about abusing the recruiting system drew bursts of laughter from audiences who were personally aware of the practices he described.
>
> But he is more than that. Shakespeare probably intended audiences to understand Falstaff as a captain – certainly the playwright's historical sources portrayed him that way. And from the late 14th century when the story is set through the early 17th century when the play was written, captains functioned as semi-independent contractors, who brought together companies of men under a colonel, who in turn contracted with a supreme commander.

In Shakespeare's dramas, Falstaff pays for his company's initial costs out of his own pocket and then tries to raise a loan to finance his venture on the eve of battle. (Sturgess 2010)

Is this analysis a use or an abuse of Shakespeare? It certainly provides illumination of the great recruiting scene in *Part Two*, which comes complete with muster book and a character called 'Shadow'. Sturgess is right about the continuance of this recruiting system until the late eighteenth century, though in terms of theatrical representation, the story is slightly more complicated: *Part Two*, in sharp contrast to *Part One*, was not staged at all frequently, not least because its comic centrepiece, the recruitment scene, kept being appropriated and reworked in popular new plays – first George Farquhar's *The Recruiting Officer*, then Isaac Bickerstaff's *The Recruiting Serjeant* – which displaced their Shakespearean original.

Sturgess is delighted to report that the original Sir John Fastolf 'was said to have left a fortune worth $18 billion in today's values, and has been described as the 51st wealthiest individual in British history ... he is a reminder that for hundreds of years, governments did find a way of contracting with private individuals for the delivery of military services, services that would today be regarded as "inherently governmental"'. At this point, Sturgess' agenda becomes apparent: he is stating the case for the privatization of military procurement. 'He may be a figure of fun, but Falstaff shows us that incentives matter': that is one way of reading the play. An alternative conclusion might have been 'state provision is burdened by inefficiency, but reliance on the private sector is liable to be tarnished by corruption and inevitably leads to the exploitation of the poor'. Still, as the new age of austerity forces government to ask what are the services that must be provided by the state and what are those that can be contracted out in the name of 'efficiency savings', there is grist in the lesson from history that a state-run as opposed to an entrepreneurially led army is a relatively new phenomenon in Britain.

Humanities research is a kaleidoscope through which we rearrange the fragments of our collective experience. An attentive, critical reading of a single document – whether Holland's 1610 translation of Camden's *Britannia* or Sturgess' 2010 essay on Falstaff and military recruiting – can throw fresh light on old and new questions. By reading Shakespeare's dramaturgy and researching the historical framework of his plays, we use the past to frame the debates of the present.

Note

1   The speech was published on http://www.number10.gov.uk but removed with the change of government in 2010. It remains available, as of the time of writing, at http://www.martinfrost.ws/htmlfiles/feb2008/brown_migration. html [accessed 12 July 2010].

Bibliography

Adams, G.B. and Stephens, H.M. (1930), 'Act declaring England to be a Commonwealth', *Select Documents of English Constitutional History*, London: Macmillan, http://home.freeuk.net/don-aitken/ast/cp.html [accessed 11 July 2010].

Bate, J. (1989), *Shakespearean Constitutions: Politics, Theatre, Criticism 1730–1830*, Oxford: Oxford University Press.

Brooke, S.A. (1877), *English Literature*, London: Macmillan.

Camden, W. (1637), *Britain, or A chorographicall description of the most flourishing kingdomes, England, Scotland, and Ireland, and the ilands adjoyning, out of the depth of antiquitie beautified vvith mappes of the severall shires of England: vvritten first in Latine by William Camden Clarenceux K. of A. Translated newly into English by Philémon Holland Doctour in Physick: finally, revised, amended, and enlarged with sundry additions by the said author*, London: George Latham.

Colley, L. (1992), *Britons: Forging the Nation 1707–1837*, London and New Haven, CT: Yale University Press.

Davies, N. (1999), *The Isles: A History*, London: Macmillan.

Dobson, M. (1992), *The Making of the National Poet*, Oxford: Clarendon Press.

Kearney, H. (1989), *The British Isles: A History of Four Nation*, Cambridge: Cambridge: Cambridge University Press.

Kerrigan, J. (2008), *Archipelagic English: Literature, History, and Politics 1603–1707*, Oxford: Oxford University Press.

Nietzsche, F. (2010), *On the Use and Abuse of History for Life*, trans. Ian Johnston, Nanaimo, BC, Canada: Vancouver Island University, http://records.viu.ca/~johnstoi/Nietzsche/history.htm [accessed 11 July 2010].

Sturgess, G. (2010), 'Shakespeare on Military Contracting: Lessons from History about Private Contracting', *Journal of International Peace Operations*, 5: 5, http://web.peaceops.com/archives/423 [accessed 11 July 2010].

Weinbrot, H. (1993), *Britannia's Issue: The Rise of British Literature from Dryden to Ossian*, Cambridge: Cambridge University Press.

5. Custodians and Active Citizens

Robert Hampson (Royal Holloway, University of London)

On English literature

Britain has over 1,300 years of literary culture from the first arrival of the English in the Celtic archipelago up to the present moment. Not only that, it is exceptional in that its literary culture has been extremely sophisticated for over a thousand years, with writing of the highest international standard manifest from *Beowulf*, *Sir Gawain and the Green Knight* and the works of Chaucer onwards. The great authors of the past are familiar names the world over: William Shakespeare, John Milton, Lord Byron, William Wordsworth, Jane Austen, Charles Dickens, George Eliot. Nor does our international literary reputation rely on authors of the past. In the last decade, there have been three Nobel Laureates: V.S. Naipaul (2001), Harold Pinter (2005) and Doris Lessing (2007). The fact that one was born in the West Indies of Indian parents, one in London of Jewish immigrant parentage and the third in Southern Africa testifies to the range and variety of contemporary 'English literature'.

   The history of English literature is a history of the migrations of peoples and cultures, and the study of English literature is an inescapable engagement with that history. The history of English literature encompasses the Germanic culture of the Anglo-Saxons; the cultural impact of the conquest of Anglo-Saxon England by the Normans, French-speaking Scandinavians; the importation of classical Greek, Latin and contemporary Italian literatures during the Renaissance; the spread of empire and the return flow of art, literature and ideas from India, China and the Arab world; the writings of new immigrants into Britain and the various 'new writings' in English that emerged during and after the age of empire. At the same time, this literature has also been the site of negotiations between the varied constituent cultures of the archipelago – in Shakespeare's *Henry V*, in Walter Scott's Waverley novels, in James Joyce's *Ulysses*, to take just three examples. *Henry V* brings together the Welshman, the Scot and the recently colonized Irishman to fight at Agincourt alongside the English, but registers also the tensions between these groups in a complex exploration of king and subject, colonizer and colonized (Greenblatt 1985). Scott's Waverley novels engage with Scottish politics and Scottish identity after the failure of the 1745 Jacobite Uprising. *Ulysses* is similarly pervaded by the national politics of the time: it is an Irish assault upon England and English culture; a painstaking attempt to locate Irish culture in relation to English colonial rule, a larger European culture and American popular culture; and an engagement with Irish cultural politics designed to influence the shape of a new Irish identity in the new Irish state (Gibson 2002).

This wealth of literature is both a cultural asset of considerable value and an unparalleled resource for future cultural work. While major literary works, such as Edmund Spenser's *The Faerie Queene*, Milton's *Paradise Lost* and Wordsworth's *The Prelude*, do not have a market value in the way that important paintings do, they have a comparable cultural value. While the loss of a painting through sale abroad often makes newspaper headlines, we are much more careless about our literary heritage – sometimes failing to ensure that it stays in print, remains available to readers and is actively read. At the same time, writers remain vividly aware of this inheritance. They are in constant dialogue with the literature of the past. The poetry of the Anglo-Saxon period, for example – in particular 'The Wanderer', 'The Seafarer', 'Wulf and Eadwacer' and *Beowulf* – was repeatedly returned to in the course of the twentieth century by poets as various as Ezra Pound, Bill Griffiths and Seamus Heaney. *Sir Gawain and the Green Knight* has prompted both a recent opera and a new verse translation by Simon Armitage. David Lodge and Colm Tóibín have turned back to Elizabeth Gaskell and Henry James, and there is an entire new genre of neo-Victorian fiction. It hardly needs saying that the novels of Jane Austen, Thomas Hardy and Virginia Woolf are continually being reinterpreted through film. But literature is more than just a source for films. Joseph Conrad's *Heart of Darkness* has been reinterpreted through films, dramatizations, graphic novels and even puppet shows, a *Rhapsodie Negre* and an oratorio; it has provided a narrative model for travel books and for other novels (from Woolf's *The Voyage Out* to Will Self's *The Butt*); it has also provided a journalistic shorthand for accounts of disasters in Africa or for reviews of V.S. Naipaul's biography. Like all literature, it provides narrative models, metaphors and points of reference by which we can attempt to make sense of contemporary events or the most profound personal experiences.

Researcher as custodian

In the first instance, humanities research in this field has an important custodial role in relation to a valuable cultural asset. This custodial role is most evident in the work of textual scholars, the editors of literary texts and the editors of authors' letters. Research into the development of the text of a literary work – which might be from manuscript to typescript, from typescript to serialized version, from serialization through various editions (with a range of authorial and non-authorial changes) – provides the groundwork for all subsequent reading and criticism. This research might arrive at a definitive edition or it might arrive at ten different, equally valid versions (as in the case of Samuel Taylor Coleridge's poem 'Frost at Midnight'), but it is important for readers to know the status and authority of the text being read. The first edition of H. Rider Haggard's *King's Solomon's Mines*, for example, features a solar eclipse; in all subsequent editions, this becomes a lunar eclipse and Haggard's protagonists have an extra half-day of activities while they wait for this event to take place. Wordsworth's *The Prelude* of 1805 is more radical in its politics and less orthodoxly Christian in its religion than *The Prelude* of 1850. To discuss Haggard or 'Frost at Midnight' or *The Prelude*, we thus need to have some sense of the writing and publication history. The annotation of literary texts – the explication of references or the provision of knowledge and information that is no longer current – is also an important service to future readers and critics. Some information about Frederick Selous, Southern African politics and the ruins of Great Zimbabwe, for example, is likely to be useful to readers of *King Solomon's Mines*.

Perhaps equally important is the identification of current knowledge which will be unfamiliar to future readers. The precise nature of Charles Olson's excitement at the graphic possibilities of the typewriter in his 'Projective Verse' manifesto (Olson 1966), for example, already has to be explained to students familiar only with word-processing, while the kitchen range upon which Bloom cooks his breakfast in *Ulysses* is passing out of the experience of all but the oldest readers (Joyce 2000: 15–26). Modern textual scholarship is also often concerned with the contexts in which work is published. For example, our reading of Keats' Odes might be affected by the knowledge that his publisher was awaiting trial for sedition at the time the 1820 volume in which the Odes first appeared was published (McGann 1985: 15–65). Similarly, it might be useful in relation to other poets and fiction writers to know what kind of magazine a work first appeared in, who else was published in the magazine, what kind of readership the magazine was aimed at and what kind of visual material accompanied the text. Electronic media permit the reproduction of such publications and the dissemination of this information, but scholarly research is necessary to locate it and understand its significance.

This also suggests how literary research, too, has a custodial role. Where textual scholarship provides the texts, literary research keeps those texts alive and current. Literary scholarship mediates between the pastness of the text, the text's original production in a quite different culture, and present concerns and interests. Through publication and teaching, literary research also mediates between the pastness of the text and present (and future) readers. It is, in part, through the debates produced by literary research that particular texts are revived and kept in circulation. This can be seen, for example, in the enhanced reputation of Elizabeth Gaskell's work over the last fifty years or the greater prominence of Gothic fiction over the same period. A wide range of women's writing, including that by women of African, Chinese and South Asian descent – and other writing formerly marginalized – has been given a broader readership as a result of literary research. In all these cases, this revival of interest is motivated not simply by an antiquarian interest. These earlier works speak to contemporary concerns. Gaskell's novels about the relations between workers and their employers, the role of unions, and the gap between rich and poor have an obvious relevance to our own times. The attention to women's writing more generally has contributed to the ongoing interrogation of women's role and identity, and attention to the immigrant and ethnic minority experience, while the interest in the Gothic reflects an increasing awareness of the literary expressions of fears and anxieties – and the reading of literary works as symptomatic of larger cultural anxieties.

Thus, there has recently been an engagement in literary studies with 'literature and terrorism', which aims to contextualize the present through comparison, for example, with nineteenth-century political 'terror'. Equally importantly, it also puts pressure on that word 'terrorism' – on the tendency to lump nationalist struggles and the resistance to occupation indiscriminately under this label together with 'terror' campaigns, or the tendency to focus on the 'low-tech' terror of home-made bombs and ignore the 'high-tech' terror of aerial bombardment. This is not to argue for a full-blown 'presentist' approach to literary studies and research; it is rather to register that literary research is inevitably shaped and nuanced by contemporary concerns. It derives from and returns to current debates within the subject and within the larger society. Similarly, it is not that earlier literature provides the answers to our questions, but rather that literary research provides an historical depth, other perspectives on contemporary issues, and an enrichment of our questioning and understanding.

The custodial role played by editors, annotators and critics has an obvious importance for other scholars and for other literary critics, but it also has important national and international functions. At its crudest, this can be seen in the heritage industry. It is often said that Wordsworth's poetry created the Lake District as a tourist destination. Certainly, Shakespeare, Austen, Dickens, the Brontës and Woolf – to name just a few – have an important role in relation to internal and international tourism. Tourists are more likely to come to visit the houses of dead writers than the houses of dead politicians. Many British writers are extremely popular overseas among academics, teachers and ordinary readers – Shakespeare, Austen, Dickens, Woolf and Thomas Hardy, for example, all have large followings in Japan. When I took my seat on a country bus in rural Bengal, I was drawn into a conversation with my neighbour about the comparative merits of Shakespeare and Tagore. Our literary heritage still wins friends for us overseas, and our writers are important cultural ambassadors. This is too often overlooked in an attempt to promote the contemporary at the expense of the past. Dickens might seem off-message to politicians keen to promote the United Kingdom as a 'young country', but Dickens' work will remain alive long after that political rhetoric will be beyond resuscitation.

Vital connections

Our literary heritage also has an important domestic role. The more than a thousand years of literary culture can be seen, as I have suggested, to constitute a continuous negotiation of national identity. It thus also constitutes an overlooked cultural resource for the current attempts to define 'Englishness'. Rather than demanding allegiance to a cricket team, a flag or a single family – a feudal notion at odds with European citizenship and in conflict with the republican traditions of many new citizens – our politicians might consider the resources of our literary culture. As Martin Kettle has argued, there are 'some potent English traditions that have nothing to do with flags and everything to do with the tradition of Shakespeare, Bunyan, Blake, Shelley, Morris and Orwell'. Kettle is arguing for a specific tradition of 'Englishness', which he sums up as a vision of 'a free, shared and inspired England that has never existed but remains, in the Albion of the imagination, the England many of us desire' (Kettle 2008: 31).

Nevertheless, what his argument shows is the value of literature as a cultural resource. We might begin to take as much pride in this literary heritage as the Germans do in Goethe or the Bengalis of West Bengal in Tagore. Professional politicians have come up with narrow, rigid and one-dimensional notions of 'Englishness'. Our literary heritage is the heritage of all of us: it constitutes a rich common culture which has the potential to provide more subtle, informed and nuanced engagements with 'Englishness', and it has this potential precisely because it has been a site of negotiation, where 'Englishness' is a text constantly being written, rewritten, interpreted and reinterpreted within a long history of the migrations of peoples and cultures.

While professional politicians have come up with impoverished notions of 'Englishness', they have also failed to articulate a national vision beyond celebrity and the accumulation of wealth. The Beckhams became the cultural icons of the 1990s, and footballers and their wives have been set up as aspirational figures. At the same time, there has been ever-increasing evidence that these values of celebrity and wealth have not produced a healthy society at ease with itself but rather a culture of debt, depression, alcohol and substance abuse, mental health problems, and a widening gap between super-rich and poor. Again, our literary heritage has the potential to provide more ambitious versions of human aspiration than our politicians currently offer.

However, one obstacle to be overcome is the disenfranchisement of the working classes here as in many areas of contemporary society. Jonathan Rose has provided a valuable account of the working-class movement for self-education, a movement which would have been familiar with the authors invoked by Martin Kettle. Rose notes the importance of the canon of 'great books' to this working-class movement: 'If the classics offered artistic excellence, psychological insights, and penetrating philosophy to the governing classes … then the politics of equality must begin by redistributing this knowledge to the governed classes' (Rose 2001: 7). Where such works provided their working-class readers with epiphanic visions of new possibilities, non-canonical literature, by reason of its formulaic nature, 'by and large did not perform the same function for proletarian readers' but operated instead as an 'escapist narcotic' (Rose 2001: 8). Where earlier generations of working-class readers were told that 'great books' were not for them but only for their social superiors, more recent working-class readers have been told that such works are elitist – and, therefore, not for them. Whatever the intention, the effect has been to exclude working-class readers from precisely those works which earlier generations found socially liberating and, self-fulfillingly, to cordon off 'elitist' literature as the preserve of an elite. Research in literature provides a constant tending and renewal of the national heritage, but changes have to be made elsewhere in the system for the working classes to receive their share of this heritage.

In the Preface to his *Mixed Essays*, Matthew Arnold asserted that 'Whoever seriously occupies himself with literature, will soon perceive its vital connexion with other agencies' (Arnold 1954: 545). Research in English literature, as Arnold suggests, involves also an engagement with those various vital connections. Recent research in literary studies into gender, post-colonialism, ethics, the spatial and economics, for example, all contributes to the exploration and understanding of our contemporary situation. This research, and the teaching based on it, feed into the public discussion of important contemporary issues. Literary research contributes to public debate through its own work and through the dissemination of that work through teaching. English literature programmes produce students with transferable skills in writing, research, organization of time, organization of material and oral presentation, but, more importantly, they also produce active citizens through their training of students to be critical and active readers, and through their varied engagements with literature's vital connections. Ronald Barnett argued long ago that 'A higher education organised around skills is no higher education' (Barnett 1994: 61). As Barnett pointed out, an emphasis on skills assumes a prior knowledge of the necessary skills and a prior judgement about the kinds of situation in which those skills are to be used. It assumes that businessmen, businesswomen and politicians are the best people to make these judgements. It ignores the short-termism that has characterized the decision-making of both business and politicians. It also assumes that the function of universities is to produce obedient employees rather than innovative, creative thinkers and critical, active citizens. The teaching of literature, by comparison, as Ben Knights has argued, engages in and fosters 'the conversations that livable societies need' (Knights 2008: 5).[1]

Beyond the immediate short-term needs of business in terms of specific skill-sets, which these programmes can supply, are other skills, less comfortable for business and politicians, which are important for the long-term health of the society in which we live: imagination and vision; a practice of critical reading attentive to language and its implications; an understanding of the narratives, myths and symbols with which we make sense of our lives or by which others try to persuade us; and the ability to bring wider temporal and cultural perspectives to bear on the present. Literary research, and the teaching that is based upon it, can thus produce citizens equipped to engage in the debates about values and social choices that should be part of a healthy democratic society.

However, above all, literature is an aesthetic experience. It derives from basic human activities such as creating and listening to stories, or taking pleasure in playing with the sounds, textures and rhythms of language. We create stories in order to make sense of the world we live in, but we play with the sound, texture and rhythm of language as part of our primary physical engagement with that world. The stories that we create and read give meaning to experience, offer models for and practice in such production of meaning, sustain memory and provide imaginative training in engagement with the unknown. They supply, in Ben Knights' words, 'a space for encounters with the unexpected' and 'mental maps for navigating complexity'. Play with the physical qualities of language is a much more basic part of our species equipment: what might be seen as the purely aesthetic dimension of literary experience. For Herbert Marcuse, the achievement of aesthetic form was the revelation of repressed dimensions of reality: 'a feast of sensuousness which shatters everyday experience and anticipates a different reality principle' (Marcuse 1978: 19). We might also see this primary physical engagement with the concrete elements of language as offering a more profound satisfaction than celebrity and the accumulation of wealth. Research in literature contributes to enhancing both our understanding of the stories that we tell and our sensual appreciation of the world, our pleasure in our senses and in aesthetic experiences. There is more to life than the market, more to life than the cycle of production and consumption. Beyond the training in transferable skills, or even the creation of active citizens, there is this understanding and enriching of what it means to be human.

Note

1   I am indebted to Professor Knights' discussion paper here and elsewhere in this essay and to Professor Kiernan Ryan.

Bibliography

Arnold, M. (1954), *Poetry and Prose*, ed. by John Bryson, London: Rupert Hart-Davis.

Barnett, R. (1994), *The Limits of Competence: Knowledge, Higher Education and Society*, Buckingham: Open University.

Gibson, A. (2002), *Joyce's Revenge: History, Politics, and Aesthetics in 'Ulysses'*, Oxford: Oxford University Press.

Greenblatt, S. (1985), 'Invisible Bullets: Renaissance authority and its subversion, *Henry IV* and *Henry V*', in J. Dollimore and A. Sinfield, *Political Shakespeare: New Essays in Cultural Materialism*, Manchester: Manchester University Press, 18–47.

Haggard, H.R. (2008), *King Solomon's Mines*, London: Penguin.

Joyce, J. (2000), *Ulysses*, with an introduction by D. Kiberd, London: Penguin Classics.

Kettle, M. (2008), 'Speak for England, Gordon, and stop all this flag-waving', *Guardian*, 26 April.

Knights, B. (2008), 'Leitch, Skills and Prosperity for All: Towards a Humanities Perspective', *HEAC English Subject Centre Newsletter*, 15: 22–4.

McGann, J. (1985), 'Keats and Historical Method', in J. McGann, *The Beauty of Inflections: Literary Investigations in Historical Method and Theory*, Oxford: Oxford University Press.

Marcuse, H. (1978), *The Aesthetic Dimension*, London: Macmillan.

Olson, C. (1966), 'Projective Verse', in R. Creeley (ed.), *Selected Writings of Charles Olson*, New York: New Directions, 15–26.

Rose, J. (2001), *The Intellectual Life of the British Working Classes*, London and New Haven, CT: Yale University Press.

6. Architectural History in Academia and the Wider Community

Deborah Howard (University of Cambridge)

Respecting buildings

How can academic research in the arts and humanities make its impact in the cultural context promoted by today's celebrity-focused media and by government policy that privileges applied research? This essay will argue that the humanistic disciplines, in reality, represent one of the country's most valuable resources. While 'Englishness' may be highlighted in travel supplements to encourage tourism, in reality our culture is, of course, not insular but continually enriched by influences from outside, a process that is accelerating exponentially in the global universe.

I am an architectural historian – which, I would argue, is not at all the same thing as an 'historian of architecture'. Architectural history is a profoundly interdisciplinary practice that explores the role of buildings as settings for human activity. It involves at least some understanding of a daunting spectrum of other fields, ranging from engineering to economics, from religion to social history and from geography to archaeology. Since every citizen inhabits and uses built structures, no one is untouched by the architectural setting. About twenty years ago I heard a lecture by a celebrated French conservation architect, Didier Repellin, who told two anecdotes that seemed to underline the value of my own subject (Repellin 1991: 109–10). In the first story, he explained how he had dissuaded the council of his home town, Lyons, from demolishing the medieval quarter on the banks of the Rhône – a drastic threat imposed by fire regulations – by simply persuading the emergency services to make smaller fire engines. Public policy, he demonstrated, can be guided by enlightened historical awareness in simple, cost-effective ways. The second story recounted his ambition to take a group of severely disturbed and delinquent youngsters up the scaffolding to see the restoration of Lyons cathedral. Somehow he managed to overcome the opposition of the Bishop who feared damage and disaster, and the boys were transfixed with wonder. They watched the restoration work with such concentration that they forgot to be naughty. My point is that every member of society has a potential to be inspired and even influenced by the built environment. The Ciceronian view that an ordered society and a well-designed townscape are inseparable still deserves recognition.

Architectural history teaches the public to respect and value buildings around them, and to take an informed interest in the places they occupy and visit. I spent a decade lecturing at Edinburgh University in the 1980s and was struck by the exceptional knowledge and involvement even of the least educated tradesman in the city's architecture. New buildings were talked about in the street and the pub, as well as in the media, while old buildings aroused pride and curiosity. Lectures and visits to historic buildings frequently attracted capacity audiences. Government should never underrate humanity's natural inquisitiveness. The fundamental question at issue in this essay is how far the research of a university scholar or department can help to engender civic pride of this kind, and how far political benefit may be claimed, directly or indirectly, from research in the field.

The word 'culture' involves growth, and obviously no civilization can exist in a vacuum. What is the role of research in the arts and humanities in today's dizzy process of cultural diffusion? In the twenty-first century the identity of specific places is threatened with dilution – or even Disneyfication – by the instant diffusion of images from across the globe at the touch of a mouse. In this overload of visual information, how can any community possibly understand the historical significance of its own surroundings? Within academia the sector is threatened as never before by lack of resources, in comparison with the competing fields of science, technology and medicine. In my own university, Cambridge, the School of Arts and Humanities is now the smallest and poorest because it lacks the massive grant income of the richer scientific schools, although we teach almost half the undergraduates.

The concept of applying for research grants is foreign to many senior figures in arts subjects. According to the traditional mode of research, the lone scholar ferrets in a library or archive, collecting material for a 'great book'. Such independent scholarship is now considered old-fashioned, but it is worth remembering that this is an extremely economical process, only requiring funding for the senior academic if the relevant source material is far from home or if the researcher needs extra sabbatical leave. The results can be groundbreaking – and eventually internationally influential through diffusion in publications, and thereafter by the internet and the media. Perhaps research by individuals deserves a more sympathetic calibration as 'extremely good value for money'. Such work can play a vital role in helping to trace the trajectory of the discipline as it evolves.

For almost forty years, my main field of research has been the art and architecture of Venice and the Veneto. As the longest lasting republic in history, Venice has much to teach a modern democracy, both positively and negatively. Fortunately, the city has preserved remarkable archives – the Venetian State Archive alone has literally miles of shelves. The historian of Venice can indulge in a captivating process of time-travel, exploring past centuries that in many respects were far more 'real' than the city of today, now depopulated and swamped by tourism. Archival research is like detective work – one discovery leads on to another, and each day brings both excitement and disappointment in varying measures – but the crucial issue in documentary research is to ask questions that have both focus and relevance. The ways in which civic buildings were erected under the patronage of elected committees, and subjected to public consultation and enquiries, resonate strongly with the issues surrounding contemporary public building initiatives (Howard 2008).

West meets East

Some years ago, I became curious about the cultural relationship between Venice and the Islamic world. Like many earlier travellers and critics, I was struck by the exotic, seemingly orientalizing qualities in the architecture of Venice, and suspected that they might reveal a long process of cultural diffusion fed by commercial exchange. Official documents tell a story of constant friction – war, piracy, extortion and espionage – yet when I began to explore other sources such as merchant letters, pilgrim chronicles, travel narratives and legal documents, I was intrigued to uncover a web of much closer and more intimate contacts between Venetians and their Muslim trading partners, sustained over many centuries.

Although the papacy and the Byzantine emperors continually tried to prevent Venetians from trading with the Islamic world, afraid – with some justification – that the exported wood and metals could be used to manufacture arms, the Venetians defended their role as protectors of the Christian faith while indulging in the constant exchange of both ideas and goods with Islamic trading partners. Many young Venetian men spent their formative years in the great emporia of the Eastern Mediterranean such as Damascus, Acre and Alexandria, where they studied Arabic and book-keeping, and learned how to trade in a dazzling array of valuable commodities including exotic spices, valuable textiles, gems and pigments. Inventories of Venetian merchants who died overseas revealed an extraordinarily cosmopolitan range of possessions, ranging from a 'German roasting-spit with counterweights' to a rare pigment known as 'dragon's blood'. Venetian merchants were the only westerners allowed by special trading privileges to wear local dress when living and travelling in the Near and Middle East (Howard and Bianchi 2003).

In 2000 I published a book entitled *Venice and the East,* in which I attempted to show how Venetian civilization in its widest sense had been deeply influenced by this dense web of cultural and commercial exchange (Howard 2000). The book sought to make a small contribution to the important process whereby Western civilization builds a better understanding of Muslim culture and religion, a matter of crucial significance to public policy. The book was followed by two major art exhibitions, both of which attracted considerable public interest. The first, *Bellini and the East*, held at the Isabella Stewart Gardner Museum in Boston and the National Gallery in London, explored a very short time-span, focusing on the period 1480–1500, while the second, *Venice and the Islamic World*, shown in Paris, the Metropolitan Museum in New York and in Venice, covered the much longer period 829–1797.[1] This demonstrates how research initially stimulated by a single academic's personal inquisitiveness can broaden out to influence the educated public over a very wide geographical area, and may even help to inform public awareness of current political issues.

Over the past two decades, brave attempts have been made to foster a new kind of academic research in the arts and humanities involving more than one individual, and often more than one institution. The idea that academics in the arts should work, like those the sciences, on major grant-aided collaborative projects has been perceived as a means of raising the status of research in the humanities. Ambitious international networks have been set up involving regular meetings of scholars and huge multi-author publications, and applications have been invited for themed research areas. Such exercises are an extremely expensive use of public money – especially now that universities can claim such high overheads – but they play a crucial role in providing opportunities for post-doctoral scholars and in creating webs of international contacts.

Sound and space

The scope of a grant-aided research project can be immeasurably more exciting than lone-scholar research. In February 2005 I began a three-year project, funded by the Arts & Humanities Research Council (AHRC), to explore the relationship between architecture and music in Renaissance Venice. How can one justify the expense of public money on such an exercise? First of all, one has to place trust in the curiosity of the taxpayer to learn about the great achievements of civilization. In the sixteenth century, Venice stood at the forefront of European achievement in both architecture and music. Its principal architects, Sansovino and Palladio, were not only gifted designers but also great problem-solvers, intrigued by the specific needs of every commission. Together they infused the Venetian townscape with a new monumentality and classical discipline, learned from their studies of ancient Rome, but they also created – or modified – ecclesiastical spaces for a range of different kinds of worship: the grand state ceremonial of St Mark's, the simplicity of parish life, the solitary routine of the monastery, the great preaching arenas of the friars and the settings for the choirs of orphan girls in the four hospitals that would eventually grow into famous music conservatories.

Meanwhile, remarkable developments were underway in sacred music, as composers began to break free from the constraints of plainchant. Although Gregorian chant could be embellished with fixed harmonies that simply followed its words and rhythms, this improvised polyphony was rarely written down. By simply adding a time signature and bar-lines, polyphonic music could evolve into far more complex patterns, using counterpoint and canons. In Venice a pathfinding role was performed by the Flemish composer Adrian Willaert, who introduced into St Mark's an early form of stereo known as *coro spezzato*, in which two spatially separated choirs sang in a dramatic form of musical dialogue. Although some church reformers were suspicious of the worldly seductiveness of the new polyphony, it was soon realized that sincere and powerful religious ideas could be expressed in this way. Andrea and Giovanni Gabrieli and Claudio Monteverdi were among the composers who revolutionized the composition of sacred music during their employment at St Mark's.

How did these groundbreaking achievements in music and architecture interact? Any act of worship involves ritual movements within a spatial setting, and depends on the communication of religious doctrine and spirituality in words and music; yet space and sound have rarely been considered together. In architectural history, a church interior is traditionally analysed in terms of its visual qualities – the plan and details of the design – while in recent decades attention has also been paid to broader issues such as patronage and ceremonial. But unlike lighting, circulation, decoration and proportion, the aural dimension is usually sacrificed, because the words and music are ephemeral, surviving only in liturgical texts and musical notation.

How can the sound qualities of a space be reinstated? Our project tackled the issue on several fronts. First of all, we pursued an intensive programme of traditional historical research into the musical, liturgical and architectural traditions of each type of religious institution, and selected a dozen case studies for detailed investigation. Meanwhile, we organized an interdisciplinary international conference in Venice, bringing together for the first time architectural historians, musicologists and acousticians. This allowed the three separate constituencies to communicate and exchange their expertise. Somewhat to our surprise, these disparate groups found they had much to learn from each other.[2]

As the project gained in momentum, the merits of international and interdisciplinary collaboration became more and more evident, as we benefited from the sponsorship offered by a range of other organizations. The most significant of these was the generous support of two leading acoustic laboratories, one in Cambridge and one in Venice.[3] These allowed us to carry out scientific assessments of the acoustic properties of our chosen churches. One of them, the church of the Incurabili hospital, was demolished in 1831, although it had been renowned for centuries for its excellent acoustics. In collaboration with the Acoustics Department of Venice University's Architecture School (IUAV), we were able to set up a student project to make a virtual reconstruction of the former church and to play anechoic recordings in its simulated virtual space in order to recreate some impression of its musical acoustic. Meanwhile, the Acoustic Laboratory of the Fondazione Scuola di San Giorgio carried out a systematic programme of measurement of the acoustic parameters of ten selected surviving churches. Qualities such as the reverberation times of the spaces and their ability to sustain different frequencies were measured, using a range of positions for both sound emission and microphone based on the evidence of our historical research.

A year after the first conference, we gathered together the same team of scholars to take part in a workshop in Cambridge to plan a programme of choral experiments. The climax of the research was to be the visit of St John's College choir to Venice in April 2007, and we needed to take the best possible advice from our experts. Of course, we were fortunate to have the services of an internationally renowned choir, but we needed to be clear about what we wanted to test. Where did singers perform in each church, and what sort of musical repertoire was involved? How far did the acoustics of each building suit the musical and liturgical needs of that particular institution? How did the audience and singers respond to the acoustic environment? The search for 'authenticity' was not a primary objective, as we were sceptical that it is an achievable goal. Instead, we sought to acquire rigorous comparative evidence by performing the same repertoire in a variety of different spaces.

The visit of the choir in April 2007 was inspiring and instructive in equal measure. The support of the choir's Director of Music, David Hill, was invaluable, as was the skill and enthusiasm of all the singers – even the boy choristers were able to sight-sing complex Renaissance polyphony. By chance, the size and composition of St John's College Choir was very similar to that of the choir of St Mark's in the sixteenth century. In other churches, we varied the composition and size of the group of singers according to the historical context. In the hospital churches, for example, we needed only children's voices: in the absence of any girls' choir with the necessary skills, we used the boy choristers of St John's (in any case, recent research has revealed no perceptible differences in boys' and girls' voices up to the age of thirteen – Howard *et al.* 2002). In the monastic churches, the college's adult choral scholars played the role of monks, usually singing in beautiful inlaid wooden choir stalls.[4]

Within the city of Venice itself, the programme of choral experiments aroused considerable local interest. The series was widely advertised, as we needed to fill the churches for acoustic reasons – an empty church is far too reverberant. The audiences included local parishioners, tourists, architectural historians and musicologists, as well as parents and friends of the members of the choir. With the advice of our Cambridge acoustics consultants, Arup Acoustics, we devised a questionnaire for the audiences, using numerical scales to assess qualities such as reverberation, warmth, volume, envelopment and brilliance. We also invited the performers to give us their own reactions to the acoustics in each church. We returned from Venice with a suitcase full of questionnaires and eight CDs' worth of music recorded using the latest all-round 'Soundfield' microphone technology, not to mention the copious scientific data from the programme of acoustic measurements.

The next stage was to set about the analysis of this material. The Music Faculty of the University of Cambridge gave us the use of its acoustic laboratory to allow further reflection on the musical recordings and comparative assessment of the acoustics of different spaces. Meanwhile, the Cavendish

Laboratory (Department of Physics) sponsored the employment of a summer student to analyse both the audience questionnaires and the scientific data. This Cambridge-based scheme, known as UROP (Undergraduate Research Opportunities Programme) paid for an enthusiastic second-year engineer with both musical and computer skills, who worked intensively for two months under the direction of physicist Malcolm Longair to collate and analyse all the data. The result was a remarkable body of unique evidence which forms the technical appendix of the project's final book.

The most fascinating outcome of this scientific offshoot of our project was that we discovered significant links between the subjective and objective data. In other words, the responses of our randomly selected audiences corresponded very closely with the measurable acoustic characteristics of the various church interiors. This is the first time in the history of acoustics research (as far as our professional consultants are aware) that such a correlation between objective measurements and audience responses has ever been attempted. The results were presented at the international conference of the Association of Acousticians in Paris in June 2008. The audience questionnaires also showed a remarkable agreement with the informed judgments of one of our acoustic specialists, suggesting that even amateur listeners have discriminating responses to acoustic environments. It is inspiring that an arts-based collaborative project can break new ground even in a complex area of scientific research, thanks to the enthusiasm of the project partners and the intrinsic interest of the specific historical question.

The final dissemination of the research took the form of a full-length book, published by Yale University Press, written with the help of my principal collaborator, a young Italian scholar called Laura Moretti (Howard and Moretti 2009). Trained as both a professional cellist and architect, Moretti has proved the ideal partner, and her input into the whole project has been immeasurable. The book is profusely illustrated, both with plans and views of the buildings themselves but also with photographs of the scientific measurements and the choral experiments in progress. The technical appendix was written by our two acoustics experts, Davide Bonsi and Raf Orlowksi, together with our physicist Malcolm Longair and the summer student Philip Garsed. The data are presented in graphs and diagrams so that they can be easily understood by a non-specialist. The book is linked to a website on which we have placed a selection of the musical recordings.[5]

The churches discussed in the book are all well known to both architectural historians and tourists. In addition to St Mark's and the principal surviving churches of Sansovino and Palladio, we included some older churches with features that influenced the acoustic conditions. We were especially interested in different types of ceilings, such as ship's keel vaults, barrel vaults, Gothic rib-vaults, mosaic domes and flat coffered wooden roofs. Even in the Renaissance, it was well understood that a vaulted roof gave greater resonance for singing, whereas a flat wooden ceiling was more suitable for the spoken word. We were also interested in the effects of wooden choir-stalls, such as the beautiful choir that still survives in the Franciscan church of Santa Maria Gloriosa dei Frari. In Venice a particularly distinctive feature of some monastic churches is the *barco*, or raised choir gallery, at or near the back of the nave. Both Palladio's most celebrated Venetian churches, San Giorgio Maggiore and the Redentore, were visited annually by the Doge and the Signoria in a huge procession accompanied by the choir of St Mark's. In each church the monks or friars sang from secluded choir-stalls hidden behind the high altar, but the ceremonial books are unclear where the singers from St Mark's were positioned. We were able to try out different possibilities and investigate what worked best musically, especially when compositions for divided choirs or *coro spezzato* were involved.

Our subsequent studies of the musical recordings reinforced our first impressions, that is to say, that the differences between the acoustic properties of the various types of churches we studied were extremely marked. The scientific analysis confirmed the listener's experience that the acoustics could be graded typologically. The most reverberant spaces were the large monasteries and friaries, where traditional plainchant sounded breathtaking, whereas the spoken word was difficult to understand. At the other extreme the parish churches were rather 'dry', an effect exacerbated in the choral experiments by the carpets and hangings put out for Easter. Here the acoustic properties would have favoured small, intimate family rituals such as baptisms, marriages and funerals. The best position for musical performance in the parish churches was the organ loft over the entrance. In St Mark's, a spacious five-domed Byzantine-style church, the acoustics were surprisingly good, especially from the position of the Doge's own throne, just inside the rood-screen. The positions of singers and the liturgical furnishings were modified during the sixteenth century, in response to the demands of the new polyphony for a more favourable musical environment.

The best acoustics, by far, were experienced in the two hospital churches: the Ospedaletto and the Mendicanti. The four hospitals all had orphanages attached, and it was the female orphans who became renowned for their musical excellence. As mentioned, Sansovino's church of the Incurabili hospital, admired for its exemplary acoustics, no longer survives, and in this case we had to rely on a virtual reconstruction. The church of the fourth hospital, the Pietà, was rebuilt in the eighteenth century, and thus fell outside the time period of our project. Its present church, popularly known as 'la chiesa del Vivaldi', was in fact rebuilt after Vivaldi left Venice for Vienna and has very problematic acoustics. At least the original orphanage of the Pietà still survives, and it was here, most appropriately, that St John's College Choir lodged during its visit to Venice.

What were the characteristics that made the Ospedaletto's acoustics so special? The amount of reverberation was just enough to give a resonance to the sound, yet every change of harmony was clear and every fast passage discernible. The music from the raised singing gallery over the high altar seemed to float along the ceiling and then gradually descend to envelop the spectator in a rich, warm glow of sound. The effect was transfixing and difficult to describe in words, but we were reassured to discover that the scientific measurements confirmed the phenomenon of sound descending vertically. The Ospedaletto has a classic 'shoebox' interior, like the musical spaces most celebrated for their excellent acoustics – the Musikverein in Vienna, the Concertgebouw in Amsterdam, and the Boston Symphony Hall.

What might be the benefits to the wider community of a funded research project such as this one? The amount of public interest in Venice during both our first conference and the choral experiments demonstrated the intrinsic relevance of the research. The buildings themselves, the music written for them and the quality of the execution by St John's College Choir are all examples of excellence, according to any international criteria. But this is not a project that speaks only to the elite – local women of the parish, who admitted to knowing nothing about either music or architecture, came along to our choral experiments. Furthermore, in any society people of any class or age group attend musical performances of one kind or another, whether in a religious or secular context. The sort of architectural characteristics that favour speech over music, or vice versa, need to be better understood in the design of a huge range of spaces from schools to restaurants, not to mention concert halls. Spaces have sound qualities that are often ignored in our overwhelmingly visual culture, yet, as we demonstrated, listeners are sensitive to acoustical differences.

The currently available technology offers the potential for interactive use of websites – for example, the listener of the recordings could choose to vary the sound by adding sound-absorbing tapestries, as we know was done in the basilica on special ceremonial occasions, or by changing the number of spectators. During the academic year 2009-10 this exercise was carried out in a follow-up project using virtual models of four of the churches made by Braxton Boren under the supervision of Malcolm Longair, with striking results (Boren 2010).

The value of grant-aided research in the arts and humanities

The project on architecture and music in Renaissance Venice was one that seemed to be beset by good fortune, and it certainly proved how exciting international and interdisciplinary collaboration can be. In parallel I led another AHRC research project entitled 'Sharing and Visualising Old St Peter's: East and West in Renaissance Rome', part-funded by Cambridge's Isaac Newton Trust. In this project a post-doctoral Research Associate Christiane Esche explored how pilgrims from Armenia, Ethiopia and Hungary gathered together in their own special national compounds on the south side of Old St Peter's. The historical research investigated the artistic contacts between each of these groups and fifteenth-century Rome, and showed how even before the discovery of the New World, the horizons of the papacy extended far beyond the boundaries of Europe. Despite the longer timescale involved in international communication, the Early Modern period, like our own, was one of rapidly increasing speed in the processes of cultural exchange. Because most of the remains of the pilgrim hostels were obliterated in the later rebuilding of St Peter's, the project used sophisticated virtual simulation techniques to reconstruct the area occupied by these foreign pilgrims, based on the careful analysis of a wide range of surviving graphic evidence. Two short films reconstructing the experience of pilgrims were made in collaboration with Stanislav Roudavski.

'Sharing and visualizing Old St Peter's' involved collaboration with local experts in three countries – Ethiopia, Hungary and Armenia – and uses state-of-the-art computer simulation skills. As in the architecture and music project, the combination of interdisciplinarity, international collaboration and sophisticated scientific procedures gave this specific historical question a far wider relevance. The virtual simulation employed groundbreaking technology that will lend itself to future research projects as well as to the wider community. At the same time, we hope that the historical investigation will help to inform public understanding of the three countries involved, especially Armenia and Ethiopia which are still relatively little known.

The scope and opportunities offered by major research grants open up the arts and humanities to an array of international opportunities and interdisciplinary collaborations that were unimaginable thirty years ago. The technology available to us offers invaluable new ways of analysing historical problems and allows innovative research to be disseminated across the world. The role of the AHRC in expanding the horizons of researchers in the arts and humanities – across disciplines, periods and geographical areas – has enabled projects of far greater ambition to be undertaken, generating new practical applications and methodologies, and providing intellectual discoveries and insights of real significance to civilization in its widest sense. The major research funding opportunities, both for individuals and for collaborative projects, have enabled British academia to retain its high status in the international scholarly community. This innovative work underpins and enriches the evolution of our national culture, which, as we saw at the start of this essay, is one of the UK's most valuable assets.

Notes

1   *Bellini and the East* was curated by Caroline Campbell and Alan Chong, and *Venice and the Islamic World* by Stefano Carboni.

2   The conference proceedings, issued nine months later in a bilingual paperback book by a prominent Italian publisher, established the state of knowledge at the outset of our research project (Howard and Moretti 2006).

3   These were Arup Acoustics in Cambridge and the Laboratorio di Acustica
     Musicale e Architettonica of the Fondazione Scuola di San Giorgio in Venice.

4   The remarkable result of a major international project such as this one was that
     additional support and sponsorship continually assisted us when resources
     were tight. As well as the two acoustic laboratories previously mentioned,
     who worked without remuneration, the Gladys Krieble Delmas Foundation
     of New York and St John's College both subsidized the choir's expenses. In
     Venice, we were given official encouragement by the Regione Veneto, while the
     organization known as 'Chorus', which manages the tourist visits to the city's
     most celebrated churches, paid for the publicity for the choral experiments.

5   http://www.yalebooks.co.uk/soundandspace.

Bibliography

Boren, Braxton (2010), 'Recreating Lost Soundscapes: Music, Architecture and
    Acoustics in Renaissance Venice,' unpublished MPhil dissertation, Cavendish
    Laboratory, University of Cambridge.

Howard, D. (1975), *Jacopo Sansovino: Architectural Patronage in Renaissance
    Venice*, London and New Haven, CT: Yale University Press.

Howard, D. (2000), *Venice and the East: The Impact of the Islamic World on
    Venetian Architecture (1100–1500)*, London and New Haven, CT: Yale University
    Press.

Howard, D. (2003), 'Death in Damascus: Venetians in Syria in the mid-fifteenth
    century', *Muqarnas*, 20: 143–57.

Howard, D. (2008), 'Architectural Politics in Renaissance Venice', *Proceedings of
    the British Academy*, 154: 29–68.

Howard, D. and Bianchi, F. (2003), 'Life and Death in Damascus: the material culture
    of Venetians in the Syrian capital in the mid-fifteenth century', *Studi Veneziani*,
    XLV: 233–99.

Howard, D. and Moretti, L. (eds) (2006), *Architettura e musica nella Venezia del
    Rinascimento* (Architecture and Music in Renaissance Venice), Milan: Bruno
    Mondadori.

Howard, D. and Moretti, L. (2009), *Sound and Space in Renaissance Venice:
    Architecture, Music, Acoustics*, London and New Haven, CT: Yale University
    Press.

Howard, D.M. *et al.* (2002), 'Listeners' Perception of English Cathedral Girl and Boy
    Choristers', *Music Perception*, 20: 1: 35–49.

Repellin, D. (1991), 'The Human Heritage: A message from the Past transmitted to
    the Future', *Architectural Heritage*, II: 109–18.

7. 'This is a local film': The Cultural and Social Impact of the Mitchell & Kenyon Film Collection

Vanessa Toulmin (University of Sheffield)

'In 1994, the history of British film changed for ever. In fact, British history as a whole would never look the same again. In a basement in Blackburn, Lancashire, three metal drums were discovered, containing more than 800 reels of original camera negatives of films languishing unseen since 1922. The past was about to be reinvented': so wrote Christopher Wood in the *Times Higher Educational Supplement* on 1 July 2005, reporting on the Mitchell & Kenyon Collection. This is the story behind the discovery and how the unimagined popularity of the BBC2 series *The Lost World of Mitchell & Kenyon*, broadcast in January 2004, together with the public engagement undertaken by the British Film Institute (bfi) and the National Fairground Archive (NFA), helped to reinterpret the first decade of the twentieth century.

Before the creators of the television series 'The League of Gentlemen' and the fictional village of Royston Vasey popularized the idea of the 'local town for local people' through their anarchic view of the vales of Derbyshire, a small film company from Blackburn called Mitchell & Kenyon were sending out cameramen to shoot local views of towns and villages across Edwardian Britain. From 1900 to 1913 they filmed the men, women and children of the time so that cinematograph showmen could reveal a new novelty – moving pictures. The footage that survived to become known as the Mitchell & Kenyon Collection is now a treasure trove of international importance that reveals snapshots of the working class at work and play, watching football (both association and rugby), participating in civic and religious events, and enjoying a range of other leisure activities. Individually, these long lost and forgotten films can be described as vignettes capturing fragments of larger and more complex events, but on a more human scale the modern audience response to them is complex and emotional. The faces frozen on nitrate now gaze out at us a century later, revealing the secrets of Edwardian Britain. Described by historians as the lost generation, since so many of them died on the battlefields of the First World War, thanks to Sagar Mitchell and James Kenyon these dead souls are now forever captured in a celluloid tapestry of smiles, gestures, motion and poetic grace, ghosts of the past who beckon the modern viewer into the dawn of the twentieth century.

How were these ghosts brought back to life? What was the process that enabled fourteen million viewers to watch the BBC2 series 'The Lost World of Mitchell & Kenyon'?[1] Why did the material release such an emotional response

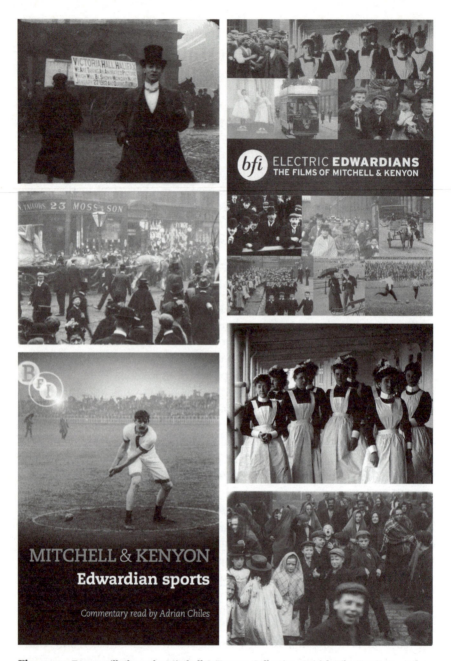

Figure 7.1 Frame stills from the Mitchell & Kenyon Collection, British Film Institute, and flyers for touring shows from 2005 to 2008. © Mitchell & Kenyon Collection, the British Film Institute

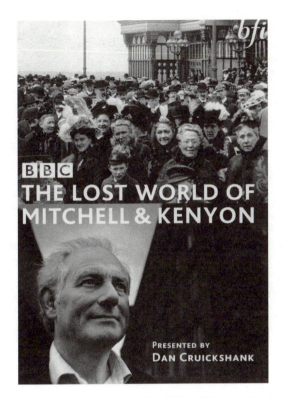

Figure 7.2 Cover of BBC2 series 'The Lost World of Mitchell & Kenyon', released in April 2005. © Mitchell & Kenyon Collection, the British Film Institute

in the British public, and how were the films researched, contextualized and brought to life? This is my attempt as the curator and primary researcher of the Mitchell & Kenyon Collection to answer these questions; to bring together the real story of the research, the collaboration and often frustrating journey behind the television series, and to demonstrate in the words of Italian art critic, Giovanni Morelli, that 'In people's faces there is always something of the history of their time, if one knows how to read it' (Burke 2001). This is the story of how we learned to read the faces of our grandparents' generation and how from 2001 onwards, with the aid of an Arts & Humanities Research Council (AHRC) grant, the British Film Institute (the holders of the Mitchell & Kenyon Collection) and the University of Sheffield's National Fairground Archive, we joined together with scholars, film archivists, historians and enthusiasts around the country to bring the treasures of the past back into the public domain.

The Mitchell & Kenyon Collection is now the third largest film collection in the world relating to the output of a single company from the early 1900s.[2] The Collection was acquired by the British Film Institute in June 2000 from Peter Worden, a local businessman in Blackburn who rescued the films, and

Figure 7.3 Child workers leaving Alfred Butterworth and Sons, Glebe Mills, Hollinwood
(1901). © Mitchell & Kenyon Collection, the British Film Institute

researched by my team at the University of Sheffield. Since then, numerous
books (Toulmin *et al.* 2004; Toulmin 2006a), articles and DVDs have been
produced on the Collection, and 40,000 copies of the DVDs have been sold.[3]
Millions of people have seen the films on television and, in venues from
Sunderland to San Francisco, Leeds to Luxembourg, and Blackburn to Boston,
over half-a-million cinema-goers have watched the films. The Collection is
now internationally recognized as one of the world's most important visual
records of Edwardian life and society, and it has been embraced by more
than just the academic community, but by the public at large. Students have
made their own films on YouTube in the style of Mitchell & Kenyon, modern
bands such as In the Nursery and Lemon Jelly have written new soundtracks,
and Flatpack Festival, an arts festival in Birmingham, commissioned new
material from local band the Destroyers in 2009. A key to understanding
why the material has been embraced by this atypical new audience is found
in the words of Lemon Jelly's Fred Deakin who remarked, 'films like this
are an emotional trigger – in song writing you tend to create your own brief
and then try to fulfil it, but when you have the Mitchell & Kenyon films as a
starting point it's already clear what your colours are' (Hodgkinson, 2006).
   However, in the period between the rediscovery in 1995 and the AHRC-
funded research project in 2001, the material was stored in a fridge in
Blackburn and was generally regarded as inconsequential in the larger

picture of film archiving and scholarship. Indeed, the small number of films that were restored at great expense by Peter Worden were rarely seen outside the rarefied and elite surroundings of film festivals and conferences. At a time when Worden was trying to persuade the British Film Institute and the University of Sheffield to work on restoration of the collection, a representative of the Film Council, the lead agency for film in the United Kingdom, queried the relevance of acquiring and preserving non-fiction local material. Fortunately, such doubts did not kill off the project.

Once the Collection was safely at the National Film and Television Archive in Berkhamsted, an extensive programme of restoration and research collaboration was discussed, planned and timetabled for the next four years, with funding for restoration to come from the bfi and support for the research process from the University of Sheffield and the AHRC.[4] It was essential that the two processes worked hand in hand, as without the restoration process the material would be inaccessible, but without the research process the newly restored material would go undated, with no location details or sense of how the 826 rolls of films could tell a story and were part of a larger picture. Only a small percentage of the material had any identifying features on the negatives, such as the name of a showman or a factory, or just a location or an abbreviated title of an event. In the case of the film of a Manchester United v Burnley football match, the date '6 December 02' was inscribed on the first frames of the negative. An extensive three-year research process funded by the AHRC was undertaken in 2001 in order to match the films to the events and locations. It was this funding that provided the key to unlocking the material, as the names and dates inscribed on the negatives directly related to the exhibition routes of travelling showmen who operated around the turn of the century.

The research trail

Tracing the showmen was relatively easy, since these larger than life personalities left a trail of advertising in local newspapers and on handbills, posters and programmes which were held by the National Fairground Archive. Linking these to the films and the locations became part of the research and two research assistants, one in the bfi and one in the NFA, scoured local archives, libraries, newspapers and private collections to put forward a pattern of exhibition that could lead to dates and locations, and then verification from the experts brought together for the project. As the working list of these dates, titles and possible locations was assembled, specialist historians and local enthusiasts came to the University of Sheffield to view the material and to help identify the content on the film, possible locations or to corroborate our findings.

One memorable afternoon saw the historians of Sunderland, Middlesbrough and Newcastle football clubs watching the local derby and reeling off the list of players, scores and match reports of games that had been played in 1901, 1902 and 1904. Programme collectors sent copies of match reports, as enthusiasts and die-hard football fanatics joined forces with academics and historians to help unlock the secrets in the newly restored material. A set of films showing Everton v Newcastle, which we believed to be from 1902, was actually two different matches played a year apart, proven because of the presence of burly centre forward Brian Appleyard, the Newcastle legend. Appleyard was spotted by Alan Candlish, the club historian. Elsewhere, the first sight of William 'Fatty' Foulkes, the Sheffield United goalkeeper, bringing his twenty stone mass to bear on a slightly built Bury centre forward brought cheers from the assembled football enthusiasts who came in their own time and at their own expense to help identify the players on screen.[5]

The Bradford City club historian verified that the 1903 title was the first home game ever played by the team in its newly reformed status as an association football club, formed when it switched from Northern Rugby Football Union (known as Northern Union) in 1902. As a thank you for his help, the bfi agreed to screen the Bradford v Gainsborough game to mark the club's centenary in September 2003. Five hundred supporters crowded into the National Museum of Photography in Bradford to see the films and laughed as they were told that Bradford not only lost the game but missed a penalty and had a man sent off! Tony Collins, the rugby league historian and Professor of the Social History of Sport at Leeds Metropolitan University,

Figure 7.4 The infamous Fatty Foulkes captured during Sheffield United v Bury (1902).
© Mitchell & Kenyon Collection, the British Film Institute

Figure 7.5 Hunslet players line up for the camera in Hunslet v Leeds (1901). © Mitchell & Kenyon Collection, the British Film Institute

explained the complexities of the Northern Union games that were filmed less than five years after the great split that separated the two rugby codes forever, and rugby league historian Robert Gate located match reports and verified the dates of the matches.

Professor John Walton brought his immense knowledge of Blackpool and all things seaside to the project and also gave us the key to understanding the social context of the time with his detailed understanding of Lancashire and its industries. This sense of sharing of scholarship and research for the greater good occurred in all the specialist areas that were reflected in the Collection. The National Tramway Museum demonstrated that expert knowledge, attention to detail and contextual understanding could bring the material back to life: they dated a film purely by viewing a tram track and made us all honorary tram enthusiasts. Hundreds of individuals allied with a team of academics to provide the contextual background that would help illuminate the world and time that the animated figures sprung from.

'The Lost World of Mitchell & Kenyon'

The three-part television series that was commissioned by the BBC and produced in collaboration with the bfi directly benefited from this intensive two-year process as the material selected by the producers had already been dated, contextualized and identified prior to their involvement. I was hired by the BBC as historical consultant and full access to the research project was granted for the purpose of identification and selection of material. However, as the research process was part of the story, it was agreed that dramatic reconstructions of some of the research visits could be portrayed by the presenter Dan Cruickshank, in order to aid the viewer's understanding of how the material had been dated. Although the BBC was not directly concerned in any aspect of the research process, because of these programmes the Collection achieved national status. The BBC brought added value to the project by interweaving the story of the films and the lives of individuals captured on camera; dramatizing personal stories was a good way to interpret the whole collection. The team from the BBC selected key individuals from the films and researched them by advertising in local newspapers, on regional television, in libraries and record offices with the intention of finding any living descendents. The grandchildren or children became living testimonies and the means of telling the story of the lives flickering in film. In addition, the BBC programmes showed the delicate nature of the archive and the scale of the investment in the Collection by the bfi in order for the films to be conserved and made available.[6]

By the end of its transmission, the three-part series had attracted over 14 million viewers, and was described by *Broadcast* magazine as 'an instant hit for BBC2' (Broadcast 2005), with subsequent repeats on BBC4 achieving audience figures of an average of 1.6 million per episode. Other reviewers referred to 'The Lost World' as the 'a near (if not parallel) equivalent to the finding of Tutankhamen's tomb or the Dead Sea Scrolls' (Jack 2005), with *The Times* critic commenting that 'they offer a startlingly vivid portrait of working class life in the North of England a century ago' (Chater 2005). The television series not only widened public access but created an insatiable public demand for more material than the two hours of actual archive footage used by the BBC. The Collection had indeed gone beyond the lecture theatre, the academy and the text, and, to paraphrase the filmmakers, the next stage of dissemination and public engagement had to be the 'local show for local people'.

'Local films for local people'

'Local films for local people', Mitchell & Kenyon's original advertising slogan from a 1900 handbill, provided the key to how the material could once again be revealed to what was and still is the core audience for the collection – local people. The local film was something that cinema historians had always known about and although it had aroused some academic scrutiny, on the whole this type of material was seen as merely a footnote in the canon of film scholarship. However, to the regional film archive the local is more than just a stepping stone: it is often the means by which an archive can engage with its public, as people become increasingly occupied with and obsessed by the history of their families, their houses and their towns. This need to look back and seek a direct link to the past is the basis of the popularity of recent television series' such as 'Who Do You Think You Are?'. The personal story format as presented in 'The Lost World ...' was certainly part of the reason for its success with the viewers, alongside the stunning visual quality of the archival footage. However, the emotional impact aroused by the films was the cry of recognition when the viewer spotted images of their town or city or village. Such was the flood of interest by cinema owners, film societies and local history groups that the bfi and the NFA offered a selection of material that combined the touring programme with local views specifically tailored to each area. By the end of January 2005, it was clear that the original 12-venue programme would have to be increased. Five years and over 100 shows, lectures and presentations later, over 20,000 people have seen the films in their home town. Events have included the Liverpool Capital of Culture show in front

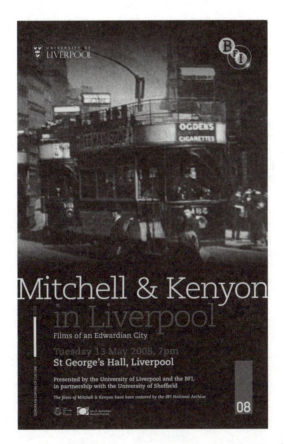

Figure 7.6 Programme for Mitchell & Kenyon in Liverpool, part of the City of Culture Programme of Events, St George's Hall, 13 May 2008. © Mitchell & Kenyon Collection, the British Film Institute

of 800 people on 13 May 2008 at the St George's Hall, while 1,000 people in Blackburn attended a show in February 2010 to celebrate the 100th anniversary of the local cinema. Ten per cent of the collection can be found on the bfi's own dedicated YouTube channel with the latest in Web2 technology enabling viewer comments and interaction between the institution and the end users.[7]

One of the highlights of the touring shows took place in Chorley in 2006. The Chorley Electric Palace, built in 1911, was the original venue where the films were once presented as part of the 1911 Coronation celebrations and 400 people packed into two sell-out shows to see views of local mills, church exits and the Coronation celebrations. Another memorable evening was the show created to help Oldham Rugby League Club to commemorate its history with a special showing in the local art gallery of the Oldham v Swinton match of 1901. Touring shows, complete with live commentary, played to packed houses in Sheffield, Derby, Bristol, Glasgow, Belfast, Dublin, Manchester, Preston, Leicester, Stoke, Lancaster, Carlisle, Birmingham, Hull and other towns and cities, with audience participation being a memorable feature of each show. Faces, places and lost buildings were brought to life not only by the images on screen but also at the end of each screening through the local response and knowledge, during the question and answer session. These sessions were good opportunities to acquire additional information about the films. Locations were always familiar to the local audience, churches were

Figure 7.7 The 'hands' leaving work at North Street Mills, Chorley (1900). © Mitchell & Kenyon Collection, the British Film Institute

Figure 7.8 Flyer for Mitchell & Kenyon show at the Grand Theatre, Blackpool, Sunday 13 January 2008. © Mitchell & Kenyon Collection, the British Film Institute

named, streets and roads identified, and the trajectory of the journey or angle filmed by Mitchell & Kenyon was as marvellous to the modern viewer as it would have been to the Edwardian audience. In addition, the questions posed by the audience at the end of the show became part of the wider research rationale for the Collection. Ultimately, the research became more about understanding the films as social and historical documents than merely the process of dating and naming a location.

For me, as curator and primary researcher, the local shows became the highlight of the project and it became apparent that the audience needed to feel part of the performance. The project was not about academics presenting their findings but more about engagement and knowledge exchange; in return for seeing the films, local people provided intimate knowledge of the area and its stories that brought the material to life. Sheffield was once again seen in its prewar splendour before the 1960s development changed the city and reactions ranged from amazement at the splendour of the Edwardian cities to shock at seeing thousands of mill girls in East Lancashire with their heads covered. A rendition of the old football chant 'who ate all the pies' rang out from the audience in Sheffield as the aforementioned goalkeeper 'Fatty' Foulkes once again patrolled the nets at Bramall Lane. Sometimes the films appeared particularly topical with the footage of the women factory workers covering their head and faces with large shawls, striking a chord with the audience with parallels drawn on the issue of British Asian girls and the hijab. The North Lancashire show saw half the audience identify a previously unknown factory exit as Vickers and Maxims of Barrow-in-Furness, with the railway bridge in Doncaster recognized as being the exit from the Great Northern Railway works. The appeal of the material was not only local or regional but also international as the touring programme *Electric Edwardians* played in over twenty American cities including San Francisco, Boston, Chicago, Seattle, Washington, DC and New York. Festivals in Italy, Luxembourg, Austria and Germany showed parts of the Collection; the *Electric Edwardians* DVD was distributed by Milestone Films and in 2007 a German language edition was issued.

Additional topics from the Collection were selected for exhibition, with leisure, sport and transport prominently featured in the material, while special subject DVDs were commissioned to curate all the sporting material and location-specific titles.[8] This proved fascinating in terms of audience popularity and expectation. The special rugby league show outstripped the specialist football programme in audience figures. This reflected my belief that football supporters are tribal as opposed to the rugby league fans who can watch the sport as a whole. (For example only 58 football fans came to the show at the Cornerhouse Cinema in Manchester as opposed to 400 rugby league fans at Headingley Stadium in Leeds). From 2005 onwards, the touring collection criss-crossed the country, and was presented at two or three shows a month in the style of an Edwardian exhibition, with musical accompaniment and a lecturer to explain the films. The modern shows often opened with the same films that would have been exhibited at the venue a century before. These events would have been impossible without the infrastructure and support provided by the BFI and the University of Sheffield; public engagement was, and still is, at the heart of both institutions' outreach activities. In terms of the South Yorkshire shows, the then Registrar at Sheffield, Dr David Fletcher, actually sponsored the holding of the two free shows to commemorate the university's centenary and also used his local knowledge to give a live commentary on some of the titles.[9]

Public interest in all types of archival material has increased. On 25 November 2005 the bfi launched its new Archival Short Film Initiative to bring national film heritage to a wider cinema public. Short films drawn from the bfi's archival collections were offered free of charge to cinemas across the UK for screening with main features. To launch the series, the bfi invited filmmaker Jonathan Glazer to make a special short celebrating Mitchell & Kenyon and the completed two-and-a-half minute film, *Mitchell and Kenyon,* was released in conjunction with Stephen Frears's new feature, *Mrs Henderson Presents.* The bfi collaborated with cinemas across the country including City Screen, a range of independent art houses and the entire Cineworld circuit to bring audiences in over 100 venues an exciting taste of a major archival collection. Specially produced Mitchell & Kenyon postcards were sent to each venue, enabling filmgoers to find out more about the Collection and about the other activities of the bfi. The short film, with the Pogues' 'Dirty Old Town' used as the soundtrack, was ultimately seen by over 150,000 people in one year alone. The funding of the trailer was partly aided by an AHRC dissemination grant which enabled the material to be shown to a younger cinema audience (ages 25 to 40) as opposed to the traditional archive audience of 50 years and over. This short film changed the demographics of the standard archival audience and challenged perceptions of where such material could be shown and enjoyed.

From the street to the archive and back

In the words of one colleague, 'the Edwardian era is now the Mitchell & Kenyon decade'. The films depict life as it was lived by ordinary people at the dawn of the twentieth century. They are images that present change and modernity, sadness and community as we gaze on the faces of a generation that in hindsight we know was lost on the battlefields of France and Belgium. Professor Mary Beard has stated that 'you can't have the superstructure without the substructure' (Reisz 2008) and without the substructure of the research funding awarded to the National Fairground Archive at the University of Sheffield by the AHRC, the films would still be largely unseen by the many millions who have accessed them in a variety of formats since January 2005. They would be unknown outside the specialized world of early cinema and lost to the wider cultural audience. For the archive community, the Collection has, according to Marion Hewitt of the North West Film Archive, transformed public perception of film archives and their usages in a variety of cultural activities for the wider community. Dr Jon Burrows, a film historian at the University of Warwick, emailed the NFA to say that 'his neighbours and colleagues were gripped by the films', while another colleague thanked me for making his dentist understand what he did for a living! The impact of the Collection widened to other disciplines when in 2007 researchers at University College London used the films to illuminate the decline of left-handedness in Victorian Britain (Elliott 2007).

The Collection has also given greater significance to the value of archival films as stories in their own right rather than as mere background illustration for other histories. The 'Lost World' idea or concept became almost a franchise or title under which to group archival film collections, with the 'Lost World of Friese Green' and the 'Lost World of Tibet' produced by the bfi and BBC largely on the back of the success of the Mitchell & Kenyon series. Within television and media circles, archival or historical programmes with large film content are now publicized or described in relation to being similar or related to the Mitchell & Kenyon Collection. Ultimately the Collection has enabled the film community as a whole to understand the wider cultural value and significance of their holdings. Archive material that was previously thought of as arcane or of little interest to the general public is now discussed on news programmes by national and international broadcasting companies (there have been over sixty items since 2005). Feature articles have appeared in the *Guardian*, the *Daily Telegraph*, the *Observer*, *The Times* and *Times Literary Supplement* to name but a few. The wider international media coverage of the Collection has also been extraordinary, with requests from newspapers and television stations throughout Europe for the use of images. ABC Nightline in the US produced a thirty-minute programme on the films that was broadcast statewide and ARD Channel One, broadcasting in Germany, Austria and Switzerland, also featured the Collection.

For my colleagues in both the archival and academic communities the restoration and research of the films, together with the phenomenal public interest, represent a sea-change in attitudes to how this material could and should be utilized. The academic and archival community as a whole has a responsibility to preserve, enhance and enable understanding of the material we collect and catalogue. Ultimately, in the case of the Mitchell & Kenyon Collection, it is a moving record of our society at work and play. From the leaving of Liverpool to the leaving of work, the growth of leisure and expansion of professional sport, and the rise of modern consumer society, all aspects of this lost world have now been recorded and researched for posterity. The past is no longer hidden away but restored to its rightful place at the heart of the communities that lived in it. Without public funding for humanities research the fantastic journey undertaken by all involved would not have been possible.

Notes

1   The three-part BBC2 series was transmitted 14 January 2005 for three consecutive Fridays. According to the website Broadcast Now, the first episode reached a peak viewing audience at 9.25 of 4.4 million, a 19 per cent capture of the viewing figures.

2   The two larger collections are the Edison Films held by the US Library of Congress and the Lumière Brothers titles held by the Cinématèque Français.

3   For the DVDs see *Mitchell & Kenyon in Ireland* (bfi 2007), *Mitchell & Kenyon: Edwardian Sports* (bfi 2007) and *Electric Edwardians: The Films of Mitchell & Kenyon* (bfi 2005), selected by Dr Vanessa Toulmin, with a 28-page illustrated essay/booklet to accompany the films, as well as *The Lost World of Mitchell & Kenyon* (BBC Productions 2005).

4   The AHRC research grant totalled £178,000 with the bfi committing to the costs of full restoration of the negatives with additional funding for post production work. Each part of the project involved the full expertise and experience of the various bfi departments ranging from distribution to exhibition. This was before its new curatorial model was introduced in 2006–7.

5   Further details of the football films can be found in David Russell, 'The Football Films in the Mitchell & Kenyon Collection' (Russell 2004).

6   This investment, according to personal communication with the bfi, totals over £4.5 million pounds from 2000 onwards.

7   For City of Culture show see http://www.liv.ac.uk/08/video/mk-video.html and for the bfi YouTube channel see http://www.youtube.com/user/BFIfilms, where over 72 titles can be viewed.

8   For an overview of the sporting material see 'Edwardian Sport on Film' (Toulmin (2006b) and David Russell, 'The Football Films in the Mitchell & Kenyon Collection' (Russell 2004).

9   The local shows still continue at the rate of six to eight per year.

Bibliography

Broadcast (2005), 'BBC Beats Bex', *Broadcast*, 17 January, http://www.broadcastnow.co.uk/news/multi-platform/news/bbc2-beats-bex/1018460.article [accessed 18 July 2010].

Burke, P. (2001), *Eyewitnessing: The Uses of Images as Historical Evidence*, London: Reaktion Books.

Chater, J. (2005), 'Television', *The Times*, 15 January 2005.

Elliott, J. (2007), 'Left-handers on roll as numbers triple', *The Times*, 16 September, http://www.timesonline.co.uk/tol/news/uk/article2461315.ece [accessed 18 July 2010].

Hodgkinson, W. (2006), 'Snapshot', *Guardian*, 21 April, http://www.guardian.co.uk/culture/2006/apr/21/2 [accessed 19 July 2010].

Jack, I. (2005), 'The Lost World', *Guardian*, 7 January, http://www.guardian.co.uk/film/2005/jan/07/1 [accessed 18 July 2010].

Reisz, M. (2008), 'Soul Searching', *Times Higher Education*, 14 February, http://www.timeshighereducation.co.uk/story.asp?storycode=400543 [accessed 18 July 2010].

Russell, D. (2004), 'The Football Films', in V. Toulmin, S. Popple and P. Russell, (2004), *The Lost World of Mitchell & Kenyon: Edwardian Britain on Film*, London: British Film Institute, 169–180.

Toulmin, V. (2006a), *Electric Edwardians: The Story of the Mitchell & Kenyon Collection*, London: British Film Institute.

Toulmin, V. (2006b), 'Edwardian Sport on Film', *International Journal of Sport in History*, 26: 2.

Toulmin, V., Popple, S. and Russell, P. (2004), *The Lost World of Mitchell & Kenyon: Edwardian Britain on Film*, London: British Film Institute.

PART TWO

Looking Around Us

8. Living Landscapes

Stephen Daniels (University of Nottingham)
and Ben Cowell (National Trust)[1]

Landscape and environment are currently matters of compelling cultural and material significance, as fields of academic enquiry, genres of artistic creativity and arenas of public concern. In the mind and on the ground landscapes are a medium for making sense of the world and people's place in it, and for expressing and exploring passionately held values about beauty, belonging, livelihood, relations with the natural and social environment, memories of the past and prospects for the future.

This is the context and strategic case for the Arts & Humanities Research Council (AHRC) programme in Landscape and Environment. The programme has researched the making and meaning of a range of landscapes within and beyond Britain, landscapes created on the page and in performance, built and cultivated in city and country, landscapes lived in, worked on, moved through and looked at. A central theme of the programme is exploring the range of values, including aesthetic, commercial, spiritual, scientific, social, historical and ethical values, which are expressed in the way landscape is seen, designed, made and managed. The programme has examined the cultural complexities, and power relations, of such values, both combining and competing: landscape as both common ground and contested terrain.

The AHRC programme reflects a resurgence in public interest and scholarly research, nationally and internationally, in the ways in which landscape is valued and managed. In rural policies the UK government has looked beyond food production to a wider cultural stewardship of the countryside, and opened up new areas to public access. A cluster of departments and agencies concerned with the landscape and the built environment, in both city and country, have addressed concepts of public value that are intrinsic rather than instrumental, that go beyond utilitarian or financial values, to a sense of place and social belonging, spiritual solace and aesthetic inspiration (English Heritage 2000; Communities and Local Government 2009). Places may have their price, as creators of tourist revenue as well as the costs of conservation, but the value of Stonehenge to the English landscape, no less than the value of Shakespeare to the English language, is a matter of public good that cannot be measured adequately in monetary terms and which arts and humanities research helps us identify and enhance (Cowell 2008). Such valuation in terms of landscape takes us beyond the protection of certain sites to the wider, changeful world of their historical and geographical significance, including taking into account overlooked places and periods, and the views of those who live and work around them as well as visit them from afar. This is a growing feature of conservation and heritage policy internationally. The Council of Europe's European Landscape Convention, now signed or ratified by thirty-six states, promotes a broad, participatory view of landscape, including natural, rural, urban and industrial areas, and sites that may be overlooked as everyday or degraded as well as those that are scenic and iconic. Similarly, new planning policy in the UK emphasizes above all the relative significance of local landscapes, as discerned through visual examination, archival study and public consultation, and whether or not they feature heritage assets that are formally designated through the planning system (Communities and Local Government 2010).

The Landscape and Environment programme has created a collaborative community within and beyond the academy, including multidisciplinary project teams in partnership with a range of people and organizations with a practical stake in landscape matters, notably on questions of heritage, conservation and public understanding. Many of these organizations themselves are actively engaged in research into landscape, much as there is also a great tradition in Britain of lay research into the deep and wide histories of localities and places. This essay focuses on two programme projects in northern England, which include National Trust properties and are centrally concerned with understanding and promoting the public value of landscape.

The National Trust is Europe's largest conservation charity. Established in 1895, it now has more than 3.75 million members (many more than all UK political parties combined) and manages an estate that encompasses 250,000 hectares of land and countryside, 1,100km of coastline and more than 300 historic properties open for public access. In total, its property portfolio comprises 1.5 per cent of the total land area of England, Wales and Northern Ireland. The origins of the Trust are associated with Victorian liberal campaigners interested in social reform and access to open space, and a concern for landscape as a public amenity, modelled on the success of similar trusts in the United States. The initial pattern was to acquire land rather than buildings, including areas of common land, while in its main expansionist phase in the mid-twentieth century it became more closely associated with the cause of country-house preservation. Since the 1960s the Trust has expanded its range of social and environmental interests, in the spirit of its founding ideals. While larger mansion houses such as Calke Abbey in Derbyshire and more recently Seaton Delaval in Northumberland have continued to feature in the Trust's acquisition policies, there is increasing contextual attention to the broader estates, and changing social and physical worlds, which give them cultural significance and material support (Daniels 1993). The Trust's portfolio of properties has expanded to embrace more subaltern forms of heritage such as the early nineteenth-century workhouse in Southwell, Nottinghamshire, and the childhood homes of John Lennon and Paul McCartney in suburban Liverpool, interpreting these sites in terms of recent scholarship on their wider cultural landscape (Daniels 2006). The National Trust has recently developed a broader concept of its role and function, going beyond the permanent preservation of land and buildings to a more dynamic concept of conservation and heritage built around changing values and significance (Gaze 1988; Newby 1995; Cowell 2008).

'Tales of the Frontier'

Hadrian's Wall, one of Britain's best-known historic monuments, provides a vantage point for exploring wide-ranging issues of landscape value. The Wall has been opened up to a wider world in the last decade, with sites made more physically accessible and publically understandable along its 117km length, coast to coast from the Solway to the Tyne, as it runs across upland pasture to post-industrial towns. As a linear insertion in the landscape, the Wall is a complex and challenging monument to maintain and manage, with over 50 organizations and 700 private individuals owning particular sections. It is a requirement of the Wall's designation as a World Heritage Site that it is both managed as a single entity along its length, and a 16km zone to either side, and that its historical significance is framed by a broad field of cultural values, accommodating the range of interests of those who conserve, use and enjoy the site, including the million or so people who live or work within the Wall's regional sphere of influence.

The scholarly concern to explore the wider world of Hadrian's Wall for its 300-year Roman history, including its dynamic relations with the land and life of the territories it passed through, is beginning to be presented to a wider public, in on-site interpretation and associated guide books. What has been much less understood, and scarcely presented, is the Wall's long, post-Roman history, and its impact on the changing fabric of the Wall and how these express changing ideas of Roman Britain. The Landscape and Environment project 'Tales of the Frontier' has pioneered this form of understanding, by researching key periods in the Wall's post-Roman history, including that of the present, to uncover contrasting and competing perspectives on its Roman past, and their material effects in developing the surroundings of the Wall as well as the structure itself.

The multidisciplinary team of archaeologists and geographers from Durham University has excavated a rich range of sources, including the rich seam of factual and fictional writings on the wall, as well as new ethnographic and observational field work. They have examined how the meaning of the Wall has been made and remade, materially and imaginatively, and variously represented and experienced, written on the page, performed in re-enactments, encoded in visitor conduct, inscribed in the earth in excavations and set in stone in restorations and reconstructions. They have also examined what these findings tell us about wider questions of national, imperial and post-imperial identity (Hingley 2008; Hingley and Nesbit 2008; Nesbit and Tolia-Kelly 2009; Witcher, Tolia-Kelly and Hingley 2010). The project has explored the landscape narratives, the framing codes of time and space, which both shape, and are shaped by, the Wall as it transects a range of rural and urban sites and episodes of the region's longer history. Here we will focus on findings at two sites, Housesteads and Wallsend.

Housesteads

At Housesteads the National Trust owns the fort as well as five miles of wall and over a thousand hectares of land surrounding it. Here Hadrian's Wall is presented to the visitor in its most iconic form, and makes its most dramatic public impact, snaking across wide open spaces, the impressive remains of its ramparts built on to the cliff-like geological exposure of Whin Sill. This sublime-looking conjunction of culture and nature, ancient social and earth history, is a centrepiece of the Northumberland National Park, and its careful stage management is part of a modern history of improved estate landscape. The earliest antiquarian visitors in the seventeenth century were keen to claim a site marginal to classical scholarship (it is scarcely mentioned in Roman texts of the time) for a field-based British history and its imperial inheritance of a Roman past, but this border country between England and Scotland was still a dangerous place, beset by bandits. As the wider landscape was improved so its Roman history was reclaimed. The nineteenth-century landowner John Clayton purchased substantial areas of the central part of Hadrian's Wall, including the fort at Housesteads, carried out excavations on the fort to consolidate and display its Roman remains, and had substantial

Figure 8.1 Housesteads Fort (Vercovicium), one of the sixteen permanent bases on Hadrian's Wall, Northumberland. © NTPL/Simon Fraser

parts of the stone rampart rebuilt. Later sites and structures integral to the long post-Roman history, including medieval buildings and arable fields, were cleared to create extensive pastures and sweeping, panoramic vistas. The site, and its historical authenticity, can be understood as both ancient and modern, a Roman site accommodated within a project of landscaping, in the tradition of antiquarian landowners who displayed and refurbished ruins on their estate as the focus and viewpoints for panoramic views, a source of both scholarly and scenic delight.

Housesteads was designated as a scheduled ancient monument under the Ancient Monuments and Archaeological Areas Act in 1928 and given over to the National Trust in 1930, one of its first archaeologically significant properties. The protection and management of the monument has meant that for last thirty years there has been an effective presumption against further intrusive archaeological excavation. Other sites, notably Vindolanda, have demonstrated how an archaeological project can work as an academic and popular initiative, fulfilling new expectations of access to archaeology (some promoted by the 'Time Team' television programmes) and a more zonal, less monumental sense of the Wall and its significance. The remains of a medieval bastle house built into Housesteads fort's south gateway have been conserved and interpreted for the visitor, beginning to communicate some of the post-Roman history of the site, and the Trust and English Heritage are endeavouring to disperse visitors more widely. But shifting public perceptions and on-site interpretation to match scholarly research is challenging, and at Housesteads the Roman flush toilets will remain a principal attraction as much as the functioning modern ones to the motorized tourist, demanding that standard measure of British amenity value, the view with a loo.

Wallsend

Wallsend, as the name indicates, is where Hadrian's Wall came to an end. In Roman times this was on the wild banks of the Tyne, but it is now in the streets of a former shipyard district of the greater Tyneside conurbation. Here, we seem a world away from Housesteads. Little remains of the Wall itself, but the local area has long been conscious, proudly so, of its presence, with a sustained tradition of municipal engagement. In 1903, a stretch of the Wall was found within the adjacent Swan Hunter shipyard; this could not be preserved in situ and was relocated to Wallsend Public Park, joined a few years later by parts of the East Gate discovered during the construction of a hotel. In 1929, the Wallsend Corporation began excavations which identified the plan of the fort and parts were marked out with paving. During the 1970s, a large area of housing was cleared for redevelopment; consequently, extensive archaeological investigation between 1975 and 1984 revealed almost the entire fort site and further commercial development on the site was halted. During the late 1990s, a multimillion pound development included the construction of a museum, Segedunum, the reconstruction of a Roman bath-house and the full display of the excavated site. Difficult to comprehend at ground level, the site is visible from the museum's 35m viewing tower, along with a wider panorama of the locality's long landscape history, including former industrial areas and residential areas. Consciously referencing Wallsend's shipbuilding heritage, the viewing tower takes the form of a ship's bridge, in a version of local heritage which twins classical and modern engineering achievement. If the fort at Housesteads is framed as a pastoral landscape park, Segedunum mobilizes another tradition of envisioning landscape history: the theatrical panorama. It does so, like many Victorian panoramas, as a form of entertainment and instruction, and like many municipal museums of the period it has a serious civic purpose: to help regenerate the area economically and culturally, and increase the cohesion of its community.

Working in partnership with North Tyneside Council, the 'Tales of the Frontier' project contributed to this civic purpose with the principal, public-centred outcome of an exhibition, *An Archaeology of 'Race'*, staged at Segedunum before moving to a venue near to the western end of the Wall, Tullie House Museum in Carlisle. Building on evidence for the multiracial makeup of the Roman garrisons, the exhibition addressed the question of landscape and citizenship in a dialogue between past and present, and gave a view of the imperial presence that was more than a military matter of coming, seeing and conquering. It focused on the period of governance of North African-born Lucius Septimius Severus, the man whose name was attached to the Wall for a period of its post-Roman history before it reverted to Hadrian. This exhibition displayed the broader culture of the Wall community, its domestic, everyday life, the growing of food and religious observance, with a range of objects – originals and replicas, material and virtual – and newly commissioned artworks including a hologram bust of Severus. It located the Wall through its community within a broader geography, its people drawn from the shores of Africa, the forests of Bavaria, the mountains of the Balkans and the plains of Iberia, a view of the Wall as a gathering place rather than a barrier, a site of contact and encounter, not just about keeping people out but about bringing in so many people and things (Tolia-Kelly and Nesbitt 2009).

At Housesteads and Segedunum the 'Tales of the Frontier' team have identified different strategies of presenting and learning about the landscape and culture of Roman Britain. It was an opportunity to deploy current modes of landscape theory, which emphasize the mobility and mutability of landscape features, even monumental ones, and the fluency of sites which may seem fixed, on the ground and in the mind. This deconstructive academic aspect of the research is connected to a socially constructive one as an integral part of the project, in the tradition of scholarly civic engagement for a university mindful of its regional commitments. The project's Durham University-based team are contributing to the efforts of various agencies charged with the custody of Hadrian's Wall to enhance the complexity as well as the complementarity of the various sites along the Wall and a new appreciation of this linear landscape as a diverse, connected whole.

Contested common land

Common land in Britain holds a special place for people concerned with the public value of landscape and research is revealing it to be highly complicated physical and cultural terrain, much less understood than many of its admirers or detractors might assume.

Common lands were usually to be found on tracts of marginal land beyond intensive farming, often on thin soils and intractable terrain, and in areas of heathland, moorland, marshland and woodland, which once covered a third of England and Wales. Such commons were conventionally condemned as wastelands by those intent on developing them for highly profitable uses, for farming or housing, but they have proved highly valuable to the communities which used them, a rich reservoir of resources, for grazing, food, fuel and materials for building and making a variety of products, from chairs and pots to dyes and medicines.

Traditionally commons were not legally public property, open to all, nor a no man's land which anyone could exploit. Yet neither were they (unlike in continental Europe) in communal ownership: commons were privately owned, the property of a manorial landowner but subject to the rights of commoners, usually local inhabitants, governed by manorial courts. The contraction of common land, to the point where it now covers just 3 per cent of the country, and its virtual disappearance from large parts of lowland England, have been accompanied by some redefinition of its meaning and use, even its reinvention.

In places the decline of effective manorial governance opened a permissive space, more customary than constitutional, for new kinds of commoners, sometimes in temporary huts and encampments, to make a living. Enclosure for agriculture prompted paternalistic plans to reserve patches of heath land for the poor to subsist or village greens for play, and building development around cities and towns provoked campaigns for commons' preservation as an urban amenity, with grants of access protected through local acts and statutes. Early conservation organizations, including the National Trust, helped re-imagine the commons, including those around cities and those in more peripheral regions made accessible by motorized transport, as a collective national resource, green spaces over which everyone may roam freely. (A quarter of the Trust's landholdings are registered commons, and it looks after 11 per cent of the commons in England.) As common land has physically shrunk, so it has culturally expanded, from a specific landscape for a local community to a general landscape for a national citizenry. It was not until the twenty-first century that there was anything approaching a comprehensive right of public access to registered common land (Everitt 2000).

Pastoral myths of commons may mask some pastoral realities, that there are still over a million acres of common land in England and Wales, most privately owned, much of it working country, grazing land, in upland regions of northern England and Wales. Within this upland region there is rich diversity in the commons' culture of landscape, their character and identity varying according to terrain, tradition, neighbourliness, custom, historical development and interaction with national legislation and designations that affect the land and its management. The long and continuing history of upland commons is rich and complicated, but often features much less than laments for lost lowland commons in national narratives of landscape history (Winchester 2000; Straughton 2004).

'Contested Common Land' is a project in the Landscape and Environment programme focused on upland commons as a continuing collective resource with multiple, and sometimes conflicting, valuations and uses. The project brings together historians and legal scholars, from both sides of the Pennines, from the Universities of Newcastle and Lancaster, to address the issue of the sustainable use and management of common land. It is focused on the implications of the 2006 Commons Act, which introduced a new legal framework for commons governance, enabling commoners to establish statutory councils, and powers to enter into binding agreements with government agencies promoting sustainable management. This Act introduced much more flexibility and collective local power than the static model of property fixed in the previous Commons Registration Act of 1965, and mobilized a long history of the landscape and its governance. Archival and field work was combined with contemporary ethnographic research, interviews, group discussions and conversations with farmers, landowners and land managers. Both forms of research helped reconstruct the collective memory of common land, as expressed in documents, embodied in custom, acted upon in practice and manifested on the ground, in the traces of present and past activity. As well as informing and improving the governance of commons the project has enhanced wider scholarly understanding and public awareness (Straughton 2008; Rodgers 2009).

The case studies of three upland commons in Cumbria, Powys and North Yorkshire reveal long and complex histories, with phases of decline and development, disuse and re-use, ruin and reconstitution, and resilience in the face of periodic pressures and predicaments, external and internal, adapting to and engaging with modern development. The modern county of Cumbria contains the largest area of common land of any county in England (some 112,786 ha). The local significance of the commons as a working country is framed by the Lake District's history as a national amenity. Large areas fell within the early twentieth-century Lakes Urban District and were designated metropolitan commons and subject to public access and demand for outdoor leisure of many forms has increased substantially since then. The commons, including its traditional farming management, is one of the elements in the Lake District's current proposal to seek World Heritage Site inscription, giving this region 'outstanding universal value'. This is thus a model countryside to chart the intersecting demands and values of farming, recreation and conservation, and the making and meaning of a variety of landscapes and environments, folded and faulted like the region's rock strata. One of the largest commons in the county, consisting of over 3,000 ha, is in Eskdale in the southern fells of the Lake District National Park.

Eskdale

The development of Eskdale Common is an integral part of the valley's landscape history as an aristocratic estate, and now as a more extensive, and highly varied, National Trust estate. It includes England's highest mountain, Scafell Pike, and its deepest lake, Wastwater, as well as the remains of a Roman fort high on Hardknott Pass and the more tranquil river scenery of the Duddon Valley.

Eskdale Common was owned for much of its history by the Earls of Northumberland and latterly by their successors the Lords Leconfield until 1979 when it was transferred to the National Trust. This substantially increased the Trust's holdings in the valley. The freehold on the high fells was donated to the National Trust early in the century, and the peaks, including that of Scafell Pike, became a memorial to Lakelanders who died in the First World War. Carrying a new meaning of commons, as an amenity of public

Figure 8.2 Taw House Farm in Eskdale, Cumbria. © NTPL/John Miller

access, the plaque on Scafell summit announces that it is 'subject to any commoner's rights'. Interviewed by members of the Contested Common Land project team, local officers of the Natural Trust maintained that the Trust's commitment to the common pasture lands, along with farm tenancies it has acquired, form a vital part of Eskdale as a working environment, though there remain, inevitably, issues of managing the pressures for public access and nature conservation.

Until the later nineteenth century the management of common rights in Eskdale was regulated by a manor court, with a jury of local customary tenants making and enforcing agrarian rules. The common then entered a period without a management institution, until the formation of a commoners' committee in 1945, largely the creation of a conservationist campaigner, the Reverend H.H. Symonds, prominent in national pressure groups for public access to the countryside. The committee lapsed when Symonds moved away from the locality. The gap was filled in 1967 by a more successful body, the Eskdale Commoners Association, endorsed by the landowner but with more significant grassroots support from the commoners. It original purpose was primarily to prepare for the registration of rights under the Commons Registration Act of 1965, and it continues now as a vehicle for collective action.

Common rights in Eskdale are of three kinds, largely pasture, but also turbary (peat cutting) and estovers (bracken harvesting). Commons pasture, mainly for sheep, remains central to hill farming and livelihood; turbary and estovers have now fallen into disuse, with the use of alternative sources of fuel, roofing and animal bedding. Their legacy in the landscape takes the form of the remains of peat tracks and huts (some re-roofed) and the rampant spread of bracken. The landscape also reveals remains of former landowners' rights to hunt game, in the form of grousebutts and hunting lodges, and to mine minerals, in the form of the ruined mine workings and the narrow gauge track of a railway which once transported iron ore and granite to the port of Ravenglass. In the mid-twentieth century this railway promoted local tourism, bringing in visitors from the industrial Cumbrian coast, including the poet Norman Nicholson, whose writings on Eskdale, in poems and guidebooks, did much to enhance the appreciation of Eskdale as an enterprising, working country, governed by its sturdy 'statesmen' farmers (Nicholson 1944; Nicholson 1949).

> ... the ESK comes from the narrowest dale
> Where the statesmen meet at the Woolpack for a glass of ale
> And a crack about herdwicks as a cure for the tick
> And how some fool has broken his neck on the rock.

Common rights in Eskdale were codified by a document originally drawn up in 1587 known as the 'Eskdale Twenty Four Book', so-called because it was prepared by a jury of twenty-four men. No less than estate maps and account books of the period, the book was part of a new, modern, rational framework of land management, precisely prescribing and demarking the time and space for commons practice. For pasture, the book designated each commoner's heaf (grazing portion of the fell) and drift (the designated route to it), conceiving the common in terms of grazing capacity, taking into account different livestock (sheep, cattle, horses), topography and ground cover, creating a patchwork of practice. The book has proved sufficiently flexible to accommodate four centuries of economic and social change, including the development of Eskdale for industry and tourism, and the transfer of government from the manor to other institutions. No original copy of the book is known but it has been periodically copied and transcribed, for example in relation to stocking disputes. It continued to be consulted as a framework for commons governance into the twentieth century, long after the manor court's demise, in conjunction with more recent texts, such as new fell rules drawn up in 1980 when the National Trust acquired ownership and legal statutes of modern environmental stewardship on grazing strategy.

The 'Twenty Four Book' deserves to be better known, not only as an enduring framework for commons governance, adapted and appropriated through a long history of practical use, but for its language of landscape. One passage reads:

> As for the tenants of Spouthouse we find that they shall take their sheep up their bank or bankedge and on the south side of Blea tarne upon their accustomed waye upon the height of Brownband and up over the How of Swinside and up at Eile Ark to the Hardrigge and if their sheep be on the north side of Bleatarn that then they shall take them and go to their drift both at cominge and going there at will and pleasure.

Here is an expressive and performative language of landscape, one of movement and process, through a detailed topography of named places and pathways, which echoes in the literature of the Lake District sensitive to places, like Eskdale, off the beaten track, mindful of their forgotten ways.

The 'Twenty Four Book' remains a talismanic text for some commoners, but a number of the younger generation and newcomers seemed unaware of it when interviewed in the course of research. The project has effectively reintroduced this text to the commoner community as a whole, as part of the initiative to restore flexibility and local custom in the governance of Eskdale Common, and to address the new requirements of environmental law; a sustainable text for a sustainable landscape. The project has done this through its online Geospatial tool, LandNote, which displays heafs and cow pastures areas mentioned in the book, along with other information from modern documents on registration and conservation. As with other forms of mapping, landscape representation is social as well as visual, representing the rights and interests of those who own, work and visit the land as well as its topography. Displayed on a tabletop screen, LandNote is used to focus discussions on future management among stakeholders, but will also be made available as an open source, a virtual commons, to a wider public, for community planning and as an educational tool. It will also be used for new forms of tourism that are mindful of the history and sociability of Eskdale as a working country, as well as its more solitary and scenic pleasures, a place of local livelihood as well as part of a bigger picture of national belonging and identity.

Conclusion: researching landscape and environment

The projects at Hadrian's Wall and Eskdale explore a variety of different concepts of landscape and environment, both in the present day and in an historical context. They do so through multidisciplinary approaches, encompassing legal, archaeological, anthropological and archival research. At Hadrian's Wall, issues of monumentality are addressed, locating the physical structure of the boundary within the fluid movement of people over time and place, from Roman imperial forces to the shipyards of the early twentieth century. At Eskdale, the community of farmers defined their relationship with the landscape through structures of governance centred on the manorial court, and later the commoners' association. In both examples, the National Trust is one of the organizations that have stepped in to protect and conserve the significance of these landscapes in the twenty-first century. Honouring this responsibility depends on sound understanding and knowledge. To present Housesteads purely as an inheritance from the Roman era is to misrepresent the way it has been reinterpreted and incorporated into the landscape in the intervening centuries. Similarly, the uplands pastures of Eskdale cannot properly be safeguarded and understood without reference to the skeins of rights practised over them by farmers and their animals over a period of at least 400 years. Landscapes are composed of multiple layers of value, accreted over time and sustained through the interactions between people and place. Understanding those values requires a kaleidoscopic approach to research, one that looks beyond the boundaries of the academy, embracing both past and present, and theory and practice, in equal measure.[2]

Notes

1   Stephen Daniels is Director of the AHRC Landscape and Environment programme and Ben Cowell is Assistant Director of External Affairs for the National Trust.

2   The authors wish to thank the project teams of 'Tales of the Frontier' and 'Contested Common Land' for their close co-operation in preparing this chapter, including supplying materials from which we have at times silently quoted. Fuller documentation of their findings, including working papers and publications, are on their project websites linked from their respective web pages of the AHRC Landscape and Environment programme (http://www.landscape.ac.uk).

Bibliography

Communities and Local Government (2009), *World Class Places: The Government's Strategy for Improving Quality of Place*, London: Communities and Local Government.

Communities and Local Government (2010), *Planning Policy Statement 5: Planning for the Historic Environment*, London: The Stationery Office.

Cowell, B. (2008), *The Heritage Obsession: The Battle for England's Past*, Stroud: Tempus.

Daniels, S. (1993), *Fields of Vision: Landscape Imagery and National Identity in England and the United States*, Cambridge: Polity Press.

Daniels, S. (2006), 'Suburban pastoral: "Strawberry Fields Forever" and Sixties Memory', *Cultural Geographies*, 13: 1: 28–54.

English Heritage (2000), *Power of Place: The Future of the Historic Environment*, London: English Heritage.

European Science Foundation (2010), *Landscape in a Changing World*, Science Policy Briefing, Strasbourg: European Science Foundation.

Everitt, A. (2000), 'Common Land', in J. Thirsk (ed.), *Rural England: An Illustrated History of the Landscape*, Oxford: Oxford University Press.

Gaze, J. (1988), *Figures in a Landscape: A History of the National Trust*, London: Barrie and Jenkins.

Hingley, R. (2008), *The Recovery of Roman Britain: A Colony So Fertile*, Oxford: Oxford University Press.

Hingley, R. and Nesbit, C. (2008), 'A Wall for all Times', *British Archaeology*, 102: 44–59.

Nesbit, C. and Tolia-Kelly, D.P. (2009), 'Hadrian's Wall: Embodied Archaeologies of the Linear Monument', *Journal of Social Archaeology*, 9: 369–90.

Newby, H. (ed.) (1995), *The National Trust: The Next Hundred Years*, London: National Trust.

Nicholson, N. (1944), *Five Rivers*, London: Faber and Faber.

Nicholson, N. (1949), *Cumberland and Westmorland*, London: Robert Hale.

Rodgers, C.P. (2009), 'Property rights, land use and the rural environment: A case for reform', *Land Use Policy*, 26.

Straughton, E.A. (2004), 'Beyond Enclosure: Upland Common Land in England and Wales since 1800', in I.D. Whyte and A.J.L. Winchester (eds), *Society, Landscape and Environment in Upland Britain*, Exeter: University of Exeter Press.

Straughton, E. (2008), *Common Grazing in the Northern English Uplands, 1800–1965: A History of National Policy and Local Practice with Special Attention to the Case of Cumbria*, Lewiston, NY, and Lampeter: Edwin Mellen Press.

Tolia-Kelly, D.P., and Nesbitt, C. (2009), *An Archaeology of 'Race'; Exploring the Northern Frontier in Roman Britain*, exhibition catalogue, Durham: Tales of the Frontier, Durham University and AHRC.

Winchester, A.J.L. (2000), *The Harvest of the Hills: Rural Life in England and the Scottish Borders 1400–1700*, Edinburgh: Edinburgh University Press.

Witcher, R., Tolia-Kelly, D.P. and Hingley, R. (2010), 'Archaeologies of Landscape: Exploring the Materialities of Hadrian's Wall', *Journal of Material Culture*, 15: 1: 105–28.

9. Making a Home: English Culture and English Landscape

Matthew H. Johnson (University of Southampton)

Every weekend, thousands of people take a walk in the English countryside. A walk in the country is about exercise, but it is also much more than that. It is enabled by the tracks and paths, the public rights of way over private property. The surrounding scenery is of fields, hedges, grasslands, moorlands, studded by the spires and towers of medieval churches, and the distant prospect of Georgian houses amidst parklands.

All these elements are and were human creations. Even the moorland has been cleared from natural forest thousands of years ago, and actively maintained since (most recently for the management of grouse); and the 'forests' themselves have been managed for millennia. In the densely settled landscape of the British Isles, the idea of a 'natural' landscape is almost always an illusion.

Furthermore, rather than being 'pretty' objects or components of pleasant scenery, these elements signify cultural and national identity.

Figure 9.1 Map-reading on a Sunday afternoon in the Devon countryside

David Lowenthal (Lowenthal 1994) has talked of a 'scenic nationalism' in which fields, villages, tracks and rolling countryside provoke affection and allegiance. To understand the English countryside is therefore to understand what it is to be English. 'England – fight for it now!' proclaimed propaganda posters during the last war, depicting a landscape of rolling Sussex downland.

Taking a walk, then, is doing much more than just stretching one's legs and enjoying the scenery. Walkers are (perhaps somewhat unwittingly) walking into a story of national identity, a story which has been partially uncovered and shaped by academic research. The date of this church tower, the architectural style of that country house, the origins of this droveway and the fields beyond – these are all elements of a very old tale. Furthermore, the way that academics have discovered more about this story – the techniques of landscape history and archaeology such as walking the fields looking for scatters of ancient pottery, poring over old Ordnance Survey maps and estate documents – has been as important as the final results of the research.

Academic writing about landscape is one of those pursuits which are inextricably linked to popular tradition and practices. Many of the 'general public' walking across rural landscapes know the details of medieval origins of villages, of the dating of this or that architectural style of church, and of enclosure of the landscape. Others (for example, English Heritage, members of rambler associations, amateur history groups, the Countryside Alliance and conservation organizations) have clearly defined 'rural' roles and identities, and consequently have an enhanced stake in the landscape. Indeed, every week some new controversy over the uses of landscape opens up, from foxhunting to second homes to the right to roam to the National Parks. Conflicts between different interests such as the Kinder Mass Trespass still resonate over seventy years after the event. These controversies reflect different views of what the landscape is really all about and, it can be argued, different views of national identity.

Given the fact that people can and do regularly negotiate their own identity and relationship with landscape, how has arts and humanities research contributed to the picture? In this essay I argue that one of the biggest contributions academic research has made and can continue to make is to show how varied the meanings and interpretations of landscape can be and how this contributes to a vibrant, lively and inclusive definition of what it is to be English. Indeed, I will argue that viewed historically, landscape research has changed the way people think about what it is to be English. However, perhaps more valuable than this is the role academic research can play in countering the view of landscape as timeless, mythical and unchanging – a view which leads directly to the appropriation of landscape by one group to the exclusion of others.

The countryside and what it means to be English

The idea of the landscape as a haven, a retreat, a source of cultural value and a repository for what is quintessentially English is not a new idea. It has been shown by academic research to be many centuries old. The notion of the rural retreat, for example, goes back to Virgil. Since the Middle Ages, prosperous merchants and industrialists have sought to purchase rural estates and set themselves up as country gentlemen. The desire for a place in the country, and a corresponding alienation from the city, has been a recurring motif of English culture (Williams 1973).

Recent legislation creating areas of open access in the countryside was bitterly fought over, in part, I would argue, because it exposed just how many histories of the landscape there are. For landowners, the history of the landscape is one of centuries of effective management, a difficult struggle in the face of an uncomprehending urban elite – a view effectively expressed on the website of the Countryside Alliance: 'Your countryside owes its great beauty and wildlife to the private and public land managers who we should encourage as they shape the land for future generations'. Conversely, for many ramblers, the history of the landscape is that of the defeat of common rights and the victory of the landowner over the community (Shoard 1999).

Who owns the landscape and how accessible it should be is an argument which has long been taking place in the history of ideas. To the Romantic poets, in particular William Blake and William Wordsworth, the English landscape was a national treasure to be shared by all. Wordsworth wrote, 'my object is to reconcile a Briton to the scenery of his own country, though not at the expense of truth', and wrote of the Lake District as 'a sort of national property, in which every man has a right and interest who has an eye to perceive and a heart to enjoy'. It was from Wordsworth's vision that the modern conception of the National Parks sprang and Wordsworth wrote one of the first guidebooks – *A Guide to the Lakes* – which opened up the Lakes as an area to be appreciated by all classes of people. Interestingly, in his reactionary later years Wordsworth bemoaned the accessibility of the Lakes as he endured the 'railway inundations' of common folk disrupting his beloved solitude (de Selincourt 1906: 92, 145, 160).

The debate was taken up with a vengeance once more in the 1950s, and it is to this period – viewed by many as a pivotal moment in academic research into landscape history (as well as the development of postwar British culture) – that I now want to turn (Johnson 2007; Sinfield 1989).

Hoskins, Crawford and understanding the countryside

It may seem a little perverse to go back to the 1950s when writing about the value of current-day arts and humanities research, but I have selected this particular generation of academic research into landscape to illustrate how research ideas, questions and practices can impact, over the very long term, on cultural life as a whole.

In 1953, O.G.S. Crawford published *Archaeology in the Field*. Crawford was an unusual and colourful character who pioneered the use of air photography (it is worth noting in passing the close links between the uses of air photos for both archaeological and military purposes during the two world wars). Crawford made the striking proposition that the whole landscape was a vast archaeological site:

> The surface of England is like a palimpsest, a document that has been written on and erased over and over again; and it is the business of the field archaeologist to decipher it. The features concerned are of course the roads and field boundaries, the woods, the farms and other habitations, and all the other products of human labour; these are the letters and words inscribed on the land. But it is not easy to read them because, whereas the vellum document was seldom wiped clean more than once or twice, the land has been subjected to continual change throughout the ages. (Crawford 1953: 51–2)

Crawford's insight was taken up by the landscape historian and academic W.G. Hoskins. Hoskins' work established six key points that are now familiar to us, but represented a major advance in their time:

1. The great antiquity of the landscape – he wrote 'everything is much older than we think' in *The Making of the English Landscape* (Hoskins 1955: 12). The villages of England are a millennium old; many of the traditional farmhouses and cottages are over 500 years old; many field boundaries and trackways date back to the time before the Romans. This insight, established by academic research and later reinforced by landscape archaeology, is now so commonplace that it scarcely seems controversial. But in its time, the notion that the landscape was of a very great age, and that its value derived from that antiquity, was quite revolutionary. This insight now sits at the heart of public policymaking, for example in the work of English Heritage on historic landscape characterization (Rippon 2007).

2. Recognition of change in the landscape. If villages are a thousand years old, then a thousand years ago they were created (Jones and Page 2006). Further, English landscapes were often transformed quite deliberately and suddenly. The eighteenth-century enclosures were only one of several major transformations in the landscape, going back to the clearing of woods and forests in prehistory. If farmhouses date back 500 years, then very many were built right at the end of the Middle Ages. Subsequent academic work established that many of the field boundaries in the English landscape are of Roman or prehistoric date – but in the process pointed to quite sudden moments of rural transformation (Williamson and Bellamy 1987; Williamson 2003).

3. Hoskins repeated Crawford's insistence on our ability to 'read' the landscape – to explore it by book and by foot, and to piece together

its history through patient research. But he did so in terms which stressed the resonance and cultural value of the experience, and how the experience of particular regions, what the French call *pays*, enhances appreciation and understanding of the country as a whole:

> One may liken the English landscape ... to a symphony, which it is possible to enjoy as an architectural mass of sound, without being able to analyse it in detail or to see the logical development of the structure. The enjoyment may be real, but it is limited in scope and in the last resort vaguely diffused in emotion. But if instead of hearing merely a symphonic mass of sound, we are able to isolate the themes as they enter, to see how one by one they are intricately woven together and by what magic new harmonies are produced, perceive the manifold subtle variations on a single theme, however disguised it might be, then the total effect is immeasurably enhanced. So it is with the landscapes of historic depth and physical variety that England shows almost everywhere. Only when we know all the themes and harmonies can we begin to appreciate its full beauty, or to discover in it new subtleties every time we visit it. (Hoskins 1955: 19)

4. Hoskins used these materials to tell a grand and emotive story about that landscape. Every hedge and track, every village and church, became one small element in a wider national story that held meaning and resonance. For Hoskins, that story was one of the loss of a traditional way of life and its subversion by the alienation of modern urban society – a story also told famously in J.R.R Tolkein's *The Lord of the Rings*, where the heroic hobbits return to find a despoiled and industrialized landscape of the Shire.

5. A populist perspective. Hoskins was committed to disseminating his academic research to anyone who would listen. His weekends were taken up with addresses to day-schools and extra-mural classes. Hoskins 'fronted' two of the earliest TV documentary series on the landscape – 'English Landscapes' and 'One Man's England'. He also gave a series of influential talks on the BBC's Third Programme, subsequently reprinted in the *Listener* (for example, Hoskins 1954b). As a result of his commitment and skill, and that of others of his generation, this story about the landscape – and the values it embodied – became firmly embedded as part of the taken-for-granted postwar English culture.

6. The problems of understanding and managing the landscape in a modern world. Hoskins' own perspective was openly anti-modernist: his most famous passage is a passionate denigration of modernity:

> What else has happened in the immemorial landscape of the English countryside? Airfields have flayed it bare ... Poor devastated

Lincolnshire and Suffolk! And those long gentle lines of the dip-slope of the Cotswolds, those misty uplands of the sheep-grey oolite, how they have lent themselves to the villainous requirements of the new age! Over them drones, day after day, the obscene shape of the atom-bomber, laying a trail like a filthy slug upon Constable's and Gainsborough's sky. England of the Nissen-hut, the 'pre-fab', and the electric fence, of the high barbed wire around some unmentionable devilment; England of the arterial by-pass, treeless and stinking of diesel oil, murderous with lorries; England of the bombing-range wherever there was once silence ... Barbaric England of the scientists, the military men, and the politicians; let us turn away and contemplate the past before all is lost to the vandals. (Hoskins 1955: 231–2)

Hoskins managed to bridge the gap between the academic and popular experience and understanding of landscape by writing academic texts and popular guides. His work was hugely popular and he made it accessible via radio, early television and teaching. Indeed, his legacy lives on in continuing education – the most popular classes being on landscape history. One of the reasons this legacy is so strong is that Hoskins gave such classes a method to find out and understand the landscape around them, quite literally, and he also gave them a wider national story into which they could fit their particular experiences and give them meaning. It can be argued that the 'Time Team' television series and its consequent effects on the popularity of archaeology (discussed more thoroughly in Chapter 2) would not have been possible without the intellectual horizon of the academic research of Hoskins and his contemporaries.

As valuable and groundbreaking as Hoskins was in making both the landscape and academic study accessible, the limits of his approach are as interesting as its possibilities. Whilst Hoskins' research posed the question 'How do we value and conserve heritage in a changing landscape?', his academic work could seem to suggest turning away from the problem, railing at modernity. Interestingly, Hoskins was committed to serving as a Liberal councillor in Exeter to fight the 1960s destruction of the ancient fabric of that city (Johnson 2007: 46). Like Wordsworth, then, he created a mental and moral climate in which questions of conservation, heritage, and cultural value in the landscape were placed centre stage; but he became unsure of how to deal with his own success, in terms of the social pressures of increased accessibility.

Another academic writing in the 1950s, Nikolaus Pevsner, did for architecture what Hoskins did for the landscape. Pevsner, a German-Jewish émigré who came to England in the 1930s, was the most profound writer of his generation on the history of architecture. But architecture, like landscape, expresses the ideas and values of the communities that create and inherit buildings. And many of those values are national ones. Many of Pevsner's ideas are summed up in his great book *The Englishness of English Art*, compiled from his Reith Lectures. Pevsner presented a vision of an essential English spirit running through the buildings of England from the Anglo-Saxon minster to modernist architecture (Pevsner 1956; Pevsner 2002).

Pevsner's impact on the cultural life of the nation was again profound (and continues to be controversial). It came through his architectural guides to English counties, in which ordinary people were told not just what buildings to look at but also how to look at them and what to deem worthy or unworthy. Pevsner's county guides are clearly meant to be read out in front of the building in question – thus descriptions of churches routinely start by describing the exterior, facade by facade, as one walks round the building, before moving to the interior.

Hoskins, Crawford and Pevsner were part of a postwar generation who engaged in academic research that indirectly addressed some of the hard questions about national identity, fairness and equity which the new democracy posed. My argument is that whilst they did not always find answers, their research helped to create a moral and cultural climate in postwar Britain that enriched the lives of people of all social classes, from Hoskins' extra-mural classes to families walking in the English countryside clutching Ordnance Survey maps and Pevsner's guides in their hands. It helped to create an engagement with the landscape and the history of that landscape that endures and is familiar to us today.

Landscapes mean things to people

Englishness is not unusual in being evidenced through landscape. Who people think they are, and what they see in the landscape around them, are ideas that fit like lock and key. For the indigenous peoples of Australia, and for other peoples across the world, landscapes can be enchanted or cursed. Places are associated with stories, and these stories are of supernatural beings or gods. Stories in turn define who individuals are, where they belong socially and geographically, and what rights they have over territory (Ucko and Layton 1999; Bender and Winer 2001).

Growing political and cultural respect for such interpretations of landscape has been fostered by academic research, for example work with the indigenous peoples of Australia. Tourists now visit Uluru, not Ayers Rock, the change in name reflecting greater awareness of and respect for indigenous traditions. Similarly, in Montana, they visit the site of the Battle of the Little Big Horn, not the Custer Battlefield. The colonial vision of a '*terra nullius*', an empty land free for white people to colonize, has been replaced by a more complex view in which different groups have different rights over the land. This conception of a natural landscape was central to the formation of the identity of the United States of America, and is celebrated by the millions of annual visitors to Yosemite or the

Grand Canyon. In reality, the landscape had been settled for millennia by Native Americans.

Western culture has a different conception of landscape from that of non-western peoples, but it is fanciful to think that 'our' culture is free from ideas of enchantment and spiritual value. The Swiss Alps, the mountains of the Auvergne, the rolling Tuscan landscape, the terraces and olive trees of Greece – all play central roles in defining who people are, and all are given a special status in national consciousness. The German idea of *Heimat,* or homeland, is a complex idea of belonging, loss and nostalgia that was abused for political ends in the last century. Urban landscapes are also given value in this way as much as rural landscapes. In the 1953 film *The Wages of Fear*, the last unforgettable frame is of the hand of the dead Yves Montand, many thousands of miles from home in a harsh, alien landscape of the New World, clutching … a Paris metro ticket.

English landscapes in a multicultural world

Hoskins' vision is more relevant today than it has ever been precisely because it is underpinned by a desire to make landscape accessible – to read stories in the hedges and churches and ridge and furrow. However, for Hoskins, the English landscape was the setting for his socially middling, Anglo-Saxon ancestors:

> My ancestors were men and women of no particular eminence even in local history, farmers nearly all of them until the collapse of local communities all over England in the early 19th century drove them off the land and into the towns and across the water to the American continent. But they were the sort of people who form the foundations of any stable society. (Hoskins 1954a: xix–xx)

Like any narrative about landscape, such romantic celebration runs the risk of becoming as exclusive and inaccessible as John Major's infamous eulogy to a Britain that is defined in terms of a stereotypical view of lowland England:

> Fifty years from now Britain will still be the country of long shadows on county grounds, warm beer, invincible green suburbs, dog lovers and pools fillers and – as George Orwell said – 'old maids cycling to holy communion through the morning mist' and – if we get our way – Shakespeare still read even in school. Britain will survive unamendable in all essentials. (Major 1993)

Recent academic research, then, has set itself the task of making landscape research actively relevant and accessible to all elements of a modern, multicultural society – a social landscape that is inclusive of the poor, the marginalized, and of different faiths and cultures.

The central problem for legislators as well as academics is how to harness the power of visions of the English landscape for people who do not have ancestors in the sense that Hoskins and Major assume – urban dwellers, ethnic minorities – and how they also 'form the foundations of any stable society'. If this intellectual work is not done, the consequences again are those that are always born of ignorance – a recent Commission on Integration and Cohesion concluded that racial tensions were more likely in rural areas of the rural lowland England than in the inner cities.

Alternative ways of reading and seeing the landscape are constantly at play. In the 1970s, the literary and cultural critic Raymond Williams was opening our eyes to the construction of the English countryside through the eyes of the 'outsider' in the form of the city dweller. Williams' academic point was that to understand Romantic and other views of the English landscape, you had to understand first the Industrial Revolution. Images of an unchanging, peaceful rural idyll did not simply exist in a vacuum, and nor were they an unvarnished version of the way the countryside really was. Rather, 'the country and the city' were intertwined (Williams 1973).

Williams' thinking, as revolutionary in its own way as Hoskins', reiterated the fact that different groups of people read the countryside in different ways and turn those readings into cultural capital in literature as well as art and cultural practice. He and his students – political and cultural critics like Stuart Hall – went on to develop his ideas of social class and apply them to questions of colonial and ethnic divisions. Their work opened up new and exciting questions such as: to what extent does the English landscape exclude as well as include?

Researching English landscapes

My argument is that a single static reading of landscape leads to a stale and reactionary view of rural society and of British society as a whole. As we have seen, an academically informed picture emphasizes change, diversity and plurality, and these are terms which have powerful currency in the local and global settings we work within in today's academic world.

To underline my point I conclude by offering four examples of the types of landscape research which have the potential to posit questions which feed back into our cultural heritage and national identity.

First, research has established how many of our most loved landscapes are the product of the slave trade. The great houses and parks around Bristol, or William Beckford's Gothic fantasy of Fonthill Abbey, were built on the proceeds of either the trade itself, or from the slave labour used on the sugar plantations of the Caribbean, as exemplified most famously by the fictional landscape of Jane Austen's Mansfield Park. As a result, many of these great sites have been reinterpreted as part of a postcolonial heritage; Fonthill Abbey is a place of meaning for black as well as white people with the surname Beckford (Williams 1944).

Second, possibly the most contested landscape of any in England, that of Stonehenge, has been studied by Barbara Bender (Bender 1998). She has shown how both in prehistory and in the present, the Stonehenge landscape has kept some people in and other people out, from Neolithic social divisions to New Age travellers. Academic research such as Bender's has again changed the climate of debate over Stonehenge; where forty years ago excavations there were the reserve of a few privileged academics, the recent excavations have been viewed by millions over the internet (BBC 2008).

Third, there is the work of the Council for British Archaeology in involving different groups in studying the landscape through its Community Archaeology Forum. Here, community groups are able to create their own webpages, such as for the Northamptonshire 'Local People: Local Past' project (Community Landscape & Archaeology Project 2010), and participate in discussion with other groups, in a genuinely inclusive process.

Fourth, there is the recent publication of the Whittlewood project, an Arts and Humanities Research Council-funded enquiry into that most fundamental of questions: the origins of the English village. The gathering together of church, houses and manor was not a natural process: it occurred in different places at different times, and in many communities of England it never occurred at all (Jones and Page 2006).

Many of the projects under the umbrella of the AHRC Landscapes and Environment programme are continuing this intellectual project, with research both on the English landscape and across the world. Scholars have been brought together from art, archaeology, geography, history and many other disciplines to address fundamental questions about how we view the landscape, how common land has been contested over the centuries, the history of elements of the landscape such as the parish church, the military and enclosed fields, and how we have constructed images of nature.

Conclusion

Every time someone takes a walk in the English countryside, they owe a debt to academic research. Through this work, individuals and families understand not just the landscape around them, but come to a deeper and more informed awareness of their own place within it.

The relationship between arts and humanities research and popular views of the English landscape is a fundamental one. I have looked at the relationship over a span of more than fifty years because it is difficult to trace in a direct manner over a short time-frame – this piece of research, that piece of social benefit. Part of the reason for this is that academic research is not, and should not be, a one-way process. Academics do not hand down the truth on tablets of stone which are then passively consumed by culture as a whole (though they sometimes like to think they do so). Different stakeholders react critically and selectively to what they hear, and have their own landscapes and landscape histories.

The influence of academic research is nevertheless profound. Different groups have taken Hoskins' story about the landscape and deployed it for their own ends. He provided people with a much needed intellectual armoury, a set of tools with which to understand what they were looking at.

Academic research also has the capacity to develop a process of learning about the landscape, and this process is as important in engaging people as the final results of any research. Landscapes are an ideal form of discovery learning: everyone is interested in the landscape around them, and exploring the countryside is a far more engaging way to learn than sitting in a dark and stuffy lecture theatre. At the same time, amateur groups do not have to dig or use complex scientific equipment to obtain important results. Groups of amateurs make exciting discoveries through the use of maps and exploring by foot, in the Hoskins/Crawford tradition.

To conclude: if you want to understand the value of academic research into landscape archaeology and history, wait until your walk or drive home through city streets or country lanes, or until a walk in the countryside this coming weekend. As you walk, look around you. The proud tower of this

Figure 9.2 Idsworth, an eleventh-century church set alone in the landscape, best known for its fourteenth-century mural of St Hubert. The winding road and woods beyond are ancient features, and typical of Hampshire chalk downland landscape. The isolated farm on the left is probably of post-enclosure, eighteenth- to nineteenth-century origin

church was rebuilt by a medieval wool merchant; that line of hedges marks a boundary that was set out centuries before the Roman invasion of Britain; this clump of trees was planted as part of a Georgian landscape park.

If you are happy with understanding what is around you as just a pretty picture, then academic research is not worth funding, and you will take home with you a sentimental, slushy and ultimately conservative and reactionary view of the landscape. Public debate will be impoverished by ignorance and stereotypes. If on the other hand you want to know about the historical and cultural processes that created what you are looking at, you will understand the worth and value of academic research. Understanding those processes may in part be sheer intellectual curiosity, but you will also come to a more positive, more informed, more liberal, more inclusive and ultimately more humane understanding of what it means to be English or British in the world today.

Bibliography

BBC (2008), 'Stonehenge – The Healing Stones', http://www.bbc.co.uk/history/ programmes/stonehenge/ [accessed 18 July 2010].

Bender, B. (1998), *Stonehenge: Making Space*, Oxford: Berg.

Bender, B. and Winer, M. (eds) (2001), *Contested Landscapes: Movement, Exile and Place*, Oxford: Berg.

Crawford, O.G.S. (1953), *Archaeology in the Field*, London: Phoenix House.

Community Landscape & Archaeology Project (2010), 'Local People: Local Past', http://www.olioweb.me.uk/clasp/LOCAL/ [accessed 18 July 2010].

de Selincourt, E. (ed.) (1906), *Wordsworth's Guide to the Lakes: The Fifth Edition*, Oxford: Oxford University Press.

Hoskins, W.G. (1954a), *Devon*, London: Collins.

Hoskins, W.G. (1954b), 'The anatomy of the English countryside: 1. The anatomy of the English countryside; 2. A hand-made world; 3. The road between; 4. The house through the trees', *Listener*, LI: 732–4, 772–4, 819–20, 864–6, 917–8.

Hoskins, W.G. (1955), *The Making of the English Landscape*, London: Hodder and Stoughton.

Hoskins, W.G. (1977), *The Making of the English Landscape*, new edition, London: Hodder and Stoughton.

Hoskins, W.G. (1978), *One Man's England*, London: BBC.

Johnson, M. (2007), *Ideas of Landscape*, Oxford: Blackwell.

Jones, R. and Page, M. (2006), *Medieval Villages in an English Landscape: Beginnings and Ends*, Macclesfield: Windgather Press.

Lowenthal, D. (1994), 'European and English landscapes as national symbols', in D. Hooson (ed.), *Geography and National Identity*, Oxford: Blackwell, 15–38.

Major, J. (1993), Speech to Conservative Group for Europe, 22 April, http://news. bbc.co.uk/news/vote2001/hi/english/features/newsid_1362000/1362285.stm [accessed 13 July 2010].

Pevsner, N. (1956), *The Englishness of English Art: An Expanded and Annotated Version of the Reith Lectures Broadcast in October and November 1955*, London: Architectural Press.

Pevsner, N. (2002), *Pevsner on Art and Architecture: The Radio Talks*, London: Methuen.

Rippon, S. (2007), 'Historic landscape characterisation: its role in contemporary British archaeology and landscape history', *Landscapes*, 8: 2: 1–14.

Shoard, M. (1999), *A Right to Roam*, Oxford: Oxford University Press.

Sinfield, A. (1989), *Literature, Politics and Culture in Post-War Britain*, Oxford: Blackwell.

Ucko, P. and Layton, R. H. (eds) (1999), *The Archaeology and Anthropology of Landscape: Shaping Your Landscape*, London: Routledge.

Williams, E. (1944), *Capitalism and Slavery*, Chapel Hill, NC: University of North Carolina Press.

Williams, R. (1973), *The Country and the City*, London: Chatto and Windus.

Williamson, T. (2003), *Shaping Medieval Landscapes: Settlement, Society, Environment*, Macclesfield: Windgather Press.

Williamson, T. and Bellamy, L. (1987), *Property and Landscape: A Social History of the English Countryside*, London: Allen.

10. Accidental Haiku, or Encouragement, Enlightenment and Raising Aspiration

Catherine Leyshon (University of Exeter)

In a classroom full of excited seven-year-olds, a sudden interest in haiku is stimulated when a child reads a three-line acrostic poem which, by chance, is just a couple of syllables shy of the magic five-seven-five formation. Thinking on her feet, the researcher quickly explains what haiku is, and everyone starts talking about it and counting their syllables. When someone's poem is shown to have the right combination of lines and syllables, a powerful sense of triumph and achievement animates the children. Does it diminish the art of haiku if a simple explanation of it encourages a group of schoolchildren to search in their own poems for this distinctive way of capturing nature, space, place, feelings and mood? Not when it means that new eagerness to create meaning about landscapes is sparked.

In this essay, I make a case for arts and humanities research that encourages, enlightens and raises aspiration. But who are the beneficiaries of such outcomes? This essay begins from the premise that the traffic is two-way: this is not only a question of what we as academics can do to make a difference to contemporary life, but how we can learn to listen better to what people *want us to do* to identify and take the lead on questions of national and international importance. In this way we can all be motivated and inspired to try harder to understand the world. This requires us to be adaptable, to think on our feet and remember that the complexity of everyday life cannot be captured by a single discipline. When the accidental haiku was made, the researcher thinking on their feet in the classroom of seven-year-olds was a geographer who, through their own interdisciplinary background and by working with a scholar from literary studies, was able to listen to, energize and invigorate the group.

This essay will focus for the most part on a project I coordinated entitled 'Understanding Landscape', which involved writers of all ages and academics from a wide variety of disciplines, to show how a group of writers and academics became involved in producing knowledge together. The Understanding Landscape project was led by academics from geography and English literature. It combined geography's traditional concern with landscape and literature's concern with text. It sought to understand the place of landscape in creative writing and explore the potential for interdisciplinary research. Before I talk about this project, let me first try to explain why I think place and landscape matter as part of people's culture and everyday lives.

Culture is everywhere

Every part of our everyday lives is saturated with the stuff of arts and humanities research, whether we realize it or not. Our every waking moment is filled with objects, people, places, memories, landscapes and ideas that make us who we are. Some of them reach back into the distant past (you could find yourself walking your dog across the rippling furrows of a medieval field system in Warwickshire), some of them are very much in the now (you enjoy the surroundings of a modern extension to an art gallery) and some are a curious mixture of the two (as you listen to Beethoven on your iPod).

As a human geographer, I am most interested in making sense of the many ways in which people use history, memory, place and landscape to forge a sense of belonging. In 1976 a geographer named Ted Relph wrote that 'to be human is to live in a world that is filled with significant places' (Relph 1976: 1). He was trying to call attention to the ways in which human beings identify what he called 'sense of place'. At the most basic level this refers to the ability to recognize different places and different identities of a place or the unique combination of architecture, topography, flora and fauna, culture, social life and landscape that makes places different from each other and gives them an inimitable character. Relph recognized the profoundly human emotional attachments that people form to places and attempted to show how very personal and individual factors make a difference to people's sense of place. Some geographers would argue that defining a sense of place is more about finding our own identities than anything else. To explain this point, the geographer Nigel Thrift has argued that places 'form a reservoir of meanings which people can draw upon to tell stories about and thereby define themselves' (Thrift 1997: 160). In other words, our sense of place helps us to define who we are and what we think is important. This undoubtedly shapes the way we interact with each other and the world.

One of the most important ways in which a sense of place is created and communicated is through landscape and its representation in words (for example, through poetry, and fictional and non-fictional writing), visual art of all kinds (from fine art, through to postcards, prints, book jackets or posters) and the media (including magazines, television, film and radio). The word 'landscape' is used rather glibly in the English language in a way that ignores its very specific meanings. It often gets conflated with words like region, area, nature, place, scenery (particularly the countryside), topography or environment. Landscape is more often used to refer to a portion of the earth visible by an observer from a particular position or location, and especially that which can be seen in a single view. But landscape is much more than this. Seeing a landscape always involves having an imaginative response to it — whether we are standing in an art gallery, looking at something on television or gazing out over the countryside from a hilltop. This imaginative factor helps to explain why different people have such different responses to places and landscapes. As a geographer I have been working with these ideas for a long time, but it was only when I started to explore interdisciplinary links with a lecturer in the English Department that I realized that I didn't clearly understand how people use landscape in their creative writing and how their creative writing formed an important part of who they are. Of course, as an avid reader of novels, I have seen how important landscapes and places are to stories like Graham Swift's *Waterland* in which the landscape of the Fens is critical to the development of plot and character, or Charlotte Brontë's *Jane Eyre*. But despite publishing scholarly articles on landscape for fifteen years, I had never had the opportunity to speak to authors about their writing. Equally, research in English literature often focuses on the analysis of the finished novel rather than conversations with the writers about their craft. From my conversations with my colleague arose the Understanding Landscape project, in which we attempted to find out how writers of all ages were developing their sense of place through their own creative writing.

Understanding landscape

In our project, we wanted to get inside the writing process rather than doing what a lot of academics do, which is to just study the finished novel. We wanted to ask writers how and why they write, where they do their writing, what sorts of stories they liked to tell, whether they appear in their own stories (perhaps as themselves or as other characters), how important place is to their stories and how they write about landscape. We were also interested in the nature of inspiration. Where does it come from? How does it happen? How does a writer capture it and then work it into their writing? We wanted to try to glimpse not only inspiration, and hear about the work of drafting and redrafting, but learn about all the messiness in between, including the possibility that the story is never finished and lies in a drawer somewhere. We were curious about how writers respond to existing literary conventions and how they use or perhaps avoid using them.

The project was based in Cornwall, a landscape that has often been written about in a very specific ways over the years, building up a set of specific images – high cliffs, wild seas, sandy beaches, fishing villages – which can almost be plucked straight off the shelf. We need only think of Winston Graham's *Poldark* novels as an example. In light of this, we wanted to ask writers how they managed to write in a place that had already been written about a great deal but was paradoxically still very popular with writers. Finally, we were interested in whether we could find some new approaches to understanding landscape and working with writers that combined the different academic disciplines with lay and non-academic interpretations. All this meant that we were not really interested in published fiction or even writing that was finished. Contrary to Daphne Du Maurier's assertion that writers should be read and not seen or heard, we were interested in talking to writers about their writing and reading some of their work, whether finished or not. In sum, we were interested in the imaginative processes of summoning landscape into being through the creative medium of fictional writing.

The project involved thirty writers, aged from seven to over seventy, and the value of the Understanding Landscape project to the participants (non-academics and academics) was both tangible and intangible. We made a difference to contemporary life by affirming to individuals the importance of their writing and creative effort in their own lives, and in their communities of practice. We were in turn affirmed by their response and willingness to participate. In the next section I sketch out some of our experiences during the research.

Events

The project centred on engaging writers through a number of events which included walking through different landscapes including coast and woodland, taking boat trips and working in classrooms to seek out and understand the writers' spaces of inspiration. We developed a set of questions for use in informal interviews to structure the conversations we would have. Our first event was with students from a local further education college and took the form of a walk and discussion at Porthcurno beach with three female A-level students (two were seventeen years old and one was nineteen years old) from the college and their tutor.[1]

We walked from the car park at Porthcurno up the cliff path to a spot beyond the Minack Theatre, with wide views of the sea and beach. Each student had been writing since they were very young and produced a mixture of stories and poetry mostly as a hobby, though they each had aspirations to have their work published. They clearly noted the place of landscape in their writing, pointing to its importance as a setting for action, or as a indicator of mood and emotion. These were often fictitious landscapes, and they rarely found themselves incorporating what they understood to be real landscapes in their work. Much of the discussion centred on the extent to which Cornwall was 'overwritten' by which they meant that their attempts to write about Cornwall were frustrated by the sheer quantity of imagery that already exists.

These themes were also picked up in our second event with three adult writers from the Writing Centre, a local resource for creative writers. One male and two female writers volunteered for the walk along a section of the Cornish coast path near Falmouth. Our volunteers were a fifty-six-year-old woman pursuing a PhD in creative writing whose work she described as life writing; a thirty-four-year-old male novelist who described his occupation as 'literary practitioner' because he uses his knowledge of writing and literature to support others through the Writing Centre; and a forty-year-old woman, professionally employed, who writes poetry, musings and fiction in her spare time. Unlike the young people, this group of adults had not been writing very long – about ten years – but all identified literature as an important part of their adult lives. These writers were either unpublished and wrote purely for pleasure or had been published in small local pamphlets or collections.

Much of the discussion centred on the meaning of craft in writing, exploring in particular how literary conventions inform the direction a piece of writing takes. We talked extensively about the importance of the notebook as a tool for writers to jot down thoughts and ideas on the spot, noting particularly that the male writer's book was a multifunctional tool with many different sections of coloured paper. We discussed the place of the notebook in the creative process, and talked about how it provides access to thoughts and ideas that are at risk of being lost. The notebooks prompted many interesting questions about the nature of inspiration and the way landscape forms part of the writing process. None of the writers did any significant amount of writing outdoors, but returned to their desks and studies to produce the finished piece, working through several drafts as they did so. We also discussed the extent to which aspects of themselves appear in their writing. The writer who produced life writing called attention to a distinction between work which is semi-autobiographical and that which is reflective, rejecting the former as a description of her own output. She preferred to think of her work as outward looking.

Later we also caught up with another member of the Writing Centre, a forty-nine-year-old working with a local theatre group who started writing letters home when she lived abroad and now writes short stories. During our walk with her in a woodland near Falmouth we discussed the way in which foreign landscapes initially provided the inspiration for writing. Standing looking out over a still quarry pond shaded by trees, we talked about the temptation to respond to landscape through conventional narrative forms (in which, for example, a quarry pond becomes the site of a mysterious event). Finally, we explored the place of the self in writing, focusing on the example of a local writer who used writing to manage and understand her grief after the sudden death of her partner.

Upon meeting the writers of the Truro Writers' Group for a walk along a river near Truro, one of the group declared, 'We're Cornish! We possess the landscape.' This set the tone of the discussion which continued over lunch and at a later meeting of the group in Truro. Apart from one twenty-year-old female member who worked at a riding stable, the group is composed of retired people who write for pleasure and who speak in a humble and modest way about their writing. They share their writing with the group but once a year produce an anthology of their best writing, which is self-published. Of the retired people, three women described themselves as sixty-plus and the four men ranged in age from fifty-five to over seventy. They wrote an eclectic mixture of poetry and short stories with historical and contemporary themes. In discussion with this group, who shared the writing that was produced as a result of the walk, several interesting themes emerged. One member, a man of fifty-five with strongly held religious beliefs, asserted that 'being in this landscape [along the river] feeds something in the soul. It feeds the soul being in the hills'. Exploring the issue of how aspects of the self emerge in creative writing, the same writer noted that 'things that fascinate you about life fascinate you in your writing'. Another male member of the group admitted that his writing, which often featured roguish characters in historical contexts, gave him the 'freedom that we all want to have but can't have'. Another member of the group who suffered a serious head injury several years ago suggested that putting his feelings and experiences into words reduced the sense of isolation he felt as a result of his injuries. Working with this group of writers also gave us insights into how generic forms are subverted or resisted in their writing. They would take conventional situations and use the very everydayness of the setting as a counterpoint to an unexpected twist in the tale.

Working in collaboration with Sense of Place, a curriculum development organization, we organized three events with local schools. This collaboration was highly significant in the research, giving us the basis of a comparative approach with the creative endeavours of young people and adult writers. The events – two boat trips and a woodland walk – gave the curriculum new relevance and excitement for staff and students alike.

During two boat trips on the Fal with pupils from two different schools we noted the influence of fairy tales and fantasy on the children's imaginations. There was also a significant gendered element with girls inventing stories with fairies, goblins and plenty of fantasy, and boys inventing stories about treasure and pirates. All the children understood the concept of landscape or setting being important to the action. One boy of seven said, perceptively, 'you have to have action to stimulate the reader'. Notwithstanding this observation, the children sometimes found it hard to think of a story that could take place in the familiar surroundings of the river Fal. One boy of eight said that he was of the view that books like *Harry Potter* and magic stories belonged in 'far away places'. Another boy of seven identified an island that does not appear on any map as somewhere that an adventure would happen involving maps, clues and buried treasure. When he was asked if that kind of adventure could happen in Cornwall, he said no because there were too many people around! Asking children, in terms they can understand, how they work out aspects of themselves in their writing is quite tricky, but elicited interesting responses. One boy told us that he had used his creative writing to work out what to do if he was being bullied.

Pupils from one of these schools followed up their boat trip by a classroom session and a performance of choral poetry inspired by the trip. In the classroom session, three groups of pupils were interviewed. The children had been instructed by their teacher to think about how to convey a sense of place through sound, so their parents or others reading the poems could imagine what it was like to be on the river or in Falmouth town. The children therefore focused on onomatopoeia ('sound effect' words such as 'splash' and 'slip'), alliteration (words beginning with the same sound) and dramatic imagery (e.g. 'houses looking like they would tumble into the water'). In the choral performance, the children read their poems out loud, using various effects, e.g. varying the volume of their voices, switching from speaking in groups to individuals and exaggerating sounds such as using sibilance ('ssss' and 'ssssh' sounds) for added effect, to convey the sense of landscape. The performances ranged from self-assured to shy, but all were extremely creative! Both the classroom session and the choral performance suggested the ways in which even child writers are socialized into understanding the conventions of literary form in depicting landscape, demonstrating the way in which the creative process interacts with conventional expectations from a young age.

Our final event with school children entailed a walk through woodland near Falmouth with pupils aged 7–10. Unlike the previous events with children, this outing was not a formal part of a curriculum unit organized by Sense of Place. Instead, with the help of the head teacher, we developed a new group exercise to be used along with the existing interview schedule. This group exercise, conducted as we sat on the river quay on the edge of the woods, entailed choosing five words of phrases that described what the children had seen on their walk in the wood, followed by five words or phrases that described what they could feel, hear and smell. They were also asked to touch things like rocks, shells, sand, wood, trees, bark and plants. In small groups they were asked to plan a story. They had to decide who their characters would be, what they would be like and what would happen to them. They were also asked to think about whether place was important to the story. This produced some intriguing plans which once again tended to be derived from popular fairy tales or magical stories (in particular *Harry Potter*, *The Lord of the Rings* and *Pirates of the Caribbean*).

Raising our game

A key argument of this essay is that academics should always be open to the possibility that their assumptions will be challenged. This can happen in many ways, for instance through new and interesting conversations across traditional disciplinary divides, but equally much can be achieved by bringing together academics and research volunteers from the public.

In the Understanding Landscape project, we introduced adult writers and academics to each other at a workshop in which writers showed us that we have far to go in understanding the creative process. The aim of this event was to bring together academics and the writers with whom we had worked in our writers' events. Several adult writers from our groups of research volunteers attended, as did a representative from a group of poets in Somerset.

The session was organized around small group discussions. Each group contained a mixture of academics and writers who discussed a series of themes that resonated with the broad themes that we believe are central to the understanding of landscape through the creative writing process:

1. Creative processes, e.g. where does inspiration come from? Does inspiration come from the landscape and place that you find yourself in or the opportunity to reflect and contemplate in a quiet place? Does the notebook become the source of information and inspiration later on in the writing process? What literary forms does your writing take? Do some forms require more drafting or 'processing' than others?
2. Influence of landscape and place, e.g. is place and setting important to the plot or characters or action of a piece of writing? How is place invoked? How does a place work its way into your writing? Do you have a preconceived notion of place before you come to write about it? If so, where does this come from? Do you find yourself inadvertently writing in a particular style or drawing on popular motifs or metaphors in your writing (e.g. Cornwall as a wild place)?
3. Auto-ethnography, e.g. how do aspects of yourself or your life experience enter your writing? Do you sometimes write accounts which deal with some aspect of your own life but which are fictionalized? Have you ever tried to write about writing?
4. Methodology, e.g. what methods are effective in understanding more about how writers write, the influence of landscape and place and the creative process? How do we understand the process by which established or canonical writers write? What can practising creative writers teach us about this process?

The small group discussion produced a lively debate on the nature of inspiration vis-à-vis landscape. This discussion was intriguing for the geographers present as these issues had not been fully thought through in that discipline. We saw the potential for a lay understanding to change thinking within an academic discipline. There was also a debate about the socially constructed nature of landscape which explored the notion that our view of landscape is not natural, elemental or organic but a product of social milieu and context. Although this was an argument familiar to geographers, academics from other disciplines felt that this discussion gave them significant new insights into how landscape forms part of social identity. Debates moved on to the purpose or role of the notebook as a means of somehow capturing the moment of inspiration in the landscape, with responses ranging from a negative view of notebooks as they act as a lightning conductor, stripping the 'flash' of inspiration of its power, to those who noted that notebooks helped fallible memories to work! There was some recognition and concern that language is a very limiting mode of expression. Some writers argued that language keeps writers separate from the essence of what is seen and felt. This affirmed our interest in focusing on the joint importance of both the text and the writing process.

Finally, the discussion turned to the question of how academics could usefully research writers and their practices. It was suggested that a sustained and long-term engagement between academics and writers would yield a better understanding of the nuances, complexities and contradictions of the writing process. However, the writers argued that they might not welcome such scrutiny because, if the creative process is laid bare, the mystique of it would be lost and they might not be able to capture it again. We knew little about the creative process when we started the research, but our writers made us ask new, more searching questions about what goes on in a writer's head, in their craft, on the piece of paper. We wanted to talk about the creative process with our writers, but they were often reluctant to put into words a process that eluded explanation, for fear of diminishing it. We quickly realized that each individual has a set of rituals that attend their writing that they did not want to disclose. This forces us to think more carefully about whether traditional research methods are appropriate or if methodological innovation will help academics and research volunteers to communicate better.

Thus, as writers humbled us as academics, and challenged our claims to knowledge, our aspirations were raised and we thought more carefully about the questions we needed to ask. We sought to make a space for our research volunteers, allowing them to make knowledge about themselves, challenging and perhaps overturning our scholarly expectations about identity, place, meaning and belonging in the process. Having created a safe and respectful research environment in which writers were encouraged to talk about and practise their writing, we were rewarded with rich textual and sometimes very private accounts. These demonstrated to us a heightened awareness of sense of place, and a clearly articulated sense of belonging.

The lifecycle of ideas

The commitment to research that is relevant and interesting for lots of people and not just the scholarly community has changed the lifecycle of ideas. In the past this lifecycle might have been characterized by research which was developed in an academic department and disseminated to other academics through conferences and scholarly publications. It is easy to imagine that academics have the monopoly on producing ideas for research that are funded by organizations like the Arts & Humanities Research Council. But shifts in the way that research funding is distributed and accounted for have rightly encouraged a change in this lifecycle. It is increasingly the case that ideas are developed collaboratively in partnership between universities, voluntary organizations, charitable trusts, government and businesses. If the stuff of arts and humanities research can be found in every aspect of everyday life, as I argue above, it would be counter-intuitive for ideas to emerge only from one group of people working in universities and for the results to be useful only to academic audiences.

Our collaboration with the curriculum development organization, Sense of Place, helped us to assess our expectations of working with children and also ensured that the research was embedded in part of the curriculum. We were encouraged to use a recently developed curriculum module on rivers, designed to help the exploration of different writing styles by children, as a vehicle for our contact with children. This approach enabled us to work collaboratively with school teachers rather than making new demands on their time and resources. We also benefited from an insight into how the literacy curriculum develops in children an understanding of generic forms such as fairy tale and fantasy. The teaching of generic forms and conventions quickly seeps into children's understanding of writing as a craft. In one school we took a slightly different approach, where the head teacher identified children to take part in the research from the gifted and talented programme for literacy from across three-year group in the school. In both cases, the input of experts changed the design and conduct of the research in positive ways. It also emphasized to us how collaborative research has the power to enable the participants and researchers to share ideas, negotiate different styles of research, choose spaces of encounter and facilitate change that makes a positive contribution to the lives of those involved.

Crucial to my argument is that the Understanding Landscape project enhanced the lives of the researchers as well as the research volunteers who took part. You might ask whether a project of this scale – just a year long with thirty writers – is significant enough to make a difference. In response I would point to the many projects of this scale which cumulatively result in new exhibitions, displays and performances, and thereby get people involved in thinking, learning and talking about the complexities of modern life and their place in it.

Although the Understanding Landscape project was small and relatively localized, it speaks to much greater concerns of the twenty-first century, because having a sense of place contributes to belonging, identity and citizenship. However, people's attachment to and understanding of different landscapes is not always easy to tease out through methods that treat people as subjects of research rather than co-producers of knowledge. Scholars in the arts and humanities have the methodological and conceptual tools to encounter, engage and inspire people but will not succeed in this unless there is a lifecycle of ideas in which dialogue and exchange between academics and others is paramount. The project highlights some important lessons about what a collaborative and inclusive relationship between people in research can achieve. But we must constantly evolve, whilst both managing and meeting people's expectations of what we can achieve together. In sum, in order to produce more innovative and meaningful research of value to the wider community, we must be alive to the possibilities that emerge from the conversations that we have along the way – including accidental haiku.

Note

1   Names have not been used to preserve anonymity.

Bibliography

Relph, E. (1976), *Place and Placelessness*, London: Pion.

Thrift, N. (1997), '"Us" and "Them": Re-imagining Places, Re-imagining Identity', in H. Mackay (ed.), *Consumption and Everyday Life*, London: Sage.

11. Thinking about Architecture

Iain Borden (University College London)

Architecture is, like all areas of the arts and humanities, a complex affair, and involves a very wide range of people and personalities, ideas and philosophies, theories and actions. But, more than any other artistic endeavour, architecture is also an inherently interdisciplinary and multidisciplinary practice, and is inextricably linked to our everyday world of business, work, leisure, health, environment and social life. We can do almost nothing in our lives without encountering architecture, whether as offices, housing, hotels, sports facilities, hospitals, train and bus stations, or architecture in drawings, films and video-games, or architecture as part of the hidden world of communications and virtual technologies. For this reason, the UK's research into architecture must – and does – deal with a wide spectrum of concerns, all of which have the potential to impact directly on our lives today.

Architecture and architects

Architecture is perhaps most often thought of as being the product of architects – that is as the product of a single person or of small groups of people, and of their thoughts, designs and actions. One of the most important areas of architectural research is, therefore, into who these figures were in the past, and who they are now and in the future. Who is 'the architect' and what does he, she or they do? (Saint Andrew 1993; Hughes 1996; Kostof 1987). There are, of course, many important architects in the UK who have made a major contribution to our society and cities. From Christopher Wren in the seventeenth century and John Soane in the eighteenth century through to Zaha Hadid and Norman Foster today, architects have used their considerable artistic imagination, technical innovation and entrepreneurship to produce some of the most significant and lasting constructions in the contemporary world. These are important figures to understand, not only in terms of themselves but also in terms of how their ideas and designs have reached out far beyond their own buildings and have had a pervasive influence throughout the world of art, design and the creative industries. Much of what we see and understand as 'architecture' in the world today is because of a relatively few number of architectural designers and thinkers, and, as a result, we need to record and explore this important historical and cultural legacy.

The more detailed results of this research are, however, frequently quite surprising, for they tell us that 'the architect' is, very often, not a single kind of person at all. Such research reveals, instead, that an architect might be a builder, a developer or a technician, or that an architect might be an artist, a sculptor, a writer. Or that they might have come from different kinds of background, whether the son of working-class parents (like Soane and Foster) or the daughter of aristocrats (like Hadid). This kind of research demonstrates, then, that our architects are not just one sort of person, and that anyone has the potential to produce and create architecture. Anyone, given the right education and training, may contribute to the design and construction of the physical world around them.

Even more tellingly, research into architects and what they actually do shows that the 'architect', rather than being an individual working solely on their own, as is so often thought to be the case, is very frequently the leader or figurehead for a much larger group of people. Or the architect is revealed as being part of a much more complex interdisciplinary team of not only architects but also engineers, planners, environmental consultants and financiers. As a consequence, this kind of research shows that there is no single way to design and produce architecture, and that many of the most prevalent forms of building design and construction in the UK today are – although perfectly rational and appropriate for their specific context – not necessarily appropriate for all buildings, in all cities and at all moments in history. Instead, this kind of architectural research shows how the design team may be formulated from different forms of contract, management and organization – such as one research project, funded by the Arts & Humanities Research Council (AHRC), on the systemization of design practices (Julier 2007), or the 'VivaCity 2020' research into how key decisions are made with regard to urban sustainability (VivaCity 2020 2010). It can also show the possibilities for different kinds of operation of the building site, for the supply of materials and for ways to extract maximum economic value from a particular building or type of construction. This kind of architectural research thus has an immediate impact on the way in which the construction and creative industries work together in the UK, leading not only to new economic efficiencies but also to new ways of creating and designing in collaborative and team-based contexts.

There is even the possibility that we do not need architects at all. After all, several research studies have shown that many of the greatest medieval cathedrals and some of the most successful contemporary housing developments have been produced entirely without the presence of anyone who might be readily equated with the figure that we traditionally understand to be an 'architect' (Rudofsky 1987). Our present-day creation of architecture has much to learn from such seemingly radical scenarios.

Buildings and design

In many ways, however, it is of little or no concern to our life in the UK if a professionally qualified architect is involved or not in the design and creation of architecture. For wider society, what matters much more than the presence of an architect is the *quality* of the actual buildings that are produced, and how these buildings impact upon all of us. As one prominent client has put it, 'All buildings are capable of good design. Good architecture should not just be reserved for signature buildings' (Loe 2000: 30). But how do we measure this quality of 'good design'? How do we know what is a good building and how do we understand its degree (or occasional lack) of success? How, we might ask, do all kinds of buildings – from housing to art galleries, from hospitals to sports stadia – contribute to the well-being and sustainability of our communities?

Writing in the first century BC, the Roman architect and theorist Vitruvius famously asserted that good architecture should have the three qualities of *firmitas*, *utilitas* and *venustas* (firmness, commodity and delight). In many ways, this trio still holds up well today, and it bears a brief explication here in the context of the value of architectural research.

Firmitas, or firmness, refers to how well a building is constructed, and to technical aspects of architecture such as structure and how a building 'stands up'. Much architectural research is then directly concerned with this essential quality, looking not only at the safety aspects of a building's construction and eventual operation (such as possible risks in housing from over-exposure to carbon monoxide) (Croxford 2010), but with how different materials are used (one AHRC-funded project shows how recycled glass can be utilized as a new building material, with considerable economic as well as environmental benefits) (Roddis 1999), or at how different kinds of structure (columns, domes, arches, vaults, grid-shells, etc.) allow for different kinds of enclosure and spaces to be created. Much important architectural research is also concerned with the more environmental conditions of building design, investigating how architecture lets in light, or how it controls sound, air and heat. In addition, given that buildings are currently responsible for approximately 40 per cent of the UK's carbon emissions (Carbon Trust 2010), this research has increasingly focused on maximizing the energy performance of buildings, whether through technological advances or through changing the way users inhabit and control their buildings (such as research into why building users choose to incorporate air conditioning) (Young 2004).

It is no good, of course, if a building stands up and has an adequate environmental and energy performance if it still does not meet our human requirements. Research into what Vitruvius called *utilitas*, or commodity, therefore enquires into the functional and social performance of a building. Does, for example, a hospital adequately meet the various and complex demands of its medical staff and patients? Do our museums meet the widely differing needs of their various groups of visitors? Is our aged housing stock, much of it over 100 years old, appropriate to the rapidly changing profile of our population? As one study has argued, 'Good design in itself does not guarantee sustainability within an urban context unless, over time, adaptability is inherent within the design' (Loe 2000: 35). For example, one piece of award-winning AHRC-funded research, called 'Flexible Housing', used over 150 historical examples to investigate ways of adapting housing to different uses and technologies over time, with the potential to considerably increase the annual rental income and reduce maintenance costs in the UK's Registered Social Landlord (RSL) sector (Till 2004). This kind of architectural research crosses the boundaries between the economic, technical and social aspects of architecture, and, given the interdisciplinary and multidisciplinary nature of architecture, shows how we cannot look at one without the others. It shows how buildings must certainly meet our needs in terms of the quantity of space and equipment, but they must also be of the right *kind* and *quality* in order to properly address our various social requirements and cultural predilections.

This is also where Vitruvius' third category comes in, that of *venustas* or delight. Very often, this kind of research is treated simply as a matter of aesthetics, and asks questions as to whether a building appears to be beautiful, or of how it fits in with the rest of its surroundings. But architectural research is generally much more ambitious than this, and shows how aesthetics is in fact about far more than what a building looks like, about how it appears to the eye. Rather, architecture can 'delight' in a great number of different ways, such as by representing ideas (the democracy of parliament, the justice of law courts), history (the commemoration of famous events and people), memories (the marking of local and personal traces), cities (the spectacular iconic buildings that make many of our great cities immediately recognizable) and communities (providing places of focus and inspiration for different peoples and groups). This is the kind of architectural research and innovation that, as the Royal Institute of British Architects (RIBA) has put it, 'transforms the demands of economic production and control into a vision of art that the spirit can respond to' (Loe 2000: 28). Thousands of books, articles, exhibitions, film documentaries, television and radio programmes are produced every year on these kinds of artistic and cultural questions, and which do a great deal to help raise our understanding of architecture in the context of UK arts of humanities.

Despite this impressive range of research activity, it is worth stressing here that much architectural research is not just a study *about, of, upon* or *into* architecture (where architecture is the subject being studied). As many experts in architectural research have shown, architectural research can also be *for* architecture (where research is conducted in order to help with a specific design application or problem) and, in addition, it can also be conducted *through* architecture, where certain kinds of architectural practice can themselves be the vehicle for undertaking research (Rendell 2004: 141–7; Frayling 1993: 1–5). That is, in creating new buildings and other projects that reflect on, respond to and help to change our rapidly developing society – see, for example, the 'BedZed' eco-community initiative described below – architecture as a form of complex and inherently interdisciplinary and multidisciplinary practice is constantly asking new questions and finding new answers to some or our most pressing technical, environmental, social and cultural problems. Much of architecture is then not just the subject of research, it *is* research.

The everyday urban environment

So far I have considered mostly the kinds of buildings which if not always designed by architects are at least a conscious attempt at producing 'architecture' – that is, I have been concerned mostly with architecture as a deliberate creative act, where someone or some group has set out to change the world around them through a new building.

In recent years, however, there has been an ever-increasing interest in other forms of building, with the kind of architecture that is created almost accidentally, seemingly without any degree of deliberate intent. This kind of architectural research considers more ordinary forms of architecture, such as mass housing and street signs, or street markets and bus shelters. What is the value, this research asks, of all of the buildings and spaces in our communities today?

The answers are often obvious, and yet are also too often overlooked. For example, some research shows that everyday street markets are just as important – or indeed more so – to a local community than might be any number of designer-focused high-street boutiques. Similar research shows that art does not have to be placed within an art gallery to have a profound effect on people – buildings can have murals, sculpture on their facades and gardens outside that allow for all manner of artistic events (Rendell 2004). Or that playgrounds and other neighbourhood sports facilities can have a more immediate local impact than Wembley Stadium, or that a good and well-designed secondary school is more connected to the specific educational achievements and standards within a particular community than may be a new national museum hundreds of miles away. Conversely, this kind of architectural research can also show the terribly debilitating and negative impact that such things as vandalism, poorly maintained housing or even just inadequate street lighting can have upon the perceived safety of a local environment.

Research in these areas thus goes straight to the very heart of our local neighbourhoods and communities throughout the UK. It shows what matters to all of us as we go about our lives, and it shows what needs to be done in order to improve the quality of life. It is research which recognizes that 'architecture' can and does encompass all of the built environment, and thus is research which directly connects, which has an immediate value, which makes a difference to all parts of our cities.

Interaction with architecture

One of the problems faced by this kind of architectural research – that which is concerned with people's ordinary and everyday lives – is that simply identifying the different ways that architecture (whether architect-designed or not) connects with different people's lives is a hugely complex affair. For this reason, much architectural research is now concerned with one of the most central problems facing us today: namely, how do we all live in a way which, while recognizing and celebrating the many differences between us both as individuals and groups, also emphasizes the equally numerous things which many of us enjoy, share and participate in together?

To properly engage with this problem – and great opportunity – of cultural interaction, much new architectural research (some of it, for example, contained within the 'Cultures of Consumption' five-year research programme co-funded by the AHRC and the Economic and Social Research Council) is now recognizing that architecture and the built environment often mean different things to different people. This kind of research therefore looks into many of the various ways architecture can give inspiration, pride, memory and a sense of community to different people, whether through their substantive characteristics of gender, class, ethnicity, age, physicality and sexuality, or through more culturally diverse criteria as to whether one might be an opera, cinema or a football fanatic, a driver, walker or a skateboarder, or an aficionado of video-games, shopping or knitting.

All of these cultural characteristics make a difference, such that to all people, of whatever group or interest, the same piece of architecture will always mean something slightly different. It is therefore one of the tasks of architectural research to track and understand this difference. This, for example, has been the focus of some of my own personal and collaborative research into public perceptions of public space (Borden *et al.* 2001), while AHRC-funded projects have looked at such diverse subjects as how people are now meeting less and less in offices and more and more in informal places like coffee houses and transportation hubs (Coyne 2009), or at how the office workplace can be adapted in order to accommodate the increasing percentage of older people who are now contained within the workforce (Myerson 2006). Given that architecture often incorporates a whole range of differing cultural and aesthetic components, large-scale research initiatives are sometimes required in order to pursue this complexity, as for example with the AHRC Centre for the Study of the Domestic Interior. This centre has developed new histories of the home, its contents and representation, led research into the changing appearance and layout of rooms in a range of buildings, as well as explored the objects that furnish those rooms, the ways in which rooms and objects are depicted, the manner in which people use them and how they think about them.

Only through these kinds of investigation are we now beginning to understand, design and create truly modern twenty-first-century architecture – architecture which meets the needs not just of a few relatively affluent and privileged individuals, but of the various cultural interests, tastes and demands of all UK citizens.

The city context

As this last area of research suggests, architecture is about far more than just individual buildings or even important building types such as houses, schools or museums. We must also appreciate and understand the relevance of architecture on a much larger, urban scale. In particular, some of the most important architectural research is now concerned with how architecture can contribute to the development of cities and urban forms.

In many ways, this is a kind of larger scale version of Vitruvius' categories concerning technical performance, social amenity and aesthetics. But the stakes here are, if anything, even higher. Regarding technical performance, the key focus of research is that of sustainability, particularly environmental sustainability (such as arrangements for private and public transport), overall energy consumption patterns (for the construction, operation and eventual demolition of projects around the UK), and new technological inventions that can be prototyped and, for the first time, properly tested on a relatively large scale. For example, UK housing schemes such as 'BedZed' in south London (Beddington Zero Energy Development (BedZED 2010), the carbon-neutral eco-community developed by the Peabody Trust, Bill Dunster Architects and environmental consultants BioRegional Development Group), or, on an even greater scale, the ongoing development of Thames Gateway to the east of London, thus offer an unrepeatable opportunity to undertake true architecture-as-research on a scale and in a manner that is already having, and will continue to have, a major impact on the ways in which we think about and create new kinds of UK city living.

But just as important is research into the social and cultural sustainability of these kinds of new forms of urban forms. For, as with buildings, there is no point in creating something which functions technically if no one actually wants to live and work there. How, then, can we create new forms of urban design and local neighbourhoods which, while meeting the demands of energy, land use and construction costs, also create the same sense of rich culture, excitement and adventure that many of us experience in our major UK cities and cultural projects? This is why groups such as the Commission for Architecture and the Built Environment (CABE) have undertaken research on the value of cultural risk-taking in architecture and public space (Commission for Architecture and the Built Environment 2005b), and it is also why the Higher Education Funding Council for England recently funded the university-led 'Urban Buzz' project in order to help bring UK academic researchers and business partners together and so help bridge the knowledge gap that too often prevents the creation of truly thriving and vital sustainable communities (UCL and the University of East London 2010). As the government's 'Best Value Programme' made clear in 1998, projects like these are those which drive up service standards, which put 'the interests of local people, who both use and pay for environmental services, ahead of other vested interests' (Loe 2000). Architectural research here is changing not only architecture as buildings, but architecture as cities and urban design, and making our future places of work and living more sustainable both environmentally and socially.

Exploring cultural discourse

As I have already shown, architecture has a pervasive presence in our cities today in physical terms, creating new spaces, buildings and technologies that we all use on a daily basis. Architecture also has another role to play, this time in a more dispersed yet equally pervasive manner. This is architecture as it engages with the wider context of other creative arts, design practices and cultural activities. Research here thus enquires into the engagement between architecture and all manner of other cultural fields, such as art, film, photography, dance, literature and industrial design.

Some of this work is historical. For example, one substantial piece of AHRC-funded research has recently been undertaken by an architect turned filmmaker, exploring the landscapes of early films made in 1895–1905, taken from the National Film and Television Archive; it investigates ways in which the city has changed over the past century, and suggests a critique of present and possible future spatial experience (Keiller 2007). Other historical work deals with similar relations between architecture and painting, architecture and sculpture, architecture and music, or, in a more modern context, with how architecture and cities are represented in photography, video, retail design and other contemporary arts (Marcus and Neumann 2008). All of this helps us to understand our creative history in greater depth, and to appreciate the considerable artistic achievements that make up the UK's cultural heritage.

Other research work in this area is more focused on kinds of creative practice, and frequently explores the different ways in which creative producers might learn from each other, work with each other and so produce new forms of artistic and design expression. For example, the recent programme 'Designing for the 21st Century', jointly funded by the Engineering and Physical Sciences Research Council and the AHRC, has supported the development of design practice so that it can play its part in tackling the exigencies of modern world (Arts and Humanities Research Council and Engineering and Physical Sciences Research Council 2010). One component, 'Spatial Imagination', brought together practitioners and academics from such diverse fields as architecture, computer sciences, creative arts, electronics, engineering design, environmental consultancy, product design, management, graphic design, psychology and urban design in order to propose new uses for drawing, writing and modelling as ways of creating spatial design (Rawes 2006). Other projects in this initiative have looked at more technical intersections of the different arts, showing how our world of increasingly virtual-and-physical spaces and communications is creating new forms of artistic invention, from video-games and creative computer software, to mobile phone interfaces and websites. Outcomes of this kind of interdisciplinary architectural and design-based research have been considerable, and have enabled the proposition and creation of, *inter alia*, new human-technology interfaces, secure ways of parking bicycles in UK cities, tensioned fabric as a material for sculpturing architectural enclosures, and interior spaces that use visceral qualities of images, sounds, lighting and other sensory factors in order to help people to personalize their individual experiences.

Through this kind of research, architecture and all of the creative arts and industries are able to learn from each other. This leads both to new and inventive ways of working among creative professionals, and to new ways for all people to engage with the arts and humanities in the UK.

Architecture is made by everybody

As I have suggested above, despite the considerable and significant contributions made by architects and other professionals, as well as by academic architectural researchers, architecture is not just the product of these relatively limited groups of people. Rather, architecture is made by all of us, everyday of our lives – for every time that we use, look at, visualize or think about a building then we are in effect remaking that architecture again in our own context, according to our views and interests. How, then, can we understand this phenomenon, and what are the ramifications of it for architecture and our cities?

Hence we have the kinds of architectural research which, for example, investigate how different people use their senses of smell, taste, touch and motion as well as vision in order to make judgments about architecture and urban spaces (Sonne 2007), or how different kinds of road offer greater numbers of human encounters to pedestrians (Worpole 2000: 38). Or research which considers the different ways in which members of the public perceive and understand their places of work and other local buildings, or research which explores the different ways in which building users might engage and interact with architecture and cities in different ways. One AHRC-funded project, for example, has looked at how digital technology can help create more socially acceptable and democratic architectural environments, such as through the use of automated monitoring in care homes or ways to vote from home through SMS text-message technology (Weaver 2010).

This kind of architectural research has profound consequences for the design of buildings and cities, for it suggests that architects and other urban managers are neither the sole producers of, nor are solely responsible for, the buildings around us. It suggests instead that not only should the thoughts, fears and aspirations of local people, buildings users and other interest groups be taken fully into account in the planning and construction of architecture, but also that these self-same people might also have a greater role to play in the continuing life of buildings, that is in the way that buildings are used once they have been constructed, and how these uses might change and develop as our society also changes and develops. The 'Designing for the 21st Century' programme, for example, has included research into participatory design practices in the UK's Building Schools for the Future (BSF) initiative, leading to increased satisfaction and greater respect for the environment among schoolchildren (Woodcock 2010). This kind of architectural research suggests a much wider responsibility for both the creation and utilization of architecture, and, above all, shows how our buildings, through the whole of their useful life, might provide the maximum benefit to the widest possible sections of the community, from the moment of construction right through to the time of major refurbishment or demolition.

The value of architectural research

Clearly, architectural research is concerned with an extremely wide range of subjects and questions. As such, it rightly deals with some of most undeniably important and pressing issues facing us today, whether they are about environmental and social sustainability, about climate change and cultural interaction, or about the role of architects and other design professionals.

Architectural research therefore investigates new technologies that help meet the challenges of climate change, it suggests new kinds of buildings that meet changing new social needs and patterns, and it proposes new ways of working that help produce buildings more efficiently and in a manner that responds to the increasingly complex cultural makeup of our diverse and integrated community groups. Following research commissioned by CABE and the RIBA (Macmillan 2006; Commission for Architecture and the Built Environment 2005a; Loe 2000; Worpole 2000), we can then say that, as a result, architectural research in the UK makes a quantifiable and specific difference in five distinct areas:

1. *Economically* (exchange value), through increasing the market or book value of a building for the owner, or through increased profit and/or rents.
2. *Functionally* (use and business values), by helping to raise productivity, profitability and competitiveness, or by making environments that are safe and which promote staff health, well-being and job satisfaction.
3. *Professionally and creatively* (practice or process value), by finding new ways of working in architecture and design, either within the architectural profession itself, within the context of the construction process, or in relation to the wider context of the creative arts and industries.
4. *Environmentally* (environmental value), through a concern for intergenerational equity, bio-diversity, management of finite resources and climate change, and through immediate benefits to local health and pollution.
5. *Socially* (social value), by creating opportunities for positive interaction, identity and pride, encouraging social health, neighbourly behaviour, safety and security.

Yet architectural research also addresses still more than these five areas. This is because of the role that architecture itself has within society – whereby architecture does not just provide for our needs, or simply reflect what we already believe in, but actually challenges us to find new and improved ways in which we might all live together. To these five areas above, and still in part following CABE and the RIBA, we then can add two other areas in which architectural research in the UK makes a difference:

6. *Aesthetically* (image value), through a contribution to the identity, vision and reputation of groups, institutions, cities, companies, and individuals, or through ways in which we can express our varied ideas, ambitions and intentions.

7. *Culturally* (cultural value), by connecting with the local grain and heritage of cities, through a concern with location, context, patterns of historical development and a sense of place, and through a consideration of less tangible issues such as cultural symbolism, inspiration and social meanings.

There is one final thing to add. Given the extremely wide scope of these seven different kinds of value, it is clear that architectural research, while focusing on architecture and buildings, necessarily not only engages with but also makes new proposals for much wider aspects of our society, whether they are new and inventive ways of working, original and successful ways of meeting environmental challenges, or creating stimulating forms of cultural expression. Research is, after all, nothing if we do not in some way change ourselves as well as our buildings. The best architectural research, of which there is a great deal going on in the UK today, is therefore that which asks us to consider not only what we understand and undertake by way of architecture and buildings, but also who we think we are and how we want to reside, play and work together. Architectural research here speaks to the very heart of our contemporary society in the UK, and not only allows us to better appreciate and understand our cultural heritage, but also asks us to consider how we want to live today and in the future.

Bibliography

Arts and Humanities Research Council and Engineering and Physical Sciences Research Council (2010), 'Designing for the 21st Century', http://www.design21. dundee.ac.uk [accessed 13 July 2010].

BedZED (Beddington Zero Energy Development) (2010), http://www.peabody.org.uk [accessed 13 July 2010].

Borden, I., Rendell, J., Kerr, J. with Pivaro, A. (eds) (2001), *The Unknown City: Contesting Architecture and Social Space*, Cambridge, MA: MIT Press.

Carbon Trust (2010), http://www.carbontrust.co.uk [accessed 13 July 2010].

Commission for Architecture and the Built Environment (2005a), *Physical Capital: How Great Places Boost Public Value*, London: Commission for Architecture and the Built Environment.

Commission for Architecture and the Built Environment (2005b), *What Are We Scared Of? The Value of Risk in Designing Public Space*, London: Commission for Architecture and the Built Environment.

Coyne, R. (2009), 'Branded Meeting Places: Ubiquitous Technologies and the Design of Places for Meaningful Human Encounter', http://ace.caad.ed.ac.uk/NonPlace/ [accessed 13 July 2010].

Croxford, B. (2010), 'Carbon Monoxide Risk', http://www.bartlett.ucl.ac.uk/web/ben/ [accessed 13 July 2010].

Cultures of Consumption (2008), http://www.ahrc.ac.uk/FundedResearch/CaseStudies/Pages/consumption.aspx [accessed 13 July 2010].

Frayling, C. (1993), 'Research in Art and Design', *Royal College of Art Research Paper*, 1: 1: 1–5.

Hughes, F. (ed.) (1996), *The Architect: Reconstructing Her Practice*, Cambridge, MA: MIT Press.

Julier, G. (2007), 'Counting Creativity: Understanding the Systemization of Design Practices', http://www.lmu.ac.uk/as/artdesresearch/pdf/CountingCreativityReport.pdf [accessed 12 July 2010].

Keiller, P. (2007), 'The City of the Future', in A. Burton and L. Porter (eds), *Picture Perfect: Landscape, Place and Travel in British Cinema before 1930*, Exeter: Exeter University Press, 104–12, http://www.bftv.ac.uk/newslet/0304p3.htm [accessed 12 July 2010].

Kostof, S. (ed.) (1987), *The Architect: Chapters in the History of the Profession*, Oxford: Oxford University Press.

Loe, E. (2000), *The Value of Architecture: Context and Current Thinking*, London: RIBA Future Studies Group.

Macmillan, S. (2006), *The Value Handbook: Getting the Most from Your Buildings and Spaces*, London: Commission for Architecture and the Built Environment.

Marcus, A. and Neumann, D. (eds) (2008), *Visualizing the City*, London: Routledge.

Myerson, J. (2006), 'The Welcoming Workplace: Rethinking Office Design to Enable Growing Numbers of Older People to Participate in the 21st Century Knowledge Economy', http://www.ahrc.ac.uk/FundedResearch/Pages/ResearchDetail.aspx?id=121507 [accessed 13 July 2010].

Rawes, P. (2006), 'Spatial Imagination', http://www.spatialimagination.org.uk [accessed 13 July 2010].

Rendell, J. (2004), 'Architectural Research and Disciplinarity', *Architectural Research Quarterly*, 8: 2: 141–7.

Roddis, J. (1999), 'Open Loop Solutions for Recycled Glass: Translucent/Transparent Architectural Structures', http://www.ahrc.ac.uk/FundedResearch/CaseStudies/Pages/ttura.aspx [accessed 13 July 2010].

Royal College of Art, V&A and Royal Holloway University of London (2010), 'AHRC Centre for the Study of the Domestic Interior', http://www.rca.ac.uk/csdi [accessed 13 July 2010].

Rudofsky, B. (1987), *Architecture Without Architects: A Short Introduction to Non-Pedigreed Architecture*, Albuquerque, NM: New Mexico University Press.

Saint Andrew (1983), *The Image Of The Architect*, New Haven, CT: Yale University Press.

Sonne, W. (2007), 'Multimodal Representation of Urban Space', http://www.ahrc.ac.uk/FundedResearch/Pages/ResearchDetail.aspx?id=121409 [accessed 13 July 2010].

Till, J. (2004), 'The Past, Present and Future of Flexible Housing', http://www.ahrc.ac.uk/FundedResearch/CaseStudies/Pages/housing.aspx [accessed 13 July 2010].

UCL and the University of East London (2010), http://www.urbanbuzz.org [accessed 12 July 2010].

VivaCity 2020 (2010), 'VivaCity 2020 project', http://www.vivacity2020.eu [accessed 18 July 2010].

Weaver, L. (2010), 'Democratising Technology', http://www.design21.dundee. ac.uk/Phase2/Phase_2_projects/democratising_technology.htm [accessed 13 July 2010].

Woodcock, A. (2010), 'Realising Participatory Design with Children and Young People: a Case Study of Design and Refurbishment in Schools', in *Designing for the 21st Century: Interdisciplinary Methods & Findings*. London: Gower, http:// www.coventry.ac.uk/researchnet/d/699/a/6774 [accessed 13 July 2010].

Worpole, K. (2000), *The Value of Architecture: Design, Economy and the Architectural Imagination*, London: RIBA Future Studies Group.

Young, A. (2004), 'Domestic Air Conditioning: Occupant Use and Operational Efficiency', http://gow.epsrc.ac.uk/ViewGrant.aspx?GrantRef=GR/S45423/01 [accessed 13 July 2010].

12. 'All this Useless Beauty': The Hidden Value of Research in Art and Design

Mike Press (University of Dundee)

'What shall we do, what shall we do with all this useless beauty?'
(Elvis Costello, 'All this Useless Beauty')

The annual Morgan Stanley 'Great Briton' awards celebrated the highest achievements in the arts, business, sport, public life, and science and innovation. Each year three people were shortlisted for each of the awards. The 2007 shortlist for the Great Briton in Science and Innovation included a theoretical physicist from Imperial College, an international expert in the pathology of dinosaur bones and John McGhee, an Arts & Humanities Research Council-funded research student based in an art school. McGhee's digital animation research on 3D visualization strategies to improve disease understanding among patient groups has twice featured on BBC News and secured the front page of the *Guardian*'s education supplement on 30 October 2007.

When crop geneticists provided printmaker Elaine Shemilt with their DNA data, their expectation of the science-art project was that it would result in some striking decorative prints that would liven up the walls of their research institute. However, the resulting prints revealed to them the occurrence of new elements and data patterns that they had previously been unable to perceive. The prints led directly to a whole new research project examining gene progression in pathogens. Within the decorative patterns, new knowledge became visible.

With a background in craft-making and product design, Graham Whiteley brought a highly idiosyncratic approach to his doctoral research on prosthetic design. To begin with, the medical physics specialist who was part of the supervisory team saw dubious value in Graham's emphasis on life-drawing and model-making as his key research methods. Six years later, his research contributed to a new bionic arm and hand that has been hailed as one of the most significant breakthroughs in prosthetics.

We look to our art schools to produce great art and design, and the buoyant state of the UK's creative industries suggests that they are continuing to deliver. However, their recently emergent research culture is producing something else as well: unique contributions to science, technology and innovation in fields far removed from 'creative disciplines'. This chapter considers the 'hidden' value of research in art and design: its contribution to other specialist disciplines, to industrial competitiveness and innovation, and to social policy. In exploring this value we will venture from hospital wards to the suboceanic world; we will examine the role of designers in defining advanced manufacturing processes and the role of artists in scientific research; we will see how art and design researchers can contribute to crime prevention, prosthetic technologies and urban planning.

Necessarily, this chapter is highly selective in the examples that it draws upon, and does not claim to provide anything close to a comprehensive survey of current research practices. However, it seeks to highlight notable and representative exemplars of research that demonstrate the new, vibrant and highly relevant directions that art and design research is exploring. It is argued here that these creative disciplines provide unique skills and knowledge that can be usefully applied to diverse real world problems. In some cases researchers are using their unique skills of visualization to help specialists in other disciplines to reveal and communicate new knowledge. In other cases, it is the intimate and exploratory use of materials and process which lies at the heart of 'intelligent making' that is providing a new source of innovation. The new research culture is providing novel opportunities and frameworks for collaborative working which are encouraging artists and designers to cross boundaries. Furthermore, the UK now clearly leads the world in research-led art and design education. This is a unique competitive advantage which we must seek to build on and exploit further, and which will serve the UK well in addressing the economic, technological and social challenges that confronts it.

'A perfect place and a perfect education'

The emergence of research in art and design education in the UK is relatively recent, but has accelerated apace over the last decade and is now both redefining the nature and concerns of its constituent disciplines, thereby providing a distinctive identity for UK art and design education internationally. Most significantly, it is now beginning to demonstrate and assert its value as a unique source of knowledge that can be applied to a range of problem areas. This new research culture is a product of a peculiarly British Victorian invention: the art school.

From the 1830s art schools were established throughout the UK to train artists and designers for the needs of manufacturing industry. Each art school was geared to supplying for the specific needs of local manufacturers – whether it was ceramic painters in Stoke, jewellers in Birmingham or cutlery designers in Sheffield. While the art schools aimed to improve the competitiveness of British manufacturing through better design, the associated development of public museums and exhibitions – such as the National Gallery and the Victoria and Albert Museum – aimed to raise the aesthetic awareness of the British consumer. Through production and consumption, the UK would design its way to industrial pre-eminence. The art schools not only helped to create competitive well-designed products, but they also produced our culture – both 'high' and popular: the Apple iPod, the Beatles, Habitat, punk and the Dyson vacuum cleaner all have their creative roots in the British art school. The educational experience of UK art schools is unique. According to Kim Howells, former Minister of State at the Foreign and Commonwealth Office, and one of the leaders of the Hornsey College of Art sit-in of 1968, 'it was somewhere you just spent all your time: painting, arguing about why you liked David Hockney, learning how to weld. Looking back on it, it was a perfect time, a perfect place, and a perfect education' (Howells 2005).

The UK art school provides an environment that nurtures creativity, and emphasizes individual development and personal direction, within a subject of study. Practically focused project work within a studio setting is the main vehicle for learning, although there is some use made of 'conventional' lecture- and seminar-based methods. Until the early 1990s 'research' played at best a marginal role in the culture of the art school. Although there is a history of formal research in design and architecture, marked by the establishment of the Design Research Society in the 1960s, this had very little impact on the concerns and practices of those who taught in the art schools. However, as a recent report for the Arts & Humanities Research Council (AHRC) argued, all changed in 1992:

> Although many art schools became part of the Polytechnic system in the 1970s and developed CNAA degrees, most other disciplines in the Polytechnics already had one foot in the university sector and for them, arguably, the shift to university status in 1992 was not a fundamental challenge to the way that academics worked or perceived their roles. For Art and Design the period following 1992 has brought some dramatic changes and in many ways Art and Design can still be seen as emergent academic disciplines despite their long history. (Rust *et al.* 2007)

Over the last decade-and-a-half, the UK's art schools – now part of the university system – have been presented with new opportunities to fund and develop research. The Research Assessment Exercise (RAE) and the establishment of the AHRC have together provided considerable funding for research in creative disciplines. In the case of the AHRC, in the eight years up to 2006 over £28 million was provided to support research in art, design and architecture. The 2,500 research active staff in art and design have also shown increasing confidence and ability in securing funding from other research councils and sources such as the National Endowment for Science, Technology and the Arts (NESTA) to pursue research. Doctoral research in art and design, which less than two decades ago was embryonic in the extreme, is now widespread in the sector and has led to the emergence of a new generation of art and design academics who are pushing their disciplines into new territories and defining a new relevance for the unique knowledge within art and design.

New ways of making

I used to go to the faculty of science and work in a lab, with a white coat and safety specs, you know, the chemistry technicians thought I was a ceramics chemist and it took ages to communicate clearly with them that I was actually a designer, an artist. Eventually they were going, 'What are you doing here?' and I was, 'Yeah, what am I doing here?' (Katie Bunnell)[1]

A decade ago, many of those seeking to undertake research in art and design found themselves working in other disciplines, simply because the visual disciplines lacked the methods, expertise or the basic infrastructure to support research. The comments above by Dr Katie Bunnell describe her experience of pursuing a research project in the field of ceramics, adding, 'It was very, very difficult because they wanted someone to do a PhD, but they didn't know what that was, a PhD in art and design. My supervisor was enthusiastic and supportive but had no experience of supervising a research degree' (Bunnell n.d.). Today Katie Bunnell leads the Autonomatic research group at University College Falmouth, which is linking craft practices with advanced digital manufacturing technologies. Her personal research journey says much about how the research culture has been transformed in recent years to create a vibrant and supportive environment for creative research that has the knowledge and confidence to address serious issues in 'the real world'.

A graduate of the Royal College of Art, Katie wished to pursue her interest in developing new technical innovation in studio ceramic practice. A short unhappy period working in 'a white coat and safety specs' led her to seek out an environment that was more appropriate for an artist who wished to use her creative practice as the engine of a research inquiry. At Gray's School of Art in Aberdeen, Carole Gray and Julian Malins were pioneering an approach to doctoral research that was *practice-led*: research questions were defined through creative practice and addressed through its application using methods that applied academic rigour. Katie Bunnell joined the Gray's team to pursue research into how digital processes could be incorporated into studio ceramics, using her own creative practice as the test bed for this research.

Practice-led research within an art and design context provided the ideal environment for Bunnell. The Autonomatic research group at Falmouth specializes in applying their craft-based knowledge and creative expertise to emerging digital manufacturing technologies that have developed through science and engineering research. They are seeking to demonstrate how such technologies can be applied by individual designers working in a 'craft' context and are exploring a new digital aesthetic. This has considerable application for micro manufacturers to exploit the opportunities of a digital manufacturing revolution. As the group explains, this revolution 'has the potential to enable mass customisation and highly responsive localised production, perhaps even in the home. Through our research we want to challenge perceptions of the boundaries between craft and industrial production and raise the profile of *making* in 21st century design culture' (Autonomatic 2010).

The Falmouth research team is representative of the new generation of design researchers – individuals who use their design expertise and creative practice, often rooted in traditional methods and materials, within a clearly defined research context to address the opportunities presented by new technologies and fast changing consumer culture. While Katie Bunnell and her team are developing a new vision and aesthetic for micro-manufacturing, others from this generation have used the knowledge arising from their creative research to connect with the needs of mainstream manufacturing industry.

Ann Marie Shillito provides a powerful demonstration of how craft knowledge, applied within art and design's new research culture, can contribute to addressing the needs of innovation in manufacturing and digital industries. Ann Marie is a jeweller whose work has been exhibited throughout Europe, including a solo show at the Scottish Gallery. However, as Research Fellow at Edinburgh College of Art, she has initiated and driven forward the Tacitus Project which has gained major external funding and has led to the establishment of a spin-out company that has attracted the interest of major manufacturing companies.

Tacitus was established to investigate how advanced virtual reality technologies could be applied as design tools for craft makers. AHRC funding was secured in 2001 to explore the potential of 3D haptic and multisensory computer tools for designers, in a project that also involved specialists from Edinburgh University's Virtual Environment Centre. This project succeeded in demonstrating the value of such research, and after three years further funding was secured from Scottish Enterprise to develop virtual design tools that had commercial application. This has led to the spin-out company being established – Anarkik3D Ltd – to provide bespoke haptic software solutions for industries that include automotive design, oil and gas, and computer animation. As the company explains:

As easy and as versatile as using pencil and paper, this digital equivalent of sketching and rough modelling, gives full movement and rotation (six degrees of freedom) and co-location within a true three dimensional environment. This application is a radical alternative to traditional CAD methods for visualisation and exploration of initial design concepts. Designers, artists, architects and animators can now construct and modify their ideas more intuitively as if it were a real solid object, entirely in the digital domain, with all the advantages this offers. (Edinburgh College of Art 2010)

The Edinburgh project has demonstrated the value of creative research within an interdisciplinary context where art and design specialists are working alongside researchers from other disciplines to develop and apply innovative new technologies. Anarkik3D is already developing an enviable client roster of world-class companies that recognize and seek to exploit the benefits that these new design tools offer.

Elsewhere in the UK, Hewlett Packard is working with a research team whose specialisms are rooted in fine art practice. The Centre for Fine Print Research is based in Bristol's School of Art, Media and Design – a part of the University of the West of England. The centre was established in 1994 as a focus for research in fine art printmaking at a time when the culture of research in art and design was only just emerging. Fourteen years later, the centre has a highly successful track record of research funding – including twenty AHRC research grants together with a number of industry-funded projects – and a strong record of dissemination through journals and research conferences. A staff of eighteen, plus doctoral students, is evidence of the centre's success in establishing robust, relevant and well-resourced programmes of research.

The centre combines historical research in printmaking with explorations into the development of new printing technologies and systems. The research approach spans both practice-based fine art and industry-focused research, which is internationally unique within its field.

As well as looking forward, our research also looks back to reappraise forgotten processes, techniques and standards that may add to, and enrich modern technological development. This strand of research has resulted in a number of fusions of old and new, which have included practical and theoretical studies of high quality 19th Century printing processes such as Woodburytype, Collotype, Photo ceramic relief casting and photogravure. We also undertake research into artist quality digital output, with a particular emphasis on wide format printing. (Centre for Fine Print Research 2010)

The Bristol team has used their expertise as artists and historians in the use of colour and print technologies in art to critique current ink-jet technologies and to explore refinement in them. As a consequence, Hewlett Packard has funded the centre to develop new methodologies for colour printing that focus on the exacting demands of fine art printmaking. As Carinna Parraman, Senior Research Fellow at the centre, explains:

Methods are being developed at the Centre for Fine Print Research that explores alternative colour sets for inkjet, modifications to the hardware and methods of programming that by passes printer driver software or the need for profiling, that explores colour mixing on a pixel by pixel level. The objective is to enable a more creative approach to colour mixing and printing that returns to traditional notions of how pigment colours are mixed. (Parraman 2008)

The centre is therefore succeeding in using the unique knowledge of fine art printmaking as a means of understanding historical approaches to the use of colour in print to inform and develop future printing technologies.

Manufacturing industry will remain vital to the UK's competitive future. The examples above demonstrate how research rooted in art and design practice can define new applications and aesthetics for emergent manufacturing technologies, develop design tools that are relevant to the needs of advanced manufacturing, and refine new technologies in fields such as digital printing.

Crafting healthcare solutions

Iraq war veteran Sgt. Juan Arredondo can grasp tennis balls and door knobs with his left hand again, now that he's been outfitted with a bionic hand that has flexible fingers. The 27-year-old former soldier, who lost his left hand in 2005 during a patrol, is one of the first recipients of the i-LIMB. 'To have this movement, it's – it's amazing,' Arredondo said Monday as he showed off the limb made by Scotland-based Touch Bionics. 'It just gets me more excited about now, about the future.'

So reported CNN on 24 July 2007 regarding the launch of the world's first commercially available bionic hand with articulating fingers. Prosthetic devices for amputees have been notoriously problematic in terms of their aesthetics and functionality, but the Scottish Touch Bionics company – a spin-out from NHS Scotland – has launched a solution that has been hailed as a major step forward in the design of bionic technologies. The UK is currently a world leader in the development of robotic systems and technologies, and the i-LIMB is one of the latest examples of this expertise.

Playing a key role in the development of i-LIMB is a company set up by a former AHRC-funded research student, Graham Whiteley. His was the first PhD to be successfully completed in design at Sheffield Hallam University and was entitled 'An Articulated Skeletal Analogy of the Human Upper-Limb', supervised by Chris Rust. Essentially, he was tackling prosthetic design research through a methodology that made considerable use of craft techniques such as physical prototyping and drawing. The research output comprises a thesis that was structured as an annotated sketchbook and a series of models and components. However, Graham is not an engineer by background, but a graduate in product design specializing in furniture and automata. His interest in the subject arose from him being commissioned to make a model of a jolly fisherman that would wave at pub customers. His ability to research in the disciplines of medical physics and aerospace engineering demonstrate not only his own personal versatility and talent, but also the value of the 'lost arts' of craft to the practice of research in these disciplines. As he and his supervisors explain:

> The making techniques used are familiar in industrial design practice, where the production of high quality prototypes is a normal method of advancing the product development process. However this approach is relatively unusual in the context of medical physics research where emphasis is placed on the analysis of data, often through mathematical models. The use of practical craft skills to represent a hypothesis and allow a rich set of evaluations could be regarded as a lost art in many fields of the physical sciences today. (Rust *et al.* 2000)

The first outcome of his research was a working model of a prosthetic arm and hand that pioneered new mechanical principles and attracted the interest of NASA scientists at their Jet Propulsion Laboratory. This success helped to launch Graham's career in establishing a robotics development company – Elumotion. Working for companies throughout Europe, Elumotion rapidly gained a reputation for innovation in the field. According to Touch Bionics, the Scottish prosthetics company 'struck a deal with Elumotion, a Bath-based business, to manufacture the prototype hand that will be used for trials and to find buyers' (Murden 2004).

The use of craft knowledge and skills to address complex issues of mechanical engineering and design within a medical context was perhaps unique, and Graham's continued success in the field of robotics demonstrates the enduring value of such an approach. An additional value was that his research gave confidence to the Sheffield Hallam design research team that their 'craft centred' approach to design research was an appropriate path for them to take from the mid-1990s as research methodologies in design were still in a state of flux and definition. In parallel to Graham's research were other projects which explored and demonstrated how 'research through making' could address complex applied research issues and result in commercial outcomes. A system for delivering vibro-sound therapy was designed at Sheffield, and manufactured successfully under licence. Another research team worked with a small local hospital communications manufacturer to develop a Nurse Call system that has led to significant commercial success. Continuing research is exploring the design of medical connection systems with the objective of reducing misconnection errors in surgical environments in partnership with medical researchers and Braun Medical.

Reflecting on Graham Whiteley's PhD and the other research projects carried out at Sheffield Hallam, Professor Jim Roddis considers that their value has been considerable:

> We have demonstrated how a hands-on approach to design research – very much workshop and process based – pays dividends in understanding problems and coming up with creative and workable solutions. But more than this, we have achieved two other things. First, we've shown how design research can make a very real difference to people's quality of life when we focus on issues of well-being. And second, we can contribute to business development and job creation, whether it's through spin out companies or SME's we have worked with.[2]

New ways of seeing

Jane Harris was always interested in tactile things. 'I knitted at 4,' said the 24-year-old graduate of the Glasgow School of Art. These days, she rarely knits. Most of her time is spent creating minutely pleated silk textiles in a rainbow of hues that shimmer and change shades as the fabric moves. Miss Harris has made fewer than a dozen one-of-a-kind garments using this fabric. But these were sufficient to bring her first place, and an $800 prize, at the Chelsea Crafts Fair here recently ... She works on commission and her works start at $4,000. 'It's a Liz Taylor kind of market, but I want to keep everything unique,' she said. (Trucco 1989)

Jane Harris remains interested in tactile things, although not quite in the same way as when the *New York Times* profiled her in 1989. Following graduation she was hailed as the future of constructed textiles – a weaver whose sculptural approach to cloth and its dynamic interaction with the body had resulted in a vibrant body of work that commanded both critical attention and the front cover of *Crafts* magazine. Within ten years she was completing her PhD at the Royal College of Art, but in place of the shimmering silks that characterized her graduation work was a projected Quicktime movie that displayed virtual textiles. Taking the place of unique pieces for an exclusive market was a unique contribution to knowledge with an application that could be enjoyed by everyone.

Jane's PhD represented an exploration of the value of material skills in developing alternative aesthetics for digital media. The interaction of the worn textile garment with the body remained a central creative focus, but the research took this in new directions using motion-capture, body-scanning 3D computer animation and other digital technologies, rather than the loom. She was interested in the potential of new creative hybrid practices that fused textiles, performance, fashion and film. As one of the pioneering 'new researchers' who helped to define PhD research in design from the mid-1990s, Jane has made a significant impact on research in textiles, and she is now Director of the Textile Futures Research Unit at Central Saint Martins College of Art and Design. Her research has attracted support from the AHRC, NESTA, the Arts Council and Channel 4. The very nature of her research has effected a fundamental shift in how she works, which reflects a wider trend in art and design research over the last decade: 'Software and hardware tooling has become more accessible and it has been possible to apply established material skills, within a broader frame of research and visual art practice. This has necessitated a shift from working as a solo maker, to collaborating and working with a range of individuals, institutions and industry' (Harris 2004).

As the recipient of the first AHRC Innovation Award, Jane had the opportunity to demonstrate the value of practice-centred research that could apply her intimate creative knowledge of material, process and clothing to the possibilities presented by computer-generated animation. Collaboration with other performance and visuals artists under her creative direction led to an innovative project for the Museum of London. On the screen she brought to life a fragile eighteenth-century dress, enabling Museum visitors to see how the garment would have looked when originally worn. As she explains, this makes museum collections more accessible and vivid: 'Once textiles and dress enter this type of (museum) environment, there are constraints on the handling of such objects. So for example, garments won't be worn again and various handling policies are required' (Harris 2004). Jane's research demonstrates how computer animation that is informed by material knowledge can create unique forms of visualization that have application in museum and other contexts.

> Design is about communicating an idea, whether it's to a product, whether it's to a graphic, it's about using the tools you have as a designer and as a creative person to try and communicate that message. The beauty of this type of research is that it shows how the designer can be brought into quite a clinical environment and be of use.[3]

John McGhee has much in common with Jane Harris. Both come from a materials-based design education, and both are now applying that knowledge in their current research in the field of computer animation. Similarly, both are applying animation in novel ways that have attracted considerable attention from specialists and from the media.

As mentioned, in 2007 John was shortlisted for the Morgan Stanley 'Great Briton' awards in the science and innovation category. This was in recognition of his pioneering work in applying computer animation techniques to a clinical context. Originally a student of product design, John retrained in computer animation, but considered that the gaming industry was too limiting an environment to explore the full potential of this fast-evolving medium. An AHRC-funded doctoral studentship at the University of Dundee has enabled him to explore the use of 3D visualization techniques to enhance medical scan data, particularly in the field of Magnetic Resonance Imaging (MRI) and Computive Tomography (CT) scanning. The work has focused on how these scans might be combined with the digital 3D visualization tools commonly used by artists in the computer animation and games industries. The aim of his research is to evaluate whether improved imagery might offer a greater understanding of illness and disease, among different patient groups.

MRI and CT imagery allows clinicians to far better understand a patient's condition and to make an accurate clinical diagnosis, but such imagery means little to the untrained eye, and can often cause misunderstandings when shown to patients. John explains how his task has been to turn this imagery into something more useful for the patient:

In this PhD research, computer visualisation techniques from the field of digital animation (storyboarding, 3-D modelling and rendering) have been used to create a hybrid image: an image that uses MRI data and artistic imaginative vision to create a new aesthetic that supports communication of complex medical data to patients. The work involved the digital artist being embedded in the hospital environment and interacting with patients, medical physicists and clinicians. (McGhee 2010)

Clinical trials with eighteen patients who suffer from hardening of the arteries have proven most positive. Not only did the patients, whose average age was seventy-one, understand what the images were showing, but it enabled them to engage with their treatment in a new way. In an interview with BBC News, John said: 'It was about imparting information but more importantly about getting a dialogue going on to help to get the patient discussing what is going on. When they talk to health professionals they now go armed with better questions and knowledge of their anatomy' (Ward 2007).

John's research is one example of an established area of expertise for design research at Dundee – the exploration and application of digital imaging techniques to fields that lie well outside those of entertainment and gaming. As we have seen from the work of Jane Harris and John McGhee, digital cinematography can be used to communicate issues and ideas in curatorial practices and medical imaging, but it has also been applied to forensics, archaeology, environmental preservation and some even more surprising fields.

In June 2007 a Russian frigate left the port of Murmansk heading north into the Barents Sea to locate Russian nuclear submarine B159 which sank four years earlier with the loss of all ten crew. A G8-funded international team and NATO unmanned submarine were aboard to help with the search and to identify the condition of the wreck, in particular the condition of the submarine's two nuclear reactors. Under heavy military supervision, the international team included the Head of Animation at the University of Dundee.

Chris Rowland has a background in television graphics and 3D animation, working for broadcast clients including Channel 4 and BBC before running a TV graphics company in Glasgow. His current research is focused on the 3D visualization of historic shipwrecks as they lie beyond the public gaze on the seabed. He has developed software tools for the aesthetic rendering of sonar data which enables far clearer and more vivid visualization of the wreck, and the impact it is having in the local marine environment. He has worked collaboratively with maritime archaeologists from St Andrew's University in developing a unique system for marine wreck visualization and analysis. They have been commissioned by government departments, English Heritage and other bodies to provide visualizations of shipwrecks such as HMS *Royal Oak*, and the *Stirling Castle*, a battleship that sank in 1703. Their work for the Russian government showed that the submarine, although damaged, is relatively intact and viable for recovery.

Our visual culture has been redefined by computer animation, providing a new richness in visual storytelling as exemplified by the wise-cracking characters in the latest Pixar movies and the massed armies of Daleks in the skies above London in the new 'Doctor Who'. But creative researchers in the UK's art schools have shown that the tales that can be told with this medium can go beyond a toy story. We can tell stories about how clothing was worn 200 years ago, we can tell stories to patients about their medical condition and we can tell the story of what has happened to a shipwreck half a mile beneath the sea.

Beyond the city limits

Innovative design has played an important role in driving down crime overall by a third over the past decade. Much of the 51 per cent fall in vehicle crime in particular can be attributed to design improvements such as immobilisers and toughened glass. The Design and Technology Alliance will seek to build on these achievements. They will champion the message that designing out crime is about sustainable and innovative design of products, spaces and places to make crime unattractive and make communities feel safe. (Home Office 2007)

Former Home Office Minister Vernon Coaker was unequivocal in his view that design plays a critical role in crime prevention when the Home Office launched the Design and Technology Alliance in August 2007. The six member alliance, which aims to raise the profile with industry of how design can tackle crime, includes Professor Lorraine Gamman, Director of the Design Against Crime Research Centre at Central St Martins School of Art and Design.

Lorraine has been a committed and vocal advocate of 'Design Against Crime', an approach to designing that recognizes and addresses its implications for crime prevention. Its Research Centre has been responsible for initiating a number of projects in partnership with police authorities, local government, the Home Office and other agencies that have focused design on addressing specific crime problems. The centre's 'Bikeoff' project has developed designs to address cycle security. As a result, Lorraine and her team won the 2007 'Best Cycling Initiative' at the London Sustainable Transport Awards. This centre has focused on a practice-centred approach to research, developing design exemplars that seek to raise the profile of design as a crime beating strategy and demonstrate the value of design thinking. While Central St Martins pioneered this within an art-school context, others have taken design against crime in more strategic directions, embedding design researchers within cross disciplinary teams to address issues of policy and planning with the objective of enabling safer public environments. Such research has been driven by the priority of addressing the urgent needs of urban development – the future of the city.

> The introduction of the notion of mixed-use, day and night-time economies has resulted in what is termed 24-hour cities. Cities such as Manchester have restructured to realise this vision, and with this has arisen conflicts of interest between stakeholders with different objectives. For example: security versus free access; the needs of older people versus conditions that support other interests such as youth culture; and commercial activity versus environmental quality. (Cooper *et al.* 2009: viii)

This passage comes from the introduction to a book, *Designing Sustainable Cities*, that arose from a five-year £2.75 million research project – VivaCity 2020 – which addresses the dimensions of sustainability in the urban environment. This major project brings together specialists in architecture and design, acoustics, air-quality and pollution, thermal quality, sociology and crime to develop new perspectives and methods to deal with the seeming conflicts facing urban development and planning. It has analysed issues of urban planning and sustainability in Manchester, Sheffield and the Clerkenwell district of London, drawing policy recommendations on design decision-making processes and new tools that can be applied to them. Led by design researchers from Salford and Lancaster who have a track record in design against crime research, the project demonstrates how design research – an embryonic field little more than a decade ago – can now play a role as an equal alongside other academic disciplines. According to project director Professor Rachel Cooper: 'Ten years ago, a major project such as this would not even have thought about design in this way, let alone have it as a central focus. We have now proved our worth as an academic community that provides unique insights and knowledge on some of the critical issues facing our future.'[4]

New roles and possibilities

The emergence of a research culture in art and design has initiated a transformation in the role of the creative practitioner, providing new opportunities to explore and redefine the scope and interests of art and design, and its relationship with other disciplines. There is evidence of this both within dedicated art schools and those which are located within research-focused universities. Crossing disciplines has opened up new possibilities and a new relevance for creative practice. Three distinctive new directions or values are now clearly developing.

First, artistic practice working within a research framework is demonstrating how it can contribute directly to other disciplines through its power of visualization. Dundee-based printmaker Elaine Shemilt explains how she worked with scientists from the Scottish Crop Research Institute, developing a series of prints and projected animations from the full genome sequence of a bacterial potato plant pathogen:

> With the screen prints I used a very subtle range of silvery blues and grays and worked with some very specific inks ... It was from looking at those prints the scientists noticed the occurrence of new elements and a very specific event of gene acquisition. My approach was to simplify the diagram into tonal variation and in so doing I recontextualized the data in such a way that it revealed information that the scientists had completely overlooked. Their scientific approach to the data was systematic and empirical. Purely by chance, my artistic reinterpretation of the scientific data contributed to a new insight ... Rather than simply identifying genes unique to a pathogen, the screen prints and animations revealed the presence of other genes present in all of the bacteria, possibly representing genes essential to all forms of bacteria. (Shemilt 2006)

This science-art project has led directly to a new programme in pathogen research.

Second, applying the methods and processes that are embedded within creative practice provides distinctive ways of thinking that can contribute to complex problem-solving. Alastair Macdonald at Glasgow School of Art has been directing a project on healthcare delivery, as part of the Designing for the 21st Century research initiative. Working with a team of senior clinicians, the project has established the case for design in playing a key role in healthcare delivery in the context of an ageing population. As one of the clinicians observed: 'Design thinking seems to be "boundary-less" or at least to cut across traditional boundaries in medicine, that is one of its strengths, and this approach can assist the patient or the staff perspective with more ease than someone who works in the medical world. The design perspective therefore brings clarity to medical problems' (Macdonald 2007).

Third, research is suggesting a new role for the practitioners in which they can act as cultural intermediaries and indeed as leaders in social and community development. At Gray's School of Art, Anne Douglas has been exploring this through the 'On the Edge' project:

> Research into the role of the artist working in public indicates that artists are uniquely placed to inform and creatively develop public life. In seeking to understand the nature of creativity in public contexts, this research focuses on the concept of 'leading through practice'. It opens up a new trajectory of thinking about leadership that is not predominantly management based, in which the role of artist operating within social, cultural and environmental contexts is scrutinised for what it can reveal about creativity in general. (On the Edge 2010)

It's a bit like the scene in Monty Python's *Life of Brian*: So what have researchers in art and design ever done for us? Isn't it all just useless beauty? Certainly art and design are disciplines that pursue beauty and meaning. But in that pursuit they create knowledge and insights that have widespread application and can contribute powerfully to our culture, economy, innovation and well-being. We see evidence of its value in scientific research labs, in declining crime statistics, in new approaches to urban planning, in new healthcare and in manufacturing technologies. We see evidence also in visual storytelling, where researchers are applying new technologies in novel ways to tell stories that help us to understand historical artefacts, clinical diagnosis and the state of wrecked nuclear submarines. And for all the stories told in this essay, there is an economic story that has been largely untold – of new products securing new markets, of new innovations that have a significant commercial potential. In their pursuit of a more beautiful, useable and understandable world, art and design researchers provide essential pathways to a better and more economically sustainable future.

Notes

1   Personal communication.
2   Personal communication.
3   Personal communication.
4   Personal communication.

Bibliography

Autonomatic (2010), 'Home', http://www.autonomatic.org.uk [accessed 18 July 2010].

Centre for Fine Print Research (2010), 'Introduction', http://amd.uwe.ac.uk/cfpr [accessed 18 July 2010].

Cooper, R., Evans, G. and Boyco, C. (2009), *Designing Sustainable Cities*, Oxford: Wiley-Blackwell.

Edinburgh College of Art (2010), 'Current research groups: tacitus/handson/anarkik3D', http://www.eca.ac.uk/index.php?id=387 [accessed 18 July 2010].

Harris, J. (1989), 'Textile Artist', *New York Times*, 19 November.

Harris, J. (2004), 'Empress's New Clothes', Proceedings of Challenging Craft conference, Gray's School of Art, Aberdeen, 8–10 September, http://www2.rgu.ac.uk/challengingcraft/ChallengingCraft/pdfs/janeharris.pdf [accessed 13 July 2010].

Home Office (2007), 'Design Alliance: fighting crime from the drawing board', press release, 14 August, http://webarchive.nationalarchives.gov.uk/20100418065544/http://press.homeoffice.gov.uk/press-releases/design-alliance [accessed 15 July 2010].

Howells, K. (2005), 'Time Shift: Art School', BBC Four, 9 September.

Macdonald, A.S. (2007), 'Ideal states: engaging patients in healthcare pathways through design methodologies', in Tom Inns (ed.), *Designing for the 21st Century*, Gower, London.

McGhee, J. (2010), 'Overview', http://www.innerpixel.co.uk/pages/research2.html [accessed 18 July 2010].

On the Edge (2010), 'Artist as Leader', http://www.ontheedgeresearch.org [accessed 18 July 2010].

Parraman, C. (2008), 'Colour in flux: describing and printing colour in art', in R. Eschbach, G.G. Marcu and S. Tominaga (ed.), *Color Imaging XIII: Processing, Hardcopy, and Applications*, Proceedings of the Society of Photo-Optical Instrumentation Engineers (SPIE) conference, vol. 6807, Bellingham, WA: Society of Photo-Optical Instrumentation Engineers.

Rust, C., Whiteley, G. and Wilson, A. (2000), 'Experimental Making in Multi-Disciplinary Research', *Design Journal*, November.

Rust, C., Mottram, J. and Till, J. (2007), *AHRC Research Review: Practice-Led Research in Art, Design and Architecture*, London: Arts & Humanities Research Council, http://www.ahrc.ac.uk/About/Policy/Documents/Practice-Led_Review_Nov07.pdf [accessed 13 July 2010].

Shemilt, E. (2006), 'A Blueprint For Bacterial Life – Can a Science-Art fusion move the boundaries of visual and audio interpretation?', Proceedings of 22nd CHArt Annual Conference: 'FAST FORWARD, Art History, Curation and Practice After Media', Birkbeck College, University of London, 10 November, http://www.chart.ac.uk/chart2006/papers/shemilt.htm [accessed 13 July 2010].

Trucco, T. (1989), 'Style makers', *New York Times*, 28 May.

Ward, M. (2007), 'Digital art aids health check-ups', BBC News website, 7 August 2007, http://news.bbc.co.uk/1/hi/technology/6934511.stm [accessed 13 July 2010].

13. A Museum Perspective

Christopher Breward (Victoria and Albert Museum)

Arts and humanities research directly informs the key activities of a national museum like the Victoria and Albert Museum (V&A). The museum serves as an international centre of excellence in the fields of the history of art and design, conservation, learning and interpretation and contemporary creative practice, and its programmes benefit from research that is designed to contribute both to the public understanding and experience of its collections, and to the methodological and theoretical advancement of relevant arts and humanities disciplines. The V&A therefore fosters a proactive research culture, both in developing public outcomes that are underpinned by current scholarship (its galleries, high-profile exhibitions, publications, conferences and website) and in fostering collaborations with academic partners.

As a frequent recipient of Arts & Humanities Research Council (AHRC) and other research grants the V&A is well practised in recognizing and capitalizing on opportunities to enhance the value of its activities and outputs through ambitious, authoritative and accessible research programmes. This essay will discuss recent examples of externally funded projects at the V&A where innovative object, collection, exhibition and archive-based research has made a demonstrable and positive impact on both specialist knowledge and the quality of the visitor experience, stimulating debate on past and present cultures, and encouraging new approaches to scholarship and the dissemination of expertise in the UK and beyond.

Much recent debate on the value of the public arts sector (including museums and galleries) has focused on its measurable contribution to the national economy via the creative industries, tourism and a vibrant art market, and to the quality of life of individuals and communities. It is certainly the case that the UK's museums play an important role in raising social capital, encouraging inclusion and kick-starting urban regeneration. Less has been said, however, on the ways in which the practice of arts and humanities research underpins these initiatives, particularly in the context of the museum exhibition and display. The following case-studies demonstrate the significant impact that such research activities can make via the public presentation of the nation's material and cultural assets.

Object-led research

The most distinctive feature of museum-based research is that it is based on objects. Prompted by artefacts from the past, museums have traditionally tended to ask very focused questions about dating, authorship, manufacture and usage. While this approach was once seen as conservative by academics, in recent years the idea that objects should be given priority – that they should determine the course of research, rather than serving as data – has become more and more accepted. Indeed, many observers agree that there has been a 'material turn' in fields such as anthropology, social history and even literary studies, comparable to the much-discussed 'linguistic turn' that occurred in the humanities some thirty years ago. The shift towards materiality has encouraged museum professionals and academic researchers to work together more closely than ever before, particularly in the UK. This has been beneficial to all concerned. UK-based museum curators have broadened the range of questions that they ask of their collections, and the focus on objects has similarly transformed the methods and goals of scholarly research and learning in the British higher education sector.

There are multiple advantages to be gained by placing objects at the centre of a collaborative research project, rather than in the margins. First and foremost, artefacts exert friction on the researcher. General theories are invariably tested by the specificity and concreteness of objects, which rarely conform to expectation. Partly for this reason, object-led research is fundamentally interdisciplinary. Fully accounting for the research potential of even a single object might require contributions by historians of art,

Figure 13.1 Beer mug inscribed '1701' and decorated in slip. © http://www.vam.ac.uk

culture, science and economics, as well as specialists in conservation and other scientific disciplines.

Take, for example, the illustrated decorated beer mug inscribed '1701'. Such an object can be studied, first of all, on the basis of its appearance. Its somewhat old-fashioned decoration in slip (liquid clay) attests to stylistic conservatism in Staffordshire, the place of its manufacture. Yet if we inquire further, we might find that the mug was implicated in new networks of distribution. The materials used to make it may have been sourced from far away, and the finished object sold in a distant city, or even abroad in America and Europe.

We might ask where and how the mug was used. Through the comparative study of objects like this one we can learn about communal drinking habits, the emergence of new venues for socialization and attitudes towards intoxication. Or we might wonder about the significance of its date inscription, which would lead to questions about attitudes to marriage, childbirth or political commemoration. The mug would probably have been used across a broad spectrum of society, from the 'plainer sorts' to the upwardly mobile mercantile class. This is a further advantage of object-led research: it often yields evidence of a wider demographic range than textual sources. In periods where many people were illiterate or semi-literate, or where documents are scarce, objects can often be the only means of accessing the experience of the majority of people – people whose descendants now form a core audience for museum displays and popular histories.

Despite all these benefits, object-based research also poses its own challenges. First and foremost, though museum collections are often defined by the goal of preservation, researchers are forced to think about the objects they hold as dynamic. Unlike most textual forms of historic evidence, material things are subject to constant change through modification, wear and repair. Though authenticity and originality are prized, the fact is that when it comes to objects from the past, alteration is the norm, not the exception.

Museum-based conservation offers a disciplinary basis for research into such issues. The techniques of the scientist and the conservator can be used to gain access not only to the moment of an object's creation, but also its entire lifespan: a principle that lies at the heart of the V&A's recent research project focusing on the Mazarin Chest (funded by the Getty Foundation and the Toshiba International Foundation, supported by the Japan Foundation and the Tobunken, and carried out at the V&A, Imperial College, Loughborough University, Dresden Academy of Fine Arts and the Institute of Catalysis and Surface Chemistry, Polish Academy of Sciences). The chest is a most unusual example of seventeenth-century Japanese lacquerwork, of a very high quality that would normally not have been exported to Europe. Its history of ownership permits us to see it in relation to a long series of people and places – from its Japanese makers to its initial owners, the Mazarin family of France, from the Romantic-era

Figure 13.2 The Mazarin Chest. © http://www.vam.ac.uk

collector William Beckford, to the V&A itself (the museum acquired the object in 1882).

The Mazarin Chest project also shed light on differing cultural attitudes to historic objects in the present day. The goal was to develop an integrated approach to the conservation of lacquer objects that respects both Western conservation ethics, in which concern with the re-treatability of objects is paramount, and Japanese conservation values, which seek to preserve the cultural continuity of objects by employing, as far as possible, materials and techniques similar to those used at the time of manufacture. The chest has thus been a basis not only for nuanced historic research but also new international exchanges of knowledge and understanding.

A final advantage of object-led research is its direct connection to physical experience. Every researcher who has worked in a museum knows that handling unfamiliar objects for the first time is among the most thrilling aspects of their work. This excitement is telling us something: through touch, we can begin to ask new questions about those different from ourselves. For those interested in issues such as comportment, the senses, and sexual and ethnic identity, materiality can provide routes into unspoken (and perhaps even unconscious) cultural values. Fashion – a subject to which we will return – is a particularly obvious example. Thinking about the self-regulating function of garments, from the kimono to the corset, is an instance in which research can make the lived experience of cultural difference immediately palpable to all.

Collection-based research

Like the objects which form their content, permanent collections such as those housed at the V&A are not inert. They are a live inheritance that requires constant reinterpretation and new models of communication if they are to speak effectively to contemporary audiences and enhance our sense of the complex, globalized twenty-first-century world as an entity with historical roots and challenging futures. Research is one of the methods by which we realize the social and cultural value of the assets that museums hold on behalf of the public, an obvious point but one that is too rarely made in press coverage and reviews of headline exhibitions and gallery developments. Two recently completed research projects help to elucidate the relevance to the UK's diverse communities of our material heritage as represented in the V&A Museum's collections.

'Fashioning Diaspora Space' was a three-year collaboration between the V&A and Royal Holloway, University of London. It was funded by the AHRC as part of the 'Diasporas, Identities and Migration' programme and examined the presence in the UK of South Asian (Indian and Pakistani) textiles intended for use in clothing. In the context of the museum, the project has expanded knowledge about the V&A's collections of nineteenth-century Indian textiles, not only in terms of identifying the objects, but also through asking how and why these collections were formed, how they have been used in the past and what they might mean to current and future generations of curators, visitors, designers and consumers. This research is also relevant to the holdings of other museum collections such as the Manchester Art Gallery, Whitworth Art Gallery in Manchester, Paisley Museum and Bath Fashion Museum, to the archives of past and present textile manufacturers at Macclesfield Silk Archives, Warners and G.P. & J. Baker, as well as to the work of contemporary fashion retailers. In comparing colonial and postcolonial forms, untangling their genesis, their cultural designations and translations, the project has significant implications for our understanding of wider British material and visual cultures and landscapes.

One of the earliest groups within the Indian textile collections at the V&A consists of examples acquired at the Great Exhibition of 1851. This was the first time that large numbers of the British public had seen what Indian textile producers were capable of creating. The quality of Indian hand-woven silk, embroideries and muslins was unmatched by industrial British textile manufacturers. In the 1860s and 1870s many of the South Asian textiles in the collection were cut up and put into two multi-volume sets of textile sample books. These were sent around the country to both inspire designers and manufacturers, and with a view to building up the sales of British textiles to the Indian subcontinent. New entries on the V&A website (the non-destructive equivalent of these nineteenth-century albums) about South Asian textiles in the museum have made relevant images and information on their history, context and use universally available to a

UK (and international) audience for the first time since the middle of the nineteenth century.

The story of the V&A's South Asian textile collection is typical of diaspora narratives in its mixture of emulation, destruction and learning. These processes – both positive and negative – are to be found in many other instances of cultural exchange, international trade and migration. Indian textiles, too, include vivid examples of objects whose very surfaces play out the action of far-flung networks in their materials and decoration. The investigation of a distinctive Parsi Chinese embroidery, consisting of a coloured embroidery on white silk depicting birds among foliage, shaped for a *jubla* or girl's shirt (figure 3) reveals longer histories and connections. The Parsis of Bombay (Mumbai) were descendants of the Zoroastrians who emigrated to the Indian subcontinent from Iran in the eighth century. Parsi-owned shipping companies traded with China, returning with highly prized Chinese goods including embroidered textiles. Some Chinese embroiderers also settled in Surat, a port city in Gujarat. This single *jubla* is thus the complex result of the interwoven histories of four nations in two continents spanning twelve centuries. New interpretations fostered through the focused research of such an

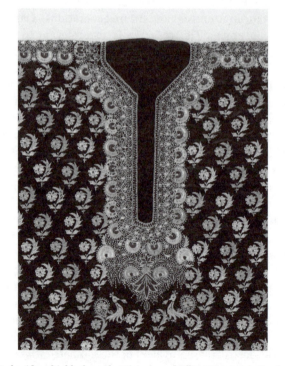

Figure 13.3 Embroidered jubla from the Victoria and Albert Museum's South Asian textile collection. © http://www.vam.ac.uk

object (amongst many others) indicate that it is time to move beyond postcolonial hand-wringing and progress in our understanding of a shared human past.

A second example focuses on an aspect of the museum's practices where research has revealed a previously overlooked area of the V&A's collecting history. The thirty-month-long project, conducted as part of a Cultural Ownership and Capacity Building Project and supported by the Heritage Lottery Fund, focused on identifying and interpreting Africa-related materials within the collections. The undertaking built on several years of engagement with black British communities, seeking to build black and minority ethnic audiences for the V&A and to develop collaborations and skill-sharing within the black heritage/cultural sector.

The V&A has always collected the art and design of Africa. Initially, its collecting focused on the northern part of the continent. Thirteen Tunisian textiles were part of the 1851 Great Exhibition purchases which formed the core of the collection. Ancient Egyptian textiles and glassware, and Moroccan and Algerian ceramics and jewellery, formed other collecting strands through the second half of the nineteenth century and the beginning of the twentieth. This same period witnessed a number of key imperial acquisitions from sub-Saharan Africa including religious, ceremonial and decorative items associated with Ethiopia's ruling family, acquired through the Abyssinian Expedition of 1868, and thirteen pieces of largely gold regalia, probably associated with the court of the Asante leader, acquired through the British invasion of Kumasi, state capital of Asante, Ghana, in 1874.

More recently, these African acquisitions have been supplemented with objects that reflect the changing political, social and cultural contexts of 'postcolonial' Africa. The Word and Image Department has been particularly active, acquiring prints by African artists including Ben Enwonwu, Tunde Odunlade, Paul Sibisi and David Koloane. The cultural influence of the African diaspora is also represented in acquisitions of work by Caribbean artists such as Winston Branch and Aubrey Williams, and Black British artists such as Maud Sulter, Lubaina Himid, Chris Ofili and Faisal Abdu'Allah. It is hoped that this fresh, research-informed awareness may fuel revisions to the museum's collecting policy and encourage a more proactive, creative approach to its Africa collections and their future development.

Exhibitions

Placed at the crossroads between scholarly enquiry and communication with a wider audience, exhibitions are ideally located to disseminate the broad cultural, social and economic benefits associated with the arts and humanities field, positively engaging visitors in a much more direct and immersive manner than other forms of media. Unlike other academic outputs, exhibitions must confront the demands of appealing to very large non-specialist audiences while making specialist knowledge widely accessible. This unique set of circumstances makes exhibitions a particularly challenging and stimulating arena within which to explore the value and impact of research.

In recent years, exhibition-based research within the UK has changed dramatically in character and scope. Museums have been at the heart of a momentous cultural shift which has transformed them from perceived passive recipients of research-led initiatives to frontrunners. Fostered by an increasing number of national and international research funding schemes and policies designed to generate active collaborations between museums, universities and colleges, this radical transformation raises important questions about the new character and purpose of exhibition-based research. This is the framework within which the groundbreaking exhibition *At Home in Renaissance Italy* (V&A, October 2006–January 2007) operated – the result of a four-year research project funded by the Getty Foundation and the AHRC.

The research leading to an exhibition differs substantially from conventional academic research. Centred on 'things', the research process must acknowledge that objects are carriers of complex visual, material, cultural and social meanings, and that as such they should generate multiple narratives and interpretations. This recognition often demands breaking out of traditional disciplinary boundaries and embracing an interdisciplinary outlook. The research for *At Home in Renaissance Italy* was carried out by a multidisciplinary team including scholars working within art, decorative arts and architectural history, social history, Islamic studies, music history, archaeology, the history of science, food history and conservation. Exploring the domestic interior in Italy between 1400 and 1600 in all its visual and material complexity, with objects ranging from prestigious old master paintings and sculptures to pins and pastry cutters, the exhibition brought together for the first time the world of Renaissance 'high' art and that of domestic material culture. Engaging with household life and everyday experience as well as cultural forms, the exhibition addressed topics as wide-ranging as cooking and dining, marriage and childbirth rituals, gambling, music-making, health and hygiene, collecting and mathematical knowledge.

The project aimed to make a major new contribution to Renaissance studies and to give revived meaning to the outstanding Renaissance collections housed within the V&A (recently presented afresh in the new Medieval and Renaissance Galleries, opened in December 2009). To achieve these objectives the project maximized its investment in original research by focusing on a wide variety of largely unpublished written documents, visual sources and objects. From domestic inventories to cookery books, from celebrated family portraits to popular prints, from ancient gems to chamber pots, the exhibition revealed a new, multifaceted aspect to Renaissance art and culture.

The multiplicity of research methods and exhibits involved in the project was reflected in the narratives accompanying the display, based directly on primary sources, which suggested different, often contrasting interpretations of the same objects. Replacing the traditional, authoritative, curatorial voice with a more challenging and active approach, this mode of display aimed at including the viewer creatively in the meaning-making process and encouraging a dialogue between specialists and a wider audience. This curatorial strategy meant that there was a direct continuity from the initial framing of research questions all the way to the labels read by members of the public.

Much recent debate has highlighted the widespread dissatisfaction with traditional arenas of social and cultural exchange and the need for alternative spaces for public discourse. As public events and experiences playing a role in the creation of shared meaning, exhibitions can be seen as a largely untapped force for debate and social cohesion. Exhibitions such as *At Home in Renaissance Italy* can respond to this demand for public engagement with culture in different ways. By presenting historical materials in an exciting and accessible form they can help to bridge the gap between past and present. By revealing everyday objects, stories or situations that resonate with the life experience of the viewer they can appeal to wider cross-sections of society. By addressing complexity and difference head-on, challenging commonly held assumptions and establishing a dynamic relationship with the viewer, they can provide potent evidence of the value of investing in research into the arts and the humanities.

Creativity and design practice

Museum-based arts and humanities research also capitalizes on and creates multiple connections within the creative industries, making links between practitioners including fine artists, graphic, fashion and 3D designers and craftspeople; manufacturers; scientists; retailers; educators; and journalists, publishers and media producers. It encourages debate and collaboration across discrete sectors to their collective benefit and offers an inspirational space in which national conversations about creative skills can take place. In the case of the V&A, research projects focusing on fashion have been particularly successful in generating productive dialogue about this high-profile, multimillion-pound industry and its economic, cultural and political meanings and impact.

The 'Shopping Routes: Networks of Fashion Consumption in London's West End 1945–1979' project was one such initiative. Jointly hosted by the Geography Department at Royal Holloway, University of London, London College of Fashion and the V&A between 2003 and 2006 as part of the ESRC/AHRC Cultures of Consumption Programme, the project had the central aim of providing a new critical history of the development of the West End in the postwar period; widening and complicating existing assumptions, particularly those associated with the powerful myth of 'Swinging London.' The project had a series of focused research objectives, seeking to provide an account of the interfaces between designers, manufacturers, suppliers, retailers, urban planners and consumers in the city. It also sought to develop recent ideas about the spatial contexts of fashion consumption, especially those situated in major metropolises, and to enhance understandings of consumption-led processes of urban renewal and transformation. It had the wider aim of interpreting London's role as a major fashion city in a comparative context, by examining the development of a range of key global sites of fashion consumption within a longer time-frame.

Through a combination of cross-institutional and multidisciplinary approaches, the research succeeded in providing a much more nuanced and extensive history of a phenomenon that hitherto has generally been approached through nostalgic accounts that focused on over-familiar sites like Carnaby Street and the King's Road, and on the emergent celebrity culture of the 1960s. It achieved this in a number of ways. First, archival research pointed to the significance of long-term features of London's fashion landscape, situating the seemingly overnight transformation of the city in the mid-1960s in the context of existing structures of retailing, wholesale, promotion and consumer behaviour, some of which had their roots in the mid-nineteenth century. Secondly, it challenged the existing emphasis on individual designers and boutiques, in favour of a framework that emphasized networks and relationships across sectors and traditions, and identified fashion consumption's interactions with other elements of urban change, particularly in architecture, planning and heritage. Thirdly, the project provided a systematic study of the concept of the 'Fashion World City', placing the specific characteristics of postwar London in a wider analysis of fashion's relationship with metropolitan modernity, which continues to have important resonance in the present.

The results of the research were disseminated through a number of channels including books and journal articles. The study of fashion in world cities formed the basis for a major international conference that brought together academics from a wide range of disciplines, and included studies of New York, Paris, Milan, Tokyo, Moscow, Los Angeles, Shanghai and Mumbai to complement the London focus. Most importantly, in 2006 the project was responsible for a high-profile exhibition on *Sixties Fashion* and an associated website at the V&A. This provided an opportunity to test some of the research findings through an engagement with the museum's collections, and through collaboration with designers, journalists and retailers active through the 1950s, 1960s and 1970s. Both display and website, together with an exhibition book, were designed to reach a broad audience and had a demonstrable effect on the popular imagination, drawing positive press comment and informing the content of the UK school curriculum. The website also provided a way of soliciting memories of the period from the public, and a means of disseminating oral history interviews with key designers, entrepreneurs, journalists and others involved in 1960s London.

In general, the project has formed part of a wider re-evaluation of the political, economic and creative legacy of the 1960s that has taken place in UK academic circles and in the popular media during the past two decades. But besides providing an important platform for debate on these retrospective issues, 'Shopping Routes', particularly in its work on fashion and the concept of the World City, also engaged with wider discussion on contemporary urban policy in relation to what has been termed the New Urban Cultural Economy. What this museum-centred research initiative has identified is the extent to which the drive towards symbolic distinctiveness by competing fashion cities needs to be considered alongside the contradictory forces that stifle urban individuality and creativity. These forces include the hyper-capitalization of property markets and the increasing power of global corporations in a hugely expanded luxury-goods sector. History does have something to teach us.

As the content of the *Sixties Fashion* exhibition suggested, connections between the new symbolic industries (media and advertising) and older craft traditions were much more dynamic in cities like London, New York, Milan and Paris in the 1950s and 1960s than they were after the massive de-industrialization of the 1970s and 1980s. The creative networks, flexible production and vibrant consumer cultures of the previous era have been replaced by the corporatized surface sheen of now. So, though 'Swinging London' was a small, local affair, its openings for new businesses, its legacy of traditional fashion skills, its affordable infrastructure and its innovative approach to consumerism offer a genuinely distinctive template to those concerned about the serious challenges faced by UK fashion entrepreneurs in the globalized landscape of the early twenty-first century.

The museum as a forum for cultural exchange

Besides functioning as platforms for creative reflection and innovation in relation to the UK's history and current cultural and economic status, museums are also ideal venues for the staging of new cultural interactions beyond national frontiers. As we have suggested in reference to projects on Japan, South Asia and Africa, because objects themselves have always traversed national boundaries they are therefore a remarkably effective way of studying historical and contemporary cultural exchange. Through intelligent juxtaposition, museums can encourage researchers, curators and the public alike to see both difference and continuity across diverse nationalities, ethnicities and geographies. This has long been a guiding principle of research at the V&A, and informs permanent displays such as the British Galleries (opened 2001), the Jameel Gallery for Islamic Arts (opened 2006) and the Ceramics Galleries (opened 2009).

The research for two exhibitions, on view in 2008–9 at the V&A, exemplified this approach. *Cold War Modern* (researched in collaboration with colleagues at the University of Brighton and the Royal College of Art) used the museum platform to reconfigure understandings of international relations in the recent past through the prism of design. Concentrating on the highly volatile years from 1945 to 1975, the exhibition examined the key themes of the period including the task of reconstruction in Europe after the Second World War and the rise of consumerism, demonstrating a continuity with the themes of modernism as they emerged in the interwar years (explored in the V&A's *Modernism: Designing a New World* exhibition of 2006). The strong influence of the Cold War upon popular culture was shown through graphics, fashion, film and product design.

Rather than focusing exclusively on the two superpowers that formed the poles of Cold War politics (the USA and USSR), the exhibition looked at countries such as Italy, France, Poland and Czechoslovakia, all of which were shaped by the era's politics but were not necessarily able to dictate them. The recovery of design history from these contexts unveiled complex lines of stylistic and technological exchange. The Soviet satellites of the Eastern Bloc, for example, experimented with surprising intersections between modernism and ideology. Across the project's wide geography, art and design during this period played a central role in representing, and sometimes challenging, the dominant ideas of the age.

China Design Now was an even more clear-cut example of the museum as a forum for cultural debate and exchange and a vehicle for truly original research. Based on extensive curatorial fieldwork carried out in Shenzhen, Shanghai and Beijing over a period of four years, and a three-day research workshop held at the Central Academy of Fine Arts, Beijing, in 2006, the exhibition provided a snapshot of the last ten years of rapid change in China's creative industries. Despite considerable recent media coverage in the UK (partly due to the hosting of the 2008 Olympics in Beijing), public understanding of the social and industrial transformations occurring in China is only just starting to take shape. In such a moment there is no substitute for on-the-ground research, and the V&A was able to provide this in depth, bringing examples of product, fashion, architectural and graphic design before the British public for the first time. In addition, *China Design Now* offered insights into the dynamics of emergent design professionalism – and lessons that might well be applied to the study of other places and times.

Public understanding

These various case studies demonstrate the vibrancy of arts and humanities research undertaken within just one national institution; many other similar examples could be cited from the activities of the V&A, and more broadly across the British museum and gallery sector. What positions interdisciplinary museum-based research in the UK as unique is its innovative focus on material and visual culture as a primary focus for explaining broader cultural, aesthetic, economic and political developments; its openness to cross-institutional and interdisciplinary research as a means of formulating such explanations; and its extraordinary capacity to further specialist knowledge whilst also informing wider public understanding. There is of course much potential for strengthening the research-base of the UK's museum sector, not least through further research that demonstrates the essential link between grounded, scholarly investigation of collections and the experience of the visitor. All must agree, however, that the simplistic dismissal of museum outputs as 'dumbed-down' versions of academic research – spectacular but empty entertainment – overlooks the tremendous innovation that underlies museum work in the UK today. This research constitutes an example to our international peers, and a major contribution to the intellectual and cultural life of the nation.[1]

Note

1   This essay has benefited from contributions by all members of the Research Department at the V&A (especially Glenn Adamson, Marta Ajmar, Sonia Ashmore and Liz Miller) and members of the museum's Management Board.

14. The Value of Music Research to Life in the UK

Katie Overy (University of Edinburgh)

Music in daily life

The powerful role of music in human experience is indisputable. Throughout history, daily musical experiences have included lullabies, children's play songs, rhythmic work songs, courtship songs, dance music, and music for religious and ritualistic ceremonies. With current technology, our daily musical experiences include music on the radio, television music, film music, advertising jingles, music in restaurants and music in shops. We are no longer restricted to hearing music in homes, pubs, concert halls, schools and on village greens – we can carry our own music library around with us and hear it on buses, in cars and on walks in the country. The fact that the music industry contributes so significantly to the UK economy is no accident. People love music and use it on a regular basis to relax, to entertain, to exercise, to socialize, and to share their tastes and experiences.

Music is thus a powerful way to bring people together. This is particularly evident in situations where people gather for special occasions, such as at weddings, sporting events and important ceremonies, but it is also evident in everyday situations such as in nurseries, primary classrooms, nightclubs and pubs. Music seems to have a special capacity to reinforce the social group; to create a sense of shared experience in which relationships are strengthened. At the same time, music can be deeply personal, stimulating strong individual emotions and memories; a familiar piece of music can trigger a memory and immediately take us back to a particular moment, place or relationship. We can also develop strong personal musical preferences and even prejudices, which help to define our individuality as well as our social group.

A key aspect of daily music-making is its extraordinary potential for self-expression and creativity. With just a voice or a pursed pair of lips, an individual can experiment with ideas, try out new sounds and begin to compose. The incredible diversity of music from around the globe and across different periods of history is a tribute to such human creativity and to the way in which we respond to social conditions and technical constraints. The drive to push conventional boundaries, and create experiences that are fresh and exciting, has led to everything from pianos, electric guitars and synthesizers to vast musical works requiring enormous orchestras and multiple choirs. While humans continue to feel the creative urge to express themselves musically, music research will afford valuable insights into the nature of the human condition and its relationship with society.

In this short essay I present some of the ways in which music is currently researched in UK universities and discuss the value of this research to daily life in the UK. In order to identify specific examples of the work of individual scholars, I refer to staff and students from the University of Edinburgh throughout the essay. The examples presented should thus be taken as a fraction of the work in the UK, reflecting similar research activity in similar institutions.

Music scholarship

Traditional scholarly, intellectual and professional understanding of music takes a number of different forms of inquiry. The Western classical music tradition has developed under royal patronage, state patronage and the church, highly influenced by religious practice, artistic movements, social change and the development of new instrument technologies. The context in which a piece of music is written thus has significant implications for our understanding of the work itself, and a great deal of historical research examines the social, religious, political and economic conditions under which musical styles have developed, sometimes within strict limitations and at other times with great freedom. Critical analysis of the works themselves also plays a strong role in music scholarship, in understanding the developing styles of individuals, the appearance of new musical techniques and ideas, the development of trends and fashions, the influences of composers on each other, in addition to the influences of composers' personal experiences and their engagement with artistic movements such as romanticism, nationalism, expressionism and modernism. Informed performance also plays an important role in such music research, with an emphasis not only on technique, interpretation and repertoire, but also on understanding the particular instruments and techniques in use at the time of composition, and how to interpret such works today.

Complementing such core scholarship, research into the history of musical instruments examines how instrument-makers developed the tools of their trade, what social factors influenced the design of musical instruments, how specific instruments have influenced the composition of different historical periods and how composers have driven the demand for new musical instruments, with their desire for wider expressive possibilities. Composition itself can also be conceived of as an expression of musical scholarship, based as it is upon extraordinary musical expertise and creative musical thinking, including deep working knowledge of various musical styles and techniques, the possibilities of different musical instruments and their orchestration, in relation to current artistic trends and personal responses to specific commissions, events and social/political circumstances.

Also of central importance to music research, are approaches that address music from a range of different perspectives. Ethnomusicology research brings fascinating and invaluable insights from the enormous variety of musical styles and musical instruments from other cultures, including detailed examination of the varied social roles of music in those cultures. Musical acoustics research examines the physical properties of musical sound, exploring the harmonic resonances of historic and modern instruments, the acoustics of rooms and concert halls, and more recently, the synthesis of new, electronic musical sounds. Music technology research explores the development and refinement of recording and production techniques, compositional software, sound reproduction systems and the design of electronic studios. Aesthetics research considers music from a philosophical, theoretical viewpoint, in terms of music's relationship with the mind, with humanity, with physical reality, with time, with emotion.

Combined and integrated, these different approaches to music research lead to rich insights into the nature of music in society, and the contribution of such scholarship to musical life in the UK is immeasurable. Ripples of knowledge and influence spread quickly and easily via concerts, music festivals, recordings, compositions, reviews, books, lectures, editions and new musical instruments, amongst other forms of communication. Taking a few specific examples from music scholars at the University of Edinburgh, Dr John Kitchen gives regular organ and harpsichord recitals throughout Edinburgh, Scotland, the UK and Europe, always programming the appropriate historical style of music for the particular organ or harpsichord on which he will be playing, as well as considering the particular concert venue and audience. Dr Noel O'Regan has conducted the Edinburgh University Renaissance Singers for twenty-four years, recently touring historic buildings around the east of Scotland, singing early Scottish music and explaining to audiences the religious and political context of the original compositions. Prof. Peter Nelson has directed the innovative concert series, ECAT, for the last twenty-nine years, bringing major national and international contemporary ensembles and experimental new works to Edinburgh. Prof. Simon Frith has been a pioneer in the sociology of popular music, regularly engaging with the UK music industry and chairing the judges of the Mercury Music prize since it began in 1992. Dr Elaine Kelly has recently gained original insights into the role of music in the former German Democratic Republic, and is currently editing a multidisciplinary book on this topic. Dr Darryl Martin gives regular tours for visitors to the Edinburgh University Collections of Early Keyboard Instruments, and builds harpsichords in various historical styles, according to commission requirements. Dee Isaacs organizes large-scale, multidisciplinary arts projects in the community on an annual basis, involving local musicians, artists, schoolchildren and students. Dr Martin Parker is a founder and director of 'Dialogues', an annual electronic music festival that brings local and international performers, sound designers and digital artists to numerous venues around Edinburgh. Prof. Nigel Osborne is known primarily as a composer, but also works internationally in

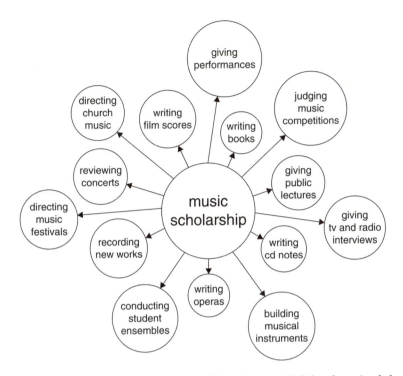

Figure 14.1 Examples of some of the ways in which University of Edinburgh music scholars disseminate their scholarship

situations of postwar conflict using music as a way to bring people together; work for which he was recently awarded the Bosnia-Herzegovina Peace Prize. These examples represent just a fraction of the various ways in which music scholarship in Edinburgh has an impact on daily musical life.

Perhaps even more important than this kind of knowledge dissemination is, of course, university teaching. Through lectures, seminars and tutorials, original musical scholarship is shared immediately with young people, who soon graduate and take their depth and breadth of knowledge into an ever greater variety of influential roles. Taking the University of Edinburgh as an example again, graduates have become performers, conductors, composers, producers, studio mangers and sound engineers. They work in the media as presenters, producers, researchers and critics. They enter the teaching profession, working in primary schools, high schools, special needs schools and prisons. They become music therapists and community music practitioners, working in hospitals and as freelance *animateurs*. Matthew Peacock, an Edinburgh music graduate, founded an opera company for the homeless, Streetwise Opera, and was recently listed as one of 'Britain's Everyday Heroes' by Gordon Brown in his book of the same name. All of these roles have a direct impact on many different aspects of society in the

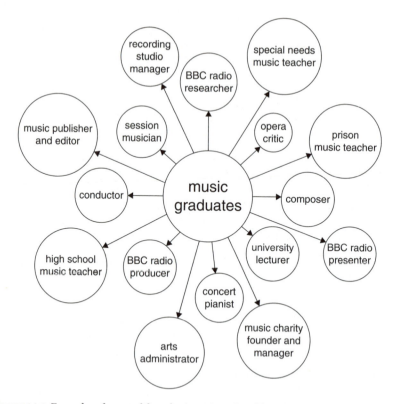

Figure 14.2 Examples of some of the roles in society played by Edinburgh University music graduates

UK, and the quality of that impact is directly influenced by strong, innovative research scholarship.

Interdisciplinary music research

An entirely different but equally valuable aspect of music research lies in the natural connection between music and other disciplines. The Pythagoreans considered music to be a branch of mathematics (along with arithmetic, geometry, and astronomy), while today music is generally classified as an art. The laws of physics are fundamental to the transmission of musical sound, and are crucial in the development of new music technology. Music is written for film and is used in education and therapy. The UK music industry is influenced by economics and the rules of business law. The history of music has been subject to the forces of politics, religion and philosophy.

The potential for interdisciplinary research is clearly enormous, and a great deal of such work takes place on a regular basis. At the University of Edinburgh there is a long tradition of collaborative research with Physics, Informatics, Psychology and Scottish Studies departments, which has led to conferences, seminar series, publications and shared teaching. There is also a growing number of collaborative relationships with other disciplines, particularly within the recently established School of Arts, Culture and Environment. For example, Dr Tom Tolley is an art historian who examines the relationship of music to the visual arts, especially in the eighteenth century. Prof. Richard Coyne is an architectural theorist who works with sound designers and electro-acoustic composers, examining the way people use voice to define spaces, particularly in the case of mobile digital media. Emily Peppers is a PhD student in music and art, examining the social context of the viol in sixteenth-century France, using evidence from the visual arts.

A strong interdisciplinary development in recent years has been the growing appreciation of music as an important topic in the fields of psychology, sociology and neuroscience. The development and refinement of musical auditory and motor skills are of great interest to psychologists, for instance, while the construction of personal, social and cultural identities through music are of interest to sociologists. Music is also a new source of fascination in neuroscience, as brain-imaging technology improves and the surprising variety of brain regions activated by musical behaviour becomes apparent, with potentially significant implications for our understanding of human communication, human intelligence and even human evolution.

Examples of some interesting work in this area can be seen in a recent special issue of the scientific journal *Cortex*, on the topic of the 'Rhythmic Brain' (Overy and Turner 2009). The special issue is the first of its kind, examining the neural basis of rhythm from evolutionary, developmental, linguistic, motor and therapeutic perspectives. Contributions include papers on the rhythmic mating 'songs' of fruit-flies, on the specific roles of the cerebellum and the vestibular system in rhythm processing and on the difficulties that Parkinson's patients can experience with beat-based rhythms. As co-editor of the issue, I found it a fascinating and challenging experience to attempt to reconcile very different conceptions of *rhythm* from a range of disciplines. There is no doubt that further interdisciplinary research of this kind has a great deal to offer our understanding of music as well as our understanding of the human brain, with far-reaching implications for education, medicine and therapy.

Music is thus central to a significant amount of academic and scientific research and is capable of informing a wide variety of other disciplines, as well as being informed by them. It should be noted then, that this interaction is particularly fruitful when the collaborative researchers involved have core knowledge of their own discipline, with no danger of making glib assumptions or surface comparisons. It is crucial that, while expanding in diversity and entering into new disciplinary relationships, music scholarship also retains its independent status and its core essence of history, analysis, performance, composition, orchestration, keyboard skills, harmony and counterpoint. If such scholarship were to be lost, we would lose our understanding of 1,000

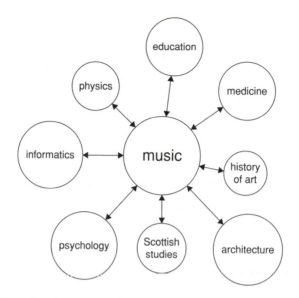

Figure 14.3 Examples of current interdisciplinary research relationships within the University of Edinburgh

years of Western musical tradition, severely undermining our ability to understand the nature of musical experience in the twenty-first century.

The Institute for Music in Human and Social Development

While the current increase in interdisciplinary music research is creating important new opportunities for deepening our understanding of human musicality, another much-needed development is research collaboration with those who use music in practice, such as music therapists, music teachers, performers and community musicians. The value of two-way knowledge exchange in this area is immense, since practice can become better informed by scientific theory and evidence, while scientific and theoretical work can become better informed by real-world insights and questions. In 2005, the University of Edinburgh established the Institute for Music in Human and Social Development (IMHSD) with the aim of bringing together research and practice from a range of different disciplines, in order to strengthen the theoretical and scientific basis of therapeutic, educational and social practice in music.

Since 2005, the IMHSD has held regular conferences, workshops and seminars involving neuroscientists, psychologists, music therapists, composers, physicists, philosophers, performers, sociologists, teachers and others. Events have focused on original themes of shared interest, such as 'Interactive Minds', 'Music and Medicine', 'Rhythm, Time and Temporal Processing', and 'Music, Language and Movement', with plenty of time set aside for interactive workshops, questions and discussions. These events have been extremely well received and have led to a variety of interesting new collaborations, friendships and networks around Edinburgh, the UK and beyond. For instance, a June 2008 Edinburgh-based conference on the theme of 'Dance, Timing and Musical Gesture' (University of Edinburgh 2010) brought together dancers, musicians, neuroscientists, psychologists, composers and dance therapists, amongst many other represented disciplines, to discuss the temporal dynamics, expressive possibilities and communicative power of dance.

The research aims of the IMHSD have also developed with immediate success, apparently meeting a need in the musical community. One recent project including musicians, physicists, psychologists, children, students and teachers, involved the design of a new musical instrument (the 'skoog') that allows children and adults with severe movement difficulties to create expressive musical performances despite their limited motor abilities. Another recent pilot project, involving speech therapists and community stroke groups, explored the potential of singing to facilitate speech recovery after a stroke and, more specifically, how best to identify any preserved singing skills when speech is severely impaired.

IMHSD postgraduate students are also conducting a range of unique studies, combining pure research with real-world practice and identifying the value of music in the lives of individuals with particular difficulties or needs. For example, PhD student Zack Moir is working with cochlear implant users and identifying new ways to improve their musical listening experiences. PhD student Kirstin Anderson is examining the potential for music classes to encourage young offenders to engage with prison education, with the ultimate aim of increasing ownership of learning and reducing re-offending.

MSc graduate Gica Loening recently piloted an intercultural music project as a way to welcome and help integrate the children of new immigrant families, involving an exchange of music and song from the participating cultures. PhD graduate Katherine Finlay studied patients with acute, post-operative and chronic pain, identifying the conditions under which musical listening can relieve some of the symptoms. PhD graduate Karen Ludke is exploring the potential of singing as a facilitator for foreign language learning, working with children and adults in experimental settings and classroom settings. Taking a more social-historical approach, PhD student Gill French is researching the brass bands of the Scottish border towns in the early twentieth century, examining the contributing factors towards their strong, long-standing support from the local community. These highly motivated and self-directed students have a significant contribution to make to life in the UK, as their research continues and their findings are disseminated and extended.

Conclusions

It should be apparent from the small number of examples presented in this short essay, from just one university, that the value of music research

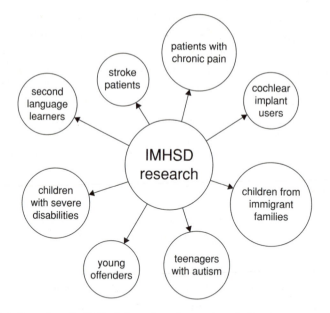

Figure 14.4 Examples of individuals in society who may benefit directly from current music research in the Institute for Music in Human and Social Development

to life in the UK is immensely far-reaching. Daily music scholarship can be a somewhat elusive and sometimes thankless task, but in between the regular duties of examining, marking, teaching, writing lectures, attending meetings, administrating courses, supervising students, reviewing papers, writing references and so forth, academic music scholars do sometimes find time to think, to explore their ideas, write new papers, perform, compose, conduct ensembles and arrange music festivals. This time is especially valuable, since it is in this space that individual expertise, passion and commitment to a particular topic, however small or currently unfashionable, moves to the forefront and progresses. Such passion and expertise needs to be nurtured, supported and respected, if the essence and reputation of UK music scholarship is to remain as strong as it is today.

At the same time, it should also be apparent from this essay that we have only begun to scratch the surface of our understanding of the role of music in human experience. The current explosion of interdisciplinary interest in the musical mind is long overdue, and will no doubt become a central feature of future research into human communication, intelligence, memory, emotion, perception, society, culture and even consciousness. If this knowledge can be tapped, influenced and translated into educational, social and therapeutic benefits for the UK population, then all the better.

What should be most clear from this essay is that music is not simply an artistic, auditory object, but an aesthetic, personal, social and physical experience that gives people joy, intellectual stimulation, creative expression and some kind of escape from their daily routine. When we listen to music we can forget everything else, or we can be driven to dance wildly around the room. Music can strengthen friendships, facilitate learning and, ultimately, significantly improve our quality of life, throughout its entire course.[1]

Note

1   Thanks to Simon Frith, Elaine Kelly, John Kitchen, Darryl Martin, Peter Nelson, Noel O'Regan, Nigel Osborne, Mary Fogarty, Jenny Triggs and other colleagues and students in Music, the IMHSD and the School of Arts, Culture and Environment at the University of Edinburgh. Thanks to Tom Howey for the figures.

Bibliography

Overy, K. and Turner, R. (eds) (2009), 'The Rhythmic Brain' special issue, *Cortex*, 45: 1.

University of Edinburgh (2010), 'Music Research', http://www.music.ed.ac.uk/ Research.

PART THREE

Informing Policy

15. Hard Cases, Hard Times and the Humanity of Law

Gary Watt (University of Warwick)

The main argument of this essay can be summarized in this simple syllogism: law has significant public value; law is a humanities discipline; so the humanities disciplines have significant public value. That law has significant public value must be self-evident in a society, such as ours, which purports to be governed by the rule of law, but the syllogism is not referring to law in practice or to law as a political fact, but to law as an object of academic research. Does 'university' law have significant public value? It is submitted that it does, not only because legislators, law reformers, judges and legal practitioners are frequently reliant on legal research, but also because a great many legislators, law reformers, judges and legal practitioners have at some point received an academic legal education informed by legal research. Thus, legal scholarship has the potential to influence the power of law even at the highest levels of its practical application, indeed lawyers tend to be peculiarly well-represented in Parliament,[1] no doubt because they are adept in those arts of argument and representation (let us not say 'and misrepresentation' – we will come to the important issue of ethics later) which are essential to the duties of a Member of Parliament. It is sobering to think how readily lawyers rise to the very highest levels of societies governed by law (Rogers 1901). Former UK Prime Minister Tony Blair was a qualified barrister, and when Blair came to power Bill Clinton, another lawyer, was President of the United States. The present incumbent of that most high of high offices, Barack Obama, is not only a former legal practitioner but also a former university professor of law.

The second premise of the syllogism asserts that 'law is a humanities discipline'. It cannot be denied that a great deal of legal scholarship employs empirical and statistical research methodologies of the sort that one associates with the social sciences, but a major component of legal research, and the one which still dominates the content of legal education, is research into the meaning of texts and, related to it, research into the meaning of texts in practical performance. In this, legal research resembles research in such humanities disciplines as literary studies, theology, classics, history and the study of theatre and film. These disciplines are not concerned to discover the merely technical or literal meaning of texts and performance; they aim to discern the manifold ways in which a text or performance is meaningful to reader and audience. Pure research in the physical sciences is immensely valuable, but it is valuable for different reasons, and it values different things. It is concerned to measure matter but it is less concerned to ask *why* measurements matter. To put it another way, it is often concerned with the material origins of life but is generally quite unconcerned with the meaning of life.

Legal research as a humanities discipline, as a search for meaning, exerts a significant influence on our laws, lawyers and lawmakers. Even at the highest level of the judiciary it has been acknowledged, albeit extra-judicially, that the interpretation of a statute 'is not a science. It is an art.' (Steyn 2003) That must be true, for no statute can exactly anticipate the contingencies of human life, and even the most technical statutes, perhaps especially the most technical statutes, deem things to be true which have no obvious connection to material reality. The statutory definition of the security interest known as the 'mortgage' is a case in point. The relevant statutory provisions do not define a mortgage in terms a layperson would understand, but describe it as if it were a *mischwese* (hybrid) made up of various abstract legal creatures.[2] It has the wings of a *charge* (that is, it takes effect as a charge), the talons of a *fee simple* (that is, a first mortgagee has the right to possess documents as if the security included the fee simple), and the scaly armour of a 3,000 year *lease* (that is, it confers the same protections, in the form of rights and remedies, as a 3,000 year lease). The fantasy is required because the mortgage of a freehold is actually a creature of medieval law that died out long ago, and all we have today is a charge 'by way of' legal mortgage.

The fantasy does not stop with statutes. In every case in civil law the task of the judge is to establish the facts on the balance of probabilities, which really amounts to producing a work of fiction that is only guaranteed to be at least 51 per cent accurate (and even that guarantee is contingent upon the accuracy of the judge's judgment). One of the first cases we teach our law students is *Bernstein of Leigh v Skyviews and General Ltd* (1978 QB 479), in which Lord Bernstein alleged that Skyviews, which was in the business of taking aerial photographs from a light aircraft, had trespassed into his private airspace. The evidence that Skyviews' aeroplane had crossed Bernstein's border was inconclusive, but the judge found as a fact that Skyviews had *probably* flown over Bernstein's land. When we ask our students if Skyviews had crossed Bernstein's land, they usually reply 'we do not know; the facts are unclear'. They are therefore surprised to be told that the judge's finding of fact is final, which means that when the judge said that Skyviews *probably* crossed the border we now know for a fact (for legal purposes) that Skyviews *did* cross the border. The law needs to abstract bright line certainties from the fog of life, and this process of abstraction is artificial. It depends upon the judge's technical skill and upon the judge's human art of judgment. The law purports to operate according to fact, but its facts are found in bare probabilities through an imaginative process of fiction. Since the statutes and decisions of our law are creative works of fiction, it should follow that more humane laws, a more humane legal system and a more humane legal profession will flow from legal research that is nourished from the founts of the other humanities disciplines. This essay seeks to demonstrate the truth of that claim with reference to a number of current issues which, if only to judge by the publicity afforded to them, are a matter of significant public concern; issues such as 'the invasion of Iraq', 'the credit crunch' and 'medical ethics'. These are the 'hard cases' of the essay's title.

The reference to 'hard times' alludes to the period of financial constraint in which we currently find ourselves, but it is also an allusion to the novel by that great humanitarian author, Charles Dickens. Dickens' *Hard Times* (Dickens 1854) observes that hard times produce a dehumanizing brand of economic utilitarianism, and that the same dehumanizing brand of economic utilitarianism produces hard times – a complaint that is as accurate now as it was when Dickens made it; but the novel also makes the positive observation that many of the qualities that are most valuable to the prosperity and well-being of human society (qualities such as 'imagination', which Dickens calls 'wonder' and 'fancy') are not qualities that can be quantified economically, but are qualities to be appreciated, and cultivated, through the arts and humanities. The main force of Dickens' critique is directed at the well-intentioned but thoroughly misguided person of Thomas Gradgrind,[3] a schoolmaster who believes that children should be 'strictly educated' and who processes them *en masse* as if he were grinding them in an industrial mill. Gradgrind is said to be a 'man of realities. A man of facts and calculations', who 'With a rule and a pair of scales, and the multiplication table always in his pocket' is 'ready to weigh and measure any parcel of human nature, and tell you exactly what it comes to'. For Gradgrind, it is 'a mere question of figures, a case of simple arithmetic'. He educates reason 'without stooping to the cultivation of the sentiments and affections'. Gradgrind is perplexed that readers in the public library wonder about 'human nature, human passions, human hopes and fears, the struggles, triumphs and defeats, the cares and joys and sorrows, the lives and deaths, of common men and women!'. We are told that Gradgrind was forever working 'at this eccentric sum, and he never could make out how it yielded this unaccountable product'; and no wonder, for Gradgrind 'proceeds upon the principle that two and two are four, and nothing over' and he 'is not to be talked into allowing for anything over'. His mind is perfectly closed. According to his cold mathematics, there is nothing of core public value that cannot be expressed in statistics; in facts and figures. When the sum is totalled, there should nothing left. And yet he finds that there is an inescapable residue of values that cannot be accounted for. He calls it eccentric, but the truth, the contrary truth, is that the unquantifiable quality of human nature is always central to what we value most. Thus he is quite right when he observes that the values of our common humanity simply do not 'add up'. Take the example of friendship: each one us can count the number of our household pets, but (as Cicero once observed) not one of us can count the number of our friends. The nature of friendship will not submit to precise definition, and the same is true of many of the qualities that are most highly prized in human life.

These cautionary observations are highly apposite to scholarship that informs the processes by which, and the people by whom, our laws are made and enforced. Numerous works of literature warn of the horrors that attend legal authorities and legal systems that process humans without concern for their humanity. Sophocles' *Antigone* is the *locus classicus*, Dickens' *Bleak House* and Shakespeare's *The Merchant of Venice* and *Measure for Measure* are classics of English literature. Most chilling of all, perhaps, are the works written in German by the Jewish, Czech-born author, Franz Kafka; a law graduate who, like Dickens, had briefly worked as a low-level legal clerk. Kafka's short story 'In the Penal Colony' (Kafka 1995) is a perfect study of mechanized 'justice' in which the central actor is a machine that inscribes a legal (and literary) sentence upon the skin of each condemned prisoner. More realistic, and therefore more terrifying, is Kafka's posthumously published novel *The Trial* (Kafka 2007) in which the unfeeling machinations of the legal process operate through the unquestioning agency of human beings. Reading *The Trial*, one would be forgiven for thinking that it was written contemporary with the bureaucratic, legalized[4] terrors of the Nazis, whereas in fact it anticipated them by more than a decade.

Now we turn to our hard cases.

The invasion of Iraq

The first is the 2003 invasion of Iraq. Sir Jeremy Greenstock, who was the UK's permanent representative to the United Nations in 2003, gave evidence to the Iraq Inquiry chaired by Sir John Chilcot in which he stated that he regarded the UK's participation in the military action against Iraq as:

> legal but of questionable legitimacy in that it did not have the democratically observable backing of a great majority of member states or even perhaps of a majority of people inside the UK ... There was a failure to establish legitimacy although I think we successfully established legality in the UN[5] ... to the degree, at least, that we were never challenged in the UN or International Court of Justice for those actions. (BBC News 2009)

The reference to 'the degree' of legality indicates that Sir Jeremy is employing a quantitative analysis: 'it was legal, but only just'; but when he states that the government established legality without legitimacy, it is clear that he is also employing a qualitative analysis: 'it was legal, but not just'. One of the lessons of Dickens' *Hard Times*, if we express it in the language of law, is that even where there is 100 per cent technical legality, the sum will leave something over. There is a quality to humanity that cannot measured by Gradgrind's legalistic 'rule' and 'pair of scales'. Law is bound to fall short of perfect justice in particular cases because the rule of law is merely shorthand for rule according to the shifting values of a constantly shifting society. It is therefore incumbent upon each member of a given society to supplement the shortcomings of the law in particular cases, and one way to do this is to question whether, in a given context, it is truly right to enforce a legal right. In the furore over personal expenses claims made by members of the UK Parliament it was notable that MPs frequently defended their conduct by asserting that they had been (to quote the spokesman of one of them) 'completely compliant with all the regulations'. Such over-reliance on the strict letter of regulations has the highly undesirable effect of limiting the popular sense of right conduct to conduct which is defensible according to a *legal* definition of 'entitlement' or 'right' or simply 'not wrong'. Thus the banker whose recklessness causes his bank to need the prop of billions of pounds of public money, still claims an obscenely large private pension;[6] and the National Health Service executive who presides over deaths caused by poor cleanliness in her hospitals still claims her contractually agreed severance pay.[7] The problem is a cultural one. We subscribe to an 'entitlement culture' which leads us to overlook the fact that it is sometimes wrong to enforce a legal right.

To counter such a culture we need to conduct research into the alternatives and to provide an education in the alternatives. This is central to the social role of the humanities departments in our universities. We need to critique and confuse our simplistic notions of right and entitlement, and there is no better way to do this than through deep engagement with the work of writers and artists who have wrestled with the complexities of the human condition. The works of Aristotle are invaluable in that regard; indeed, it was Aristotle who provided the first lengthy exposition on the ethical character of the person who does not insist upon the strict letter of the law. He called that person '*epieikes*' which we translate as 'equitable' or 'foregoing' or simply 'reasonable' (Aristotle 2004).

The works of Shakespeare are equally valuable. To take just one example, near the beginning of *Henry V* there is a scene in which the need for ethical scrutiny of the technical letter of the law is brilliantly played out. The Archbishop of Canterbury embarks upon a comic masterpiece of legal circumlocution in order to establish that there is no legal bar to Henry's claim to the throne of France, but Henry asks the Archbishop, 'May I with right and conscience make this claim?' (Shakespeare 2007) In the words that Sir Jeremy Greenstock applied to the 2003 invasion of Iraq, King Henry demanded to be satisfied that his cause was not merely legal but legitimate. We may doubt the sincerity of Shakespeare's Henry and his Archbishop (the invasion went ahead), but historical records reveal that the real Henry V made frequent, and apparently sincere, reference to 'right' and 'conscience' as inseparable legitimators of state conduct and, crucially, that he sought legitimation of both kinds from his clerical counsellors (the Lord Chancellor, in particular) (Palgrave 1834: 77). Are we satisfied that Tony Blair was exposed to any equivalent institutional critique prior to the invasion of 2003? Or do we suspect that a plausible legal argument would have provided his legal advisors (and the lawyer in him) with quite enough confidence in the *right* to invade without having to question, as an additional consideration, the *righteousness* of the proposed course of action? Humanities scholarship reveals that notions of legitimacy are more complex and contestable than a simplistic doctrinal and definitional reading of legal technicality would have us believe.

The 'credit crunch'

This brings us to our second 'hard case': the 'credit crunch'. When Queen Elizabeth paid a visit to the London School of Economics late in 2008, she asked her distinguished academic guide why nobody had seen the credit crunch coming, to which he replied that, 'At every stage, someone was relying on somebody else and everyone thought they were doing the right thing'. That is perfectly true, but a humanities perspective reveals that another cause of the credit crunch was uncritical reliance, not upon systems and officials, but upon abstract legal and economic language. Myths were spun from the thinnest threads of economic logic and a credulous commercial community began to believe its own tall tales. This is the belief that gives true meaning to the concept of 'credit', and the 'crunch' comes when the ones spinning the yarn suffer a crisis of faith. Cheap credit was a good story that too many people were too ready to buy into.

One cause of the 'credit crunch' is the fact that we are naturally powerless to resist the persuasive power of a good story, and one clue to this cause of the 'credit crunch' is indicated by the phrase itself. The phrase has taken hold on the public imagination not only, or even primarily, because of the logic (the *logos*) of the idea, but in large part because of the *pathos* aroused by the conjunction of those two words 'credit and 'crunch'. The phrase has an intense rhetorical power to stir the human senses and the human spirit. Part of its appeal resides in the alliteration of the initial 'c', and in the equally obvious onomatopoeic quality of the word 'crunch', but there is also power in the grating repetition of the 'cr' sound, which snags the phrase on the mind and memory. Most powerful of all, perhaps, is the way in which the immediate *gradatio* of the two syllables of 'cre-dit' to the monosyllabic 'crunch' conveys the sudden spatial contraction that is the very essence of a 'crunch'. Everything about the phrase speaks of swift and violent contraction in a way that is moving and memorable, hence its undoubted popularity. It is because we are naturally powerless to resist the rhetorical power of a sound-bite, still less to resist the power of a whole story, myth or saga, that it is essential to cultivate individual and collective capacity to resist the power of persuasion through disciplines of critique. The humanities disciplines are best equipped to supply the critical faculties that we need.

Uncritical popular repetition of the phrase 'credit crunch' mirrors the way in which uncritical reception and repetition of legal and economic fictions helped to cause the credit crunch in the first place. Let us return to the word 'mortgage', a word located at the very core of the economic meltdown. It is a word we all use, but very few of us know what it means. Before the credit crunch most people blithely assumed that their banks would give them a mortgage. The truth, the quite opposite truth, is that banks never did grant mortgages to their customers. A mortgage is a security interest which the borrower grants to the lender, not the other way round. The customer grants the mortgage; the bank makes a loan of money; the bank gains a mortgage, the customer acquires a debt. One of the key causes of the credit crunch was the over-selling of mortgages, and one wonders if it might have been in any degree averted if lenders had made it clear that they were not in the business of selling mortgages but in the business of peddling debt. A little misunderstanding as to the technical meaning of the word 'mortgage' will not cause a financial meltdown, but it is symptomatic of a more general habit, prevalent in financial professionals, of uncritically repeating legal and economic abstractions. It is this habit that directly produced the credit crunch. The abstract unreality of the mortgage allowed banks to collect their mortgages into notional funds or 'pools', in which they imagined that mortgages from high-risk borrowers would balance with mortgages from low-risk borrowers (as if, like water in a natural pool, the risks would find a natural equilibrium). The next level of abstraction was to transfer the notionally calm pool of securities to a company and then to issue shares in the company to investors.

A mortgage myth was spun from legal and popular fictions, and a whole commercial culture was built upon the myth. The culture collapsed when it turned out that too many borrowers (the euphemistically styled 'sub-prime' group) were unable to repay the loans secured on their homes and the pools turned out to be poisoned by bad debt. Banks and other investors went bust and the rest is history. It is recent history, but already we sense that key professionals and key politicians are unwilling or unable to abandon the rhetoric which caused the problem in the first place. The language is still the language of eternal 'growth' (Woodcock 2009), with a perfectly sanguine disregard for the fact that, outside the sphere of economic science, growth is just another name for inflation, and growth is the thing we observe in bubbles before they burst. How are we to break the cycle of repeating error without the insights of historians? How are we to break into the closed circle of professional vernacular without the assistance of scholars versed in the humanities and critical arts?

Medical ethics

Our third 'hard case', is the case of medical ethics. It is in relation to health and physical well-being that the cold front of financial figures collides most violently with the warm front of human hopes and aspirations; it is here that tears rain. The political challenge is to balance a limited supply of resources against an unlimited and sometimes desperate demand. There is no poetic solution to this conundrum, but, even here, humanities research reveals alternatives to the sterile discourse of number and scales. The point can be illustrated with reference to the 2001 decision of the Court of Appeal in the case of *Re A (Separation of Conjoined Twins)* (Court of Appeal 2001).

This was the hardest case of all. Baby girls, referred to as Mary and Jodie, were born in a physically conjoined state; Mary's heart and lungs were weak, so both girls were sustained by the heart and lungs located in the skeletal structure of Jodie. The parents of the twins had travelled to the UK from their home on the rural Maltese island of Gozo to seek safe delivery of the twins and advice on the possibility of surgical separation. When the parents were advised that separation surgery was necessary to save Jodie but that the same surgery would kill Mary, the parents decided that they could not consent to the killing of one child, even to save the other, and advised the doctors of their decision. The Court of Appeal acknowledged that the doctors would have been perfectly free to abide by the parents' decision, but in the event the medical professionals resorted to legal professionals and separation was sought against the parents' expressed wishes. There could be no easy answer to the dilemma posed by Mary and Jodie, so the challenge for the judges was to address the question with sensitivity and humility and to reach a decision in which the dignity of each child was maintained and the unique quality of their conjoined state respected. Their lordships expressed genuine anxiety with the dilemma, but the language employed was, at root, the standard language of scientific calculation and legal confrontation. In his leading speech, Lord Justice Ward framed the issues in terms of competition between the twins:

> In this unique case it is, in my judgment, impossible not to put in the scales of each child the manner in which they are individually able to exercise their right to life. Mary may have a right to life, but she has little right to be alive. She is alive because and only because, to put it bluntly, but none the less accurately, she sucks the lifeblood of Jodie and she sucks the lifeblood out of Jodie. She will survive only so long as Jodie survives. Jodie will not survive long because constitutionally she will not be able to cope. Mary's parasitic living will be the cause of Jodie's ceasing to live. If Jodie could speak, she would surely protest, 'Stop it, Mary, you're killing me'. (Court of Appeal 2001: 197)

The legal language of individualism and competition was hardly appropriate to describe this least individualistic of all human states (Bratton and Chetwynd 2004: 279–85), but, from the judge's perspective, the process of separating the twins in thought and word was necessary preparation for separation by scalpel. Such is the power of an official pen.

Professional habits of script and speech, whether of politicians or press or doctors or lawyers, dominate discourse in the public arena. One role of the humanities is to humiliate their dominance. Where professionals use and abuse the power of speech as if it were a neutral tool to be fitted to their tasks, the humanities respect the inherent rhetorical power of speech and reveal where there has been recourse to myth, cliché, stereotype and unthinking adherence to scripts set out in official form. Lord Justice Ward was aware of the need to employ humane speech. His lordship even refused to label Mary 'an unjust aggressor', on the basis that this 'American terminology' would be 'wholly inappropriate language for the sad and helpless position in which Mary finds herself' (Court of Appeal 2001: 197). Still, his lordship could have improved his own speech (quoted earlier) by avoiding the implication that Mary was a 'blood-sucker', 'parasite' and sister-killer.

The humanities alert us to those places where humanity itself has silently fallen from the scales of logic. Not that the humanities are unconcerned with logic; only that logic is not their only concern. Hopefully the reader has been convinced of the logic of the syllogism with which this chapter began, and convinced also of the logic of the argument and proofs that followed. If not, the reader might at least accept this chapter as an essay in praise of a certain kind of folly. Let it be the folly of Shakespeare's 'allowed' (*Twelfth Night*: 1.5.69) and 'all-licensed' fool (*King Lear*: 1.4.149), whose calling is to speak uncomfortable truths to those in power, when others are content to confirm the comfortable follies of routine. Politicians and professions are enthroned where kings once sat. It is in hard times and hard cases, when their power is greatest, that the humanities are most required to play the wise fool. It is when the forces of efficiency press hardest that the risk of efficient evil, which is the worst evil, must be most guarded against. The public value of law as a humanities discipline resides first and foremost in its capacity to critique, as Charles A. Reich observed:

> the study of law as a subject matter must be a study of society in the moral sense of ought and should. Herein lies law's true kinship with literature and with the other arts which seek a critique and an overview of society. Herein lies law's responsibility to be, not merely in apostrophe but in reality, the queen of the humanities. (Reich 1965: 1402, 1408)

The reader might not share our belief that the arts and the humanities represent the best hope for the best of civilizations, but the reader will hopefully be convinced that they at least protect us from the worst of all possible worlds. Some of the most iniquitous societies have been those in which laws have been applied too strictly, in which people have been analysed too scientifically and in which the powerful have taken themselves too seriously. Every society needs an independent voice to speak in the language of its history and culture and arts against the consensus of those currently in power. No voice can be relied upon to speak that language with more freedom and authority than the voice of the academy of the humanities.

Notes

1   In 2005, 30 per cent of all Members of Parliament with any professional qualification were solicitors or barristers, and one can speculate that other MPs would have studied law academically without proceeding to a practising qualification. It is not clear how many of the legally qualified MPs had studied law as an undergraduate degree, but almost certainly a clear majority, and those who did not are quite likely to have come to the law from a background in one of the other humanities' disciplines. The 30 per cent figure has remained more or less constant since 1987, when lawyers made up exactly one-third of professionally qualified MPs (Cracknell 2005).

2   Law of Property Act (1925) s 85(1); Law of Property Act (1925) s 87(1) and (1)(a), emphasis added.

3   Commonly thought to represent Jeremy Bentham.

4   For a list of the official decrees issued against the Jews under the Third Reich, the reader might consult the http://www.jewishvirtuallibrary.org [accessed 13 July 2010].

5   In particular, through UN Security Council Resolution 660 (2 August 1990) UN Doc S/RES 660, UN Security Council Resolution 678 (29 November 1990) UN Doc S/RES 678 and UN Security Council Resolution 1441 (8 November 2002) UN Doc S/RES 1441.

6   Witness the example of Sir Fred Goodwin.

7   Witness the example of Rose Gibb, who successfully appealed against the High Court's decision to uphold a ministerial instruction that she should be denied £175,000 in severance pay.

Bibliography

Aristotle (2004), *The Nicomachean Ethics*, London: Penguin.

BBC News (2009), 'Iraq war legitimacy "questionable" says ex-diplomat', BBC News online, 27 November, http://news.bbc.co.uk/1/hi/8382194.stm [accessed 13 July 2010].

Bratton, M.Q. and Chetwynd, S. B. (2004), 'One into two will not go: conceptualising conjoined twins', *Journal of Medical Ethic*, 30: 279–85.

Court of Appeal (2001), *Re A (Children) (Conjoined Twins: Surgical Separation)*, Fam 147, Court of Appeal, London: Court of Appeal, http://www.mentalhealthlaw.co.uk/images/Re_A_(Conjoined_Twins)_(2001)_Fam_147_report.pdf[accessed 13 July 2010].

Cracknell, R. (2005), *Social Background of MPs*, London: House of Commons Library, 17 November, Standard Note: 1528.

Dickens, C. (1854), *Hard Times*, London: Bradbury and Evans.

Kafka, F. (1995), *Metamorphosis, In the Penal Colony, and Other Stories*, New York: Schocken Books.

Kafka, F. (2007), *The Trial*, London: Penguin.

Palgrave, F. (1834), *An Essay Upon the Original Authority of the King's Council*, London: printed by command of His Majesty King William IV.

Reich, C.A. (1965), 'Toward the Humanistic Study of Law', *Yale Law Journal*, 74: 8.

Rogers, H.W. (1901), 'The Lawyer and the State', *Yale Law Journal*, 10: 8: 301–8.

Shakespeare, W. (2007), *The RSC Shakespeare: The Complete Works*, edited by J. Bate and E. Rasmussen, New York and Basingstoke: Macmillan.

Steyn, Lord (2003), 'The Intractable Problem of the Interpretation of Legal Texts: The John Lehane Memorial Lecture 2002', *Sydney Law Review*, 25: 1: 5–20.

Woodcock, A. (2009), '"Growth, jobs and fairness" to shape pre-Budget Report', *Independent*, 9 December.

16. The Value of Genocide Studies

Jürgen Zimmerer (University of Sheffield)

Rwanda

The day after the president died, houses started burning in our commune. Refugees began streaming in from other areas. We panicked as we saw *interhamwe* [literally translated: 'those who fight together'; these were basically Hutu death squads] following people everywhere. The second day we left home and went to look for protection in the church of Ntamara. But we were not to find any protection in the church.

About five days after we had been there, there was an attack against the church ... They threw a few grenades ... But most people who died were killed by machetes ... The attackers were *interhamwe* but they were not from our sector. They were ordinary villagers from somewhere else. They surrounded the church to knock down anyone who escaped ... People could not leave. But it was also intolerable to remain in one's position as the macheting continued. So like mad, people ran up and down inside the church. All around you, people were being killed and wounded ... The macheting continued all round me.

This was far from being an isolated case, as confirmed by an eyewitness:

I tried to get up but it was in vain. I was very weak from my injuries and there were so many bodies everywhere that I could hardly move. A few children, perhaps because they were unaware of the dangers, stood up. I called one of the children to help me. She was a girl of about nine. She replied that she could not help me because they had cut off her arms ... Finally I saw a young woman I knew, a neighbour. I called out to her. At first she did not answer. I insisted finally she responded. When I looked closely I saw she too had her arms cut off.

Both of these eyewitness reports describe the indescribable. In the early summer of 1994, Hutu militias in the central African country of Rwanda killed more than 800,000 of their compatriots, at an average of 9,000 people per day – an intensity that even exceeded the Holocaust. They indiscriminately murdered almost all Tutsi they could get their hands on and up to 200,000 moderate Hutu.

Anyone who would like to understand how this could happen, what consequences it had and whether it could be repeated, needs humanities, in the same way as anyone who would like to help the victims or prevent similar occurrences. Humanities are central for understanding the worst crimes in human history, as they alone allow a comprehensive insight into the complex processes that lead to people having their hands cut off in a central African church (but it could happen anywhere), and babies and children being hacked to death at road blocks. However, we need humanities not only to understand the past and the present, but above all for the future. Climate change, which many regard as the central problem of modernity, confronts humankind with challenges that can no longer be solved by one single discipline. Three hundred years after the division of universal science into 'humanities' and 'sciences', and the subsequent triumphal procession of the latter, a second fusion of the two disciplines is inevitable. Genocide Studies is one of the areas in which different disciplines are already co-operating to the benefit of all. Here, the humanities are not just a cultural add-on for the actual sciences, but are actually making a leading contribution.

The historical disciplines in particular play a crucial role in this area, and this will be illustrated below, taking the genocide in Rwanda, the memorialization of the Holocaust, the Australian apology for the 'Stolen Generations' and, above all, the consequences of climate change as examples. So how did the events come about that the two introductory quotations described so grimly? The killing began in Rwanda after the aircraft of the Rwandan President Juvénal Habyarimana – which also had the Burundi Head of State Cyprien Ntaryamira on board – was shot down with rockets as it prepared to land in Kigali, the capital of Rwanda. Radical forces (Hutu Power) in the military and the government used this opportunity to launch their long-planned genocide. Armed Hutu militias possessed lists produced in advance with the names of the Tutsi and any Hutu who were in opposition to the Hutu Power party. They systematically 'worked their way through' these lists, i.e. they killed everyone whose name appeared. They also set up road blocks where passers-by were checked. If their passports indicated that they were Tutsi – the passports had to specify the ethnic origin (Hutu or Tutsi) from the days of Belgian colonial rule – they were generally murdered immediately, and women were often raped first. The persecuted sought safety in hospitals and churches, but the introductory quotations reveal what awaited them there.

In an orgy of violence, neighbours killed neighbours and thousands were robbed, mutilated, raped and murdered. After three months, the Tutsi rebel army Rwandan Patriotic Front (RPF) quickly marched up from its Ugandan exile into Kigali and put an end to the massacre. Hundreds of thousands of Hutu then fled from the country in turn, particularly to neighbouring Congo where the humanitarian catastrophe continued: tens of thousands died because of the pitiful humanitarian conditions or fell victim of the revenge of the Tutsi militias. In a vicious cycle of victim-perpetrator-victim, the underprivileged and discriminated-against Hutu became masters of the life and death of the former upper class, the Tutsi, before becoming victims themselves once again. By that point the latest, mass violence was endemic in East Congo, playing its part in intensifying the conflict in and around Congo which cost an estimated total of over three million lives between 1998 and 2005.

In Rwanda, Paul Kagame, the leader of the RPF and the conqueror of Kigali, is now the President. From a superficial point of view, the country is at peace, but the consequences of the genocide are evident everywhere and not only in the form of orphan children whose fathers and mothers were butchered (in 1999, an estimated 45,000 to 60,000 households in Rwanda were headed by minors because the parents had been killed; these households included approximately 300,000 children), but also the hundreds of thousands of HIV victims who were infected by the mass rapes (UNICEF assumes a total of 250,000 to 500,000 rape victims). Many observers anticipate a new outbreak of violence in the short to medium term.

Rwanda reminded the world again that genocide prevention, as established after the horrors of the Holocaust in the 1948 UN 'Convention on the Prevention and Punishment of the Crime of Genocide', was not effective. Bosnia, East Timor and Darfur are further proof of this. Alongside Armenia and the Holocaust itself, they have become symbols of genocidal violence and of what man is capable of doing to his fellow man. And this list does not even contain wars and violations of human rights.

If the concept of promoting and extending Genocide Studies as a discipline needed any further impetus, Rwanda clearly proved the necessity for it. Genocide Studies is devoted to a crime defined by international law according to the UN Convention quoted above as:

> any of the following acts committed with intent to destroy, in whole or in part, a national, ethnical, racial or religious group, such as:
> (a) Killing members of the group;
> (b) Causing serious bodily or mental harm to members of the group;
> (c) Deliberately inflicting on the group conditions of life calculated to bring about its physical destruction in whole or in part;
> (d) Imposing measures intended to prevent births within the group;
> (e) Forcibly transferring children of the group to another group.

The central criterion for the presence of a genocide is therefore the intention to destroy a specific, clearly defined group of people. In this sense, genocide is an 'identity crime', based on the precise definition of the victim group. This definition need not necessarily be based on ethnic markers, i.e. it does not have to be a question of actual or perceived 'races', even though this has particularly frequently been the case in historical terms.

Understanding and possibly preventing genocide primarily involves understanding these identity constructs. The humanities are therefore central for understanding genocide, because assignments of identity within human societies are complex, discursive constructs. In order to decode them, the historical and philological disciplines have developed a sophisticated array of instruments: hermeneutics, deconstructivism and postcolonial theory, to name just a few.

Identity constructs exist in all societies, but genocide requires not only the definition of various identities, but also absolute, binary opposition. The victim group, which in cases of genocide is always defined by the perpetrator, and for that reason alone can be loaded with content at will, is not regarded as one group among many with which it could be possible to arrange a peaceful coexistence, but rather as an irreconcilable 'other' which must be driven out or, best of all, destroyed. This was the role imposed on the Jews by the Nazis or on the Tutsi by the Hutu.

It is the centrality of the identity, which leads to the fact that other measures apart from murder can be genocidal. The forcible transfer of children in order to raise them outside their original cultural group, as seen in Australia in the twentieth century, belongs to this category: namely, if the transfer is carried out with the aim of forcing the child to 'forget' its origins. As a result, the sustainability of cultural identity is impaired, and in the long term the group would be destroyed.

The construction of cultural identity in the initially quoted example of Rwanda is a complex procedure because the ethnic character of Hutu- and Tutsiness has been contested in recent scholarship, stressing instead the social construction of both group identities.

Historically speaking, identities grow over a long period of time, based on collective memories and they are constructed in a discursive process both within the respective groups and also between the groups. This is another reason why humanities, and in this sense above all the historical disciplines, are crucial for understanding them.

Yugoslavia

A good example of the significance of history in the collective formation of identity and its relationship with violence is found in the former Yugoslavian head-of-state Slobodan Milošević's now-famous speech on the Battle of Kosovo (1389) – in which a Serbian army was destroyed by the Ottoman Empire. In his 1989 speech, which he held at the Amselfeld battlefield on the occasion of the 600th anniversary, Milošević not only affirmed the Serbian claim of sovereignty over Kosovo (which led ten years later to the bombardment of the remainder of Yugoslavia, i.e. Serbia, by NATO), but he also used the opportunity to suggest that the defeat in battle was down to Serbian disunity. He called for Yugoslavian unity under a Serbian hegemony. Just a few months later, he reacted to the devolution of Slovenia and Croatia from Yugoslavia by declaring war. In the opinion of many commentators, he did not even flinch from ordering genocidal violence in order to support his claim of sovereignty over at least the province of Bosnia-Herzegovina. During the years 1992–5, the war raged throughout the predominantly Muslim country and cost the lives of between 100,000 and 200,000 people. This was one of the reasons that led to Milošević being handed over to the International Criminal Tribunal for the Former Yugoslavia (ICTY) in The Hague, which indicted him for his involvement 'in a joint criminal enterprise, the purpose of which was the forcible and permanent removal of the majority of non-Serbs from large areas of the Republic of Bosnia-Herzegovina'. However, before a final verdict could be reached the former President of Yugoslavia died in custody on 11 March 11 2006.

Remembering

History is not only important for understanding genocidal perpetrators; historical appraisal and reconstruction are also a central concern for the victims. As genocide as a crime not only aims at the physical destruction of the victim group but also seeks to eliminate all memory of it, as if it had never existed – even though the Nazis, for instance, wanted to place some Jewish artefacts into museums – a historic reconstruction itself can become an act of resistance against genocide. By keeping the memory of and knowledge about lost worlds alive, it is possible to counter the plans of genocidal criminals.

Moreover, memorial sites such as the central memorial of Yad Vashem in Israel or the United States Holocaust Museum in Washington, DC, to name just the largest on the Holocaust, can become crystallization points of a new identity. Because genocide has interrupted many traditions and destroyed cult objects and locations, it is mostly not possible to simply continue old traditions. Historical appraisal – and particularly also scientific examination, which can prevent the risk of drifting into myths and legends – is an important part of a process that is also central for healing deep wounds. Moreover, both healing and reconciliation between the dependents and descendants of the former perpetrators and victims, which is essential in the interests of a stable coexistence for the future, must begin with an acknowledgement of the historical reality and guilt.

The prime example of this is the German attempts at reconciliation with Israel after the Second World War. They included the merciless historical uncovering of the German crimes in the Third Reich, the reconstruction of Jewish life before the catastrophe and the rewriting of the national curricula from a post-racist perspective.

However, Germany is not the only country in history where conflicts are raging about an alleged or actual genocidal past. As an open investigation into the genocides at the end of the Ottoman Empire is not permitted, and as the debate about the United States' own genocidal past is not yet really a subject of national interest in the USA, Australia must be granted the dubious honour of being the site of the most bitter battles concerning the genocidal elements of settler colonialism. Without doubt, the treatment of the Aborigines is an open wound that has been festering for decades, and for which the healing process began only recently.

The issue of genocide in Australian history is divided into two parts. On the one hand, it involves the conquering and settlement of the country in the nineteenth century and, on the other hand, the so-called 'Stolen Generations', the victims of the government policy of removal, in which 'children of Australian Aboriginal and Torres Strait Islander descent' were taken away from their families in order to be brought up in white foster families and to make them into good, white Australian citizens. In the century between 1869 and 1970, up to 100,000 children were stolen from their parents in this way and made into de-facto orphans.

The significance of this issue in Australian society was indicated by the speech by the newly elected Australian Prime Minister Kevin Rudd on 13 February 2008 at the Opening of Parliament. He apologized to the Aborigines in the name of the Australian government. There were surely more significant events in daily politics at the time, but on a symbolic level it is hardly possible to think of a more radical renunciation of the course of his conservative predecessor John Howard, who had always refused an apology.

The debate focuses on nothing less than the self-image of a society that would like to regard itself as 'Anglo-Saxon white' but has not been so for a long time, if indeed it ever was. It confronts a country that regards itself as a Western, enlightened enclave in a hemisphere that is coming more and more under the influence of Asia with its own history and with the fact that its foundation, as many historians argue, was based on genocide. In the raging history wars, the central theme is nothing less than the national identity, based on two mutually exclusive master narratives. One deals with the civilizing mission of the Europeans who, after a long exodus, settled in the Promised Land of Australia, cultivated it and made it fruitful; the other tells a story of violence, robbery, oppression, rape and murder against the Aborigines. While the Europeans are the victims of a wild nature and terrifying 'natives' in the first narrative, they are the perpetrators in the second.

The fact that Rudd fulfilled his campaign promise at the constitutive session of the new Parliament shows just how important is the question of how to deal with the past. Without any digression, he declared outright both the crime and the suffering of the 'Stolen Generations'. Although the campaign was described for a long time as a measure of social welfare, it clearly had racist overtones. In particular, the 'half-white' children were to be rescued from the 'damaging influence' of the Aborigines, and radical supporters believed that the consistent application of the plan would destroy the Aborigine culture as such over the course of several generations. Many observers describe these actions as genocide. Rudd was reluctant to use this term, just as he declined to mention the violence and land theft accompanying the European settlement.

However, the question about the continuity of genocidal violence, that is whether the policy of the state removal of children forms part of a longer tradition of a policy of destruction practised against the local people from the outset, is a much more serious question as it concerns no less than the legality of the acquisition of territory and so, in practical terms, the (moral and economic) basis of Australian society, and the issue of compensation.

The self-image of a nation is always partly based on its history. Critical monitoring is central, especially when such serious accusations as genocide are involved. Anyone who does not want to give up all hope of compensation and reconciliation, even if it is just a symbolic acknowledgement of past suffering, must recognize the central contribution of historical appraisal in the moral economy of present societies. This is crucially significant especially in the Western societies, whose claim to leadership is largely based on their moral integrity.

Rudd is therefore not alone with his apology. In recent years, there has been an international tendency towards an obligation to apologize publicly for crimes in the past, especially mass colonial crimes and the related excesses of violence. The reluctance and the rhetorical ambiguity involved indicate the importance of the issue of historical self-perception. For instance, although President Bill Clinton expressed regrets for slavery on a trip to Africa in 1998 and also condemned the profiteers in North America, he rebutted any direct responsibility by saying that the USA had not yet existed. In 2003, George W. Bush made a similar statement, once again in Africa. At home, such clear words are lacking, just as much as a central memorial on the Washington Mall, something which Afro-American representatives have demanded for years. The theme of slavery and more precisely its abolition moved the British Prime Minister Tony Blair in November 2006 to words of regret about the crimes of European slave trading; although he criticized the criminal involvement of British shipbuilders, ships' captains and merchants, he simultaneously linked the crime to the good deed by referring to the abolition of slave trading by the British Parliament. So it was possible to infer that the British Empire was not entirely bad: it also enabled the battle against slavery.

In this respect, Germany has gone the furthest: since it became public knowledge that there had already been a German genocide before the Holocaust, perpetrated between 1904 and 1908 by German colonial troops against the Herero and the Nama in the former German South-West Africa (today: Namibia), the public pressure on the government grew. In 2004, Germany therefore apologized officially to the Herero for the genocide. However, financial compensation was only extremely limited.

Nevertheless, questions of guilt and responsibility are only one part of the historical appraisal – even though it takes the limelight because of the emphasis in the international law definition on the punishment of the culprits; the other part involves the issue of healing and reparation. The latter also includes the practical question of aid for the victims and their descendants.

Genocide Studies deal not only with forms and causes of mass violence, but also with its consequences, including processes of remembering and appraisal. Here again, there are learning processes, and a comparison and a comparative transfer can reduce suffering and help people. And not only in regions where genocides have taken place. As a consequence of the violence, the dependants of the victim groups have often been driven out of the country, and have fled all over the world. The Armenian diaspora is just one outstanding example. Directly affected people can be found everywhere, even in the rich countries of the west and north. It is also perfectly possible in increasingly multicultural societies that the 'victims' and the 'perpetrators' have to live together in a host country. It must therefore also be a priority for people in the rich host countries to prevent any export of violent structures into their own societies.

Prevention

Healing, reconciliation and punishment are not the only tasks in Genocide Studies: they also include prevention. However, this requires an understanding of the ongoing processes. The hope is that analysing them will help to prevent a repeat in the future.

Firstly, the question of understanding: How can perfectly ordinary men become mass murderers? How can the fathers of families become child murderers? How is it possible, as described in the opening quotation, that men hack off the arms of women and children? Can we understand at all? Probably not completely, but we can attempt to explain it. As one cannot simulate specific murder situations in a laboratory, the historical examples play a crucial role. They offer the advantage that it is easier to distinguish the causes and effects, the central facts from the superfluous details and the necessary from the sufficient conditions at a historical distance. Much information that was unknown to the contemporaries is accessible to the historian.

The best researched example is doubtless the Holocaust. This is partly due to the high level of scientific interest and partly to the fact that the perpetrating regime in Germany collapsed completely in 1945. As a result, no subsequent regime wanted to cover anything up, so all the archives were largely made accessible and both international and German courts could conduct criminal investigations, securing valuable sources (including cross-examinations with both victims and perpetrators) in the process. This remains the best foundation for establishing a profile of a perpetrator.

One of the most unsettling findings of the investigation of German firing squads, some of whom massacred thousands of people per day, was doubtless that peer pressure, together with excessive use of alcohol and a general brutalization due to the events of the war and earlier homicidal actions, proved to be sufficient to lead people to murder innocent victims on command. Superior orders, or the explanation that they only killed on command, and only did so because otherwise they would have been killed themselves, proved to be a convenient postwar legitimation, but did not actually play a directive role during the actions themselves.

However, it proved to be significant that the soldiers no longer regarded the victims as humans of equal value. This process of dehumanization is again linked to complex processes of identity construction based on a binary coding of the world, as already discussed above. On the one hand, this finding is reassuring because it shows that most people do not simply become child murderers or rapists, but it is also unsettling because it suggests that other people would act in a similar way in similar circumstances. The events in Abu Ghraib and elsewhere provide a frightening confirmation of this.

It also means that the prevention of genocide must above all begin with the analysis, the critical appraisal and the possible avoidance of such binary discursive constructions and their Manichaean identities. The entire range of instruments of international law and the potential for intervention by the international community or by individual states will be useless if a genocidal situation is not recognized at all, or not in time. It is precisely here that Genocide Studies, with its basis in humanities, can play a crucial role. Historical and philological disciplines are therefore not an end in themselves, but also have a genuine task, apart from their purely intellectual involvement with literature, art and history, to which they must face up: the mechanisms of stigmatization and of 'othering', social inclusion and exclusion, the construction of superiority and inferiority, of authority and subservience, are discursive, and their effects can be felt in the daily lives of everyone. That is why they have to be revealed and deconstructed. And the humanities possess the historically developed, methodological and theoretical tools that are needed.

The significance of Genocide Studies, and of the humanities in general, are likely to increase further in the short and medium term. Climate change is altering all our certainties. It is the central challenge for the modern age. For our purposes, the question of whether it was triggered by humankind or is simply part of a normal cycle is secondary. Global warming, whether it is natural or not, will have far-reaching consequences, which will shake even the rich societies of the north to their very foundations. If the ocean water level rises by just 100cm, and almost all scientists in this subject agree on this, extensive coastal regions in Africa, Asia and even Europe will be flooded. If you superimpose a map of the initially flooded areas over a map of the most densely populated regions, they coincide to a frightening degree. This can all be modelled on a scientific basis, but the possible consequences go beyond the realm of the sciences. For instance, we can predict relatively certainly that the floods (not even to mention the consequences of climate change such as storms and droughts) will lead to massive flows of refugees, although it is not yet possible to say how many millions will be affected. Like spreading waves, these fugitives will distribute themselves in all areas in the vicinity that are less affected by the floods, with a higher density in the more wealthy or generally better positioned regions. Presumably, two things will then happen: on the one hand, there will probably be violent reactions by the original population, where the intensity will depend on the shortage of resources that already existed or is worsened by the inflow of refugees; on the other hand, there will probably be a further migration of refugees towards neighbouring states and ultimately to the rich countries in the north (and possibly also China). In such cases, rich and poor are relative terms; the only certainty is that those who have lost everything in the floods will be relatively low in the social hierarchy.

Thus far, the forecasts are straightforward. It is much harder to predict when and where the provision and rejection of aid will turn into actual physical violence, or even genocide. It is far from certain that the violence will break out with equal intensity everywhere, or will automatically be aimed at the refugees. This depends on the social fabric of the respective regions. Here, definitions of identity, and the way in which they have come about, are key factors. In many regions, members of groups that regard themselves as related may live on both sides of a border. If refugees are received here, they may well be regarded as brothers and sisters. An example from European history should clarify this point. In the years between 1933 and 1945, non-Jewish Germans were persuaded to regard the 500,000 Jews living in Germany as a life-threatening danger that had to be eliminated. The Holocaust was a consequence of this. After the war, a total of 12 million ethnic Germans came from the Eastern German regions into the reduced territories of Germany. In the general state of need, these people were not popular. However, no-one called for them to be driven out or even murdered. One of the reasons for this was that they were regarded as brothers and sisters, as Germans – even in terms of racial ideology – whereas the Jews, who were both formally and culturally German, were seen as 'absolute others'. This also means that migrations of refugees do not always have to end in genocide everywhere, but that this is certainly possible. This represents a large, vitally important and scarcely researched field for Genocide Studies and the humanities.

Environmental change, with its thousands of consequences, demands that the humanities take their task seriously. Science alone, which played a decisive role in causing the problem, is no longer capable of solving it. Any ideas of tackling environmental change with major technical projects should be approached with scepticism. Above all, there should be a dialogue between the advocates of this solution and the experts responsible for the results and unintended consequences of previous major projects, in order to show the supporters of technical progress the potential fallibility of their own position. There is plenty of historical evidence. As environmental change will fundamentally alter human society, it is time for the humanities to take over their role within scientific analyses.

Problems such as genocide are a concern for the whole of humankind. In a globalized world, in which images from afflicted regions in the world flash across the screens every evening, pictures of the wealth here also find their way to the poorest people on the planet. Trade and economics are global, but so are violence and misery. However, genocide is everyone's concern, even above and beyond the specific effects. It attacks the cultural diversity of human society and produces irreversible losses. It reduces people to mere objects and so represents a fundamental attack on human coexistence. As long as genocide is regarded as a viable political option by some leaders, stable peace will be impossible. The humanities are on the front line in this particular battle.

17. History and Public Policy

Simon Szreter (University of Cambridge)

Why history and policy?

History can be studied in many ways and for many reasons, including the sheer pleasure of learning about other times, people and places for their own sake. One of the values of history in a liberal democracy can be to inform the deliberative process of policymaking (Tosh 2008). However, busy policymakers, immersed in the advice proffered by economists, sociologists, psychologists and medical professionals, while also keeping an eye on the electoral weather vane, will not have the time, even if they did have the inclination, to become regular readers of academic history.

Historians can grumble among themselves about this absence of genuine historical 'literacy' among the governing class and lament the general lack of a critically informed historical perspective among opinion-formers and political figures. But are they entitled to do so? If I do nothing to make the fruit of my historical research available and accessible to those working in the contemporary arena of policy discussion and formulation, who is at fault? The challenge for historians is therefore twofold. Firstly, it is in communicating the value of history to a policy audience, then, if this value is accepted, to persuade policymakers to listen to and act on these historical insights.

In the UK there has been an almost complete absence of any institutionalized vehicle for the communication of historians' research to this important audience. Apart from the possibility of occasional features in the broadsheets, there has been no recognized outlet for publicizing the fruits of historical research to reach this audience. There is consequently a considerable gap between, on the one hand, the monograph or the journal article and, on the other hand, the 'popularization' or 'public history' of the television series, with the student textbook as the only other standard product available.

None of these media are designed to bring historians' specialized research specifically to the attention of the policy community and none of these are of much help to the time-pressured policy advisers and policymakers who require focused historical knowledge. By presenting history in an accessible form in the public forum where policy is debated, historians can also provide an introduction to historical perspectives on current political problems and examples of historicist ways of thinking about causation, evidence, context and process in human affairs. This will provide a healthy counter-weight to the preponderance of largely unhistorical theories, models and projections that characterize the kind of policy advice offered by other influential disciplines. This represents the rationale behind 'History and Policy' (History and Policy 2010).

What is History and Policy?

History and Policy began as a website in 2002, edited by two historians at Cambridge University, myself and Alastair Reid. We publish short, accessible articles aimed at non-historians, summarizing and drawing out the contemporary policy implications of high quality, recent, historical research. In 2006, a History and Policy external relations office was established in the Centre for Contemporary British History at the Institute of Historical Research, with initial funding from the US-based Philanthropic Collaborative and a second phase of funding from Arcadia and the Esmée Fairbairn Foundation.

Since its initial launch History and Policy has become a growing partnership and an expanding network. The network comprises, on the one hand, an increasing number of historians (over 250 by February 2010) who have agreed to make themselves and their expertise available for consultation by policymakers and the media. For instance, following the publication of his History and Policy paper on 'Rationing returns: a solution to global warming?' (Roodhouse 2007) and associated publicity in the press, Mark Roodhouse of the University of York was invited to submit a memorandum to the Environmental Audit Select Committee inquiry into personal carbon allowances.

The complementary half of the network comprises individuals working in the print, news, radio and television media, in Parliament and the civil service, in think-tanks and NGOs, who wish to be kept in touch with the publications appearing on the website and the increasing range of History and Policy events, seminars and conferences, organized to engage audiences from the policy world with historians. Our first such event was a debate on pensions policy held within the House of Commons, chaired by Frank Field and attended by James Purnell MP, then Minister of State for Pensions Reform and Nigel Waterson MP, his Conservative shadow (Pemberton *et al.* 2006). History and Policy's official launch in December 2007 was another event of this kind. It took place at the Churchill War Cabinet Museum in Whitehall under the title 'Why Policy Needs History' with an audience of over 140 academics, politicians, civil servants, journalists and members of think-tanks and charities. The event stimulated widespread public discussion and media coverage in *The Times*, *Guardian* and *Independent*, as well as interviews on television and BBC Radio 4's 'Today' and 'Start the Week' programmes.[1]

However, reading or hearing a new argument once is unlikely to be enough to change deeply entrenched ideas about the present and assumptions about the past. In most fields of activity regular interaction and gradual familiarization with new ideas is usually required to bring about a real transformation of understanding. So, the History and Policy project involves not just the introduction of new information about the past as a background to the present, but a new way of using the past to think about the present, opening up policy possibilities which may have previously been unthinkable or simply invisible.

It therefore seemed worth exploring the potential of setting up an ongoing 'policy forum' bringing together small numbers of key practitioners with relevant historical experts to see what would emerge from a series of regular discussions. We expected that such interactions would not be one-way streets, but that the scholars involved would also be learning from the practitioners' accounts of their experience and from observing their responses to different types of historical argument.

The group chosen was trade unionists as my colleague Alastair Reid had recently published a general survey in this field and come into contact with James Moher, a legal official with a history PhD and a long track record of experience in different types of unions. The Trade Union Forum has now met several times, with sessions re-examining postwar collective bargaining, the issue of trade union political funding (marking the anniversary of the landmark 1909 Osborne Judgement) and apprenticeships. It is clear that there is an appetite for this sort of discussion among the target group but also that it will take time to build up an effective mix of historians and practitioners, to create an atmosphere of familiarity and trust, and to establish a shared framework of historical and intellectual reference points resilient enough to permit the exploration of new ideas. But there is no good reason to expect that making a constructive impact on public life should be any quicker or more straightforward than carrying out fundamental research or engaging in high quality teaching and learning.

The History and Policy website has also been redesigned and relaunched to make it more useful and accessible to its users. At the time of writing there are almost 100 policy papers classified into 20 searchable categories ranging from 'Climate change and environment' to 'Families and children', 'Economy, taxation and finance' and 'International affairs and security'. History and Policy also works with the BBC journalist Chris Bowlby to publish a monthly feature on topical issues in *BBC History Magazine*. Recent articles in the series have included: 'Have we lost the spirit of the Hustings?' (Bowlby 2010) and 'Did we ever have trust in our MPs?' (Bowlby 2009). The website also features shorter opinion articles and 'rapid responses', both of which encourage and allow historians to react quickly to topical events such as the Budget or the Queen's Speech. History and Policy has also run a myth-busting 'Bad History' feature, modelled on Ben Goldacre's influential 'Bad Science' columns in the *Guardian*, in partnership with *Times Higher Education* (Reisz 2009). All our activity is promoted through the monthly newsletter and on Twitter.

What is intellectually distinctive about the History and Policy initiative is its ambition to bring to the notice of policymakers and the wider public an understanding of the implications for contemporary public policy discourse of any and all kinds of historical research and of the historical perspective.

It is *not* therefore a vehicle for research exclusively on 'policy history', the history of previous government policies in various branches of government, a subfield of history already addressed by the *Journal of Policy History*. Nor is it a body attempting to promote narrowly conceived, instrumental, policy-relevant research in history, with all its attendant un-historicist problems of presentism, anachronism, teleology and selectivity.

The History and Policy initiative is run by and for professional historians and shares with them the premise that valuable history is based on research that has attempted to engage with the records and texts of the past on their own terms. Having done the painstaking historical research, we believe that the fruits of historians' labours merit being shared more widely. Historians generate important new knowledge and challenging, often disconcerting insights, which can change perceptions of the nature of current policy issues and expand the imagination of today's policymakers. Without this, the policy process can remain trapped by unexamined and misleading assumptions about the present and how it came to be. Policies for change in the future are much more likely to bring about their intended outcomes if formulated on the basis of an informed, open and critical perspective on the past.

The value of History and Policy

The strongest general argument both for the importance of bringing history into dialogue with policy and policymaking and for historians to take it as their social duty to bring about this expansion in contemporary public discourse is that history is already there, all the time, in the policy formulating process. The only question is what *kind* of history is going to be used by decision-makers?

Without the explicit input of critical and reflective professional historians, the 'history' which policymakers use is likely to be naive, simplistic and implicit, often derived from unconscious assumptions or vague memories from lessons in school. As such, it is likely to be highly selective, to be used to suit predetermined purposes and to be largely unverified. The (ab)use of history in this form not only represents a problem of commission but also of omission, in that it both invokes 'bad' history and denies the policy process the vast reservoir of imaginative and critical resources available from contemporary historical research.

In 2007 Virginia Berridge carried out a study, funded by History and Policy, into the current use of history by policy advisers and decision-makers in the health policy field. Her conclusions deserve to be cited in full:

> My interviews reveal just this; that history is being used in an ad hoc way, mostly without the involvement of historians. Historians are mainly seen as providers of the raw materials for analysis. Policy makers like to use history but they do not usually see historians or historical

interpretation as a necessary part of the frame. There is little knowledge of the interpretative role of history, and views of history are dominated, in the view of historians, by out-of-date perceptions or by mistaken views of personalities and 'great men'. Invoking Nye Bevan is a cottage industry among health ministers.

Despite the presence in the current [2007] government of many historically-trained ministers, including a prime minister in-waiting [sic] with a history PhD, the use of history as a tool to make better public policy is currently under-developed. In the health field, the past is mined for historical clichés to support current policies. The repetition of NHS folk histories has become a cottage industry among health ministers, while expert historians are excluded from policy discussion and the insights they could offer are wasted. (Berridge 2008)

Professor Berridge's interviewees identified social scientists in policy positions and politicians with historical backgrounds as potential 'history brokers'. But, despite recognizing the value of history in policymaking, many operate in a historian-free environment, relying instead on 'folk histories' to interpret the past and inform decisions in the present.

The policy world uses history all the time but it tends to be a highly selective, convenient and amateur kind. Am I, as a historian, happy to stand by and allow the use of 'folk histories' to continue? Policymakers like to invoke history for their own convenience, often using history without actually consulting historians. The point of the History and Policy network is to deny that option by providing an alternative. Historians have no right to complain about this state of affairs unless they make the effort to promote a more discerning and up-to-date awareness among policymakers of the findings of current historical research and its understanding of context, process and difference.

The purpose of History and Policy is to facilitate this. Apart from bringing pertinent historical evidence to public attention, and challenging comfortable and convenient myths about the past, fighting for a wider public hearing for the discipline of history brings with it several methodological precepts about 'thinking in time' or 'thinking with history', which are of value to those contemplating policy interventions (Neustadt and May 1986; Schorske 1998).

As John Tosh has clearly formulated in his recent exposition of the philosophy of 'critical applied history' or 'practical historicism', which underpins the History and Policy initiative, these are constituted by the profound respect which all good historical research gives to three methodological issues: questions of context, the study of process, and questions of difference when addressing human and social affairs (Tosh 2008: 36–46; Tosh 2002: 9–12). To these we would add of course the discipline's high level of critical sensitivity to the provenance of information of all kinds and its commitment to a self-critical, reflective awareness of the historian's own time and place – though it is fair to point out that the discourse of public policymaking probably has rather less time and attention available for pursuing in depth these more epistemological issues. However, it is certainly enough of an achievement to be going on with, and a substantial one at that, if historians can contribute to a heightened awareness among the political class of the importance of Tosh's three historical precepts of context, process and difference.

For example, policymakers are subjected to a plethora of forms of knowledge from the economics, management and policy science fields, which appear to be able to predict in advance specified outcomes (policy goals and their 'targets'), regardless of local contexts, and which purport to be sufficiently 'scientific' and powerful as to be relied upon for guidance by decision-making funders, officials and ministers so they can set targets and deadlines for policy delivery. Yet this creates a self-defeating problem. Such forms of context-free policy science promise interventions which will supposedly negotiate the process of change without unforeseen consequences and reactions.

They are, therefore, severely handicapped as detailed guides to practical action because policies of any kind have to be applied in particular contexts with their specific local conditions and history. Yet the differences of specific times and places from each other and from the mental universes of the policy-planners – all of this 'messy' detail of historical context and difference – have been excluded by design from such abstracted, 'scientific' policy models. History provides a way of thinking about society and its component parts, about the messy, conflicted and negotiated process of change and about the differences between perspectives of different agents, a disposition which potentially can assist in the field of policy formulation and implementation.

There can be an assumption that scientists provide objective, factual advice and that they all agree. Yet, as David Edgerton has demonstrated, even the government's science policy is itself based on erroneous historical assumptions. In presenting oral evidence to the Select Committee on Innovation, Universities, Science and Skills (arranged by History and Policy and the Arts & Humanities Research Council), Professor Edgerton debunked 'invented traditions' such as the 'Haldane Principle' that have distorted science policy for generations, and succeeded in bringing history into the frame of understanding government science policies (Edgerton 2009; House of Commons Innovation, Universities, Science and Skills Committee 2009a; House of Commons Innovation, Universities, Science and Skills Committee 2009b). The findings of science have no more intrinsic 'objective value' to policymakers and politicians than those of the social sciences and humanities. This became particularly clear with the controversial sacking in October 2009 of Professor David Nutt as the Government's Chief Adviser on drugs policy, sparking a debate about the tensions between academic freedom and the role of official government advisers. Home Secretary Alan Johnson insisted that: 'Professor Nutt was not sacked for his [scientific] views, which I respect but disagree with. He was asked to go because he cannot be both a government adviser and a campaigner against government policy' (Jones and Booth 2009).

In addition to the methodological lessons of paying attention to context, process and difference, and to the debunking of convenient but misleading myths, history can also offer policymakers imagination and inspiration. Historians are not just naysayers and the counsel of complications. Historians themselves can too easily overlook the extent to which certain aspects of the past, which are familiar or even mundane to the historical specialist, can strike those facing policy problems in the present with remarkable power as a novel insight.

Indeed, what is novel and inspiring to contemporary policymakers about a period in the past may have been known for some time to historians. In order to effectively purvey their historical knowledge to the policy arena, it is important for historians to keep a weather-eye on the contemporary world and the issues being addressed in the media. As Professor Berridge's work revealed, it often helps if historians have personal or professional contacts within the relevant policy networks, but also with academics of other disciplines who are already active in the policy arena, and it also helps if they occasionally seek to publish in the academic journals which serve these disciplines. The following case study from my own experience illustrates this relationship perfectly.

From history to policy: an example

As a lecturer in British eighteenth-century social and economic history, the Elizabethan parish-based Poor Law features in my teaching. An important comparative article published in the specialist journal, the *Economic History Review*, by Peter Solar in 1995 had brought to the collective attention of the British historical profession the unusual nature of the English Poor Law's universality of provision. By the mid-seventeenth century it covered not only the urban poor, as found in many other parts of Europe, but also all the poor in every rural parish as well (Solar 1995). Solar argued that the development of this precocious, universalist social security system could have played a significant role in contributing to England's rapidly rising agricultural productivity and associated urbanization during the two centuries following its statutory creation by Elizabeth I.

I had long idly wondered about England's system of extensive parish registers and why they had been so assiduously kept and preserved that enough of them had survived for the Cambridge Group for the History of Population to mount its extraordinary exercise of historical demographic reconstruction in the 1970s and 1980s. Solar's article helpfully suggested to me a possible inter-relationship between these two institutions. After some further research on this, in 2007 I published an article in the policy-oriented journal, *World Development*, which primarily aimed to bring a historical perspective to bear on the contemporary issue of the scandalous neglect, from a human rights perspective, of identity registration at birth among around 36 per cent of the children born today in the world's poorest countries (Szreter 2007). My historical contribution was to point out how the citizens of England, the world's first successful 'developed' economy, had long benefited both from a universal identity registration system (the parish registers from 1538 onwards) and a universal social security system (the 'Old' Poor Law, 1601–1834), as precursors to economic development. This publication then generated at least two further significant policy-related consequences.

Firstly, I was asked to join a large team of public health epidemiologists and social scientists who were writing a commissioned set of articles on the current neglect of civic registration in the world's poor countries. They did not have a historian on the team and the *World Development* article drew their attention to the potential significance of incorporating a historical perspective into their work on this contemporary policy issue. I found that one of my main contributions was to counsel extreme care in advocating the creation of new identity registration systems in the world's poorest countries because they could be open to tragic abuse by maverick political regimes – as in Rwanda in the 1990s and Nazi Germany – and must be designed with this risk in mind.

The team's work has borne fruit in a set of four articles in the *Lancet*'s online publication ('Who Counts'). This publication has, in turn, been extensively cited in the final Report of the World Health Organization Commission on the Social Determinants of Health, chaired by Sir Michael Marmot, which included the admonitory statement that, 'Improving civil registration systems requires the trust and participation of citizens. Their privacy needs to be protected through functioning data protection systems. Individuals, in particular vulnerable groups, should be protected from abuse of civil registration by governments and others' (Commission on Social Determinants of Health 2008).

Secondly, I was asked by the organizers to speak at the 'Social Protection for the Poorest in Africa' conference, sponsored by the UK Department for International Development (DfID), in Entebbe, Uganda. This addressed the practical problems of constructing social security systems in sub-Saharan Africa. Clearly this is a long way from the 'comfort zone' of an historian of modern Britain! However, what the conference organizers wanted from me as the lone historian was a tale of inspiration for an audience of hard-bitten contemporary social practitioners and decision-makers (including one of Uganda's Treasury ministers, who was going to take a lot of persuading that money should be spent on welfare support for the poor rather than on 'productive' investment in roads, hospitals, schools, etc).

Many in the audience, which included policymakers and practitioners from across the developing world, had no detailed knowledge of the historic English Poor Law; some had never heard of it. Their main focus of activity was to contemplate and discuss the mountain they would be attempting to scale over the coming years and decades, firstly in trying to convince politicians and donors to implement ambitious and costly schemes of social protection among the world's poorest, and secondly in getting to grips with very difficult practical problems such as developing systems for cash-payments to HIV-AIDS depleted households, sometimes headed by young children.

They told me that what they found helpful and inspirational in my presentation was simply the fact that history showed that complex, large-scale welfare systems were not solely the property of rich nations, the luxurious fruit of achieved development. In a country such as early seventeenth-century England – which had been as poor in per capita GDP terms as sub-Saharan African countries today, which had literacy rates way below even those of the poorest African countries today, which had been riven with religious division for decades and even open civil war – it had nevertheless been possible to construct and maintain a fully functioning, universal social security system and associated identity registration system.

For all historians of modern and early modern England, these historical facts are nothing new and to reiterate them would not hold the attention of an audience at a professional early modern history conference. But for my audience in Entebbe this was highly significant, new information. The detailed history of the Old Poor Law and its locally diverse *modi operandi* are, of course, the subject of lively and ongoing historical scholarship and debate.[2] This, too, can offer some stimulating analogies and insights to contemporary policy planners and implementers operating in the entirely distinct context of Africa today, though of course nobody would want to claim that the practicalities of Poor Law administration in England's early modern past can provide any precise template for practical and specific guidance. However, what is much more important to the policy practitioners in Africa today is simply to know of the elemental and undisputed fact of the old Poor Law's widespread existence in a 'poor' society and to ponder the pregnant fact that it long pre-dated modern economic development and infrastructure.

Since the conference I have continued to remain actively involved in international development policy. I have recently given several invited presentations on the history of civil registration and social protection in England, including to the Overseas Development Institute, Institute of Development Studies and DfID. My most recent session at DfID was praised by the Permanent Secretary, Dr Nemat Shafik as 'a good opportunity to look back to our own history and see how a social safety net was created in England when the country had a low-income agrarian economy, not unlike the countries [DfID] works with today'.

Conclusions

The historian's knowledge and the historicist perspectives are valuable precisely because they provide different and challenging intellectual resources to those available from other disciplines. As exemplified here in the case of contemporary civic registration policies, historical research and the historicist approach can – and should – provide policy practitioners, advisors and decision-makers with equal measures of both admonition and inspiration. History and Policy provides the channel through which academics can purposefully present their historical research in relation to a current policy area.

This transfer of knowledge is not just one-way. The practice of studying history is of course a two-way dialogue between past and present. History and Policy believes that it can only be helpful for historians to be as critically well-informed as possible about those aspects of the present which most preoccupy the policy world. The organization keeps network members updated with policy debates, particularly those which could benefit from historical reassessment. Historians are regularly asked to contribute to these debates, reinforcing the relevance of this two-way dialogue to both parties.

History and Policy has just completed an evaluation of its services amongst its network of professional historians. All of those interviewed believed that a source of support to link historians and policymakers was probably or definitely important and 93 per cent said the need for an organization like History and Policy was probably or definitely increasing.[3]

Some network members believed History and Policy was important because the organization, by its very existence, reinforced the importance of history to policymaking and justified the attempts of historians to become more involved. Further, History and Policy was credited with actually impacting on policy – several network members talked about their research being incorporated into policy debates. Others talked about the need for historians to dispel self-serving myths and assumptions about the past, used in misleading or simplistic ways to justify current policies, and to show how policy 'disasters' happened in the past to forewarn those at risk of taking a similar path in the present.

The most glaring, recent example of policymakers' failure to learn from history remains the Iraq War, on which Tony Blair confidently pronounced in his speech to the US Congress that, 'There has never been a time ... when, except in the most general sense, a study of history provides so little instruction for our present day' (Blair 2003). History and Policy is proud to record that in spring 2003 it published two papers which, in retrospect, were prescient in their warnings about the coalition's unrealistic approaches to winning the peace in Iraq (Dower 2003; Milton-Edwards 2003). These are among the most powerful papers on the History and Policy website, not because the authors adopted a radical political line, but simply because of their insistence on presenting a clear and full historical account to cross-examine current policies.

This chapter began by agreeing that history is valuable on its own terms and can be studied in various different ways, including for the sheer pleasure of learning about different times, people and places. This remains true, but the value of History and Policy also lies in its role as an established, independent channel through which to present accessible policy-relevant historical insights. History and Policy enables academics in the humanities to share more widely the value of their hard-won findings and insights, and those in the policy world genuinely interested in open debate to enhance their intellectual resources to deal with the very difficult problems they face.

In its relatively short lifespan, History and Policy has become an increasingly important forum for communication between historians and the policy world and both the AHRC and British Academy have cited History and Policy as an example of best practice in this respect. In 2009, Baroness Onora O'Neill, former President of the British Academy, highlighted History and Policy in her oral evidence to a parliamentary select committee saying, 'it would often be extremely useful if those who know what worked and what did not work in the quite recent past were there to say, "By the way, you tried this in 2002 and you gave it up for the following reasons"' (O'Neill 2009). Or, indeed, in 1902, or 1802 or even earlier! However, there is a long way to go before History and Policy achieves the kind of profile and acknowledged status enjoyed by some longer-established, policy-facing institutions. At the time of founding History and Policy with Alastair Reid I thought that the Institute for Fiscal Studies (IFS) provided an excellent example for long-term institutional emulation. While the field of historical knowledge is of course much more diverse and no less contested than the politics of taxation, the IFS showed that it was possible to establish a position of publicly respected authority and maintain a reputation for political impartiality and the highest professional standards. We have also quickly learned that the skills and energy of communications specialists are as vital to the effectiveness of this project in reaching its target audience in the policy world as the website with its high quality papers written by our historians. I still view History and Policy as a venture that is in youthful growth and expansion, though perhaps no longer in its infancy.

Notes

1   For details of media coverage, see 'Why Policy Needs History' at http://www.historyandpolicy.org/newsarchive/index.html#practice.

2   Solar's article stimulated debate with Steve King: King (1997); Solar 1997; King 2000. Other recent major historical studies of various aspects of the Old Poor Law have included: Taylor 1989; Lees (1998); Slack (1998); Sokoll, (2001); Hindle (2004). For a stimulating recent contribution, written with a contemporary policy audience in mind see Smith (Smith 2008).

3   Evaluation interviews with random sample of historians in the History and
    Policy Network, December 2009–February 2010; a summary of findings was
    published at http://www.historyandpolicy.org in spring 2010.

Bibliography

Berridge, V. (2008), 'History Matters? History's role in health policy making',
    Medical History, 52: 311–26.

Blair, T. (2003), 'Prime Minister's speech to the United States Congress', 18 July,
    http://www.number10.gov.uk/Page4220 [accessed 14 July 2010].

Bowlby, C. (2009), 'Changing Times: Did we ever have trust in our MPs?', *BBC
    History Magazine*, September, http://www.bbchistorymagazine.com [accessed
    14 July 2010].

Bowlby, C. (2010), 'Changing Times: Have we lost the spirit of the Hustings?', *BBC
    History Magazine*, January, http://www.bbchistorymagazine.com [accessed 14
    July 2010].

Commission on Social Determinants of Health (2008), *Closing the Gap in a
    Generation. Health Equity through Action on the Social Determinants of Health*,
    Geneva: World Health Organization.

Dower, J.W. (2003), 'Don't expect democracy this time: Japan and Iraq', *History
    and Policy*, 10, http://www.historyandpolicy.org/papers/policy-paper-10.html
    [accessed 14 July 2010].

Edgerton, D. (2009), 'The Haldane principle and other invented traditions in
    science policy', *History and Policy*, 88, http://www.historyandpolicy.org/
    papers/policy-paper-88.html [accessed 14 July 2010].

Hindle, S. (2004), *On the Parish? The Micro-politics of Poor Relief in Rural England
    c.1550–1750*, Oxford: Clarendon.

History and Policy (2010), 'Home', http://www.historyandpolicy.org [accessed 14
    July 2010].

Innovation, Universities, Science and Skills Committee (2009a), *Uncorrected
    transcript of oral evidence, Wednesday 25 February 2009, Q133*, London: Houses
    of Parliament, http://www.publications.parliament.uk/pa/cm200809/cmselect/
    cmdius/uc168-ii/uc16802.htm [accessed 14 July 2010].

Innovation, Universities, Science and Skills Committee (2009b), *Uncorrected
    transcript of oral evidence, Monday 16 March 2009, Q146-Q204*, London: Houses
    of Parliament, http://www.publications.parliament.uk/pa/cm200809/cmselect/
    cmdius/uc168-iii/uc16802.htm [accessed 14 July 2010].

Jones, S. and Booth, R. (2009), 'David Nutt's sacking provokes mass revolt against
    Alan Johnson', *Guardian*, 2 November 2009, http://www.guardian.co.uk/
    politics/2009/nov/01/david-nutt-alan-johnstone-drugs [accessed 14 July 2010].

King, S. (1997), 'Poor relief and English economic development reappraised',
    Economic History Review, 50: 360–68.

King, S. (2000), *Poverty and Welfare in England 1700-1850. A Regional Perspective*,
    Manchester: Manchester University Press.

Lees, L.H. (1998), *The Solidarities of Strangers. The English Poor Laws and the
    People 1700–1948*, Cambridge: Cambridge University Press.

Milton-Edwards, B. (2003), 'Iraq, past, present and future: a thoroughly-modern
    mandate?', *History and Policy*, 13, http://www.historyandpolicy.org/papers/
    policy-paper-13.html [accessed 14 July 2010].

Neustadt, R. and May, E.R. (1986), *Thinking in Time. The Uses of History for
    Decision Makers*, New York: Free Press.

O'Neill, O. (2009), 'Putting Science and Engineering at the Heart of Government Policy', House of Commons Innovation, Universities, Science and Skills Committee, Examination of Witnesses (Questions 120–37), 25 February, http://www.parliament.the-stationery-office.co.uk/pa/cm200809/cmselect/cmdius/168/9022508.htm [accessed 15 July 2010].

Pemberton, H., Thane, P. and Whiteside, N. (eds) (2006), *Britain's Pensions Crisis. History and Policy*, Oxford: Oxford University Press.

Reisz, M. (2009), 'Past Mistakes', *Times Higher Education*, 15 October.

Roodhouse, M. (2007), 'Rationing returns: a solution to global warming?', *History and Policy*, 54, http://www.historyandpolicy.org/papers/policy-paper-54.html [accessed 14 July 2010].

Schorske, C. (1998), *Thinking with History. Explorations on the Passage to Modernism*, Princeton, NJ: Princeton University Press.

Setel, P., Szreter, S. *et al.* (2007), 'A scandal of invisibility: making everybody count by counting everyone', *Lancet*, 370.9598: 1569–77.

Slack, P. (1998), *From Reformation to Improvement: Public Welfare in Early Modern England*, Oxford: Clarendon.

Smith, R.M. (2008), 'Social Security as a Developmental Institution? Extending the Solar Case for the Relative Efficacy of Poor Relief Provisions under the English Old Poor Law', Brooks World Poverty Institute Working Paper 56, http://www.bwpi.manchester.ac.uk/resources/Working-Papers/bwpi-wp-5608.pdf [accessed 14 July 2010].

Sokoll, T. (2001), *Essex Pauper Letters 1731–1837*, Oxford: Oxford University Press for the British Academy.

Solar, P.M. (1995), 'Poor relief and English economic development before the industrial revolution', *Economic History Review*, 48: 1–22.

Solar, P.M. (1997), 'Poor relief and English economic development: a renewed plea for comparative history', *Economic History Review*, 50: 369–74.

Szreter S. (2007), 'The Right of Registration: Development, Identity Registration, and Social Security – A Historical Perspective', *World Development*, 35: 67–86.

Taylor, J.S. (1989), *Poverty, Migration and Settlement in the Industrial Revolution Sojourners' Narratives*, Palo Alto, CA: SPOSS.

Tosh, J. (2002), *The Pursuit of History*, 3rd rev. edn, London: Pearson Education.

Tosh, J. (2008), *Why History Matters*, London: Palgrave Macmillan.

18. 'Sorting the Sheep from the Sheep': Value, Worth and the Creative Industries

Richard Howells (King's College, London)

Economic value?

Quite some years ago, while I was a PhD student, a train I was travelling in stopped in a railway cutting. It was a cold night out; the train was packed and, clearly, we were going nowhere soon. Fortunately, I had my books with me. I was working on a study of prime-time television, reading furiously and making detailed pencil notes in the margins. To me, this seemed like a perfectly normal activity – but not to the man sitting opposite.

He asked me to explain. It turned out he was a sheep farmer from Scotland, and he was also singularly unimpressed. He pressed me hard to justify not only my reading, but also the value of learning, doctoral study and – effectively – arts and humanities research as a whole. He compared both its rigour and its utility, unfavourably, to 'birthing sheep at four in the morning.' He concluded: 'It isnae *work*, is it?'

I have to admit that I did not put up a very good fight. To me, the value of this work (and it was work) was self evident. But it wasn't to the farmer – nor, it seemed, to the rest of the carriage, who had now become quite fascinated by the exchange. I could see that I was losing the fight and eventually retreated, silently, back to my books.

The French have an expression: *l'ésprit d'escalier*, which is what you wished you had said at the time – that brilliant, put-down riposte that in reality (and sadly) only seems to come to you after the event. At the time of course, I had none, and I also had no desire to put this man down because his question was a fair one – and anyway, what I might have construed as rapier-like wit would probably have been interpreted only as arrogant or rude. But more than that (and I have thought about this quite a lot over the years) there really isn't one simple answer to his question. On the other hand, because it is not easy, it does not mean that it is also unimportant. Indeed, the response is even more critical now than it was then: we live in a time in which old-fashioned notions of the intrinsic value of art and even education no longer 'go without saying' (Barthes 1993).[1] On the contrary, the arts and humanities have become something of an endangered species, and so has their study and research. Our farmer had concluded that it wasn't *work*, but nowadays there is a far more widespread concern about its *worth*. Its value is changing from the intrinsic to the instrumental, and that is something that needs to be challenged or (at the very least) realigned. But how would I explain that now to the sceptical sheep farmer? Actually, I would bring it back round to sheep, but not in ways that he might have expected. But I'd begin with the fashionable argument of the day, hoping that the rest of the carriage were listening, too.

The fashionable argument actually goes back to 1997 with the landslide victory of New Labour in the general election. It was the height of 'Cool Britannia', epitomized by that famous photograph of Oasis front-man Noel Gallagher, champagne glass in hand, shaking hands with Tony Blair at a media-friendly cocktail party at Number 10. 'Cool Britannia' faded, along with the memory of Spice Girl Geri Halliwell's Union Jack dress, but the government's newly created Department for Culture, Media and Sport continued the legacy of taking what it now called the 'creative industries' seriously. The DCMS was originally the rather cosier-sounding Department of National Heritage, but in its new form it proudly promotes: 'the *economic contribution* and educational benefits of the arts, media, sport and our national heritage' (Prime Minister's Office 2003). I've emphasized that 'economic contribution' because while 'Cool Britannia' went the way of Ms Halliwell's diminutive dress, it is the arts' contribution to the economy that continues to be seen as most important today. Underlying it all was the discovery at the end of the last century that the arts, rather than being a drain on the public purse as 'heritage', were in fact an enormous contributor to the economy as part of the 'creative industries'.

We can see the farmer starting to get much more interested here: some facts and figures might even clinch the deal. According to the DCMS, two million people are already employed in this creative sector, contributing some £60 billion a year to the British economy, a contribution that since 1998, has grown at twice the rate of the economy as a whole (according to DCMS figures for 2008). The then Culture Secretary Andy Burnham, launching a government strategy called 'Creative Britain, New Talents for the New Economy', stated in 2008 that in order to continue the success story, the creative industries 'must move from the margins to the mainstream of economic and policy thinking'. He had a vision of a Britain 'in ten years' time where the local economies in our biggest cities are driven by creativity ... We want to take raw talent, nurture it, and give people the best possible chance of building a successful business' (Department for Culture, Media and Sport 2008).

It doesn't stop there. According to NESTA (the National Endowment for Science, Technology and the Arts), the creative industries are not just an island to themselves but appear to support innovation throughout the entire economy. As a result: 'no longer is it sufficient to support the creative industries alone and for their own sake – policy should encourage and embed linkages between them and the wider economy' (Bakhshi *et al.* 2008: 3).

On the face of it, this makes a hugely persuasive case: the creative industries make a significant and growing contribution to the economy, even beyond the parameters of their own sector. Research in the arts and humanities, therefore, makes enormous economic sense. Such research can only help the sector and therefore the economy as a whole. So, instead of having to justify itself to its critics, or even having its funding cut, arts and humanities research should now be seen as a sound investment in the future of Britain. More than that, such research could help demonstrate how productive that investment has been. I can almost see the nods of approval from the railway carriage: the farmer smiles and the whole train lurches back into motion.

The economic argument is in many ways a good one, and many people in the arts thank Chris Smith (the first Secretary of State for Culture, Media and Sport) for bringing the creative sector up to join the top table of government policy. The trouble is that more than ten years on, the argument has not been sufficiently developed. There is a growing realization that there is far more to the arts and humanities than economics. People who participate in the arts, either as artists or audiences (both broadly defined) don't do so entirely under the stark, guiding light of economic rationalism. The arts are different. Indeed, there's increasing evidence that the whole idea of rational economic behaviour is a bit of a misconception anyway.

Behavioural economics and cultural production

Let's take the example of tipping after a meal. When we go to a restaurant, we nearly always leave a tip, no matter how mediocre the food or service has actually been. What is more, when we leave a tip we are voluntarily paying more than the agreed price for the meal, and doing so after the service has been provided. In terms of sheer economic self-interest, this at best makes only partial sense. Tipping makes far more sense, however, as a cultural act which says more about our social selves than the service.

This may be a fairly simple example, but the principles behind it constitute the growing field of behavioural economics. Behavioural economics is a fusion of economics and psychology. It seeks to explain why people behave the way they do in contrast to the way in which classical and neoclassical economics suggests they ought. Craig Lambert, describing the growing strength of the discipline at Harvard, explains that 'Economic Man makes logical, rational, self-interested decisions that weigh costs against benefits and maximise value and profit to himself.' The only problem with this convenient theory is that Economic Man 'does not exist' (Lambert 2006: 50).

The idea that people do not act entirely within their own financial best interests is not new. Herbert A. Simon, working at Carnegie Mellon University in the 1950s, developed its new Graduate School of Industrial Administration on the basis of both economics and 'behavioural science'. Simon famously argued that in practice, people make decisions only within the concept of 'bounded rationality' (and went on to win the Nobel Prize in Economics in 1978). Since then, new generations of behavioural economists have applied such thinking not only to the financial markets but also to areas such as pension planning, developing countries, interest rates and even giving to charity (which in purely financial terms has to be a pretty poor investment). Harvard economist Edward Glaeser has gone still further, using behavioural economics to try and explain hatred and vengeance within both the market and beyond (Lambert 2006).

The point of this brief foray into a still emerging field is simple: if rational economic models are not adequate to explain economics, then they certainly won't tell us everything we need to know about the arts and humanities. Indeed, this is a sector considerably more behavioural than economic; a field in which people are demonstrably motivated by factors other than economic self interest. More than that, the French sociologist Pierre Bourdieu was able to argue that 'the field of cultural production' was in fact 'the economic world reversed' (Bourdieu 1993: 164).

At this point I can see my adversary narrowing his eyes. French sociologists probably don't go down too well with people more used to 'birthing sheep at four in the morning', and hadn't the whole French farming community once taken exception to importing British lamb? But French sociologist or otherwise, Bourdieu still has a lot to tell us.

Bourdieu argued that the economic was only one kind of capital. If we wanted to understand more complex things such as art and literature, we had to recognize both symbolic capital and cultural capital as well. Symbolic capital was concerned with notions such as prestige, recognition and honour, while cultural capital was the accrued formal and social education that enabled one to understand the arts (Bourdieu 1986). Now, we might dispute some of the details of what is, of course, a much more complex argument, but the overriding point remains that to equate the arts and humanities only with economic capital is a mistake. There is much more at issue, and it is also clear that cultural capital, just like its economic equivalent, is not equally distributed. Professional footballers, it might be argued, may be rich in one but not the other, while the converse may be true of poets, museum curators or even university academics. Cultural capital, though, still has its uses – one of which is creating distinctions between social groups via matters of taste. But again, these distinctions are not straightforwardly hierarchical, and neither do they equate simply with economics. All manner of subcultures, for example, have very clear ideas of what constitutes style and taste, even though they could not hope to compete with the dominant culture in matters of wealth. When it comes to understanding culture, then, the economic field is only one among others.

This is especially true of Bourdieu's theory of 'the field of cultural production' in which he analyses the way in which what he calls 'symbolic goods' are made, circulated and consumed. Although Bourdieu uses words like 'production' and 'goods', it is clear that he is not talking about traditional manufacturing because these 'goods' are clearly defined as symbolic. A car tyre or a microwave oven might have a distinct practical purpose, but the same could not be said for every product of the arts (some of which, like a symphony, do not even exist in a physical state). And although symbolic goods are different, he certainly doesn't think they are so very different that they can only be understood internally, as though works of art could in practice be autonomous. In reality, they have to be understood, he argues, as part of a complex social system within which they are made, distributed and received. This is not to say that they don't have any aesthetic value of their own, but that is never the whole story. Neither, on the other hand, is the whole story economic. For Bourdieu, literary and artistic production takes place within the field of power relations, which is in turn set within the field of class. Again, we may argue about the detail, but the point remains that the cultural field is not purely or even mainly economic.

More than that, Bourdieu argues that there are two different categories of cultural production. The first is the one most easily recognized from the current 'creative industries' perspective. Here, mass-cultural goods are created on an industrial scale mostly for consumers who are not themselves active in the arts. It is primarily concerned with economic capital and prioritizes what business often likes to call the 'bottom line'.

The second category, though, is significantly different. Here, production is much more 'high' cultural and it is aimed mostly at others who are themselves active in the arts. It is far more concerned with prestige and critical approval than economic capital and the mass-cultural 'bottom line'. Crucially, though, commercial success here is perceived to be the very opposite of critical value and artistic worth. As Bourdieu puts it, the 'loser wins' because in this restricted but highly influential cultural field we see nothing less than 'the economic world reversed' (Bourdieu 1993: 169).

I hope our farmer does not misunderstand me at this important stage. I am not arguing for a precious, misty-eyed, pursed-lipped, aesthetically autonomous understanding of the arts and humanities that denies any kind of financial influence or economic context. What I am doing is harnessing thinking from areas as seemingly diverse as behavioural economics and social theory to show that the purely economic, creative-industrial, one-size-fits-all approach to the understanding of culture leaves a gaping, art-shaped hole in the arts. Trying to make the arts and humanities comply entirely to this crude, one-dimensional economic model is like the ugly sisters trying to push their swollen feet into a glass slipper. Try as they may, it just won't fit. The arts are different. And if this is true, then to see the arts simply as a form of business is not only bad for the arts, it's even bad for business.

Now that I've risen to something of a rhetorical crescendo, I might be tempted to sit back and wait for the applause from a train-full of passengers hurtling happily to their final destination. More likely, however, someone is likely to object that the creative industries still make money, don't they? What about that £60 billion a year? Certainly, the Blair/Brown government thought so, and the DCMS policy document 'Creative Britain: New Talents for the New Economy' viewed this as vast job creation opportunity with a plethora of training and other initiatives to support it. NESTA saw the potential of the creative industries to boost innovation throughout the wider economy, but one doesn't have to be an econometrist to see what a thriving cultural and creative sector has done for urban regeneration in places like Shoreditch in London and (famously) Bilbao in Spain. This has led to phrases entering the vocabulary even beyond planning professionals. When a well-connected mother and daughter team in West Sussex commissioned Thomas Heatherwick to design the new East Beach Café, the down-at-heel seaside resort of Littlehampton braced itself (according to the media) for 'the Bilbao effect' (MacLeod 2007; Bayley 2007).

The limits of instrumentalism

The creative industries, it is held, are good not only for the economy, but can be good for society, too. In addition to their economic benefits, it is believed that they can be useful in pursuit of all manner of well-intended objectives, such as social inclusion. The argument, then, is that one should invest in the arts because of what one can get out of them. This leads to a focus on aims, objectives, targets, 'impacts' and predicted 'outcomes'. These in turn need to be audited to see if the desired results have been delivered, and ultimately provided 'good value for money'. This is, then, a social variation on the business model in which the usefulness of the arts is measured according to its return on investment – even though those returns are not necessarily financial. Its focus, therefore, is on the instrumental as opposed to the intrinsic value of the arts, in which we ask not we can do for the arts, but what the arts can do for us. In some ways, this is an eminently sensible perspective, applying a stern cost-benefit analysis to a field previously thought to be too precious for such a steely gaze.

Not everyone is comfortable with this, however. First, it is a prescriptive approach to the arts and humanities that defines 'upfront' what their specific benefits are going to be and defines their success only by the extent to which these predefined objectives are realized. This clashes with more traditional (but not necessarily invalid) notions that the arts are intrinsically ennobling, or at least that one should accept their undoubted benefits *a priori*, without daring to know in advance precisely what those specific benefits are going (or indeed ought) to be. Second, this instrumental approach fails to account for the reason why so many people, in spite of everything, continue to engage with the arts not for reasons of expedience but out of sheer and apparently mystifying passion.

To practitioners in the arts, of course, the mystery is the other way round. Their world is one in which the simple equation of culture with commerce can lead to equal bafflement. Surprisingly, a subsequent report and policy briefing by NESTA (a generally 'policy friendly' organization much more typically a supporter of the 'cultural industries' model) has gone so far as to acknowledge this discontinuity. Its research into fine arts graduates and innovation accepted that any reforms to art education must accept the real motivations and aspirations of art students. The briefing pointed to: 'a strong suspicion of formal "business" education amongst art students, who regard it as promoting commercial gain at the expense of other values' (National Endowment for Science, Technology and the Arts 2008: 3). Indeed, the research revealed that fine art graduates use the term 'creativity' very differently to policymakers, while the term 'creative industries' is hardly used at all (Oakley *et al.* 2008: 6). They maintained a clear distinction between symbolic and utilitarian production. A running shoe, the report found, may have 'cultural inputs', but according to the respondent fine art graduates: 'it is not a piece of art' (Oakley *et al.* 2008: 38). Could this, coming from NESTA, signify a policy shift – or at least a growing concern?

A problem with opposing the instrumental value of the arts and humanities is that this might seem to rule out any kind of benefit as instrumental. If we were to argue, like John Ruskin, that the arts are ennobling, then that could be portrayed as an instrumental value, as would the argument that the arts, quite simply, make life better. It's the same with education: if we were to argue for an entirely intrinsic justification of education (education for education's sake), then we would presumably be happy if education had no demonstrable benefit at all! The argument, though, presents us with something of a false dichotomy, for it is in fact possible to argue for the benefits of something without determining in advance precisely what (and only what) those benefits are going to have to be. This is especially the case when we consider the value of arts and humanities research to education and, by extension, to democracy, too.

One of the drawbacks of democracy, it is argued, is that everyone has the right to vote regardless of their education, seriousness of purpose and knowledge of current affairs. Walter Lippmann, the Pulitzer Prize-winning American journalist and political commentator, feared that the average citizen was just not sufficiently informed to participate meaningfully in the democratic process. The media, he argued, were not up to the task of their civic education. Others have been less pessimistic. John Grierson, the early pioneer of the British documentary movement, was convinced that cinema had a vital role to play in 'modern citizenship' and, indeed, 'civic appreciation, civic faith and civic duty' (Grierson 1946: 174). The film medium, in other words, both could and should be used for the 'civic education' that Lippmann thought impossible – or at least inadequate – for the task. Now, whether we side more with John Grierson or Walter Lippmann, both agreed that there was a vital connection between education and democracy. More than that, both understood that one's civic education does not end with one's formal schooling. This leads us to two further positions. First, that if we think an informed democracy is still worth working towards, then education still has a vital role to play in that, no matter how hard the struggle. For that education to be in any way complete, the understanding of human affairs has to include the study of the humanities. Our humanity, it may be argued, depends on it. Second, it follows that if our formal education stops when we leave school (or, if we are fortunate, university) then our civic education needs to continue long afterwards and by other means. And if education in the arts and humanities is to continue, then so must research. The research may take place at university (or similar) level, but its benefits are disseminated to the benefit of the country as a whole (Howells 2004: 141–55).

What is (joyfully) missing from this picture is the hardline instrumentalism that seeks to regulate both the practice and the study of the arts and humanities. In a truly liberal democracy, we must be prepared to allow both the arts and education to flourish regardless of what specific enrichment or enlightenment they proceed to provide. We must be unafraid to let the population be exposed to ideas and reach conclusions with which we may not necessarily agree. To seek to regulate the consequences (nowadays the 'impacts' or 'outcomes') of art, culture, creativity and education may be well-intended, but it has an authoritarianism that sits uncomfortably with them all. Far better a crucible from which the best (rather than the simply preferred) emerges.

There is, I think, something of a backlash brewing over both the economic and instrumental justifications of the arts and humanities in both practice and research. Yes, we know that culture and creativity takes place partly within the economic realm, but not exclusively so. The old Marxian argument that economics are the base and everything else is mere superstructure is reductionalist folly – as is its disturbingly close monetarist relation, which says much the same thing from a seemingly opposite perspective. It isn't *just* 'the economy, stupid'.[2] Similarly, we realize that the arts and humanities have their uses, but may at the same time interpret these as agreeable consequences rather than their *raison d'être*. There is clearly much more going on here, including that seemingly irrational passion to which I referred earlier. All this still needs to be explained at a much more complex and sophisticated level. Today, the Economic and Social Research Council's 'Business Engagement' wing operates under the slogan 'Making Business More Successful' (Economic and Social Research Council 2010), but one doesn't have to be a bearded, wild-eyed, sandal-wearing sociologist of the old school to believe that there is far more to culture, creativity and modern society than that.

It is important to remember that the expression 'the culture industry' was originally coined as a derogatory term. It was first used in the 1940s to describe seemingly identical, mass-produced cultural products (including radio and the cinema) of poor aesthetic quality, forms which, according to Theodor Adorno and Max Horkheimer: 'no longer pretend to be art. The truth that they are just business is made into an ideology in order to justify the rubbish they deliberately produce. They call themselves industries' (Adorno and Horkheimer 1972: 121). How usages (if not times) have changed! What has also changed is our understanding of what we mean by 'industry'. When we had plenty of it (and when we took it to mean manufacturing), we were wont to deride it. But in this country we don't really make things anymore. We have witnessed a rapid and overwhelming decline in our manufacturing strength, and this has had a detrimental effect on our national self-esteem. We are suffering, then, from a marked case of post-industrial angst in which activities (tourism was an early example) are rebranded as industries in compensation for the traditional industries that we have, in reality, lost.

What makes people creative?

Research in the arts and humanities is particularly well placed to see what is both gained and lost in this transition. More than that, it is uniquely qualified to demonstrate what is missing from the current economic/instrumental paradigm. We need to think anew about why people are so driven to be creative, and what the analysis of these cultural texts tells us about our humanity and ourselves. But just in case I am losing our farmer again, I'm going to use a very good case study – which just happens to have some sheep in it.

The Navajo people, the native Americans who live in the desert south-west of the United States, are very passionate about their sheep. In 1966, a group of visual anthropologists were seeking permission to run a documentary project among a Navajo community in Pine Springs, Arizona. The Medicine Man asked them: 'Will making movies do the sheep any harm?' They assured him not. The man responded: 'Will making movies do the sheep good?' Again, probably not. 'Then why make movies?' (Worth *et al.* 1997: 4).

Sheep are central to the Navajo culture and economy: they are a source of both food and wool. The wool is needed for weaving into the famous Navajo textiles which are still hand-made and collected around the world. It is thought that the Navajo learned to weave from the Pueblo Indians, but that the real leap came with the introduction of the resilient Churro sheep into the Americas by the Spanish in the sixteenth century. The wool was ideal for the distinctive blankets woven originally by the women for purely Navajo use, but with the increasing establishment of trading posts in the nineteenth and twentieth centuries, a growing market emerged within the rest of the United States. Modern American homes wanted rugs as much as blankets, and the Navajo, under the guidance of traders such as the Hubbell family, adapted to the demand while at the same time incorporating new colours, dye-stuffs and (to an extent) designs. The older examples are very much sought after today, but production still continues using techniques very similar to the earliest examples. As these are individual, hand-made pieces by skilled Navajo craftswomen, these pieces remain a significant source of income for those who make and sell them.

To an extent, then, we could interpret this as a long-established creative industry that has adapted to changing markets and demand. This economic understanding, however, is at best only partial, for the Navajo relationship with their textiles remains significantly cultural. Navajo culture is essentially oral and visual. Their textiles, then, carry a great weight of the Navajo people's view of the world and sense of themselves. Paul G. Zolbrod, who has both studied Navajo textiles and translated their (oral) creation story into English, discovered: 'An entire culture might be woven into a single textile: its mythic and historical associations, its ceremonial practices, its need for balance and order, its sense of place' (Willink and Zolbrod 1996: 4). To be sure, dealers and traders had some influence on Navajo designs for the American market, but the Navajo perspective still remained paramount, for as Zolbrod says: 'Things came together in rugs; what was said went into the rugs as much as did the yarn. Weaving was a way of life. To live as a Navajo was to weave; to weave was to live as a Navajo' (Willink and Zolbrod 1996: 2). This may seem, at first, to be a little sentimental, but when one considers the sheer inhospitability of the Navajo landscape, one realizes the remarkable lengths to which the Navajo go to weave. The land is arid and the vegetation poor. Even to be able to dye and wash the yarn takes incredible effort and ingenuity in an environment so clearly lacking that basic raw material: water. It would have been far easier to have made purely practical textiles without colour and design, but the creative drive clearly eclipsed the logistical and economic constraints.

This was painfully demonstrated during the Navajo people's internment by the US Army at Fort Sumner and the Bosque Redondo reservation in New Mexico in 1864–8. Although they had been forcibly removed from their homelands and marched some 300 miles to incarceration, they continued to weave, even unravelling (it is said) cavalrymen's red woollen underwear in order to have something with which to work. As an elder explained: 'When you want to weave badly enough you find wool no matter how' (Willink and Zolbrod 1996: 2).

This overriding need to create, to encapsulate and to articulate Navajo experience in visual form can be understood though the Navajo concept of *hózhǫ́*, a word that is best equated in translation by harmony, balance or order. To the Navajo, *hózhǫ́* must be maintained, recovered or, if need be, remade at all times. That is why it is so crucial to weave, creating something that is beautiful from the raw materials of human experience. It may even point us to the Utopian function of art and literature, representing a better world as it ought to be or, at the very least, making a better job of the one we have already got.

The case of the seemingly distant Navajo helps us better to reflect upon ourselves. Sometimes we need the example of others to do this. The late Clifford Geertz was a great exponent of case studies as part of an interpretive, comparative anthropology in which we could often see glimpses of ourselves in unexpected places. This, at the same time, provided a wider rationale, theory and methodology for the study of culture. His most famous case studies included an analysis of ritual sheep-stealing in Morocco, together with cockfighting in Bali, which he argued was for the Balinese what *King Lear* or *Crime and Punishment* were for us. Wrapped up within the cockfight was a symbolic representation of Balinese culture and experience, 'a story they tell themselves about themselves' (Geertz 1973: 448). This is true, of course, throughout human experience: cultural and creative texts (which we might still, on occasion, be permitted to call the arts) are shining vehicles for our needs, dreams, fears and aspirations; our identity writ large. They are visions of ourselves; visions both of whom we are and the people we might rather be. They have a value beyond the economic and a purpose beyond the instrumental, so our mission is to discover not just their uses but – crucially – their *meaning*. The arts and humanities are uniquely qualified to do this. Of course, meaning is complex and interpretation is often very difficult indeed, but that is the challenge, the purpose and indeed the necessity of arts and humanities research.

As Geertz explained (and surely our sceptical farmer must finally agree): it's figuring out what 'that rigamarole with the sheep' is all about (Geertz 1973: 18).

Notes

1   This expression is also used, with some irony, by Roland Barthes to suggest that things that 'go-without-saying' usually don't.

2   A phrase used by Bill Clinton as part of his 1992 presidential campaign against incumbent George Bush Sr.

Bibliography

Adorno, T.W. and Horkheimer, M. (1972), *The Dialectic of Enlightenment*, trans. by J. Cumming, New York: Seabury Press.

Bakhshi, H., McVittie, E. and Simmie, J. (2008), *Creating Innovation: Do the Creative Industries Support Innovation in the Wider Economy?*, Research report, London: National Endowment for Science, Technology and the Arts.

Barthes, R. (1993), *Mythologies*, translated by A. Lavers, London: Vintage.

Bayley, S. (2007), 'Fresh Seafood Served Here: Thomas Heatherwick's stunning beach cafe reverses 120 years of decline in Littlehampton', *Observer*, 10 June.

Bourdieu, P. (1986), *Distinction: A Social Critique of the Judgement of Taste*, trans. by R. Nice, London: Routledge.

Bourdieu, P. (1993), *The Field of Cultural Production*, edited by R. Johnson, Cambridge: Polity.

Department for Culture, Media and Sport (DCMS) (2008), 'From the Margins to the Mainstream – Government unveils new action plan for the creative industries', 22 February, http://www.culture.gov.uk/reference_library/media_releases/2132. aspx/ [accessed 18 July 2010].

Economic and Social Research Council (2010), 'Business Engagement Strategy', http://www.esrc.ac.uk/ESRCInfoCentre/KnowledgeExch/BUS.aspx [accessed 18 July 2010].

Geertz, C. (1973), *The Interpretation of Cultures*, New York: Basic Books.

Grierson, J. (1946), 'The Challenge of Peace', in H. Forsyth Hardy (ed.), *Grierson on Documentary*, London: Faber and Faber.

Howells, R. (2004), 'Beyond Lippmann: Media and the Good Society', in F. Inglis (ed.), *Education and the Good Society*, London: Palgrave, 141–55.

Lambert, C. (2006), 'The Marketplace of Perceptions', *Harvard Magazine*, March–April: 50–7, 93–5.

MacLoed, T. (2007), 'The East Beach Café Littlehampton', *Independent*, 14 July.

National Endowment for Science, Technology and the Arts (2008), 'Fine Arts Graduates and Innovation', NESTA policy briefing FA/28, September, http://www.nesta.org.uk/library/documents/Fine-arts-graduates-and-innovationv8.pdf.

Oakley, K., Sperry, B. and Pratt, A. (2008), *The Art of Innovation: How fine arts graduates contribute to innovation*, Research report, ed. by H. Bakhshi, London: National Endowment for Science, Technology and the Arts.

Prime Minister's Office (2003), 'Department for Culture, Media and Sport', 4 February, http://www.number10.gov.uk/Page1576 [accessed 18 July 2010].

Willink, R.S. and Zolbrod, P.G. (1996), *Weaving a World: Textiles and the Navajo Way of Seeing*, Santa Fe, NM: Museum of New Mexico Press.

Worth, S., Adair, J. and Chapman, R. (1997), *Through Navajo Eyes*, Albuquerque, NM: University of New Mexico Press, 1997.

PART FOUR

Using Words, Thinking Hard

19. Language Matters 1: Linguistics

April McMahon, Will Barras, Lynn Clark, Remco Knooihuizen,
Amanda Patten and Jennifer Sullivan (University of Edinburgh)

It is hard to think of a more fundamental question than what makes us human. Naturally, fundamental questions have many possible answers; a particularly pithy and engaging one is Francis Evans' 'two legs, thing using and talking' (Evans 1998). Evans argues that humans are essentially bipedal, technological, linguistic animals, and in this essay we will focus on the last of these – the idea that humans are humans because we talk. If we accept this definition, it follows that understanding language better will help us understand ourselves, our context and our lives better. As we shall show, language bears strongly on identity; it conveys our attitudes, and in subtle ways, also shapes and determines them; it changes as we change, through the lifecourse and over generations. Research on language variation and change can help people navigate the complexities of modern society, partly because it illuminates our histories. But initial research is vital. People generally feel they are experts on language – after all, we all speak (or sign) at least one – so one of our main tasks in this essay is to convince readers that they need to know more about something they feel they understand already, and that this additional knowledge, achieved through research, will add value in sometimes unexpected ways.

Language and wider society

Given the central role of language in virtually every aspect of our lives, it seems obvious that, put simply, we should try to understand how it works. Indeed, linguistic research has a number of extremely practical applications that are directly relevant to contemporary life in the UK. For example, the children's communication charity I CAN has found that 'One in ten children ... in the UK has communication problems that require specialist help. This represents approximately three children in every classroom' (UK Parliament Website 2008). They add that '46.3 per cent. of children with a statement of SEN [Special Educational Needs] have identified speech, language and/ or communication difficulties'. However, despite this, 73 per cent of staff who work with children have not had Special Educational Needs training focusing on language (Hancock 2008). In order to correctly identify, diagnose and treat speech disorders, it is important to understand language structure and the linguistic abilities of 'non-impaired' language users; this means linguistic research must contribute to training for professionals in these areas.

Linguistic research has also been usefully employed in a legal context. One of the pioneers of research on language variation, William Labov, contributed to an early forensic linguistics case in 1987, after Paul Prinzivalli was jailed for making bomb threats to an airline (Labov 1997). Labov demonstrated that Prinzivalli had a Boston accent, while the bomb-threat caller was a New Yorker. He explicitly comments that his theoretical work was what made his forensic contribution possible:

> All of the work and all of the theory that I had developed ... flowed into the testimony that I gave in court to establish the fact that Paul Prinzivalli did not and could not have made those telephone calls. It was almost as if my entire career had been shaped to make the most effective testimony on this one case.

Prinzivalli was found not guilty, and afterwards wrote to Labov 'saying that he had spent fifteen months in jail waiting for someone to separate fact from fiction ... nothing could be more satisfactory for any scientific career than to separate fact from fiction in this case'.

Research into language varieties can also contribute to voice recognition on a much wider scale. For instance, voice-recognition software has clearly improved efficiency and contributed to the economic performance of many businesses. While telephone switchboards using voice-recognition may be the bane of office-workers' lives, it is clear that with further research, voice-recognition capability can only improve. Indeed, the development of these technologies brings further, often unseen challenges for linguistics research; for instance, a 'Brain Training' video game has been shown to have difficulties dealing with northern English accents (Gibbon 2008). The differences in sound systems between accents of English need to be fully understood in order to improve accuracy. Moreover, if it was not initially thought important for voice-recognition systems to deal with accent variation, we might ask what this tells us about attitudes to accents: we return to this question below.

In today's multicultural and multilingual society, issues concerning language variation are relevant to an increasing number of bilingual speakers. Antonella Sorace is currently developing 'Bilingualism Matters', 'an advice and information service for bilingual families based on current research' (Sorace 2010). Reference to research results is needed because there are many misapprehensions about bilingualism – as Sorace notes, 'people are ready to believe that handling two languages at the same time is too much of a burden for the infant's brain, or that the languages compete for resources in the brain at the expense of general cognitive development', whereas evidence strongly suggests that bilingualism confers significant cognitive advantages. Opportunities for bilingualism are increasing in our own society – one person in twelve living in the UK in 2001 was born overseas (UK National Statistics

2005). This means increasing numbers of UK citizens are encountering languages other than English in their day-to-day lives, and may be deciding whether to bring up their children bilingually. If linguistic research could shape more positive attitudes towards bilingualism, it would also play a vital role in determining how our increasingly linguistically diverse environments are managed. Languages die out when they are not used, and when children are not encouraged to learn them. Within the UK this is an issue both for languages like Scots, Gaelic and Welsh, which are threatened by the social and political status of English, and may be limited to increasingly restricted contexts; and for languages like Mandarin, Gujarati and Polish, which may thrive elsewhere in the world, but are spoken only within specific communities in the UK.

The loss of minority languages is an issue of great concern worldwide. Linguists can provide historical information on languages that have been lost or survived in the past (the focus of Remco Knooihuizen's research), in contexts before the development of modern nation-states, thus informing language policy today. The relative monolingualism of European nation-states, unusual in global terms, has led to ungrounded assumptions about the potential hazards of raising a child to speak two or more languages natively. It is essential to address these unfounded concerns with real data and analysis, particularly for minority languages, which may require long-term bilingualism to survive. Linguists have a broader perspective through studying patterns of language change and death, whereas individuals may only know what is happening in their own community. Linguistic research can also influence the success of attempts to standardize languages, providing symbols of national or community unity for their speakers; if users see a particular language as socially useful, and can be convinced that it has intrinsic structure and coherence, with rules of its own and a historical pedigree, there is a greater chance of survival. This task is currently being undertaken with Scots, which has recently been recognized as a minority language by the European Union. The Scots Language Centre is actively involved in raising the status of Scots by promoting its use among Scottish communities (Scots Language Centre 2010).

Language and smaller communities

Historically, accents and dialects diverge and become new languages; the dividing line between language and dialect is therefore an unclear and shifting one. Greater mobility and the diversity of the modern media mean individuals are also increasingly likely to hear more accents and dialects. Even showing that minority languages or dialects are worthy of study can be instrumental in changing attitudes: Damien Hall has researched Norman French for his PhD, and reports that:

> In the rural area in particular, people were very pleased that I was studying their language ... It seems to me that they might have been pleased about it

because it showed that their communities, traditions, lives were important from a wider point of view and might play into something bigger that I or others could say about French, or about social matters.

Dialect variation clearly causes strong feelings, as shown by an online BBC 'Have Your Say' page, which received many responses to the question 'How do you feel about regional accents?' (BBC News 2005a) People view regional dialects as an important marker of social and cultural identity and as something that should be preserved (BBC News 2004); but dialect variation is also regarded as problematic in the present day economy (BBC News 2005b). As a researcher collecting dialect data from participants, Will Barras has encountered both attitudes, often from the same people. Potential participants are very interested in the idea of studying local accents and dialects, and very keen to share their knowledge and intuitions. The possible loss of local features with older speakers is regretted, and documenting traditional dialect features is regarded positively. However, these same participants often have a low regard for their own dialect, sometimes describing their speech as 'lazy' or 'bad'. Academic work on dialect data can help to elevate the status of dialect forms, through shifting cultural stereotypes, and fostering pride in local identity. Given the current government focus on citizenship, in schools and in the wider community, this is clearly a positive and relevant application of academic research.

These attitudes to accents and dialects are clearly among the most emotive issues in public debates on language, and, again, linguistic research is central, sometimes confirming and providing evidence for intuitions, but sometimes showing that these are not well-founded. People do not just listen dispassionately to the talk of others, but draw geographical and social conclusions based on the nature of that speech. Studies on language attitudes and stereotyping show that we regularly characterize and evaluate people according to the way they speak, regardless of what they actually say. We often (unconsciously) attribute character traits like (un)friendliness or (lack of) intelligence to someone we have only just met, because of associations we have made in the categorization process between a variety of language, and the type of person (we think) speaks that way. This can have serious consequences for our interactions with others; indeed, it may determine whether we are willing to talk to another individual at all. The speaker in the following excerpt, taken from Lynn Clark's ongoing work in west Fife in Scotland, discussed his experiences of going to St Andrews University with a broad Fife accent, and becoming uncomfortably aware that not only did he judge others based on their accents, but they also judged him:

C: See when a started gaun tae St Andrews an a wiz having tae deal wi sortaefolk fae different sortae places like America an English, **couldnae understand ma accent eh**. So a wiz immediately a barrier between me an the lassie that a got on really well wi fae doon in Manchester, Jill, she said for the first couple eh months, couldnae come an talk tae me eh.

LYNN CLARK (LC): mm

c: an a says well a thought that's cos ye didnae like me. She just says well no it's just cos **a wiz so intimidated eh, an a couldnae understand yer accent** an yer awfie, ye seemed awfie sortae rough sortae, **ken local Scotsman.**

LC: [laughs] aye

c: couldnae come an talk tae me eh **she wiz quite posh speaking eh**.

LC: aye

c: so I allwiz thought, an a said that tae her as well a said well a allwiz thought ye were a bit eh **a snob sortae posh thing** eh, so **for months there wiz that barrier there** we just never really got on. It wiz just oer time that we got oer it an fund oot, best pals ye ken still in touch efter like six year eh graduating. So a think, eh, an **that wiz just fae the way she talked**.

Recent research has shown that these judgements can be linked to a single sound segment (Labov *et al.* 2006). The researchers ran experiments to determine whether listeners can discriminate variation in the use of the form of [ING] e.g. *walking* or *walkin'*, and whether it was also evaluated socially. They constructed a passage of news script containing ten instances of 'ing' forms, and had people read the passage with 100 per cent of the non-standard form (where the 'g' is 'dropped'); 50 per cent non-standard and 50 per cent standard; and 100 per cent of the standard form (where the 'g' is not 'dropped'). They played these recordings to members of the public and asked them to rate the speakers on a scale of 1–7 for their suitability as a newsreader. The stimulus passages were exactly the same except for the frequency of 'ing' as a standard or non-standard form. The results showed that tapes which contained 100 per cent of the standard form were more likely to be rated as acceptable newsreaders than those with 50 per cent or 0 per cent of the standard form. The substantial agreement in the results obviously reflects a more widely held stereotype about people who tend to use forms like *walkin'* rather than *walking* as being unsuitable to perform jobs like reading the news. Such language prejudice could have very real negative consequences for speakers of non-standard varieties of English.

Similar patterns were found in Giles and Powesland's famous research (Giles and Powesland 1975). A researcher, who was also a university lecturer in psychology, went to a school in Birmingham to talk to seventeen-year-olds about studying psychology at university. He used his Birmingham accent to deliver the talk to one group of pupils and a Received Pronunciation (RP) 'guise' to talk to another group. The content of both talks was exactly the same; the only difference was the accent he used. The pupils were then asked to comment on his ability as a lecturer and evaluate how intelligent they considered him to be. The pupils rated the lecturer as significantly more intelligent when he used his RP 'guise' than when he used his Birmingham 'guise'; they also wrote more positively about his capability as a lecturer in his RP 'guise'. Although this is an example of the prejudices that pupils can hold towards teachers based on their accent, teachers can hold prejudices of their own; Giles and Powesland also suggested that teachers may base their first impressions of pupils on the way that they speak, even when they are presented with other examples of schoolwork. This could lead to problems in pupil/teacher relations for a child who creates a negative first impression by (typically) bringing a non-standard variety into the classroom. Perhaps this child will have to perform much better in class in order to make a favourable impression on the teacher, or perhaps negative expectations by the teacher will lead to negative performances by the pupil.

Dick Hudson, of University College London, argues that 'one of the most solid achievements of linguistics in the twentieth century has been to eliminate the idea (at least among professional linguists) that some languages or dialects are inherently "better" than others' (Hudson 1996: 203). However, while linguistic research is vital in explaining accent differences and the social judgements which may accompany them, combating accent prejudice also requires these issues to be communicated clearly and effectively.

Linguistic research could counteract misapprehensions about accent and dialect variation in a number of other ways. First, there is great concern about ongoing changes, often resulting in an emotional response that the English language is suffering at the hands of lazy or ignorant users. Both the introduction of the *walkin'* form and 'h'-dropping, which produces pronunciations of *happy* as *'appy*, are seen as signs of lazy articulation. Yet from a linguistic point of view, such ongoing changes are natural, inevitable, and even somewhat predictable; this is the area of Amanda Patten's research. Rather than being haphazard, many changes 'tidy up' the linguistic system. Languages typically have 'pairs' of sounds; so, for example, the sounds 'f' and 'v' are both articulated by placing the lower lip next to the upper teeth; the only difference is that while the vocal folds remain still in the production of 'f', they vibrate when sounding 'v'; 'h' is the only English consonant with no 'partner'. Consequently, the gradual loss of 'h' shows how languages often develop in the direction of regularizing patterns in the linguistic system, which may bring advantages for learning or perception.

Understanding the history of individual features can also alter attitudes to them. We still see regular letters to newspapers complaining about sloppy and ungrammatical speech patterns; but historical knowledge of dialect formation has the potential to widen the community's perspective. Irish

English speakers' use of 'do be', as in 'She does be reading books' (all the time) is a classic example. Widely berated by speakers themselves, it has, in fact, been argued to be a relic of Early Modern English, in which case it might represent an older feature than modern standard equivalents. Others have argued this structure reflects contact with Irish. Either way, the conclusion to be drawn is that 'do be' is not inherently 'wrong' in any sense, but has simply developed in a different way from modern Standard English.

Without input from linguistics research, however, it can be difficult to appreciate, communicate or, if necessary, argue against claims about accents. In April 2008, various news organizations reported a study by psychologists at Bath Spa University into perceptions of intelligence based on accent variation (BBC News 2008). This clearly has news value: people feel strongly about the way they are perceived. However, in the reporting of this story, there was no mention of *how* the different accents vary: labels like 'Yorkshire', 'Received Pronunciation' and 'Birmingham' were given with no explanation of what features make up these accents. Another recent news story reported on a study of the Queen's Christmas broadcasts which tracked changes in her pronunciation over fifty years. In this *Daily Telegraph* article, there *is* an attempt to discuss changing features of the Queen's speech, but it is not entirely clear what accent features the journalist means to indicate by writing 'I yem speccing frem ar herm en the grends ev Beckingham Pals' (O'Hagan 2006). Similarly, the cover story in a recent issue of *New Scientist* is headlined 'English as she will be spoke', and discusses the history of English, present-day variation in World Englishes and predictions for the future development of English (Erard 2008). Even in a publication aimed at a fairly informed readership, there is none of the accessible, shared vocabulary or 'meta-language' that would be necessary to describe language clearly. For instance, the author notes that 'the "l" of "hotel" and "rail" ... is often replaced with a vowel or a longer "l" sound as in "lady"'. In fact, the 'l' of *lady* is not longer at all – what is important is what vocal organs are used to articulate the sounds. The 'dark' 'l' sound of *hotel* and *rail*, pronounced with the back of the tongue raised towards the roof of the mouth, is more amenable to being replaced by a back vowel, to which it is more similar in articulation.

Variation in sounds is interesting for a general readership, but it is very difficult to explain without recourse to some academic apparatus, such as the International Phonetic Alphabet. This presents a challenge to linguists in terms of communicating interesting knowledge in an accessible manner. We all have intuitions about language: linguists have the wherewithal to discuss these precisely. It would be helpful if there were ways of sharing this meta-language with non-linguists, and this might profitably be pursued through Continuing Professional Development courses for teachers, or indeed by further integration of knowledge about language in the school curriculum.

Language and education

Connections with schools provide other practical ways for academic, university-led research to have a positive effect on wider society. Raising literacy rates among school pupils is a vital and highly politicized example. While there is a prescribed scheme (in England) for teaching reading through phonics, this scheme does not take account of phonological variation in regional accents – thus, *saw* and *door* will rhyme in most varieties of English which do not pronounce a final 'r' sound, but in Scotland, and some parts of Lancashire and the south-west of England, the presence of 'r' in *door* means they sound very different. University academics have created guides for teachers to adapt the prescribed teaching materials for use with pupils with different regional accents. Here, academic research into phonological variation has a very practical application (Education Committee of the LAGB 2008).

In Scotland, the Committee for Language Awareness in Scottish Schools, chaired by Graeme Trousdale, and the Education Sub-Committee of the Scottish Parliament's Cross Party Group on the Scots Language, with Matthew Fitt as Secretary, aim to help teachers become more confident in presenting aspects of knowledge about language in the classroom (Trousdale 2008; Fitt 2010). At present, 'English' in Scottish schools in particular primarily means literature; and while studying literature is important, presenting language only through its connection with literature is like studying maths only through physics – one particular application of a body of knowledge which is highly relevant in its own right. There are, for example, many non-literary examples of the connection of language with power or persuasion, and it is surely of relevance for school students to be taught to recognize and analyse 'loaded' language, repetition and confusing jargon, whether in newspaper articles, adverts or political speeches. An increased, analytical awareness of language would also allow schools to encourage their pupils to use and value their own dialects in appropriate contexts, while empowering them to use a standard dialect (which might perfectly well accompany a regional accent) in more formal circumstances. Just as understanding more about the history of our languages contributes to awareness and value of our cultural heritage, so more information about present-day variation helps us to appreciate and maintain our accents and dialects. Every high street might increasingly look the same these days, but they still sound refreshingly different.

Extending our knowledge

If knowledge about language is to be shared more widely, there must also be ongoing academic research to push back the limits of our understanding, and to refine and build on our theories of how languages work. One example from ongoing research by April McMahon and Warren Maguire involves measuring the similarity between sounds. Until recently, claims that

Newcastle English is more like Sheffield English than Edinburgh English would be supported purely by intuition; now, we can measure the differences and confirm this hypothesis, partly due to a new database of the same words being pronounced in a wide range of present-day varieties of English, and partly through a purpose-built computer program (Sound Comparisons 2010). Jennifer Sullivan is extending this cross-accent comparison to prosody, and specifically to intonation, the 'tune' of speech. The capacity to compare accents quantitatively has many potential benefits. It might allow us to compare the speech of children, people with language difficulties or second language learners with a model pronunciation, to calculate divergence or improvement. We might be able to provide some indication of the cut-off point between language and dialect, even if this were necessarily probabilistic rather than absolute.

In linguistics there is not a one-way channel of communication from specialists to non-specialists or 'outsiders': linguists rely heavily on speakers and listeners for production data and perceptual judgements. The interaction has mutual benefits. Naive intuitions do not always correspond to expected linguistic categories and this can lead to development and revision of theories; but intuitions can appear messy and even incoherent, and we often need trained specialists to spot the more abstract patterns in the complexity. Knowing more about these patterns, in turn, can affect our views on what is or is not a possible human language, with enormous implications for the nature-nurture debate, and for questions of the structure and capacities of the human brain and mind.

The benefits of research can also be subtle and unexpected. School students, properly advised and guided, can gain enormously from conducting their own language experiments in their community, coming to understand both the theoretical aspects of linguistics and the social issues with which language is intimately linked. In the heavily exam-oriented school and undergraduate curriculum, there may be a place for introductions to research in the interests of academic development somewhat apart from external benchmarks and from the performance of others. Research has the potential to cultivate a 'Socratic dialogue' between researchers and develops our ability to think. We may draw a very tentative parallel with quantum theory in physics, which has made major inroads into studying matter at a level more minute than the atom. Many people think that subatomic particles like quarks have nothing to do with their everyday lives; yet they are part of every piece of matter we interact with each day. Turning to language, we find that it is an intrinsic part of every human culture. So exploring questions about language means exploring questions about who we are, about matters that are intrinsic to the human condition; and through combining insights with those from other disciplines, in studying the evolution of language, we can understand better how we came to be human.

Conclusion

William Labov, the pioneer of sociolinguistics, suggests that, 'You can defend any piece of research by saying that it is "theoretical" and "basic" research, and you may be able to get the grants you need. I myself have always felt that theory can only be justified if it fits the facts, and that some facts – the ones that affect people's life chances – are more important than others' (Labov 1997). We believe that theoretical subjects must be pursued for their own sake, because you do not know what you might discover until you spend time looking for it. However, in the case of linguistics, there *are* also clear practical benefits for society arising from the research carried out in universities.

All the authors of this essay are researching language variation and change. We have all heard comments that we are being selfish because we have chosen to be researchers rather than 'giving something back' to society; but for all the reasons given above, we do not see researching and contributing to society as being in opposition. Some of us have had other careers (Will Barras taught in secondary schools for six years); others have chosen between research and an alternative career path. None of us would be doing what we are doing if we did not find it intrinsically fascinating: of course, we all enjoy the detective work of research, gathering the data, constructing and testing hypotheses, arguing with others in our field to come up with the best solution. But we also feel what we are finding is of deep significance to everyday life, and that our research on changing languages illuminates the experience of living in changing societies. Ongoing work in linguistics might involve computational methods, statistical analysis, and experimental paradigms, but it also continues in the best and highest traditions of historical scholarly enquiry, seeking to explain both what makes us human, and what makes us modern. Interdisciplinary research on language, in connection with psychologists, biologists, archaeologists and anthropologists, can tell us more about the history of our species, and hence about the sources of our contemporary lives and values. Only the arts and humanities disciplines can provide this historical context, simultaneously revealing and interpreting.

All the areas of linguistics we have highlighted, however, rely absolutely on prior research, which needs to be thorough and independent; and the value of that research for other disciplines, or in practical applications, may not become obvious until long after it has been done and debated within the discipline – after which it also needs to be communicated to a wider public. In the sciences, courses in Science Communication and academic posts in the Public Understanding of Science are becoming commonplace; in the arts and humanities, we face an extra challenge in convincing people that everyday parts of our lives, like language, are also objects of scientific enquiry. We all use language natively and unconsciously; and grammar lacks the glamour and mystery of quarks and chromosomes, which can only be revealed through special machinery and techniques (though note that *grammar* and *glamour* come ultimately from the same linguistic root word). In subjects like linguistics, investing in a knowledgeable cohort of excellent future communicators is therefore even more important, and we crucially need to train those who will conduct and publicize research in future; with this in mind, it is worth noting that five of the six authors of this essay are currently, or were recently, PhD students funded by the Arts & Humanities Research Council. All of us share a common goal: through our research on language, we want to open people's eyes to what happens when they open their mouths.

Bibliography

BBC News (2004), 'Website aims to preserve accents', 13 February, http://news.bbc.co.uk/1/hi/england/cornwall/3484835.stm [accessed 17 July 2010].

BBC News (2005a), 'Have Your Say: Regional accents: Your experiences', 16 August, http://news.bbc.co.uk/1/hi/talking_point/4153102.stm [accessed 17 July 2010].

BBC News (2005b), 'Regional accents "bad for trade"', 29 December, http://news.bbc.co.uk/1/hi/england/4566028.stm [accessed 17 July 2010].

BBC News (2008), 'Perceptions "affected by accent"', 3 April, http://news.bbc.co.uk/1/hi/uk/7329768.stm [accessed 17 July 2010].

Education Committee of the LAGB (2007), 'Accents and phoneme-grapheme correspondences', 27 July, http://www.phon.ucl.ac.uk/home/dick/ec/accents.htm [accessed 17 July 2010].

Erard, M. (2008), 'How global success is changing English forever', *New Scientist*, 29 March, http://technology.newscientist.com/article/mg19726491.300-how-global-success-is-changing-english-forever.html [accessed 17 July 2010].

Evans, F.T. (1998), 'Two legs, thing using and talking: The origins of the creative engineering mind', *AI and Society*, 12: 185–213.

Fitt, M. (2010), 'Cross Party Group on the Scots Language Education sub-committee', 10 March, http://www.scotsinschools.com [accessed 17 July 2010].

Gibbon, D. (2008), '"Brain Training" slammed by "Watchdog"', 6 February, http://www.digitalspy.co.uk/gaming/a88706/brain-training-slammed-by-watchdog.html [accessed 17 July 2010].

Giles, H. and Powesland, P.F. (1975), *Speech Style and Social Evaluation*, London: Academic Press.

Hancock, M. (2008), 'MP backs calls for teachers to have more training to support children with communication difficulties', 10 January, http://www.mikehancock.co.uk/news/34/34/MP-backs-calls-for-teachers-to-have-more-training-to-support-children-with-communication-difficulties/ [accessed 17 July 2010].

Hudson, R.A. (1996), *Sociolinguistics*, Cambridge: Cambridge University Press.

Labov, W. (1997), 'How I got into linguistics, and what I got out of it', http://www.ling.upenn.edu/~wlabov/Papers/HowIgot.html [accessed 17 July 2010].

Labov, W., Ash, S., Baranowski, M., Nagy, N., Ravindranath, M. and Weldon, T. (2006), 'Listeners' sensitivity to the frequency of sociolinguistic variables', *Penn Working Papers in Linguistics*, 12: 2: 105–29.

O'Hagan, A. (2006), 'Who cut off the Queen's Vowels?', *Daily Telegraph*, 5 December, http://www.telegraph.co.uk/opinion/main.jhtml?xml=/opinion/2006/12/05/do0502.xml [accessed 17 July 2010].

Scots Language Centre (2010), 'Scots Language Centre', http://www.scotslanguage. com [accessed 17 July 2010].

Sorace, A. (2010), 'Antonella Sorace: homepage', http://www.ling.ed.ac.uk/ ~antonell/generalpublic.html [accessed 14 July 2010].

Sound Comparisons (2010), 'Accents of English from Around the World', http:// www.soundcomparisons.com [accessed 17 July 2010].

Trousdale, G. (2008), 'Committee for Language Awareness in Scottish Schools', http://www.lel.ed.ac.uk/class [accessed 17 July 2010].

UK National Statistics (2005), 'People and Migration: Foreign-born', 15 December, http://www.statistics.gov.uk/cci/nugget.asp?id=1312 [accessed 17 July 2010].

UK Parliament Website (2008), 'House of Commons Hansard Debates for 16 January 2008', 16 January, http://www.publications.parliament.uk/pa/cm200708/cmhansrd/ cm080116/halltext/80116h0004.htm [accessed 17 July 2010].

20. Language Matters 2: Modern Languages

Michael Kelly (University of Southampton)

Walk down the shopping streets of any city in the country and you are bathed in a rich array of languages and cultures. Many people tune this out and walk through a reduced landscape of their own language and culture. The sights and sounds of other languages, and the cultures that accompany them, then appear as no more than a background radiation of foreignness. However, a little knowledge rapidly brings the background into clearer focus. It reveals meanings that were otherwise concealed and brings life to the landscape. In this way, knowledge of other languages and cultures can transform and enrich everyday life.

A knowledge of languages can transform and enrich many other aspects of life in the UK. It contributes to economic prosperity, social and political relationships and cultural pleasures. This has been broadly recognized by recent governments and was acknowledged succinctly in a language strategy document of 2002: 'The ability to understand and communicate in other languages is increasingly important in our society and in the global economy. Languages contribute to the cultural and linguistic richness of our society, to personal fulfilment, mutual understanding, commercial success and international trade and global citizenship' (Department for Education and Skills 2002).

Languages can be learnt or acquired in many ways, through formal education or through personal learning. But both routes rely on the work of scholars and researchers who produce the knowledge, who communicate it in ways that can be assimilated and who develop strategies that support teaching and learning.

In this chapter, we shall show how languages contribute to knowledge, how they enrich our culture, how they help to build a more open society, and how they contribute to prosperity. We shall look at how public policy in this country has recognized that, and could do more to strengthen our capacity as a country to function in other languages.

How languages contribute to knowledge
Knowledge of other languages and cultures provides access to a broad range of research resources. It includes the ability to understand material of contemporary or historical importance in libraries and archives in other countries. Consider the internet, which provides a voice to those wishing to impact on global society for good or ill. Almost all languages are now represented by virtual communities in which the whole range of online

services is available. These communities conduct their affairs behind virtual closed doors since users without the appropriate language background are in practice excluded, even though they may have ready access in principle. This process of closing off whole areas of the virtual world is likely to accelerate if the language competences of native English speakers continue to decline. Those wishing to enter these virtual communities will need a knowledge of the relevant languages. They may want to do so for many reasons, for example, to assess the social needs of minority groups or to investigate the activities of suspected terrorists. And the languages they need will not be confined to the major Western European languages.

Some of these issues concern the security services, who have always been obliged to grapple with the language factor in intelligence activities. More conventional armed forces are also familiar with the language challenge, and have usually invested heavily in linguistic and cultural preparation for conflict situations. This has often worked out rather differently in practice, and current research is seeking to draw lessons from conflict experiences as diverse as the NATO-led multinational peace-keeping action in Bosnia in the 1990s and the Allied occupation of continental Europe at the end of the Second World War (Footitt 2007).

In civilian terms, though, the study of foreign languages can and does enhance the study of a range of subject areas. The editors of the most recent edition of the *Dictionary of Human Geography* lament the Anglo-American bias in dictionary's coverage (Johnston *et al.* 2000). And the UK Benchmarking statement for History recommends that: 'all single honours students should be assessed in some way or another on their understanding of and their ability to handle primary source material' (Quality Assurance Agency 2007). Topics based on non-English speaking countries remain popular with students, but they find it difficult to grasp the nuances of primary sources not written in English. For that, they need at least a reading knowledge of the original language.

The researchers who teach the students have even greater need of language competence. Recent evidence has shown that the UK is struggling with this. The British Academy has noted that: 'With the increasing development in collaborative work, and the large sums of money attached to such work by national and international agencies, lack of language skills inflicts a real handicap on scholars in many parts of the British university system, and therefore weakens the competitive capacity of the system itself' (British Academy 2009). The 'increasingly insular' perspective represents a knowledge deficit for the UK. The result is that Britain has less understanding of the wider world. This is a dangerous position to be in if we are to address worldwide issues, such as global economic movements, international terrorism or world climate change.

The knowledge value of language competence goes beyond its role in providing access to information. Without some knowledge of another language, it may be difficult to grasp concepts that have developed in non-English speaking contexts, and to understand and engage with the finer points of debates around them. In sociology, for example, the terms '*Gemeinschaft*' and '*Gesellschaft*' are widely employed in German in scholarly discussions because the common English translations ('community' and 'society') are not adequate for understanding the ideas of a theorist like Ferdinand Tönnies, who developed these tools for understanding the social world.

Important breakthroughs in science have been published in languages other than English. Knowledge of the German language was once essential for studying science at university level, and knowledge of the other languages continues to be a benefit for developments in science. French social theorists such as Henri Lefebvre, Michel Foucault or Pierre Bourdieu have made substantial contributions to the development of the social sciences in the English-speaking world, but most academics in these subjects are still dependent on the translation into English of very complex ideas. The more complex the thought, the less easy it is to understand without consulting the language in which it was originally composed. In many subjects, a 'linguistic turn' has radically changed the way we think about subjects. It has provided new paradigms of thought, in which language plays a key role. As a result, the nuances of particular languages can no longer simply be ignored. If anyone needed proof of this, they need look no further than Jacques Derrida's celebrated essay on translation, whose title 'Des tours de Babel' remains obstinately untranslatable (Derrida 1987).

Languages enrich our culture

Access to other languages and cultures does not only extend our knowledge and understanding, it also gives a richer texture to the cultural life of our own country. Simone de Beauvoir is not on our television screens as often as Germaine Greer, but she is nonetheless a basic point of reference for UK debates on feminist issues. Leo Tolstoy and Fyodor Dostoevsky are not as popular in the UK as Charles Dickens and Jane Austen, but they are nonetheless part of our mental landscape. Similar comments might be made about film makers (Fellini, Bergman, Almodóvar), playwrights (Ibsen, Chekhov, Molière), philosophers (Confucius, Kant, Foucault), cultural critics (Bakhtin, Habermas, Barthes), and many other writers and artists whose work comes to us from other languages and cultures. The well-known names are but the tip of the iceberg.

The works of the most prominent writers are often available in English and can be enjoyed on their own terms. But even when a tale of love and death seems to have a universal meaning, it is still situated in a time and a place, and draws the reader into worlds that are different from our own and not simply reducible to human universals. A majority of readers may do no more than dip into these worlds, but they will still be aware that they have crossed a threshold to enter complex cultures that will repay further exploration.

The pleasure of deeper understanding is increased by a greater knowledge of the social and cultural contexts, and even more by some knowledge of the language. There is a special delight in being able to watch a foreign language film without subtitles or read a poem in the original, even with a translation or a dictionary to hand.

The work of researchers and scholars plays an important role in making the great monuments of world culture available to a wide audience, through translations, introductions, reviews and critical analysis. Scholars bring a grasp of languages and a deeper knowledge of cultures with which they can shine a light that illuminates the wider context. They help us to see the underwater dimensions of the iceberg.

An important part of cultural research consists in engaging with researchers from other countries, especially the countries in which particular works were written. A British reader's pleasure and understanding is greatly enhanced by the insights of editors and commentators who share the language and cultural milieu of the work in question. And a UK-based scholar is well-placed to act as a mediator, offering a bridge between the British reader and the linguistic and cultural life of the country from which the work originated.

The role of intellectual mediator is not just about high culture. Increasingly, the circulation of popular culture also requires well-informed cultural intermediaries to make it accessible to UK audiences. This is obviously the case with cinema and fiction, both of which reach across the cultural range. But it is also true of television, sport, popular music, comics, festivals or circuses, where the resonances of language and the cultural contexts of a work or an event hold the key to understanding what is happening. UK researchers are playing a leading role internationally in creating a vibrant culture of enquiry in this area. The increased understanding of popular culture not only opens a window on the life of a society, but also provides conceptual tools for the growing media industries that produce it.

Whether high or popular, culture is principally concerned with making and sharing meanings, and language is therefore the main means by which culture may be understood: Chris Barker and Dariusz Galasiński point out that:

> The shared meanings of culture are not 'out there' waiting for us to grasp them. Rather, they are the product of signifying practices, most notably those of language. Language constitutes material objects and social practices as meaningful and intelligible, it structures which meanings can or cannot be deployed under determinate circumstances by speaking subjects. To understand culture is to explore how meaning is produced

symbolically through the signifying practices of language within material and institutional contexts. (Barker and Galasiński 2001: 4)

In other words, language is the most fundamental way in which a community's set of beliefs, values and norms is codified. And the linguistic construction of a community's culture is not an activity which occurs predominantly through the use of English as a lingua franca, nor can it be adequately carried out monolingually.

A good deal of the impetus to learn about other languages and cultures is motivated by travel. As Alison Phipps has suggested: 'the experience of detachment from places we call "home", from "community", from the normal locations of our work, comes to provide a strong symbolic and experiential set of possibilities through which we can develop common-feeling with others, both at home and abroad' (Phipps 2006: 29–30). Travel and communications are leading to greater mobility and migration, and intensifying the transnational patterns of linguistic and cultural exchange. For example, around 1 million Britons live in Spain and 17 million UK tourists visit the country each year (Foreign Office 2009). This coincides with the continuing increase in students studying Spanish at all levels of secondary school and through into higher education. No doubt the flamboyant appeal of Latin American popular culture has played a part in this, too.

Contact with other cultures is not an automatic result of travel, however, since many forms of travel provide a moral or physical shield between travellers and the community whose space they cross. The business hotel, the all-inclusive holiday resort, the cruise or the guided tour will shepherd the traveller into familiar paths, designed to minimize strangeness. This is a loss, reducing the wonder of new and unfamiliar experiences. It also takes away the opportunity to view our own culture through other eyes. There is a sense of discovery that accompanies children's learning about other languages and cultures. As one educator put it 'Viewing the mother-culture through the eyes of the target culture can be an enlightening experience.' (Morgan 1993) The confrontation with other cultures is an important part of a broad education, and can wean us away from a blinkered monolingualism.

Languages help to build a more open society

Languages and cultures are a fundamental part of identity. They serve to build up and express the sense of who we are and where we belong. They can provide a privileged form of access to the cultural resources and complex patterns of life in other countries. And they have an important place in promoting relationships and mutual understanding between countries. This is particularly important as the population of the UK becomes increasingly diverse. A clearer understanding of linguistic and cultural differences is necessary if we are to maintain social relationships and foster a more inclusive society.

The connections between language, culture and social identity are well documented. Research in this area gives us a better understanding of the factors that shape individual and group identities in relation to gender, ethnicity and other types of belonging. Languages are a fundamental factor. They are 'more than skills; they are the medium through which communities of people engage with, make sense of and shape the world' (Phipps and Gonzalez 2004).

Research on multilingualism in the UK has highlighted the wide variety of languages and language experiences found within the population. It reveals the complex nature of the relationship between communities and their languages, examining the way in which language choices change from one generation to another, how people make decisions to maintain or abandon a particular language and how they switch effortlessly between different languages, perhaps within the same sentence. These patterns have important implications for language policy, including issues of schooling and public communication, for example. In this way, research on the many languages and cultures that contribute to the multicultural landscape of the UK plays an important part in developing a clearer understanding of differences and fostering a more open society.

Learning to understand other languages is closely connected to the development of active citizenship on a national, European and global scale. Language learning is never content-free, and it often involves learning about issues that have an impact on people in another community or culture, considering different perspectives and trying to understand how communities work. A participative pedagogy in language learning can also give learners the experience of democratic decision-making, involvement in the local community and respect for different opinions and approaches (Anderson and Chaudhuri 2003). Foreign language learning has the potential 'for offering alternatives to inward-looking insularity, for addressing a lack of preparedness to engage with the notion of otherness and for tackling negative stereotypes' and is a means to 'foster cross-cultural understanding as well as peaceful co-existence, mutual respect and integration in a multi-cultural society' (Pachler 2000: 72).

Along with developing a general sense of intercultural understanding, research has shown that language education has a political and moral role in developing learners' sense of engagement with other cultures and nations. This is increasingly important in the context of the European Union, 'where the usefulness of language teaching will be evident in the preparation of young people to live in the multilingual and multicultural democratic polity' (Byram 2002: 45).

Language learning itself is an implicitly political proposition. John Trim makes this argument in his report for the Council of Europe, suggesting that language learning is a way to: 'promote the personal development of the individual, with growing self-awareness, self-confidence and independence of thought and action combined with social responsibility as an active agent in a participatory, pluralist democratic society and a well-informed, positive attitude towards other peoples and their cultures, free from prejudice, intolerance and xenophobia' (Starkey 1999: 156).

Language learning may also involve explicit political education as students learn about political institutions in other countries, allowing them to reflect on their own political institutions and perhaps develop a more active sense of citizenship in their own country. Research in this area, including research on the discourses surrounding ideas of citizenship and political participation in different countries, can have an impact on language policy, language learning and broader political awareness. Languages are clearly essential tools in diplomacy and international relations, and research has argued that learning languages is essential to the development of flexible identities and mutual understanding in such situations: 'Multilingualism and "linguistic flexibility" and the more "provisional loyalties" that they necessarily engender are routes to both the preservation of identity as opposed to the nihilism represented by the events of September 11, and to the mutual intelligibility that will rescue us from that destruction at all its levels' (Davies 2003: 54).

The increased diversity of the UK population increasingly requires a clearer understanding of linguistic and cultural differences, to maintain social relationships and foster a more inclusive society.

Languages contribute to prosperity

As well as being a social marker, the ability to use a foreign language is, by any definition, a useful acquisition and one which is held in high regard by many employers. Graduates in languages and related studies have high employability rates. This is not only a result of their academic knowledge and skills in language and culture, but also a result of the other skills that they acquire, such as critical thinking, independent learning, working with people and the ability to take risks, often acquired during their experience of working or studying abroad.

The success of the UK economy is strongly affected by our ability to engage with markets and trading partners in their own languages, notwithstanding the widespread (but overestimated) role of English as a language of international communication. As James Foreman-Peck put it recently, 'Lack of a common language is a barrier to trade. Overcoming the barrier is costly but there are widespread benefits from doing so that may warrant public intervention' (Foreman-Peck 2007: 21).

The inability of some businesses to function in a foreign language effectively acts as a tax on trade, reflected both in the loss of business opportunities, and in the economic and social costs of using translators and interpreters. Linguistically challenged businesses are less able to explore and identify opportunities that would have otherwise been apparent. It may be, as Foreman-Peck has suggested, that the lack of investment in languages by small and medium-sized businesses is an example of market failure, from which the economy as a whole suffers (Foreman-Peck 2007: 14).

Various surveys have suggested that a significant number of firms recognize they have lost business because of the language skill factor or cultural barriers. One recent study argued that 'a significant amount of business is being lost to European enterprise as a result of lack of language skills' (CILT and InterAct International 2007). Many companies have reported difficulties in trying to expand in key emerging markets such as East Asia, South America and Eastern Europe.

In June 2010, Simon Nathan, senior policy advisor on education for the Confederation of British Industry (CBI), argued that fluency in languages such as French, German, Mandarin and Arabic can open new doors for traders. He pointed out that, 'Obviously employers greatly value language skills, particularly for overseas trade and breaking ice with clients. I think in general business terms it is a very good thing to have, in terms of building client and business relationships, if you can speak to someone in their own language.' (Parish 2010) He suggested that possessing language skills can help to reduce costs, but also help communicate with overseas companies on their own terms. He did not believe that pure fluency was a prerequisite, but that it was valuable to be able to hold a conversation in a different language, in order to 'break the ice'.

Incoming business is also affected. The UK tourism industry is currently going through rapid changes with implications for the language support it needs. For example, between 2005 and 2008 tourist visits from Poland, India and Russia grew by more than a quarter, and as a result of the recent recession Britain has been more reliant on visitors from long-haul destinations (VisitBritain 2010). Having staff who can communicate in the languages of these countries is clearly of some importance for the development of the tourist industry, but in the absence of British workers with this ability, it seems that firms are generally meeting their needs by recruiting staff from abroad.

Beyond competence in speaking a language, it is important for people in most industries to be able to understand the cultural context of their business partners. Unless they can navigate cultural differences and intercultural relations, they are not likely to be successful in their dealings with non-UK customers and suppliers. The experience of learning a language and engaging with another country is an important key to understanding the cultural practices of others. 'The ability to adapt ... to unfamiliar environments is becoming one of the key skills demanded by an internationalised economy and rapidly changing domestic social contexts' (Campbell 2000). Language is the important key to understanding the cultural practices of others. This is in turn critically important in business.

Naturally, business has become sharply aware of these issues and there are now thriving industries offering language tuition for business purposes and cultural briefing for international trade relations. Many of these services are offered by universities through language centres and enterprise units, creating direct links between higher education and the business world. Their work benefits directly from the research of specialists in language learning and intercultural communication, which can make the difference between amateur and professional teaching.

Languages in public policy

The importance of languages in everyday life is deeply felt, and many writers have explored its intricacies (Sherringham 2006). We began by suggesting that knowledge of languages reveals meanings that are otherwise concealed and brings life to the landscape. We can go further and suggest that it also empowers the individual, giving them greater knowledge, enabling them to play a fuller role in the life around them and giving them access to a wider palette of ways to present themselves. This is perhaps the meaning of the Slovak proverb, '*Kol'ko jazykov vieš, tol'kokrát si človekom*' ('The more languages you know, the more of a person you are') (European Commission 2005). In a more physiological sense, there is also evidence that language learning may have unexpected health benefits. Controlled experiments have demonstrated that bilingual elderly people are less likely to develop senile dementia than their monolingual peers (Bialystok *et al.* 2004).

While a considerable onus lies with the individual to extend their language capacities, it is also the responsibility of policymakers to find ways of making this empowerment available to as many citizens as possible. This was part of the reasoning behind the Roberts Committee which advised the Higher Education Funding Council for England (HEFCE) that languages were among the strategically important and vulnerable subjects (Roberts 2005). The report has led to a number of policy initiatives, providing funding and other forms of support for languages. It is an increasingly important task of research in languages to provide the ideas and evidence that can inform public policy. This is already happening on a greater scale than in the past.

There is a growing requirement for research that is able to identify wider changes in language use and language contact to which governments and state agencies will need to respond. In the UK, much of this work concerns the international role of English (Jenkins 2007). Otherwise, the main focus of policy-oriented research is on issues of language teaching and learning within formal education. Only the state is able to intervene where the market cannot, especially where timescales for education greatly exceed the tolerance of business rhythms. And certainly the thirteen-year education cycle from starting in primary school to the end of secondary school stretches well beyond the planning horizons of any Western enterprise.

Language learning requires research

Research into language learning has shown that the process of learning a foreign language engages learners in developing a wider awareness of other cultures and ways of life. This learning may be mainly concerned with giving students increased experience of a specific culture, but it also involves an increased awareness of cultural models themselves. Their increased awareness allows students to reflect on their own ways of life and cultural assumptions, leading to the development of intercultural understanding. This is a critical skill applicable to interactions at home and abroad. Research in this area can help develop these skills both within a language classroom and outside it.

Language learning in schools has undergone a severe decline in recent years in the UK, with examination uptake of French and German spiralling downwards. In contrast, learning languages in informal setting and particularly for tourist purposes is booming. As Phipps points out: 'The democratisation of travel in the west has brought about a democratisation in the learning of languages for tourist purposes, but not yet in mainstream study' (Phipps 2006: 4). Her study of tourist language learners offers a new paradigm for research into language learning. She argues against the criticism that tourist language learning undermines serious language learning. Instead, she highlights the motivations of learning language for travel, of becoming 'linguistic guests' and the resultant strengthening of intercultural dialogue. Much more than a set of functional skills, she suggests that languages and intercultural dialogue are:

> an everyday quest, amongst other things, for alterity and as an encounter with other ways of living and speaking and acting. Such a quest, or engagement with the shifting realities of social life, leads to a re-attunement of the whole being, to an education of attention that does not change who we are, but expands our horizons and enskills us to dwell in different worlds. (Phipps 2006: 19)

Increasingly, language learning also requires an effort to overcome the 'smart monolingualism' of contemporary information technology. This effect is generated by the increasingly sophisticated way in which interactions through the internet are designed to present the user with the material most likely to appeal to them. As a result, the user who has frequently accessed material in English will generally find only English language material in the early pages of a browser search and may be under the impression that no other languages are used on the internet. When we access a webpage, the further links offered are also generally in the same language. However, language skills can enable the user to gain access to the rapidly growing resources of the internet in other languages. 'Wiki', Hawaiian for 'quick', is now an everyday word. Most internet users are familiar with Wikipedia, which is now available in about 266 languages, of which around 30 offer more than 100,000 articles (Wikipedia 2010). Criticisms of Wikipedia are widely expressed, especially among academics, who have a more demanding view of the knowledge process. But this online encyclopaedia does at least raise awareness of the wealth of knowledge not accessible in the English language.

Conclusion

The impact of research in languages is felt across the whole of UK society, though it is usually the unseen hand behind the use of language in different domains. Nowhere is this clearer than in the process of education. A graduate in languages entering the job market carries sixteen or seventeen years of education with them, for two-thirds of which they will have learned languages. They embody research, and the entire process of their education has been informed by research.

It is often only toward the end of their higher education that the student makes direct contact with the activity of research, when they begin to produce knowledge and insights from their own study and investigation. At an earlier point, at university, they have met teachers who are engaged in research. Earlier again, towards the end of their secondary schooling, they have made contact with the direct results of research in the form of books written by scholars on the subjects they are studying. Their teachers from primary-school days onwards are also the product of a research-informed process, and have experienced research on the pedagogy of language learning and teaching, both directly and indirectly, as part of their teacher education. They may also engage in pedagogic research themselves.

A similar scenario can be sketched for the other social domains, where research contributes to greater prosperity, to the development of an open society and to a rich cultural life. Research in languages and cultures provides important insights into each of these domains. It enables us to develop tools and approaches that underpin the UK's capacity in languages and cultures. It enables the country to reap valuable benefits, which we need in the new global age. And it provides the means by which every one of us can become more of a person.

Bibliography

Anderson, J. and Chaudhuri, M. (2003), 'Citizenship and community languages: a critical perspective', in K. Brown and M. Brown (eds), *Reflections on Citizenship in a Multilingual World*, London: CILT (The National Centre for Languages).

Barker, C. and Galasiński, D. (2001), *Cultural Studies and Discourse Analysis: a Dialogue on Language and Identity*, London: Sage.

Bialystok, E., Viswanathan, M., Craik, F.I.M. and Klein, R. (2004), 'Bilingualism, Aging, and Cognitive Control: Evidence From the Simon Task', *Psychology and Aging*, 19: 2: 290–303.

British Academy (2009), 'Language matters: A Position paper', London: British Academy, http://www.britac.ac.uk/policy/language-matters.cfm [accessed 14 July 2010].

Byram, M. (2002), 'Foreign Language education as political and moral education', *Language Learning Journal*, 26: 43–7.

Campbell, A. (2000), 'Cultural identity as a social construct', *Intercultural Education*, 1: 1: 31–9.

CILT and InterAct International (2007), 'ELAN: Effects on the European Economy of Shortages of Foreign Language Skills in Enterprise', London: CILT, http://www.cilt.org.uk/home/research_and_statistics/research/cilt_activities/the_economic_case.aspx [accessed 30 June 2010].

Davies, V. (2003), 'Tools of diplomacy: the language policy of the Foreign and Commonwealth Office and what it means for higher education', in D. Head, E. Jones, M. Kelly and T. Tinsley (eds), *Setting the Agenda for Languages in Higher Education*, London: CILT.

Department for Education and Skills (2002), *Languages for All: Languages for Life. A Strategy for England*, London: Department for Education and Skills.

Derrida, J. (1987), 'Des tours de Babel', in J. Derrida, *Psyché: Inventions de l'autre* (Psyche: Inventions of the Other), Paris: Galilée.

European Commission (2005), 'A New Framework Strategy for Multilingualism: Communication from the Commission to the Council, the European Parliament, the European Economic and Social Committee and the Committee of the regions', European Commission, http://ec.europa.eu/education/policies/lang/doc/com596_en.pdf [accessed 16 July 2010].

Footitt, H. (2007), 'Languages and war', Subject Centre for Languages, Linguistics and Area Studies, http://www.lang.ltsn.ac.uk/resources/paper.aspx?resourceid=2681 [accessed 14 July 2010].

Foreign Office (2009), 'Country profiles: Spain', http://www.fco.gov.uk/en/travel-and-living-abroad/travel-advice-by-country/country-profile/europe/spain?profile=all [accessed 16 July 2010].

Foreman-Peck, J. (2007), 'Costing Babel: the Contribution of Language Skills to Exporting and Productivity in the UK', Cardiff Business School, http://www.cf.ac.uk/carbs/research/centres_units/wired/babel3d.pdf [accessed 14 July 2010].

Jenkins, J. (2007), *English as a Lingua Franca: Attitude and Identity*, Oxford: Oxford University Press.

Johnston, R., Gregory, D., Pratt, G. and Watts, M. (2000), 'Introduction', in *Dictionary of Human Geography*, edited by R. Johnston, D. Gregory, G. Pratt and M. Watts, Oxford: Blackwell.

Morgan, C. (1993), 'Attitude change and foreign language culture learning', *Language Teaching*, 26: 2: 63–75.

Pachler, N. (2000), 'Review Article', *Language Learning Journal*, 22: 70–4.

Parish, S. (2010), 'CBI says foreign languages skills help boost overseas trade', Microsoft Small Business Centre, 21 June 2010, http://www.microsoft.com/uk/smallbusiness/sbnews/work-together-better/CBI-says-foreign-languages-skills-help-boost-overseas-trade-19848823.mspx [accessed 14 July 2010].

Phipps, A. (2006), *Learning the Arts of Linguistic Survival: Languaging, Tourism, Life*, Clevedon: Channel View.

Phipps, A. and Gonzalez, M. (2004), *Modern Languages. Learning and Teaching in an Intercultural Field*, London: Sage.

Quality Assurance Agency (2007), *History 2007*, Mansfield: Quality Assurance Agency, http://www.qaa.ac.uk/academicinfrastructure/benchmark/statements/history07.pdf [accessed 14 July 2010].

Roberts, G. (2005), 'Strategically important and vulnerable subjects: Final report of the advisory group', London: Higher Education Funding Council for England, http://www.hefce.ac.uk/pubs/hefce/2005/05_24/ [accessed 24 April 2008].

Sherringham, M. (2006), *Everyday Life: Theories and Practices from Surrealism to the Present*, Oxford: Oxford University Press.

Starkey, H. (1999), 'Foreign Language Teaching to Adults: implicit and explicit political education', *Oxford Review of Education*, 25: 1: 155–69.

VisitBritain (2010), 'UK Tourism Trends', http://www.visitbritain.org/insightsandstatistics/trendsandforecasts/uktourismtrends.aspx [accessed 14 July 2010].

Wikipedia (2010), 'List of Wikipedias', http://en.wikipedia.org/wiki/List_of_Wikipedias.

21. Making Meaning: Literary Research in the Twenty-first Century

Francis O'Gorman (University of Leeds)[1]

After Arnold

The celebrity scholar is with us. There he is in Dan Brown's hugely popular *The Da Vinci Code* (2003), and less popular *The Lost Symbol* (2009). Art history has rarely been so intimate with life and death as in the brutal violence of those narratives. In Jennifer Lee Carrell's blockbuster *The Shakespeare Secret* (2007), it was a literary scholar rather than a Professor of Symbology who took the stage. Literally. This new star scholar-heroine is on the trail of Shakespeare's real identity. She is the literary critical answer to Brown's recognition of the deep cultural attractiveness of the man or woman of letters, in the broadest sense. Serious fiction knows that well. Knowledge of books is alluring, as Dorothea Brooke, the heroine of George Eliot's great realist novel, *Middlemarch: A Study of Provincial Life* (1871–2), finds to her cost in marrying the scholarly but unproductive Edward Casaubon. The outcome is disastrous. But the appeal of the scholar is real. George Eliot, the partner of the polymath George Henry Lewes, knew it personally. In Carrell's lively novel, serious expertise in European Renaissance drama powers a plot of multiple murders, betrayal and the destruction of libraries, which leads to the temporary recovery of Shakespeare's actual 'lost' play *Cardenio*. During the book, a literary scholar saves lives, argues whether Shakespeare wrote Shakespeare, and escapes from burning archives. A real critic's career this is not. But in imagining the attraction of literary research, Carrell makes a revealing move. She presents Kate Stanley, her savvy heroine, as someone who has given up university work to direct Shakespeare on the stage.[2] Being a critic, however much at the forefront of literary research, is insufficient.

It is not merely in popular fiction that the work of literary critics is hard to sell. There is genuine and widespread doubtfulness about what it is that literary scholars achieve and why they might be valuable. Even among literary scholars. Of course, that is not new. Indeed, it is one of the small advantages for literary and cultural historians that they know the place of the arts and humanities in national education has been debated before.[3] The nineteenth century saw the foundation of English literature as a formal academic discipline. But what use was such a subject, together with disciplines including history or classics, to society? Could it develop skills or civic values? Should it focus on particular sets of knowledge or the formation of particular habits of mind? Did a university train or educate?

These were nineteenth-century questions as much as they are ours. For many Victorians, the disputes were partly articulated through a contest – sometimes more perceived than actual – between 'arts' and 'science', as the new empirical practices of science established their authority in the formal institutions of learning. Leading intellectuals framed the arguments in support of the educational value of the humanities. In the best-known defence, Matthew Arnold – poet of loss, school inspector, literary critic – thought that they satisfied something within human beings that was ineradicable. Men and women desired knowledge with which they could make human connections. They wanted more than facts or logic from knowledge. Science, Arnold said, provided hard, objective knowledge. But what of the moral or aesthetic faculties, what of a human being's 'sense for conduct' and 'sense for beauty'? (Arnold 1960–77:63). The arts and humanities, to use the modern labels, addressed the fullest conception of the human being and responded to, and shaped, what ought to be their best desires.

Arnold's notion has remained consequential for educational theory, and the place of the arts and humanities within it. Indeed, it is hard to shake off Arnold even if one knows his argument will no longer quite do. On the old issue of the relation between the arts and sciences, the debate has certainly moved on (Arnold was hardly describing it accurately in his own day) (Cosslet 1982). Few are now persuaded of the former claims that the sciences offer 'objective' knowledge and arts 'subjective'. But literary criticism, like the humanities in general, has entered a newly intensified relationship with science's role in culture, broadly defined. Against those branches of the hard sciences with their potential for direct intervention in material life – engineering, medicine, climatology, plant genetics, water management, animal science – such criticism cannot claim the physical relevance, social utility, economic potential, and ability to change material lives that such practices of human research and development can. The challenge for the humanities to articulate themselves in terms of cultural value is greater still when the university is reconceived as a distinctive generator of economic prosperity, and measured in part on its capacity to address through research and skills training the challenges of a fragile planet, a turbulent political world and economic volatility. Where, indeed, can the advanced practice of literary criticism, especially that which is primarily – as in the UK at present – sustained by public funds, begin to have a place amid the buoyant claims of such disciplines?

There have been robust arguments in the past about the political utility of literary criticism understood in definite terms of protest and resistance. These are not focused answers to the question of why research in the humanities deserves support from public money, but they have been partial formulations of the social or moral gains of literary scholarship. Some literary movements over the past half a century have argued for their significance by emphasizing that imaginative writing expresses resistance to oppression. Marxist critics, once a real power in university English departments, found literature, for instance, immersed in the debates and struggles of practical life, of class struggle and economic determinacy, and thought literary and critical writing could make a manifest difference when understood as forms of political protest. But they were not able to agree, finally, on *how* literature engaged with political ideas, and certainly not on the relationship between reading and change in the world beyond the page.

Those problems persist for other critics who have remained loyal to the idea that their business is political or moral in its essential nature (that is not to overlook, of course, political change that really is motivated by ideas). Feminist literary historians, recovering female voices from the past and from the margins of modern culture, have perceived themselves as actively resisting contemporary forms of gender oppression. Their writing has sometimes similarly been framed as political in its conflict with societal norms. But how far, and on what scale, resistance has spread beyond the intellectual commitment of the critic has never been easy to say. And now postcolonial critics and theorists pay attention to lives lived under oppression or with the legacies of it. This critical enterprise is grounded in acts of protest, and is, again, committed to giving space to the marginalized. But if the rhetoric is sincere, it is, like a host of literary critical arguments about political intervention into the gritty world of the real, easy to make from the relative comforts of the scholarly community. It is hard to object to such moral claims, but difficult to persuade the actually oppressed of their credibility. It is hard, too, to forget the controversial American professor of English and law, Stanley Fish, who salutes Michael Bérubé's sharp words from 1994: 'it's one thing to realise that intellectual work is political ... it's another thing to think you've conquered hegemony just by talking about it' (Bérubé 1994: 121).

None of this, though, means that literary criticism, in its fullest range, is without real social value that is political in the most enabling, contributive and generous sense. Literary research, at its charismatic best, is not about a monolithic conception of what is culturally worthwhile: it is not about describing the fixed coordinates of a 'civilized' life. Those days are gone. But the intellectual activity of thinking hard about literary production, about the testimonies of other men and women through the imagination, is predicated on values that are implicitly involved in deepening our engagement with the world in which we live, and the men, women, and ideas that surround and define us. Literary research, like other research in the humanities, is an activity predicated on open-mindedness, just as it insists both on how difficult it can be to understand other people and their achievements, and how necessary is the effort is to try to understand. This is not to make a difficult-to-substantiate claim about the role of literature in political protest, in objecting to this or that oppressive political practice. Rather, it is to argue that a liberal democracy is in part built from values that the literary scholar understands as constitutive of the very act of sensible, informed and purposeful criticism.

Human dialogue

How do the humanities, with such qualities, contact their audiences most influentially? Of course, in part, they do so through publication and print dissemination in 'academic' and 'commercial' presses, through public lectures, journalism, broadcast media and the internet. But the habits of mind nurtured and developed by literary thinking, fundamental in the act of criticism, are communicated primarily through teaching, which is the principal outlet of all endeavours to comprehend the corpus of literary writing and to express and experience the public value of the humanities. One cannot exist without the other. Advanced research is nothing without the seminar room. And teaching literature well in a university is inconceivable without research (though that is not necessarily the same thing as publication). The responsible, tolerant and rigorous patterns of thinking, the bequest of the humanities, are born of the page and the classroom, and reading attentively is the foundation of both.

Advanced literary research is always concerned with understanding better what others say or have said. That research is generous, humane and properly selfless in its primary instincts, however clouded they may sometimes become by individual vanity. Charles Dickens (1812–70) reminded readers of *Great Expectations*, one of the most celebrated novels of growing up in the nineteenth century, that reading was about others when he affectionately described the chaos that results from the opposite assumption. Joe Gargery is the moral centre of the novel (if an uncomfortable one). He cannot read. But he can recognize the two letters that spell out the sound of his own name. Texts for him are, in turn, only the confirmation of what he already knows: how (nearly) to spell his name. '"Give me," says Joe, "a good book, or a good newspaper, and sit me down afore a good fire, and I ask no better. Lord!" he continued, after rubbing his knees a little, "when you do come to a J and a O, and says you, 'Here, at last, is a J-O, Joe,' how interesting reading is!"' (Dickens 1993: 47)

This is not a scene in which the reader is invited to laugh cruelly at Joe, and Dickens – absorbed by questions of education throughout his life – is too serious a writer for this moment to be less than several things at once. He has, certainly, a sober point to make about books. Joe's idea of them, however charmingly limited, is an oblique confirmation of a reader's responsibility to look beyond themselves, to understand the voice and imagination and presence of others.

Literary research reminds a reader of how hard reading is and that we cannot take things too easily. It shows that what texts were thought to mean is sometimes insufficient, incomplete and even wrong. The intentions of the literary critics are, in this respect, always to clear the air, to pin down better ways of thinking about what was thought to be known; to discern new contexts for knowledge that provides a better understanding of what human verbal expression means and has meant. That is a serious training of the mind, and it nurtures as it develops the quality of public debate itself. Literary research brings readers into contact with ideas and language that challenge because they are different from those readers' own, and because they require readers always to be ready for newer, deeper and fuller acts of comprehension. Such reading is about sympathy and tolerance, about imaginative comprehension of what it is like to see things from someone else's view point. George Eliot was not mistaken in believing in the capacity of reading literature to extend sympathy and understanding, to change the way we comprehend things beyond the page. Eliot spoke neither of uncritical sympathy, nor that which was merely ignorant or naive. But her understanding of the tolerance that serious reading nurtured was a lasting contribution to a modern understanding of the work of the humanities. Some of the dons of the unreformed ancient universities of Oxford and Cambridge in the nineteenth century looked askance at 'research'. The idea of it revealed an unhealthy state of mind, an uncertainty of opinion, a lack of commitment. That was before Mark Pattison (1813–84), Rector of Lincoln College, Oxford, helped create the new, 'research-intensive' don. But, now, openness to the new and readiness for difference are what criticism celebrates.

Intellectually flexible, analytical and articulate, students of the humanities are ready to think about things afresh in the world of words in which men and women live. Serious literary study is, certainly, a continual invitation to compare the world within the page alongside that without. It has always that dimension of the potentially political in the sharpest sense. Whether ancient or modern, from one's own culture or another's, literary writing always invites its reader to make a comparison, to take the meanings found in writing out into the world beyond that writing. Texts travel, and they take their readers with them. In the friction between the two worlds, the imagined and the real, are always new possibilities for change, development, reconfiguration and realization. Utopian and dystopian writing allows such comparisons most obviously. But all literary writing refuses to be bound merely by its historical moment and prompts assessment, however delicate or provisional, of that which is beyond the page: ourselves and the world in which we live. Literature may need to be read with a sense of its historical context (though not *always*, not every time). Yet it is never, if it is of any substance, merely confined by or to the aspic of history. In the creative interrelation between text and world, between words and self, is a bracing source of intellectual energy, of drivers for innovative conceptualization and new realization, of difficult but stimulating inquiry, of the freshest perceptions of our own lives and those of others. Here is a contest with familiarity, even a struggle with what Stefan Collini, the historian of the British intellectual, neatly describes as that 'deeply entrenched cultural prejudice that we already know the answer and know that it is not very interesting' (Collini 2006: 502). Literary research is not unique in laying claim to these habits of mind. But those qualities are intimately part of its identity all the same.

The necessity of difficulty

Literary criticism need not forget, or keep to itself, what is tough to communicate or difficult to understand in words. It should not give up asking questions that are, plainly, difficult. Because an idea cannot always be explained in straightforward terms, or takes some time to be articulated, does not mean that its place in a culture is of necessity dispensable or suspect. Criticism should certainly not disinherit readers from the fullest understanding of the written text by avoiding the challenge of speaking about, of trying to get to the bottom of, complicated matters that are sometimes almost too complicated for words. This willingness to brave the difficult can lead to dismissive bafflement or to ridicule, and sometimes that ridicule is justified. Literary critics have been caught out by imposture or empty rhetoric more often than they care to admit. But there is vibrancy and confidence in a culture that allows itself to be confronted by ideas that are too large or complex for easy summary or generalization. There is resilience and determination in a culture that permits itself to know that important things cannot always be dealt with in a few words.

The North American scholar Caroline Levine has reiterated the point that literature's long-standing commitment to pluralism and the representation of marginal voices has made it a sure-footed antagonist to the oppressive practices of non-democratic states (Levine 2007; Carey 2005). Her focus is on the avantgarde and that which stirs actual legal controversy about censorship. Such an argument might well seem oppressive itself in the forms of art practice that it values and the patterns of reading it requires. But there is no trouble in perceiving the value of a practice of thinking that endeavours to grapple with the greatest complexity of verbal conceptions and, through teaching, to embolden us to be doubtful of the sufficiency of simplicity – and to think harder. And this is all the more valuable in a culture that has, like ours, become persuaded by the adequacy of the briefest accounts of difficult issues, the sound-bite, the newspaper summary, the thirty-second media digest, however deft and witty. Literary critics do not cease to communicate an assumption that we should be analytical, thoughtful and questioning in our lives as well as in our reading, and that the best ways of developing and meeting the challenges of modern existence come from real knowledge and proper thought, without fear and without favour, and without the disabling errors of over-simplification.

Stanley Fish remarked with what have become notorious words in 2008:

> To the question 'of what use are the humanities?', the only honest answer is none whatsoever. And it is an answer that brings honor to its subject. Justification, after all, confers value on an activity from a perspective outside its performance. An activity that cannot be justified is an activity that refuses to regard itself as instrumental to some larger good. The humanities are their own good. There is nothing more to say, and anything that is said ... diminishes the object of its supposed praise. (Fish 2008)

That was a blunt version of his *Professional Correctness: Literary Studies and Political Change* (Fish 1995). Yet, for all its commitment to value, it is hard to see this as an argument at all. 'The humanities are their own good' is an empty statement. For the humanities play many valuable roles and the largest good, the greatest of their roles, could hardly be further away from that stark misjudgement, 'none whatsoever'. Literary criticism cannot cure the sick, but it can open up texts that can change us. Like the humanities at large, the serious understanding of literary writing allows men and women to make more of life. That is significance almost too capacious to grasp. Literary criticism, the fullest understanding of imaginative writing itself, has a role to play in the formation and reformation of minds and lives. Like the humanities in general, such criticism proposes a way of deepening the preciousness, the value, of existence itself.[4] Real ambition is required to think, in political contexts, about more things than mere survival. But literary interpretation always resists a desire to think only of the minimal requirements, and invites men and women to experience a deeper sense of meaning in the world that we inhabit not only as bodies with distinctive needs, but as sensitive, feeling, thoughtful beings with other forms of need, too.

Literary criticism concerns itself with the meaning of words, including those meanings that cannot always be expressed in the language of reason or logic or explanation. That is most obviously true in endeavours to 'explain' and understand human beings themselves. Memoirs, said the modernist novelist Virginia Woolf in 1939, often 'leave out the person to whom things happened ... they say "This is what happened"; but they do not say what the person was like to whom it happened' (Woolf 1978: 75). That is a perpetual challenge, but not merely for memoirists or memoir readers. Literary writing, in its whole gigantic imaginative reach, deals with meanings that slip away from other forms of expression or are lost behind them. It addresses meanings that are consequential in part because they are deeper than merely logical explanations. Art, says Robert Browning at the end of his detective-novel-in-verse, *The Ring and the Book* (1868–9), 'may tell a truth/Obliquely' (Browning 1971: Book XII, lines 859–60). And sometimes only the distinctive repertoire of literary art to communicate sense beyond merely straightforward and rationally explicable statements can approach the most significant forms of sense and value that shape us and give purpose amid what Amanda Anderson, studying the different ways in which contemporary disciplines and professions describe and analyse the world, calls 'the way we argue now' (Anderson 2005).[5]

A resource for living

Properly understood, the subject of the literary critic is a life resource not a recreation, it is enriching not decorative and it is not merely one for spare moments, for the privileged wealthy, or for those with large amounts of free time on their hands. Part of the responsibility of the scholar working in English literature is to make that literature more widely available, better understood and more intellectually, emotionally and imaginatively productive. This is no easy question, and it is not difficult to underestimate the challenges of communicating with a broader audience, of engaging meaningfully with reading communities beyond the academy, let alone of fulfilling the role of a 'public intellectual', whatever precisely that means (Small 2002: 1–39).[6] But for all this, it is true that literary criticism acts unwisely if it turns only inwards. Certainly, it jeopardizes some of its purposes if it puts up unnecessary barriers between readers and the texts that might amply offer sustenance and inspiration. That is not to say that literary criticism should cease to struggle with the complicated, or to listen to meanings that are difficult to put into words, or somehow give up on the 'canon'.[7] However, it should renew its commitment to sense and human experience, and to the determining and transformative meanings of aesthetic forms in their fullest and most rewarding powers.[8]

The case for the value of the humanities is more than a faith position, but it needs to be believed in by its practitioners as well as by others. And good arguments are not good if they are merely a veil for self-interest. Many humanities scholars first took up their profession because they had been intellectually and emotionally rewarded by their activities. That is a respectable starting point. It might seem that few have begun with a strong sense of the *public* value of what they were beginning to do as researchers, but research without teaching is barren, and teaching is always a vocation, an act of commitment to others, a statement that there are others with needs, desires and ambitions apart from oneself. The fullest force, though, of the public arguments about the values of serious literary thought, the shared understanding of a scholarly community about what it offers to the world, develops further with practice, reflection and engagement. For those who have spent some significant portion of their lives in literary study, in seminar rooms and lecture theatres as well as in libraries and in front of computer screens, the public value of literary criticism becomes most meaningful after its transformative power has been seen and seen again.

The peril of the economist is to confuse 'should' with 'will': to anticipate or theorize human behaviour through assumptions about how men and women should behave rather than how they do. That, said John Ruskin, the Victorian art and social critic, in 1860, was like designing a theory of gymnastics that began with the assumption that human beings had no skeletons: it was a science perfectly coherent and, he said, waspishly, 'deficient only in applicability' (Ruskin 1902–13: 26). Economists have been wrestling with the unruly disinclination of human beings to conform to models for centuries. And in thinking about the value of literary research, it is worth not overlooking that. For whatever else is compelling about the value of literary thinking and the transformative powers of literary criticism, it would be to fashion another science of boneless bodies to assume that human beings should or will stop caring for books, or that they should or will stop hoping to understand them better. Literary criticism will remain keenly valued, and a source of value, until mere survival *is* the best for which we can hope.

Yet we should not be tempted to rest too contentedly in such a thought. Or, rather, we should take from the ineradicable persistence of reading and desire to understand better one other pointer to the largest role of literary understanding in the shaping of our fragile lives and futures. We live, in real and meaningful ways, in and through language, in what Anthony Grafton aptly calls 'worlds made by words' (Grafton 2009). We make our meanings through words, and literature is a form of meaning in words. Serious consideration of worthwhile writing is, in turn, one of the best allies for us all as thinking and feeling creatures endeavouring to live in societies, as men and women with troubles and a capacity for joy, as human beings with inner lives and with the ambition to live responsibly and well. And, if science and technology in the industrial world may help provide some solutions to the problems we face, it is primarily with changed human behaviour and altered human values that the future of human society in the face of contemporary problems lies. It is easy to think that science and engineering offer us the promise that we can live into the future in the same manner as we live now, simply with different and more sophisticated technology. But that is a mistake. Transformed human behaviour, assisted by technology, is our only chance. And such a transformation can only come with a shifted sense of what is important, a redefined sense of what is meaningful in and from life.

Thinking of that kind of change is to enter the world of values which, especially for those without religious conviction, is quintessentially the domain of the humanities. Despite the exceptions, despite the evidence that reminds us of murderers and tyrants who were enthusiastic about literature or music or painting, the humanities are the precious help in a secular world, and vital in reminding religious thinkers of ways in which meaning is made and felt among conscious beings here and now. As verbal creatures, we can only have a limited sense of 'living' on this planet without the humanities, as we can only have a limited definition of 'health' from those who think exclusively of the body. In such times as the present, when altered values, reoriented priorities and principles, are needed more than ever, the humanities have a chance of being, in no merely metaphorical or foolishly indulgent sense, human practices that help save us from our current values and their devastating consequences on a precarious world. It is hard to envisage a better sense of public value than that.

Notes

1　Sincere thanks to Professor Dinah Birch, Professor Tony McEnery and Dr Katherine Mullin for their invaluable contributions to this essay.

2　Stanley's career echoes something of Carrell's (http://www.jenniferleecarrell. com/Bio.htm). The celebrity critic is sometimes the victim. See, for instance, Bartholomew Gill's *The Death of a Joyce Scholar* (Gill, 1989).

3　For the most recent argument about the relation of Victorian arguments about the value of the arts in education, see Dinah Birch, *Our Victorian Education* (Birch, 2008).

4　The history of such a claim is long. In recent history, it was formulated as a self-declared non-ethical understanding of art through the Aesthetic Movement in the second half of the nineteenth century but the notion of art providing intense meaning for human lives is an ethical claim. Other re-statements in explicitly ethical terms include 'What is Valuable?', in *Poetries and Sciences: A Reissue with a Commentary of 'Science and Poetry' (1926, 1935)* (Richards 1970: 35–46).

5　In relation to literature, see Helen Small's response in 'On Conflict' (Small 2010).

6　On this difficult concept, see also Chapter 14 of Grafton's *Worlds Made by Words* (Grafton 2009) and Collini's *Common Reading* (Collini 2008).

7　There is a long history to this argument which, only twenty years ago, was conceived as an opposition to 'theory'. See, for instance, Frank Kermode (Kermode 1989). Now, one is more likely to hear it expressed through assumptions about readers' class and educational background.

8　There is no more stimulating book on this subject than Rónán McDonald's *The Death of the Critic* (McDonald 2007).

Bibliography

Anderson, A. (2005), *The Way We Argue Now: A Study in the Cultures of Theory*, Princeton, NJ: Princeton University Press.

Arnold, M. (1960–77), *The Complete Prose Works of Matthew Arnold*, vol. X, edited by R.H. Super, 11 vols, Ann Arbor: University of Michigan Press.

Bérubé, M. (1994), *Public Access: Literary Theory and American Cultural Politics*, London: Verso.

Birch, D. (2008), *Our Victorian Education*, Oxford: Blackwell.

Browning, R. (1971), *The Ring and the Book*, Harmondsworth: Penguin.

Carey, J. (2005), *What Good Are the Arts?*, London: Faber and Faber.

Collini, S. (2006), *Absent Minds: Intellectuals in Britain*, Oxford: Oxford University Press.

Collini, S. (2008), *Common Reading: Critics, Historians, Publics*, Oxford: Oxford University Press.

Cosslett, T. (1982), *The 'Scientific Movement' and Victorian Literature*, Brighton: Harvester.

Dickens, C. (1993), *Great Expectations*, edited by M. Cardwell, Oxford: Clarendon.

Fish, S. (1995), *Professional Correctness: Literary Studies and Political Change*, Cambridge MA: Harvard University Press.

Fish, S. (2008), 'Will the Humanities Save Us?', *New York Times*, 6 January.

Gill, B. (1989), *The Death of a Joyce Scholar*, London: Macmillan.

Grafton, A. (2009), *Worlds Made by Words: Scholarship and Community in the Modern West*, Cambridge, MA: Harvard University Press.

Kermode, F. (1989), *An Appetite for Poetry*, Cambridge, MA: Harvard University Press.

Levine, C. (2007), *Provoking Democracy: Why We Need the Arts*, Oxford: Blackwell.

McDonald, R. (2007), *The Death of the Critic*, London: Continuum.

Richards, I.A. (1970), *Poetries and Sciences: A Reissue with a Commentary of 'Science and Poetry' (1926, 1935)*, New York: Norton.

Ruskin, J. (1902–13), *Unto this Last*, in *The Library Edition of the Works of John Ruskin*, vol. XVII, edited by E.T. Cook and A. Wedderburn, London: Allen.

Small, H. (2002), *The Public Intellectual*, Oxford: Blackwell.

Small, H. (2010), 'On Conflict', in *Conflict and Difference in Nineteenth-Century Literature*, D. Birch and M. Llewellyn (eds), Basingstoke: Palgrave Macmillan.

Woolf, V. (1978), *Moments of Being*, London: Grafton.

22. The Value of Art and the Art of Evaluation

Rónán McDonald (University of New South Wales)

Move lips, move minds and make new meanings flare.
(Seamus Heaney, 'Beacons at Bealtaine')

Value and excellence

Most people can tell you their values. Some embrace them, live by them. A few even die for them. Values are ubiquitous, impossible to do without. Even a renunciation of life or the world is based on a value judgement, albeit a negative one. Yet at the same time values, like soap in the bath, are notoriously slippery and hard to pin down. They differ from statements of fact and observation in that values are not inherent in the object that is valued but rather come from the person doing the valuing. This is not to say that all values are down to individual whim (though many would claim, so far as literary and artistic value goes, that beauty is indeed in the eye of the beholder). But it is to suggest that values are a matter of culture not nature, of ideology and not fact, of history not timeless reality. Whilst we may hold our values dear, it is hard to hold them tight. We cannot define, measure and weigh values. We cannot isolate and pinpoint a moral and aesthetic property in the same way as sulphuric acid or the laws of physics. This is to say that, while scientific research is certainly motivated by values of various sorts – the cure for disease, the search for military supremacy – value itself is not a subject on which the hard sciences have much to say. Science tells us about the 'what' and the 'how', but seldom the 'why'. This is the domain, rather, for the humanities whose values lie, self-reflectively, in the articulation of what 'value' means. The humanities, including the subject of English, help elaborate and nurture our ideas of the ethical and the aesthetical, help us arrive at the 'meanings' of things in both senses of that word. On the one hand 'meaning' neutrally indicates a message or a sense which we discern (the 'meaning' of a word, image or metaphor). On the other hand, it touches to the very quick of significance, purpose, moment (something which gives life 'meaning').

The elusiveness of value has many consequences for the value of art and the art of evaluation. But at the same time it makes the area all the more important, all the more in need of interrogation and understanding. There are some basic distinctions that might help. In quite an old, arguably outworn distinction, people sometimes separate so-called 'instrumental' and 'intrinsic' values, those which are good *for* something and those that are good *as* something. Money is instrumental. It is valuable in order to obtain something else: it is of no use at all on a desert island, except maybe as kindling. By contrast health or human life may be regarded as intrinsically valuable, 'ends' in themselves. Instrumentally valuable actions always depend on obscured but consensual intrinsic values. This is the 'why' that motivates any action, enterprise or goal. So, for instance, few people would hold that economic benefits are good in and of themselves. But, in a just society, prosperity can help achieve those other values which we might regard as coming closer to the 'intrinsic': alleviating poverty, creating employment and opportunities, reducing crime, and helping to secure justice and fairness.

There is much overlap between the instrumental and the intrinsic and, often, when the intrinsic is pressed a bit it starts to look like an instrumental value in disguise. There is no agreed endpoint towards which all actions should aim; not even the utilitarian aim of the greatest happiness for the greatest number commands universal consent. One might agree that increased library opening hours is an instrumental good. It allows one to read more books and become better educated. But is education an intrinsic good? Or is it just another instrumental value on the road to a richer, fuller life? What constitutes such a life anyway? Who decides and on what basis? It is hard to settle on an endpoint or a still centre, an agreed source for value; especially since, as a glance at history will attest, values shift and mutate across the ages. What is self-evident to the drafters of the US Declaration of Independence – that 'all men are created equal' – would not be so to most cultures throughout known history. If we wish to preserve the value of equality, a value which underpins huge swathes of our legislature and civic life, then research into how ideas and values gestate and germinate can help us do so. This is inseparable from investigation into the history of ideas, language, philosophy, culture – the domain of the humanities.

When it comes to the arts and literature the question of values is particularly slippery and befuddled. The arts may well have social and economic benefits but defenders of artistic or educational innovation are often unhappy about understanding artistic value solely in these instrumental terms. There is a lingering notion in our culture that art is, or should be, intrinsic. The point of practical artefacts, from toothbrushes to dishwashers, resides in the extent to which they are good for something. Artistic value is different. Here, at least to some extent, the object is prized not for what it does but for what it is: because it is good as something. The 2008 government report by Sir Brian McMaster, 'Supporting Excellence in the Arts: From Measurement to Judgement' signals a return to the more non-utilitarian emphasis, away from the metrical basis towards one of merit and value (McMaster 2008). State funding, the review proposed, should move away from 'measurable' social benefits, such as audience size and ethnic minority participation, to an emphasis on artistic 'excellence'.

But how do we identify excellence? What criteria do we have for recognizing it? And who decides what constitutes value in the arts? There is considerable blurring between intrinsic and instrumental so far as artistic value is concerned and one of the challenges, for public policymakers and for academics, is to steer a course between the two. On the one side lurks the Scylla of 'practical benefits', on the other the self-Charybdis of 'art-for-art's-sake'. We may agree with the McMaster shift away from measurable quantifiers to the more elusive notion of excellence. But at the same time publicly funded bodies such as museums, theatres and university humanities departments should surely deliver some return, some public value, even if that is not measurable in quantifiable terms. Who decides what constitutes 'public value', a phrase that has become something of a buzzword in political discourse in recent years? (Moore 1995; Crabtree 2004). A 2006 report by the Work Foundation on behalf of the Arts & Humanities Research Council suggests that public value needs to be determined democratically, in consultation with the public. However, the report emphasizes that it should *not* simply follow the diktats of the market place, or uninformed consumerism. Public value should aim for 'responsiveness to refined preferences'. To this end it is necessary to 'harness professional expertise' in order to 'shape and guide' public choices about value (Horner and Bevan 2006).

This notion of 'refinement' is swathed in its own evaluative assumptions and begs the old question: 'Who shall educate the educators?' Nonetheless, the idea that democracy is improved when popular judgement is elevated by education is of a venerable tradition. It is a belief, so far as the arts are concerned, that is a charter for the role of evaluative criticism as traditionally understood: critics have often provided the 'professional expertise' in this area, providing the dialogue with the public that is implied in the notion of 'refined' public responsiveness. Joseph Addison's famous adage that critics are the 'arbiters of taste' comes to mind. In this role of evaluative arbitration, English research in the humanities has a vital part to play. A vibrant humanities research environment, which addresses in an informed and accessible way the values of literature and of the arts, can contribute to a mature and reflective conversation about the creative industries in wider society.

By interpreting, analysing and, not least, evaluating literary works, English studies enrich intellectual life and the reception of culture. This improves the quality of life of the people of Britain. There are also benefits for this country's image abroad and for the sense of belonging and identity of British citizens. Any nation's cultural image, and self-perception, is important to the identity, pride and vibrancy of its people, and the attitudes and assumptions of those who might want to work or invest in it. University English studies act as the custodian of a literary heritage that includes Chaucer, Shakespeare and Woolf. But it also, crucially, taps into new literary seams, finding neglected literary works and casting new light on those that are already celebrated. English studies are responsible for the literary inheritance of future generations but the discipline is also engaged in a project of critique, evaluation and revaluation, whereby the meanings and merits of literary works past and present are made manifest and articulate.

The word 'heritage' often makes academics and writers cringe. Not least because of its associations with a commodified and sentimentalized view of the past, sepia-tinted and preserved in aspic. But heritage need not be frozen in this way. It can be dynamic and evolving, a literary past that lends itself to continual re-evaluation. The literary and cultural inheritance of future generations is their birthright. Amongst other responsibilities, literary scholars have a duty of care. But their role is not simply curatorial. It is also engaged, active and selective. One of the most important achievements of the last thirty years of English research has been the politically motivated reclamation and rediscovery of unjustly neglected or excluded voices, those of women or of ethnic minorities for instance. Crucially, though, the rise of feminism and postcolonialism broadens the wavebands not just of our political imagination, but of our aesthetic one, too. By this I mean that we have not just rediscovered neglected writers who fit into our canon according to fixed criteria – but rather that the criteria themselves have been challenged and elasticized. We have tuned our ear to the literary qualities of non-standard languages, the creole, the dialect, the demotic. We have learnt to appreciate qualities of previously neglected forms like the letter and the diary, forms that have been brought under scholarly scrutiny as a way of detecting the traces of forgotten peoples, but have in the process tutored our aesthetic sensibilities to new registers.

This is an example of that dynamic, evaluative response to literary history. Literary research at university adds to our knowledge about the literary past in a systematic way. But it also continually asks what it is in this past that is valuable. And what it means to ask this question. For if values are often taken for granted as natural and self-evident, cultural presupposition often gravitates most tellingly to them. What is self-evidently valuable to one historical moment or culture is not so to another.

The function of criticism at the present time

The McMaster's report and the attention to public value as a matter of *refined* public preferences might seem to signal a rejuvenated function for evaluative criticism. Yet in the wider culture, the signs for such a role seem inauspicious. In recent years the role of professional literary critic has been challenged and supplanted. Unavoidably, the critic occupies a hierarchical role: someone who knows more about an artform than we do, whose opinion or interpretation is worthy of special regard. This hierarchical aspect has fallen victim to the wider shifts in social relations, away from deference and authority. We are often told that people nowadays feel able to make their own choices about what they watch or read, without genuflecting to the 'so-called expert'. The proliferation of blogs and internet discussion groups are held up as signs of popular empowerment, whereby consumers of the arts make their own choices and share their own enthusiasms with their peers. The tweedy academic or critic seems, from this point of view, a figure from a more hierarchical era, now going the way of the rag-and-bone man and the bus conductor.

Even without these modern developments, the critic is a figure who has long been reviled. Of those who make their living in the creative industries, critics come pretty close to the bottom of the food chain. They are often seen as parasites, unable to create art themselves. 'Critics are like eunuchs in a harem', Brendan Behan once remarked, 'they know how it is done, they've seen it done every day, but they're unable to do it themselves'.

Yet the critic has performed vital cultural services. The standing of many of the most esteemed writers of the twentieth-century – T.S. Eliot, James Joyce, Virginia Woolf – is intimately linked to the academic and critical attention they have attracted. In terms of public value, academic critics have helped to refine the public appetites for the surge of alienating and often difficult art that emerged from the social and political turmoil of the past 100 years. So-called 'modernism', a term used to include the most significant and innovative art of the first half of the twentieth century, would have been inconceivable without the criticism that accompanied it, often by modernist writers themselves but also, frequently, by academic critics like Hugh Kenner, Richard Ellmann and Harold Bloom.

The visibility of English dons has evolved over the decades, but public critics have often been university professors, sometimes writing in newspapers or for high-end magazines like the *Times Literary Supplement* and the *London Review of Books*. Some would argue that the specialist theoretical languages and concepts that came into vogue in English studies since the 1970s have eroded this public role. But, nonetheless, the crossover has often been to the benefit of both Ivory Tower and Grub Street. It remains a visible example of how work in the humanities can enrich the cultural and social life of the UK outside the university.[1]

Academic criticism is most often read outside specialist fields when it is evaluative (which is not to say that non-evaluative criticism is not important or has no public penetration). Looking over the history of the discipline of English, it is clear that when evaluation was emphasized, by figures like F.R. Leavis or Lionel Trilling, the gap between scholarship and high journalism was narrowest. Equally, the academics of today who emphasize evaluation, disparate figures like Christopher Ricks, Helen Vendler and James Wood, are often those who are most read by non-academics. English dons have historically helped not only to answer the sociological questions about how literary texts can help us understand society, but also the thornier question: 'What in writing and culture is of merit and why?' English has a public role not only for its cultural analysis but also for its cultural judgements.

'Why should we devote time and energy to reading particular novels or poems?' 'What is it that makes celebrated writers worth the time and effort?' It is not surprising that these are the questions in which the general public might be interested and, hence, a way for academic English to find a non-academic audience. But, like many value judgements, the discernment and identification of literary quality is a deceptively complex and contested business.

It is for this reason that, throughout its history, English has often tended to steer clear of the whole area of value or to render it settled in a permanent canon of great works. Evaluation had the whiff of the personal, the subjective or the impressionistic – not qualities one wants to enshrine in a relatively new academic discipline eager to find rigour and respectability. Often the same critics who renounced evaluative approaches, figures like the Canadian Northrop Frye who dominated the field in the 1950s and 1960s, would nonetheless focus on canonical writers, like the Romantic poets, taking on trust the evaluative decisions of previous generations. Questions of value often have a habit of springing up in literary studies, even when they have been most ardently repressed in the interests of quasi-scientific impartiality.

Interdisciplinary borders

However important literary criticism has been, the role of English research takes in many other areas, analytical as well as evaluative. The borders between English and the other humanities disciplines are perforated. To an unusual degree, English is enriched and impoverished by the fortunes and troubles of its neighbours. If we are going to identify the public values of history, for instance, the benefits that accrue to society though a better understanding of the past, then some of these will reflect on to English too. Works of literature can provide us with a unique perspective on other societies, a way of accessing other attitudes, values and ideologies in all their contradictions and tensions. One benefit of studying nineteenth-century novels or medieval fabliaux, therefore, is to deepen our understanding of those periods and thereby to cast comparative light on our own condition. The historical method has been a prominent strand in English in recent years, as witnessed in the renewed interest in archival research and the history of the book.

But if literature has a fertile relationship with history, it has also often shared its spoils with sociology, psychology, anthropology and linguistics. The university humanities in recent decades have tended to view interdisciplinary innovations with ecumenical approval. Few would disagree that it refreshes and ventilates a subject to open itself to the methods and insights of another. But if other disciplines sometimes need to bend themselves for this crossover, it is hard to think of 'English' existing without it. Of its nature, English is one of the most porous and promiscuous of the humanities disciplines. This works both ways and we often see specialists in other disciplines dipping into literature for material. Philosophers since Aristotle have drawn on myths and stories to elaborate on moral dilemmas. But one could nonetheless conceive of the historian and philosopher getting on without the aid of literature. English on the other hand incorporates history and philosophy as part of its warp and weft.

Perhaps by way of compensation, during the history of English as a discipline there have been efforts to close up its borders in the interests of disciplinary integrity and coherence. The most well-known such effort resulted in the so-called 'new criticism', often known as 'practical criticism' in the UK, which became the dominant method in the universities during the 1940s and 1950s. This approach gave valour to close, rigorous literary analysis, striving to cut out all objects of attention other than the words on the page. Historical digression, including into the life of the author, was regarded as an ancillary distraction. But new criticism tended to have a strong evaluative remit, striving to show why it was that poems worked aesthetically. For this reason it had significant cultural penetration outside universities, in magazines and journals aimed at the educated general reader.

The methods and approaches of new criticism have been pushed aside over the last thirty years by the interdisciplinary ethos of literary theory and cultural studies. French linguistic philosophy became the preoccupation during the 1970s and 1980s, as structuralism and post-structuralism gained in their ascendancy. Related to this, various politically accented approaches developed such as feminism, Marxism and, later, postcolonialism. These developments opened the window on literary studies. They routed the idea that literature was separable from its context and that literary value occupied a stable, unchanging and permanent fixture.

The phrase 'literary theory', used by admirers and detractors of these new developments, is a misnomer. As I suggested earlier, an important feature of literary criticism is its habit of considering its own proper agency and purpose, doubling back on itself to ask the question what it is or should be doing. Criticism has theory running through its veins, much more so than many of the refuseniks of 'theory' might like to think. This is one reason why the practice of literary criticism often functions best in proximity to the self-reflectiveness afforded by universities. And why, at its best, it is adept and restless in addressing values, in seeking for the 'why?' as well as 'what?' The closeness between the words 'critic' and 'critique', the latter with its philosophical connotations in the work of Kant and Hegel, indicates this quality of criticism, its double-jointed tendency to question its own purpose and procedure.

So 'literary theory' is not new, and not an abstract intrusion into the proper business of criticism. What is striking, though, is that for all its philosophical daring and diversity, the different strands of modern theory have tended to have quite a tentative, even hostile, attitude to artistic (if not political) value. Partly, this is because aesthetic values are so culturally contingent. A neoclassicist will praise an artwork for its accordance with pre-given generic forms; a Romantic poet for its originality and intensity of expression; a puritan, if he allows art at all, for its inculcation of virtue and discrediting of vice. There are many reasons for valuing the arts and they evolve with changing social attitudes. As ever, value is not something that can be pinned down permanently and this makes it very difficult to discuss with disciplinary rigour. This is an anxiety that goes back to the origins of English as a university subject.

But there were also political reasons for the turn from literary merit and the canon in the 1970s. The various strands of Marxist theory and cultural studies tended to view the whole notion of the aesthetic with suspicion. It became something to be historically located, unmasked as ideology – at best as mere dilettantism, at worst as complicit in oppressive power structures through its exclusion and silencing of marginal voices. The canon of Great Literary Art was no longer judged in some decontextualized, timeless forum, it was no longer neutrally 'great', but rather a selection of works that reinforced prevailing values and, often, political, social and gender hierarchies. In the universities during the 1970s and 1980s the battle against 'discrimination' in the negative, racist or sexist sense often had as an early casualty 'discrimination' in the sense of evaluative judgement or discernment.

There are signs in recent years of a renewed hospitality to the category of the literary and the aesthetic, and to the idea of cultural value in English literary studies.[2] English research at university is about more than evaluative criticism. But if one abandons the evaluative dimension altogether then the foundations of its disciplinary integrity start to disappear. If English literature is not distinguished by quality considerations, then why not merge English with sociology or cultural studies? Without recognition of literary merit, then the interdisciplinary proclivities of English make the subject look more like an outpost of history or a handmaiden to politics. The essential question of English, which precedes the analysis of the object of study, is *why* it should be studied in the first place. What does literary quality mean? How do we identify and articulate it?

Returning to value

When we ask what the value of humanities research is we go consciously or unconsciously to the humanities themselves, to subjects like philosophy, history and the arts. But this role of the humanities as a crucible wherein we test and judge values is part of their value, or perhaps more accurately, 'meta'-value (in the sense of the value of value). The values our society embraces are too important not to be given serious academic investigation and reflection. This is perhaps most evidently true for ethical values. We rightly involve moral philosophers in applied ethical decisions about such issues as stem-cell research or the use of torture. But behind this very obvious contribution of philosophy to the non-academic context, the work of moral philosophy interrogates the basis for value judgements that, though they may seem self-evident in our culture, are historically variable. It is 'self-evident' to us now that we should no longer burn witches or put the insane on public display. It was not always so. There is a complicated overlap between the ethical and the literary such that many evaluative critics praise the artistic qualities of an artwork precisely because of its moral intelligence. This is most notably true of the novel, where moral dilemmas and situations are embodied in narrative and character. The esteem in which novelists like Jane Austen or Henry James are held is in no small measure down to the finely filamented moral ironies they craft. Literary study can feed the capacity for moral questioning.

However necessary it is to navigate them, these are perilous waters. How values gestate, where they come from, is a highly complex area of philosophical investigation. Everything we do in life, from brushing our teeth to organizing international summits on global warming, is influenced by values of one sort or another. If usually unarticulated or unexamined, they are, nonetheless, inescapable. Academic enquiry is saturated in value judgements, even when it is ostensibly value-free. The decision to be impartial or to dispense with interested analysis is itself an evaluative decision, one which implicitly holds up 'value-free' procedures as *better* than evaluative ones.

Scientific investigation generally seeks to avoid prejudice and subjective viewpoints. It does not seek to prescribe but to describe, using as its cardinal procedure empirical observation. At the same time scientific research takes place within a context that is highly charged with evaluative ends. Those scientists seeking a cure for cancer will use the neutral laboratory techniques of impartial testing but the decision to direct scientific resources towards finding such a cure is clearly not neutral and non-evaluative. But science does not, of itself, inevitably aim at the beneficial and the enlightened. It has been deployed for mass murder as well as medicine. Decisions about its ends (if not its means) occur in a context shot through with ideology, assumptions and values about the good. One word that describes this context is 'culture'.

The aim of the humanities is to analyse and assess this culture, to subject our values to academic and historical consideration. As the philosopher John Gray puts is (significantly in an essay on the novelist Joseph Conrad): 'Human beings use the power of scientific knowledge to assert and defend the values and goals they already have' (Gray 2004: 106). These values and goals are not the subject matter of the sciences; but they are the proper subject of the humanities, pedagogically and in research terms. Society benefits from having a specialized academy that includes reflection on what constitutes values, including the aesthetic values of its cultural inheritance.

The tremendous prestige science has accrued – through its unprecedented advances not only in knowledge about the universe but also in the applied fields of technology and industry – sometimes obscures this point about values. And it is not to say that the humanities cannot benefit from using scientific methodology. Scholarship in literary studies often relies on the scrupulous, painstaking, objective compilation of evidence and, indeed, on various applied technologies, such as that afforded recently by digital technology. But nonetheless science cannot invent or discover values. In one of the most notorious intellectual controversies in twentieth-century Britain, the so-called 'two-cultures' debate, the novelist C.P. Snow claimed in a lecture in 1959 that science should be ranked alongside the arts as the fountainhead of civilized values. In a notably heated exchange the leading literary critic of the age, F.R. Leavis, riposted that distinctions between the provinces of science and art are central so far as values are concerned. Science may, as Snow proclaims, be valuable and beautiful, but it does not reveal these 'qualities' in the laboratory or through the microscope. Values are not empirical. This is not to say that they are subjective, but rather that they are nurtured and cultivated through what Leavis called elsewhere the 'collaboratively created human world' or, as he puts it here, through the processes of 'human responsibility':

> Science is obviously of great importance to mankind; it's of great cultural importance. But to say that is to make a value-judgement—a human judgement of value. The criteria of judgements of value and importance are determined by a sense of human nature and human need, and can't be arrived at by science itself; they aren't, and can't be, a product of scientific method, or anything like it. They are an expression of human responsibility. (Leavis 1972: 140)

All the values our society holds dear are not timeless, absolute or innate, but rather gestate within the processes of human civilization, generated by culture. The university humanities are the arena where these values can be reflected upon, analysed and intuited. As part of the sphere of the humanities, English shares in this remit.

A central part of English is the judgement of literary merit. Literary merit cannot be contained within some neat formula or catch-all definition. Like the discernment of all values, it must adopt a dynamic rather than a static measure. The canon is fluid, not fixed, but this is precisely why evaluative literary criticism has a role to play. There has been a renewed hospitality to the concept of the aesthetic and the literary in English studies in recent years, a growth of what has come to be called the 'new aestheticism'. This is not a renunciation of the political preoccupations of the past thirty years but rather a development of it. The new interest in aesthetics is theoretically sophisticated and often intimate with the imagining of politics and ethics at the level of form. The advocacy of interpretative tact, the renewed concern with the particular instance rather than the general rule, the allowance that texts might have a literary quality that is ineffable or inexhaustible: these have an implicitly political and progressive dimension in that they curtail the totalizing impulse. There are no strict criteria against which human creativity is held to account. Allowing literary criticism to be free from such controls, attending the particular artwork as well as the general rule, leaves a space for values to mutate and develop. This is a key value that the humanities offer within society: it provides a space in which new values can germinate.

The values tested in university humanities can grow outside the boundaries of the academy and into the ecology of the wider society. To allow this to happen, though, it is vital that the strictures of value are not formulaic. There are, as I have argued above, instrumental values for literary criticism. It has, historically, had a rich connective role with the world of letters outside the academy. It can provide a vital role in the 'refinement' of public preferences that, as we have seen, contribute to the identification of 'public values'. But the humanities also need to keep a privileged intellectual space for the values of which we do not yet know. This is why it is necessary to defend literary and intellectual enquiry, for all its bountiful social benefits, as an end in itself, too.

The deepest benefits might be the ones we cannot put a finger on so easily. There are, to borrow Donald Rumsfeld's distinction, 'known unknowns' and 'unknown unknowns'. It is easy to see the dark areas that the systematic application of established methods can illuminate. It is easy to appreciate how identifiable academic activities can add value, judging by criteria long-established and accepted. But giving our society a space to stumble on the unknown unknowns, the values we have not yet arrived at, may prove the greatest value of all.

Notes

1   For a history of the relationship, see *Grub Street and the Ivory Tower: Literary Journalism and Literary Scholarship from Fielding to the Internet* (Treglown and Bennett 1998).

2   A symptom of a renewed concern with literary value can be found in enterprises such as the AHRC-funded project at Shakespeare Institute at the University of Birmingham entitled 'Interrogating Cultural Value in the 21st Century: the case of "Shakespeare"'.

Bibliography

Crabtree, J.H. (2004), 'The Revolution that Started in a Library', *New Statesman*, 27 September 2004.

Gray, J. (2004), 'Joseph Conrad: Our Contemporary', in J. Gray, *Heresies: Against Progress and Other Illusions*, London: Granta Books.

Horner, L. and Bevan, S. (2006), Presentation on 'Public Value' at the Arts & Humanities Research Council (AHRC) seminar on 'Impact Assessment in the Cultural Sector', London, 15 March.

Leavis, F.R. (1972), *Nor Shall My Sword: Discourses on Pluralism, Compassion and Social Hope*, London: Chatto and Windus.

McMaster, Sir B. (2008), 'Supporting Excellence in the Arts: From Measurement to Judgement', London: Department for Culture, Media and Sport, http://www.culture.gov.uk/images/publications/supportingexcellenceinthearts.pdf [accessed 16 July 2010].

Moore, M.H. (1995), *Creating Public Value: Strategic Management in Government*, Cambridge, MA: Harvard University Press.

Treglown, J. and Bennett, B. (eds) (1998), *Grub Street and the Ivory Tower: Literary Journalism and Literary Scholarship from Fielding to the Internet*, Oxford: Clarendon Press.

23. 'And your point is ...?'

Chris Gosden (University of Oxford)

Prologue

My daughter Emily and her best friend chat at our kitchen table, unaware that I can hear them. Her friend says 'My dad's a philosopher, it's sooo boring.'

'Yeah,' replies Emily. 'My dad's an archaeologist; all he can talk about is potsherds.'

Later, and not entirely coincidentally, Emily and I are talking. I'm explaining about a project I have going, with philosophers amongst others, on issues of human intelligence and creativity. The line we are taking is that intelligence is not so much an all-in-the-head, cerebral, rational activity, but is rather about practical knowledge, held in our bodies, about how to make and use objects so as to influence people in desired manners. Emily and I get talking about clothes, a specialist subject of hers, and in particular how to choose a new party dress (for her, not for me). Such a choice requires an intimate knowledge of cloth, cuts, colour, celebrity fashion, price and what everyone else will wear. This is a prime example for our project, I point out, where the choice is largely intuitive, using knowledge which is felt and emotional, with a clear feel for fast-changing forms of aesthetics. A party-dress model of intelligence is miles away from calculus, logic and reason, long the mainstays of human intelligence, and has the distinct advantage of tapping into decisions of incredible complexity that people make every day, deploying in the process masses of knowledge of the material and the social.

The party dress takes us off on a slightly unlikely journey into those two key elements of human life: to know and to be known. Party-going is not altogether easy, especially if, as a teenager, you are trying to define yourself and influence others. Clothes make the party-goer and here the difficulties are felt most acutely. The current world of fashion is one of minor variations, trends of colour and cuts from different decades and no real novelties. To get a grip on this world means working through magazines, regular trips to the shops, an understanding of television, film and music, discussions with friends and so on. Emily worries that when talking to me she seems like a fashion victim, but I'm mainly impressed by the range and depth of knowledge required to dress in the latest style. Party-dress knowledge is complex and material. But it is also very definitely social knowledge displaying an understanding of what the group as a whole values or scorns, a feel for social aesthetics and a display of belonging and the importance of the group. Staggeringly, this is a group which is global, with very similar fashions in Shanghai and Sydney, Oxford and Ottawa. When I put this point to Emily she strongly demurs – 'Dad, you only find Harajuku girls in Japan'. A slight regional exception that I feel proves the rule.

Emily goes off to do her homework, leaving me to ponder how much of this knowledge is developed and located in the body, and how much can be put into words. I've felt for a long time that the capabilities of the body are underrated and under-explained, so that we don't really know what the human body can do, beyond a rather functional appreciation of the mechanics and biochemistry. Our lack of understanding of bodily knowledge and capability is due in large part to the obscuring nature of mind. For many centuries the disembodied mind was both the centre of understanding and of rationality, a particular and privileged form of knowing and acting in the world. The body, with its senses and emotions, its sheer physicality, its mundane nature and volatility, was deeply suspect. A mind could only work properly if it gained distance from the body.

Bodies and emotions

Now the body is fighting back, becoming again key to understanding and to acting knowledgeably in the world. There are many aspects to this resurgence, but two elements can be picked out. One particular organ of the body, and a surrogate for the mind, was the centre of immense attention at the end of the last century and the beginning of this. The brain is an old territory newly opened up to scrutiny by the techniques of neuroscience. The impact on the social sciences and humanities has been profound, with new, hybrid disciplines springing up such as neuro-aesthetics, neuro-economics and neuro-philosophy. The prospect of grounding human sensibilities and decision-making in the workings of synapses and neurons is enticing, perhaps grounding seemingly ephemeral choices of dresses or suits in an empirical reality. We might be able to trace the complex of interactions in human brains and link these to shopping malls and clubs where social life takes place. In fact, the practical and theoretical difficulties of mapping of this kind are immense, when most brain scanning takes place on isolated individuals lying flat on their backs in a laboratory setting which is a long way from the bustle of a shopping centre.

A second area offers less empirical rigour, but more human richness: the arena of the emotions. Writers like Antonio Damasio in *The Feeling of What Happens* are moving towards a whole-body view in which the brain's integration into the workings of the body is key and not separated into brains, arms, legs, eyes and ears (Damasio 1999). The brain, Damasio shows, spends a lot of time monitoring the biochemistry, the mechanics and dispositions of the body, working out background mood, energy levels, dispositions to actions and the emotions. For Damasio and an increasing number of thinkers the emotions are not confusing and wayward emanations of the body which the rational mind must avoid or control. Rather feelings and emotions provide us with a complicated, diffuse but critical set of information about how we are feeling and how others are affecting us. Emotions cannot always be controlled, nor are they easy to make sense of. Feelings of pain, anger, loss or helplessness after someone close has died may come whether we want them to or not. They are felt in the belly, the arms or the head in a way linked to physical pain. For us to break down and put into words or thoughts what someone's death means to us may take a considerable time, but our emotions are vital, felt guides to our change in state. Emotions are becoming more acknowledged both culturally and academically, a tricky business for the English. Academic interest in the emotions helps construct an holistic view of the body in its material and social worlds. Anger, shame, fear, disgust and so on also connect the processes by which we know and are known.

By our emotions are we known. By our emotions we come to know. An outburst of anger, an obvious display of fear or a generally sunny disposition have ramifying social effects through our network of contacts. As people face our anger with their own, try to placate us or keep out of our way, we learn more about our social position and power, and, centrally, this allow us to continue or modify our actions accordingly. What we have come to see in the West as our internal psychological and mental life may not be so internal after all, but our physiologies, our biochemical and synaptic states are networked to those of others in ways that are predictable and surprising. The global world of youth fashion provides a field in which reactions can be coordinated and shared over vast areas, but also surprises can be had.

In humans, knowing and being known are linked in unique manners compared with all other species. Archaeologists, amongst others, are interested in the links between knowing the world and the presentation of the self. Many animal species, we now know, make and use tools, these ranging from Caledonian crows, who can make hooks from straight bits of wire to pull food out of narrow-necked bottles, to chimpanzees that crack open tough nuts with stones. Animal technical ingenuity is widespread and fascinating, but lacks a key component as compared with people. Chimpanzees, we now know through a series of fascinating studies, have very rich and dynamic social lives. But social relations if you are a chimpanzee are direct and unmediated, being about fighting, grooming or sex. Material things don't figure in building friendships or alliances, so that especially effective or attractive nut-cracking stones are not exchanged, as far as we know. Food-sharing is important, but here items of food are generally not modified or culturally altered in any way. The party-dress model of life does not apply to chimpanzees and, hence, the sad absurdity of chimps being dressed up for shows or tea adverts. For chimpanzees and Caledonian crows the mechanical processes of the world which have to be mastered to fish food from a bottle or crack a tough nut have nothing to do with presenting and developing themselves as socially competent or innovative members of the group.

To be human is to be material; mastering the physical properties of things whilst appreciating their social impacts. The first stone tools we know of date from 2.6 million years ago, found in the area we now call Goma, Ethiopia. Over the many generations since then the human material world has exploded into one of buildings, fields, trackways and motorways, plastic and baseball caps. Material things are useful in a practical sense, but they also help carry emotional charges and sustain our social lives. People have come to understand the world in lots of ways and we now generally feel that science is the best (the only?) way to understand the workings of the world. This official view can be challenged by how we actually live.

Magic and onions

In a pub call the Barley Mow in the small town of Wellington, Somerset, on a Sunday lunchtime a group of men sat supping their beer. The year is 1894. A gust of wind blew four objects down from one of the broad chimneys of the pub on to the floor in front of them. On inspection these turned out to be onions around which strips of paper had been wrapped and secured by pins. On each strip of paper a name had been written and it seemed clear from the outset that the onions were forms of magic and sorcery intended to do people harm. Partly resident in Wellington at that time was E.B. Tylor, who lived for the rest of the time in Oxford where he had been Keeper of the University Museum since 1883. Tylor, who is often described as 'the father of British anthropology', spent much time in Wellington, the home of his wife's family, the Foxes. On hearing of the events in the Barley Mow he summoned the drinkers to Linden, the Foxes' large family house. Here he quizzed the men on what they knew of the onions and local attitudes to magic, without, as far as we can tell, getting very satisfactory answers. The evasiveness of the men, if that is what is was, may partly have derived from the inhibitions the British class system imposed on the encounter. For Tylor, the class divide was felt differently so that he was interested in survivals of so-called primitive beliefs amongst local labourers.

As he was due to give a lecture on magic in London that week, Tylor requested two of the onions as illustrations and one of them, now very shrivelled, is held in the Pitt Rivers Museum in Oxford to this day, an object of wonder and puzzlement (see the Pitt Rivers' website for more information on this and many other extraordinary objects).

For Tylor, anthropology was ultimately about the history of the human mind. He developed an historical scheme in books like *Primitive Culture* whereby human understanding had three key phases: magic, religion and science (Tylor 2010). Tylor felt that according to a magical view of the world, entities do not have the properties that a scientific notion attributes to them, nor does cause and effect work as we have come to think. Stones, rivers, plants and animals can all be active and purposive, so that any of them might possess a personality, will or ability to act. In a magical view an onion could have a causative power when combined with paper with people's names on and the correct spells. In Tylor's view religion concentrated the active powers of the universe in many gods or a single god so that their intentions and actions were determined. Science took both magic and the gods out of the world, leaving mechanical or biological forces and rational human wills.

What made Tylor's thought anthropological is that he did not just take belief in magic seriously, but kept a small part of his mind open to the possibility that magic might work. He himself tried dowsing and participated in seances and in these activities the central question was not so much a sociological one – 'Why do people believe in this stuff?' – but rather an empirical one – 'Might some of this work?' Mainly his answer to this question was 'No, it does not.' But there were always instances and occasions (some dowsing and one or two seances) which he could not dismiss totally. Tylor's intriguing openness to the way in which the world works is the mark of an arts and humanities scholar today. If we can see that all views of the world, including our own, are historically and culturally contingent, might we be mistaken or too narrow in our views of cause and effect or the place of human beings within the world? New views of understanding and the body are important in many ways, not the least because they open up less mechanical, more diffuse, intuitive and felt modes of grasping the world. Tylor's relative openness, to which we have made a partial return, might be due to the organization of knowledge in which he operated.

One of my current mild love affairs is with the intellectual world of the later nineteenth century, of which Tylor was an important part. The attraction of such a world is its relative lack of disciplinary boundaries. As mentioned above, Tylor was Keeper of the University Museum, Oxford, an institution which opened in 1860 as part of an effort by John Ruskin, who held a temporary Professorship in Art History in Oxford, and Henry Acland, Professor of Anatomy, among others, to create a unified home for the sciences in Oxford. Subjects we would now call Physics, Chemistry, Anatomy and Zoology were allotted space around the court of the museum for laboratory work and teaching. The central court drew them all into it, reminding individual workers that they were part of a broader whole, the aim of which was to understand the material and the living worlds. The eastern side of the court was allotted to the human world and the space was only actively made use of from 1884, when General Augustus Pitt Rivers gave his collection of archaeology and ethnography to Oxford. Tylor's post was supported by the money the University agreed to put up in accepting this collection. From the first, the Pitt Rivers Museum, as it quickly became known, represented a wonderful profusion of human products, from hand axes to lacemaking pillows, but understood against a broader context of the material world as a whole.

Tylor and others in the museum were both practical, experimental scientists and documenters of human history and cultural variety.

The social and the material were not two things, but one. Tylor was a proficient knapper of stone tools and famously set his beard on fire when demonstrating a fire drill at a lecture. The University Parks in Oxford had until recently a sign which read 'No boomerangs' because Henry Balfour, a younger colleague of Tylor's, had been trying out some of the museum's boomerangs when one fell into a baby's pram, not injuring anyone, but shocking all involved.

The museums of the later nineteenth century were places where people could discuss crystalline lattices, locusts, human skull shapes or the nature of gift-giving in Aboriginal Australia. In a recent book Frances Larson and I have documented a little of this world in the spirit of exploring something of a foreign country to which we can never quite return (Gosden and Larson 2007).

For the archaeologist and general student of material culture these are exciting times. Human artefacts are being recognized to have a charge and a power denied them for some time. Bodies and objects are also becoming connected up in new ways, bringing about novel academic collaborations. A philosopher like Andy Clark, in his book *Being There*, shows that human life is given direction and texture by a great complex of what might be called low-level skills of making and doing things in interaction with materials (Clark 1998). I have a coffee mug in front of me. I can reach out and pick up this mug. As I do so, very complex things happen – my hand takes on the shape and size of the mug without me consciously willing it to do so, being influenced by the shape of the mug itself. The force I use to lift the mug is influenced by the weight of the mug and the liquid it contains, something that varies every time I drink. I am more cautious drinking hot coffee than a cooler liquid, and so on. I can do all this without consciously thinking about it, but rather while attending to what I am writing. Of even greater difficulty is drinking very hot coffee from a flexible plastic cup on a moving train. The fact that we achieve these feats, which no other species can, without too much conscious effort, means that we have ignored them, only now starting to give them all the academic attention they deserve.

Our world is weighed down by objects which are in turn freighted with all sorts of significances. Once, when teaching a class on material culture in Melbourne, I asked people which of the things they owned had most significance for them. One member of the class said that he had actually to make this decision a few years previously when he and his family had to leave their home in a hurry when it was threatened by a bush fire. All they could take was what would fit into their car. The things they rushed for were the family photograph albums, his violin, paintings done by his wife, kids drawings, etc., as well as a change of clothes, toothbrushes and a few practical things. Happily, they came back to find that their house had not burned down.

The family is most obviously made up of its human members, but they are in turn held together by photographs, paintings, favourite clothes and so on. Cultural groups more broadly are linked by familiar objects, the skills to use them properly, the histories they evoke and the futures they point towards. A collection of poems, like Seamus Heaney's *Seeing Things*, evokes the tiny, everyday marvels of our lives – the heft of a full basket, the frittering of a straw in the spokes of a turning bicycle wheel (Heaney 2002). A poet of Heaney's ability can evoke in words physical sensations and material things, but for most of us much of the time there is a profound gap between what can be felt and what put into words.

Large questions derive from teacups, armchairs and ironing boards. If we want to know how people live well, when they feel deprived, cut off or excited by new possibilities, then it is key to look closely at people and their objects. We are consuming at rates that will be difficult to sustain, which is an ecological problem but also a social one. If our social lives in the West have become based on such a profusion of goods, what happens if this supply dries up? Thinking more globally, how does the scale of our consumption impoverish others? Can other views of the world, magical, religious or scientific, throw light on the dilemmas posed by people and things? As an archaeologist I am excited by the possibilities that the mundane things of past and present contain. But I am happily aware that my skills of description and measurement or of scientific analysis need to be complemented by those from many other disciplines who know more about bodies, aesthetics, performances and detailed recent histories than I do. The material and social worlds are far too complicated to be the province of one discipline. The issues arising from people and things are too pressing for our society not to address them. The arts and humanities community is not the only one to study human artefacts and their effects, but without the skills we have to offer this study would be greatly impoverished.

Coda

Emily comes back into the room to find her father scribbling and sighs gently in a 'get a life' sort of way. I explain that in my own fashion, getting a life is exactly what I am trying to do. I don't go into all the detail I could, as it is getting late. Emily does appear somewhat intrigued when I talk a little about party-dress knowledge and where it might lead. I am happy, temporarily, to acquire some minor relevance in Emily's eyes, avoiding in the process her killer question – 'And your point is ...?'

The arts and humanities community also worries it will be asked this, aware that utilitarian justifications for what we do are hard to come by. We are confident that philosophers are not boring, nor are the conversations of archaeologists limited only to broken pots. And when brought together these and other disciplines can start to do justice to the richness of the world in ways that speak directly to everyday, contemporary issues. This then is my point.

Bibliography

Clark, A. (1998), *Being There: Putting Brain, Body and World Together Again*, Cambridge, MA: MIT Press.

Damasio, A. (1999), *The Feeling of What Happens*, London: Heinemann.

Gosden, C. and Larson, F. (2007), *Knowing Things*, Oxford: Oxford University Press.

Heaney, S. (2002), *Seeing Things*, London: Faber and Faber.

Tylor, E.P. (2010), *Primitive Culture: Researches into the Development of Mythology, Philosophy, Religion, Art and Custom*, Cambridge: Cambridge University Press.

24. Philosophy and the Quest for the Unpredictable

Nicholas Davey (University of Dundee)

An 'adventure of ideas'?

Philosophy delights in being mischievous and somewhat sceptical. To ask its advocates to explain the social and economic return on their research can invoke ribaldry from die-hard conservatives along with a degree of not unjustifiable derision. Three questions immediately arise.

1. What does philosophical research mean? Is it like research in physics or medicine?
2. What is a quantifiable output in philosophical terms? Is it a proven technique, a new concept, or does it achieve a fresh interpretation of a classic text by Marcus Aurelius or Arthur Schopenhauer?
3. How is the reception of philosophical work to be judged? The number of times it is cited on Radio Three discussion programmes or is the timescale completely different? A Chinese adage would have it that 2,000 years would be too soon to judge!

Each of these questions invites a variety of responses. On the negative side, if philosophy is more an 'adventure of ideas' rather than a verifiable form of experimentation, how can insight and understanding ever be articulated in terms of predictable, let alone reliable, returns? Is not the social impact of a philosophical work extraordinarily difficult to assess accurately? On the positive side, protagonists of the discipline will cheer Plato's and Nietzsche's appraisal of philosophers as value-makers and legislators, moulders of world views. Who, after all, could reasonably doubt the continuing impact of John Locke on American constitutional and liberal thought, of Karl Marx on the development of social history or of Wittgenstein on the understanding of how language shapes how we think about the world? Fair point, it might be conceded, but none of these thinkers filled out a grant form and only one of them worked in a university and only for a very short time. Yet, the impact of their work has been immense and on a scale that certainly was not predictable. Perhaps history might settle these questions but that is no help to those who, in increasingly stringent economic times, must anguish over decisions as to what research ought to be publically supported. Is work on the concepts of terror and the sublime more or less urgent than understanding the operational contexts from which scientific judgements gain their legitimacy?

Perhaps our problem should be reformulated. Is the substantial question not whether it is socially preferable to support research into an ethics of state torture as opposed to issues in modal logic, but what is to be gained by promoting a certain type of research culture *per se* whose chosen topics, whatever they may be, are but a means to the broader and more substantial end of promoting the skills and values of that culture? It is a poor view of research activity that defines it solely in terms of advancing knowledge in a specialism. Knowledge may be power, as Francis Bacon once suggested, but that power is a promiscuous one. Advances in one discipline often promote the serendipitous transfer of new insights into other disciplines. Martin Heidegger's impact on modern theology, Walter Benjamin's influence on the development of visual studies or Michel Foucault's indirect shaping of much contemporary social thought suffice to make the point. The demonstrable transfer value of philosophy research is hugely underestimated.

To some, the transfer value of research into the history of philosophy or the arguments concerning virtue in ancient philosophy may seem contentious. What relevance can Plato's view of the just society have to us today, we who live in entirely different social and economic circumstances? Of course, there is an immediate and obvious relevance to scholars in the classical community but to chide the impact of this research as narrow is to fall into the trap of thinking that most philosophical research is, or ought to be, monological, i.e. that it approaches a specific problem with a well-defined method of analysis. The virtue of such single-minded and rigorous research is that it is in fact dialogical. Getting to grips with voices and arguments shaped by intellectual parameters that are very different from our own is far from being an exercise in accommodating strangeness but rather allows the strange, and the historically distant, to bring us up short against our intellectual assumptions about pressing contemporary problems.

One of the largest obstacles to creative thought is overcoming the prejudices of what is regarded as acceptable current good practice. We fall all too readily into the convenience of habitual assumptions. An important virtue of research into the works of previous philosophers is not the increase in knowledge about the past that it brings (important though that is) but how it challenges the scope and adequacy of our present intellectual orientation. By indirectly informing public debate, the dialogical dimension of philosophical research has a social relevance that reaches well beyond the definition of a specific project. The dialogical consequences of philosophical research reveal something of the distinct character that such research achieves.

Beyond problem solving

A great deal of philosophical research can be undervalued if it is understood just as problem solving. A problem in logic or mathematical reasoning disrupts a certain line of thinking. If a solution can be found, the hindrance can be overcome and a thought procedure can resume. However, many of the problems which philosophy deals with are not properly to be called problems but are issues which, like questions concerning justice, goodness or the meaning of loyalty, will never permit a technical solution. Far from being non-problems, they involve normative questions which can only ever be better or more deeply understood, rather than resolved in any technical fashion. The questions are far from abstract. They involve the socially strategic issues of how human life is to be understood and the meaning of childhood, and concern the appropriate direction for education. By bringing different analytic and historical skills to these concerns, philosophical research extends social and political awareness of what is at stake and at the same time increases the repertoire of possible practical responses. The difference between problem solving and achieving a greater reflective understanding of an issue highlights the nature of these two modes of research. In a great deal of philosophical and humanities research knowledge is 'accumulative' rather than 'progressive'. It does not progress by overcoming the problems of previous generations but rather thickens and extends an understanding of the issues involved. Once again, such research contributes to extending the informed nature of public debate and, hence, to the generation of new responses to canonical issues such debate can engender. Research into the character and nature of human rights and especially the rights of women over the last twenty years has indeed been game-changing.

Accumulations of insight in philosophical research can often be serendipitous. The history of ideas demonstrates that solutions to problems are not always achieved in a conventional manner, nor do they always emerge from expected professional sources. Indirect approaches can prove more productive. And so, at first glance, philosophical research into the language of religion or the nature of artificial intelligence may not seem relevant to a hard-pressed economy or to a society whose conventions and self-understandings are under constant pressure to change and adapt. There is still a quaint and no doubt endearing perception of the philosopher as a quite useless and impractical person, a reputation of ancient pedigree. It allegedly starts with the contemporary scorn heaped upon Thales, a pre-Socratic philosopher, for being more enamoured of the celestial beauty of the stars than the earthly charms of an amorous admirer. 'Useless' is a not an uncommon description of much modern art but few hard-headed politicians now dispute the utility of new urban art centres for the rejuvenation of depressed communities. Does the analogy work for philosophy, too?

The demand for social utility is not always a philistine call. If the public purse underwrites higher education, philosophical academics must expect to justify their salaries and research funding. Residues of a long-standing and mutual suspicion between, on the one hand, academics who see calls for justification for their research as an unwarrantable attack on academic freedom and, on the other hand, administrators who can regard research funding as money for relieving overspent budgets continue to have a negative influence on university communities. There is, however, a serious point that anxious philosophers and predatory administrators tend to overlook. Calls for demonstrations of the worthwhile nature of research investment are often myopically short-sighted. It is not long ago that 'Useless!' summarized the consensus judgement concerning the productive economic value of research in the humanities.

In the late 1960s and early 1970s the economic mandarins of both principal political parties started to doubt whether there was a demonstrable connection between the high cost of public investment in higher education and research, and the general level of economic productivity. Against the background of worldwide student unrest not just over the Vietnam war but also concerning the political complacency of post Second World War Western society, the Japanese industrial model of hiring staff at eighteen and training them for life in a company ethos seemed to promise a stable economic return. Deliberate government attempts were made to draw potential students away from university and into the workplace by diminishing the graduate employment premium. State postgraduate research grants were very hard to come by.

Events, of course, then intervened. The major OPEC oil price increases after the second Arab-Israeli conflict and the extraordinary collapse in city office rental values, brought about by the computerization of office procedures, initiated what has now become the familiar culture of 'rationalizing', whose practices quickly pervaded private and public sectors. The anarchic independence of free-thinking individuals, which had just previously been anathematized, once again became a highly tradable commodity. Their open-minded flexibility held precisely the qualities major economic players found themselves urgently needing: the ability both to think independently outside conventional boundaries, and to draw and utilize insights from a wide variety of economic and political sources. During this period philosophy graduates and researchers became one of the more employable groups of graduates and researchers. Useless? The reasons are obvious: philosophy's research skills require an ability to grapple with the logical structure of complex problems, to review unfamiliar ideas with an open mind, to acquire the patience for both listening and for long-term reflection, and to examine issues in a multi-perspectival way. Does history repeat itself? Perhaps, only for those who have not learned its lessons. The Higher Education Statistics Agency and major US employers all recently reported on the current economic relevance of philosophical skills of analysis.

What is often unsettling about demands for justifying research in the humanities is that the defining criteria for output and research productivity are inappropriately set. This is not the place to revisit the C.P. Snow's 'two-cultures' debate, but it is clear that within many aspects of humanities and philosophy research reasoning is not always demonstrative in the deductive sense. Knowledge in the humanities is not universally advanced by the scientific model of reasoning ably articulated by Karl Popper as 'conjecture and refutation'. In philosophy and other humanities subjects the procedure can be both more speculative and serendipitous. Many great philosophers from Immanuel Kant to Ernst Cassirer freely admit that the full conceptual entailments of an idea are rarely if ever grasped by their authors. The limitations of a particular discourse often blind researchers to what is held within a central concept.

Creative enquiry is rarely able to predict, prior to commencement of research, the extent and significance of its anticipated outcomes. What is held within a concept often only becomes apparent when it is placed alongside other interpretations. I remember very well how the limitations of something I was researching in its own right – Nietzsche's rather romantic and individualist concept of language – suddenly became apparent not because of an internal analysis but because of a chance exposure to a study of Hans-Georg Gadamer's analysis of the cultural foundations of language. To borrow an image from Wittgenstein, to get an idea as to what wheels a concept can turn, see what work it might do in a different framework. In philosophy and, indeed, the humanities generally, diligence in constantly maintaining sound research practices, reading widely and being open to new discourses will be rewarded by those *eureka* moments in which the really useful insights will spring forward as an unexpected consequence of the main investigation. This is also the great advantage of interdisciplinary research. A pattern of argumentation and an association of ideas in one discipline can expose previously unseen analogous structures of reasoning in another. What is of significant value in an enquiry is often a consequence of maintaining the momentum of a research practice rather than pursuing a predefined goal. Three further points can be made in this context.

First, senior scientific researchers have become sensitive to the negative aspects of research defined and supported by predictable outcomes. The latter tend to constrain enquiry within the predictable and attainable, reward the cautious instead of the adventurous and tend to 'embroider' known territories of operation rather than discovering access to new ones.

Second, the more serendipitous nature of humanities research (especially when in an interdisciplinary format) actually creates circumstances capable of generating new and unpredictable transformations of insight. Given the strong tendency of research in well-defined communities to talk only to itself, a great deal more support should be given to interdisciplinary research, not just in its own right (though desirable that would be), but also because the bringing together of two research frameworks has a greater chance of generating provocative new understandings.

Third, research in philosophy and the humanities is, in a certain sense, capable of being more objective than work undertaken in the sciences. Rarely does scientific research lead to a radical questioning of the methodological paradigms supporting it. However, in philosophical research those *eureka* moments of sudden and abrupt insight often bring the researcher up short against the very presuppositions of the inquiry itself. A research project in philosophy that does not lead to a serious questioning of its grounding assumptions does not really pass muster as a philosophical project. Philosophical research is always in search of the unpredictable. Once again, we see why the results of philosophical research are difficult to predict. Yet, there is some wisdom in this. That significant shifts in understanding are achieved serendipitously suggests that we should be very cautious about placing our faith too exclusively in administration and management systems. Good research should disrupt and alter expectations. What matters is not a devotion to a method but the willingness to methodically engineer those circumstances either in a discipline or between disciplines that might induce the sudden eruption of those *eureka* moments which can transform understanding of a problem. The encouragement of research with no obvious outcome may, in the present climate of severe financial restraint, seem rather fanciful. However, we should look for and need research impacts that reach well beyond current fiscal horizons.

Public debate

Striving to manage the economic determinants of a society is clearly necessary for its health and well-being. Power and wealth are, however, merely means and not ends. It is important that the voices that raise the question of values either in book form or in open debate continue to be audible. Without values management systems are blind and directionless. Values determine the direction of travel. Once again, it is not the specifics of a given research project that matter but more that such research keeps the debate about guiding values alive. It is said, 'Judge a philosopher by his or her attitude to death!' There is no morbidity here, merely an appraisal of what it means to live a healthy life. Apart from the question of whether the maintenance of life at all costs is a contradiction in terms, recent philosophical work on assisted death and on the ethics of non-intervention in terminal circumstances raises at least two important questions. Should a life, no matter how painful and compromised, be maintained in all circumstances? Some are fearful that humans should not assume the power of gods over the life and death of individuals. Others protest that this is agnosticism of the worst order, abnegating the power of decision to chance or to a divine will. In the mind of some thinkers this is indicative of a failure to face up to what it means to be human, i.e. taking responsibility for our judgements no matter how agonizing or painful. If control over the quality of life is of greater value than life at any cost, the autonomy of a healthy life carries a greater premium than mere existence. If so, the debate may favour the classical Roman virtue of *choosing* to fall on one's own sword once the threat to autonomy or well-being becomes intolerable. Whatever the ethical, legal or political resolution (and it will be an instance of Cicero's uncomfortable description of politics as the art of having to choose between two unpalatable options), the emergence of this debate and the sizeable ethical research informing it indicate a reassuringly healthy aspect of our community. There is, perhaps, something unsettling about a society unwilling to confront the question of death for, ultimately, that unwillingness betrays a reluctance to face up to the difficulties of life.

Research in favour of assisted death and moral debate about the irresponsible burden placed on others by maintaining a life that lacks all autonomy raises difficult and uncomfortable issues. However, no community can afford to be complacent about its values. In this respect the broad responsibility of philosophical research is to challenge and probe the foundations of established attitudes, especially when they are called upon as a justification to intervene in other communities. Philosophical research can remind us of the great need for caution when we make practical judgements which influence the lives of others. Recent research in political thought has started to question the Western world's rather unthinking response to what has been misleadingly described as fundamentalist religious terrorism. It suggests that this response needs to be tempered by the realization that the West's own secularist faith also promises a Utopia, albeit a secular one and one which, as recent events show, is rarely implemented without violence. Contemporary philosophical research into the notion of the community is also being invoked against the tendency of centralist governments to take unto itself the management of education and welfare. In the latter instance, medieval conceptions of community are being revised to challenge the lethargy that has settled around the question as to whether issues of individual responsibility are properly the concerns of state. As our society questions the dominant liberal values of recent years, influential philosophical research is exploring the paradoxical if not contradictory notion of progress. If progress requires peace and stability and if the latter requires a major investment in potentially highly destructive defence systems, the pursuit of progress in a world of diminishing resources may indeed be a road to annihilation. The thesis invites an exacting debate about guiding social and economic values.

Philosophical research will not itself settle these questions but it can rightly unsettle the complacent and self-satisfied disregard of their urgent nature. More important is the ability of philosophical research to enrich wider debates about community, society, individual responsibility and legitimate aspirations, questions which the 'unacceptable face' of capitalism, as a former Conservative Prime Minister (Edward Heath) once described it, has now made so urgent. Useless? Apart from the obvious observation that the facts speak otherwise, what Theodor Adorno and Jean Paul Sartre once said of art and the imagination equally applies to the philosophical imagination and its researches. In the ability to think in ways that refuse the current ideology or belief, and in the power to speculate about the different and the otherwise, lie the seeds of political freedom, the seeds of a belief in the possibility of real and significant individual engagement and intervention and, most important, the seeds of a faith in a future where things can indeed be made otherwise.

The encouragement of 'blue sky' research with no predictable outcome is in the present climate of severe financial restraint perhaps rather fanciful. Yet in times of crisis it can be more damaging not to adopt a long-term view. A species such as ours, which most likely as not has no predetermined nature, relies for its survival upon what it learns not just directly but also indirectly from experience. The value of such lessons is never timeless. Environments change and change calls into question long-standing operating assumptions. What has proved useful to a community in the past can prove a liability in the future. The role of scepticism in philosophical research is important precisely because it deliberately probes and tests those experientially acquired assumptions which habit and convenience can persuade us are actual truths. The skill of questioning is central to promoting the cultural powers of innovation and adaptation well beyond the walls of the university.

In addition to the productive promotion of scepticism, it is just as important for an experience-dependent community to nourish those 'blue sky' buccaneer channels of creative and imaginative reflection which push at the tried and tested. In times of social and economic difficulty, experience-based communities can ill afford to disinvest in innovative research but rather should accelerate investment in their stock of creative resources. Within any community there is always the need for a balance between consolidation and innovation. Research insights do not emerge *ex nihilo*. They require the long-term consolidation of research practices. Yet consolidation can breed self-satisfaction and complacency. Adventurous research into the more speculative dimensions of thought is equally needed. Philosophical creativity can not only challenge complacent assumptions within consolidated social practices but it can also offer a repertoire of alternative thought frameworks. Whether the research involves Buddhist logic, medieval conceptions of beauty or seventeenth-century notions of the individual, there is no telling when and where such frameworks will achieve their full application.

Those who regard such research as a privileged indulgence miss the contemporary point. Understanding how the Greeks thought about *aletheia* (truth) or how Chinese philosophy grasps the interdependent nature of all things does not only introduce us to a different way of thinking (always an intellectual challenge) but enables us to think differently about our own ways of conceptualizing the social and cultural challenges we face. Twenty years ago, funded philosophy research into the concept of emptiness (*śūnyatā*) and the related non-essentialist notion of 'dependent origination' may have seemed a liberal indulgence. Now it appears as commendably prescient. This philosophical research into Buddhist conceptions of the interrelatedness and dependence of all living beings assumes a pressing urgency as we learn more and more of the horrendous consequences of having treated our environment over the last four centuries as a mere resource. If there is any degree of certainty here, it is this. It would surely seem unwise for an experience-dependent community to demand an immediate economic justification for all of its research outputs. Who can be certain of the eventual worth of such investments? Are such wagers defensible? Let us remember this. The corridors of power that tend to demand such justifications utterly failed to predict the dramatic demise of the Eastern Bloc and were almost criminally negligent in their inability to foresee the recent world banking crisis. If a community is unprepared to trust in the possible transformative outcomes of its research activities, that community betrays its faith in its own future. Such a lack of a faith undermines the ability to respond to the challenges of the contemporary world, and compromises the material *and* spiritual health of our community.

The genius of public debate is that it can give rise to ideas that its participants would not have anticipated before the discussion started. The quality of those emergent ideas depends in large part upon the information that shapes the debate. It is of paramount importance for an open community that it be as well-informed as it can about significant ethical, environmental and legal issues. Philosophy contributes to the broad exchange of ideas. A community that does not regularly expose itself to the risks and challenges of this exchange has little hope of adapting to the rigours of social change. For that exchange to be of consequence, 'free spaces' are needed for reflection to generate transformative ideas.

Philosophers who teach in universities are subject to the increasingly dominating bureaucratic pressures of all professions. Yet the promotion of research establishes those free spaces within which reflection can be nurtured. The individual projects are not as important as the research habits and practices that surround them for it is these that will, for the most part, generate new ideas and insights. The justification of such spaces lies, then, not just in the scholarly worth of the work produced, but in what the production of such work enables beyond the individual researcher; its contribution to the discipline of philosophy, its serendipitous impact upon other discourses, and the way it shapes and informs the public debate and exchange of ideas. Philosophical research may indeed generate the unexpected but that is the point; only the unexpected will prove transformative within and outside the discipline.

In conclusion, there is no doubt that the skills philosophers and their research bring to the social economy are highly relevant and have, in previous crises, been proven to be so. Intellectual flexibility and an innovative capacity for creative analysis and judgement are primary assets for any community whose material and spiritual resources are put to the test. This much is known. What is not fully appreciated is both the nature and transfer value of the practices of philosophical research itself. The worth of a research practice often lies in its manner of operating rather than in its planned results. Research into the works of leading philosophical figures of the past is not an arcane excuse for an antiquarian escape from the intruding pressures of the contemporary world. To the contrary, it offers to a community, by way of comparison with previous modes of thought, a route to challenge the advantages and limitations of contemporary prejudices about its primary cultural values. It would be irresponsible to judge a piece of research by its most immediate outcomes. There is no way of predicting its eventual consequences.

What is clear, however, is that the research practices that support individual philosophical projects do bring an immediate return. Nurturing informed enquiry, strengthening patient reflection and enhancing powers of critical analysis represent an investment in the ability of society to respond creatively to times of test and trial. Philosophical research celebrates the serendipitous and the willingness to be open to the strange and unusual. It bolsters a spirit of intellectual adventurousness precisely because it has learned from its own experience of the untold insights that are held within the unexpected. In this respect, philosophy research addresses contemporary anxieties about the conservatism of output-driven scientific research. Philosophical research as an adventure of ideas is always in search of the unpredictable. This is because it seeks not just to challenge the predictable, the habitual and the customary, though this does have the virtue of establishing what is of genuine worth within everyday practices. Philosophy pursues the unpredictable insight precisely because of its transformative power. The new understanding it brings is indeed the proper reward for sustained and open inquiry, virtues without which any experience-based community such as ours is unlikely to rejuvenate itself, even to survive.

Index